Medieval Religion

A sourcebook

**Edited by
Roberta Anderson and
Dominic Aidan Bellenger**

Routledge
Taylor & Francis Group

LONDON AND NEW YORK

First published 2007
by Routledge
2 Park Square, Milton Park, Abingdon, Oxon, OX14 4RN

Simultaneously published in the USA and Canada
by Routledge
270 Madison Ave, New York, NY 10016

Routledge is an imprint of the Taylor & Francis Group, an informa business

© 2007 Roberta Anderson and Dominic Aidan Bellenger

Typeset in Baskerville by
Taylor & Francis Books
Printed and bound in Great Britain by
MPG Books Ltd, Bodmin

British Library Cataloguing in Publication Data
A catalogue record for this book is available from the British Library

Library of Congress Cataloging in Publication Data
A catalog record for this book has been requested

ISBN10: 0-415-37027-2   ISBN13: 978-0-415-37027-1 (hbk)
ISBN10: 0-415-37028-0   ISBN13: 978-0-415-37028-8 (pbk)

Contents

Illustrations

Plates

Preface

In the medieval West the life and thought of the Christian Church was crucial in building up the pattern of Europe. Christendom's identity was constructed by the clerics who formed the literate elite from the fall of Rome to the discovery of America. The wealth of material available from this period is reflected in this collection, which is drawn from a wide range of sources, from hymns and poems to papal bulls.

The Church was not only about elites, and this book opens up the obscured areas of popular religion and the magical, as well as giving a place to the writings of women in what can appear to be a male dominated period. It also attempts to reach beyond the Christian consciousness into the parallel experiences of the Jews and Muslims.

This sourcebook is intended to assist students in their understanding of the richness and imaginative force of a world in which the great works of art and architecture were inspired by the Christian ideal. It also suggests that the sublime sometimes accompanied the banal.

Acknowledgements

This book, like its predecessor, is not only a result of the collaboration of the editors but owes much to previous scholars and translators.

We are indebted to Dr John Crook, FSA, of Winchester for providing the photographs for this volume.

The authors would like to thank both Downside Abbey, especially the Monastic Library, and Bath Spa University for their assistance in producing this book of sources.

We acknowledge permission for the use of the following copyright material:

A Description or Briefe Declaration of all the Ancient Monuments, Rites, and Customes Belonging or Beinge within the Monastical Church of Durham before the Suppression. Written in 1593 (Llanrech Press: Felinfach, 1998).

A Word in Season: monastic lectionary for the divine office (Augustinian Press: Pennsylvania, 1991).

R. J. Armstrong; J. A. Wayne Hellmann and W. J. Short (eds) *Francis of Assisi: early documents, vol. 1: The Saint* (New City Press: New York, 1999).

Augustine of Hippo, *The Monastic Rules*, with a commentary by G. Bonner (New City Press: New York, 2004).

D. Ayerst and A. Fisher, *Records of Christianity, vol. I: in the Roman Empire* (Blackwell: Oxford, 1971).

D. Ayerst and A. Fisher, *Records of Christianity, vol. II: Christendom* (Blackwell: Oxford, 1977).

J. F. Benton (ed.) and C. C. Swinton Bland (trans.) *Self and Society in Medieval France: the memoirs of Abbot Guibert of Nogent* (Harper and Row: New York, 1970).

J. Bertram (trans.) St Aelred of Rievaulx, *Life of St. Edward the Confessor* (St Austin Press: Southampton, 1997).

R. N. Bosley and M. M. Tweedale, *Basic Issues in Philosophy: selected readings presenting the interactive discourses among the major figures* (Broadview Press: Ontario, 1999).

W. Butler-Bowdon (ed.) *The Book of Margery Kempe, 1436* (Random House/Cape: 1936).

D. Dales, *A Mind Intent on God. The Prayers and Spiritual Writings of Alcuin: an anthology* (Canterbury Press: Norwich, 2004).

M. L. Del Mastro (trans.) *Revelations of Divine Love of Juliana of Norwich* (Random House/ Doubleday: New York, 1977).

J. France (ed.) Radulf Glaber, *The Five Books of the Histories* (Clarendon Press: Oxford, 1989).

C. Garton (trans.) *The Metrical Life of St Hugh* (Honywell Press: Lincoln, 1986).

D. Geanakoplos (ed. and trans.) *Byzantium: church, society, and civilization seen through contemporary eyes* (University of Chicago Press: Chicago, 1984).

M. Goldstein, *Jesus in the Jewish Tradition* (Palgrave MacMillan: New York, 1950).

P. Henderson (ed.) *A Pilgrim Anthology* (Confraternity of St James: London, 1994).

J. Hogarth (trans.) *The Pilgrim's Guide: a 12th century guide for the pilgrim to St James of Compostela* (Confraternity of St James: London, 1992).

Hugh of Saint-Victor: selected spiritual writings, translated by a religious of CSMV with an introduction by Aelred Squire, OP (Faber and Faber: London, 1962).

Idung of Prüfening, *Cistercians and Cluniacs: the case for Citeaux. A dialogue between two monks, an argument on four questions* (Cistercian Publications: Kalamazoo, 1977).

K. L. Jolly, *Popular Religion in Late Saxon England: elf charms in context* (University of North Carolina Press: Chapel Hill NC, 1996).

M. H. King (trans.) *The Life of Christina of St-Trond by Thomas of Cantimpre* (Peregrina: Saskatoon, 1986).

C. Kirchberger (ed. and trans.) *Richard of Saint-Victor: selected writings on Contemplation* (Harper and Row: New York, 1962).

H. Lawrence (trans.) *Documentary Sources for the canonisation process for Edmund of Abingdon, Archbishop of Canterbury, 1234* (Westminster Diocesan Printing: London, 1990).

T. Mackintosh-Smith, *The Travels of Ibn Battutah* (Pan Macmillan: London, 2003).

J. Marcus, *The Jew in the Medieval World: a sourcebook, 315–1791* (Jewish Publication Society: New York, 1938).

J. McCann (ed. and trans.) *The Rule of St Benedict* (Ashgate: Aldershot, 1952).

C. E. McCracken (ed.) and A. Cabaniss (ed. and trans.) *Early Medieval Theology*, Library of Christian Classics 9 (Westminster Press: Philadelphia, 1957).

J. Parkes, *The Conflict of the Church and the Synagogue: a study in the origins of antisemitism* (Jewish Publication Society: New York, 1934).

B. Pennington (ed.) *The Works of Aelred of Rievaulx, vol. 1: treatises and the pastoral prayer*, Cistercian Fathers series, no. 2 (Cistercian Publications: Massachusetts, 1971).

E. Peters (ed. and trans.) *Heresy and Authority in Medieval Europe: documents in translation* (Ashgate: Aldershot, 1980).

M. Philippides, *The Fall of the Byzantine Empire* (University of Massachusetts Press: Amherst, 1980).

B. Pullan, *Sources for the History of Medieval Europe from the Mid-eighth to the Mid-thirteenth Century* (Blackwell: Oxford, 1971).

J. E. Rotelle (ed.) *Augustine's Heritage: readings from the Augustinian tradition* (Catholic Book Publishing: New York, 1973).

A. Saunders, J. Hillier, A. Halliwell and C. Rudge, *The Chichester Reliefs* (Otter Press: Chichester, 1989).

P. Schaff and H. Wace (eds) *A Select Library of Nicene and Post-Nicene Fathers of the Christian Church* (Eerdsman Publishing Co.: Grand Rapids, 1955).

H. J. Schroder (trans.) *Disciplinary Decrees of the Ecumenical Councils* (B. Herder: St Louis, 1937).

D. Scott, *An Anglo-Saxon Passion* (SPCK: London, 1999).

J. Scott (trans.) William of Malmesbury, *De Antiquitate Glastonire Ecclesie* (Boydell and Brewer: Woodbridge, 1981).

D. Sherlock, *Signs for Silence: the sign language of the Monks of Ely in the Middle Ages* (Ely Cathedral Publications: Ely, ND).

C. Stephenson and F. G. Marcham (eds and trans.) *Sources of English Constitutional History: a selection of documents from AD 600 to the present*, vol. VI (Harper and Row: New York, 1937).

C. H. Talbot (ed. and trans.) *The Life of Christina of Markyate: a twelfth century recluse* (Clarendon Press: Oxford, 1959).

N. P. Tanner (ed. and trans.) *Decrees of the Ecumenical Councils* (Continuum: Georgetown, 1990).

N. P. Tanner, *Heresy Trials in the Diocese of Norwich, 1428 – 31*, Camden Fourth series, vol. 20 (RHS: London, 1977).

The Bible: new revised standard version (Continuum: London, 1993).

C. Waddell, *Cistercian Lay Brothers: twelfth-century usages with related texts* (Citeaux ASBL: Citeaux, 2000).

D. Wright (trans.) Geoffrey Chaucer, *The Canterbury Tales* (Oxford University Press: Oxford, 1986).

S. A. Zenkovsky (ed. and trans.) *Medieval Russian Epics, Chronicles and Tales* (Penguin/Plume: New York, 1974).

Abbreviations

Ayerst and Fisher, *Records*	D. Ayerst and A. Fisher, *Records of Christianity, vols I and II: Christendom* (Oxford, 1977).
Bosley and Tweedale, *Philosophy*	R. N. Bosley and M. M. Tweedale, *Basic Issues in Philosophy: selected readings presenting the interactive discourses among the major figures* (Ontario, 1999).
A Word in Season	*A Word in Season: monastic lectionary for the divine office*, part iv, Santoral (Pennsylvania, 1991).

Introduction

The Middle Ages has often been described as the Age of Faith, and from a documentary point of view such identification is justifiable. In the corpus of surviving medieval texts the Christian faith is predominant. This reflects the fact that while Roman imperial power had evaporated in Western Europe by the beginning of the fifth century the established religion of the Empire, the Catholic Church, continued to thrive, and its Latin language and theological concerns gave Western Europe a common culture. Moreover, the clergy were the principal record keepers of Christendom.

This book is a companion to the editors' *Medieval Worlds* (2003) and attempts to provide a range of sources which show both the universality of the Church in the activities of Western Europe and the diversity of Christian principle and practice. The word 'church' itself suggests the wide possibilities inherent in the title of this compilation. The English word 'church' has its roots in the Greek word which means 'belonging to the Lord', and was originally confined to a church building, but the Latin word *ecclesia* meant something much nearer to an 'assembly' or 'congregation'. In their turn these words could be used to define either the local or universal Christian community. Frequently the 'assembly' was further defined as consisting of clergy, professional churchmen, and the laity, the people of God, who made up the majority of the faithful but were not part of its hierarchical structure.

The 'hierarchy' is the word which has been used since the late Roman Empire for the ordained body of Christian clergy whose organisational pattern mirrored that of the Roman Empire with its imperial, provincial, diocesan and parochial agencies. Theodosius I [d. 395] had made Christianity the official religion of the Roman state and to some degree the ghost of that state continued to live in the Church. Roman imperialism, with its centralising tendency, did not predominate, however, in a world where Christianity propagated itself as a missionary body beyond the boundaries of the Empire and adjusted to local conditions.

Alongside the hierarchical Church were a numerically significant group of 'professional' religious who were neither quite 'clergy' or 'laity': the monks and nuns. These were individuals who attempted to live out their Christian life in community and simplicity with the blessing of the hierarchical Church and under religious vows. Their way of life was a challenge to their fellow Christians and a reminder of the primacy of the Kingdom to come, prayed for by Jesus.

Prayer and learning, especially in the reading and preservation of texts, were characteristics of all medieval religious houses to a greater or lesser degree, and the monks were for a time the librarians of Europe. The great flowering of medieval ecclesiastical learning was not confined to the monastics. With the continuing rediscovery of the texts of antiquity and an abiding sense of wonder in the acquisition of knowledge, the Middle Ages is punctuated with a string of renaissances, including those associated with the Carolingians and that sometimes referred to as either the Renaissance or the Reformation of the twelfth century. Such concepts are highly appropriate for medieval Christian learning, which seems to have had as its ideal a return to original purity and the wellsprings of truth.

The quest for perfection was not confined to the religious and intellectual elites of the period. The medieval Church, through its sacramental system, attempted to sacrilise the whole of society, and every member of the people of God was called to holiness. Some dissented from the Church's official viewpoint, which became more closely defined with the passage of time, and this collection of texts includes items concerning those who were outside the Church, either by birth or by choice. Medieval Christianity, for all its striving for unity and uniformity, was never monolithic.

The documents in this book present a wide variety of material, ranging from the administrative and the legislative to the poetic and the philosophical. They reflect a Church that was both self-confident and questioning. They describe, too, a body which for most of the period covered by this book was a divided Church, or rather the Western part of the Christian body broken by a fundamental disparity between Latin and Greek culture: a Latin culture which increasingly looked northwards and westwards, and a Greek culture which looked to the east and the south. Yet, looked at from a distance, the medieval Church possessed a deep integrity and force. In these Christian centuries, half the history of the Christian Church, Christianity was no longer a minority faith but became what it remains, one of the great world religions. This book attempts to mirror the life and achievements of that Christian millennium.

Further reading

J. H. Arnold, *Belief and Unbelief in Medieval Europe* (2005).
M. Barber, *The Two Cities: medieval Europe* (1992).
R. Bartlett (ed.) *Medieval Panorama* (2001).
P. R. L. Brown, *The Rise of Western Christendom* (1996).
A. Cameron, *The Mediterranean World in Late Antiquity: AD 395–600* (1993).
B. Hamilton, *The Christian World of the Middle Ages*, 2nd edn (2003).
—— *Religion in the Medieval West*, 2nd edn (2003).
J. Herrin, *The Formation of Christendom* (Princeton, 1987).
D. Knowles, *The Evolution of Medieval Thought* (1962).
F. D. Logan, *A History of the Church in the Middle Ages* (2002).
R. W. Southern, *The Making of the Middle Ages* (1953).

1 Saints

The saints were the heroes of medieval religion and saints' lives provide one of the most important sources for the study of the period. Hagiography, the lives of the saints, is a specialised department of biography and often says more about the ideals of the holy life than the details of an individual's story. Saints come in all shapes and sizes and reflected contemporary ideals. The martyrs of the Early Church were the first Christian saints and monks, holy women, and miracle workers followed them. The intervention of the divine in the life of all the saints is crucial, as is the example which they provide for the ordinary Christian in their life. Many individual early saints were the subject of popular acclaim and their cult was localised. By the time of the Fourth Lateran Council a more thorough process for canonisation had emerged, emanating from the Holy See and part of the move towards greater Church centralisation. Throughout the Middle Ages the patronage of the saints was regarded as essential for protection and prosperity, and calendars of saints' feasts revealed the complexity of what became a characteristic feature of medieval Church life.

Those Christians whose virtue was recognised as heroic and were acknowledged to be in heaven form part of the communion of the saints in which all good Christians had a part. The feasts of All Saints and All Souls commemorated those known and unknown who were in heaven and those who were dead and needed the prayers of the Church. Odilo, abbot of Cluny (d. 1049) popularised the commemoration of the saints and the dead on the first two days of November.

A Word in Season: monastic lectionary for the divine office, pt iv, Santoral (1991) pp. 206–207

From a sermon by Saint Anastasius of Sinai (d. 599)

How can we explain our zeal in attending this solemn gathering today, beloved, if not by the fact that our brothers and sisters who have been called away from us to Christ have summoned us all here? Gladly then let us come to Christ with songs of praise, for our departed ones have inspired us to glorify God for them on earth, while they join the choirs of angels in praising him in heaven, and provide a spiritual meal for us. Filled with the delights of paradise, they place before us the wine of compunction. They now enjoy the consolations of heaven and are kindling a light to enlighten their own hearts as they move toward the unapproachable Light.

The saints already with Christ have drawn away the saints from among ourselves. Those who were once with us have departed from us, returning to their true homeland

and leaving us orphans. They have passed from a state of corruptibility to one of incorruptibility; they have gone from this world and risen again in Christ, exchanging their tent-dwelling for the heavenly Jerusalem. Leaving to us the emptiness of this life, they have attained to the bliss of heaven; leaving to us our earthly worries, they have passed to a land without worry. They have left behind the winds and waves of this world and have anchored in harbours of perfect calm.

Yet even while they seemed to be with us they were not so in reality, for their minds were turned to God. They lived on earth as citizens of heaven. Having here no lasting city, they sought a heavenly one; having no earthly riches, they sought the riches of heaven. They were strangers and sojourners as their ancestors were. Strangers to the world, to the things of the world, and to the ways of the world, their whole heart was absorbed in the things of heaven; these were the things they thought about and were concerned about. They longed for the beauty of heaven, its mansions and dwellings, its choirs and hymnody, its feasts and its eternal blessedness.

The saints contemplated, sought, and hastened toward these things, and so at last they attained them. Their striving was rewarded by admission to the heavenly bridal chamber. Because they laboured they now exult. Because they were not negligent they now rejoice. *Precious in the eyes of the Lord is the death of his saints.*

A Word in Season, pp. 207–208

From a homily attributed to Saint Bede (d. 735)

Today, beloved, we celebrate in one joyous festival the feast of all the saints in whose company heaven exults, in whose patronage earth rejoices, and whose triumph is the crown of holy Church. The more steadfastly they confessed their faith by suffering, the more highly are they honoured, for the glory of the contestants is in proportion to the intensity of the struggle. Sufferings of many kinds went to make the martyrs' triumph, and the greater their torments were, the greater was their reward.

Our mother, the Church catholic extending far and wide throughout the world, learned from Jesus Christ her head not to fear insults, sufferings, or death. Having herself gone from strength to strength by enduring rather than resisting, she inspired all that noble band as they came up to the starting post to enter the contest with a zeal like hers, and achieve a glorious triumph.

O truly blessed is Mother Church thus resplendent with the honour of divine grace, adorned with the renowned blood of victorious martyrs, robed in the virgin purity of an inviolate confession of faith! Her crown lacks neither roses nor lilies. Beloved, let each of us now endeavour to gain the high degree of merit attached to both these honours, whether it be the dazzling white crown of virginity, or the red crown of suffering. The court of heaven has crowns for the soldiers of Christ whether they served in war time or in a time of peace.

Moreover, in his unutterable, his boundless goodness, God arranged that the time of toil and suffering should not be endless or even of long duration, but short and one might even say momentary. In this poor brief life we have to wrestle and work, but in that other life which is eternal we shall be crowned and rewarded as our deeds deserve. The work is soon done, but the reward we earn lasts for ever. When the night of this world is over the saints will behold a light of surpassing brilliance and will receive a blessedness outweighing the anguish of any suffering. To this the Apostle bears witness when he says: *The sufferings of this present time are not worthy to be compared with the glory which shall be revealed in us.*

From a sermon by Saint Odilo (d. 1049)

Christians are absolutely certain of the divine promise that the dead will rise again. Truth himself made the promise and Truth cannot lie. The promise given by Truth concerning the resurrection of the dead is reliable because, since Truth cannot lie, he must fulfil all he has promised. Moreover, to give us certain proof that bodies will rise again, the Lord himself deigned to demonstrate this to us in his own body. Christ rose so that Christians may not doubt that they too will rise: for what happened first in the head will happen later in the body.

Now we should realize, beloved, that there are two deaths and two resurrections: scripture speaks of a first death and a second death. The first, moreover, has two parts: in the one the guilty soul forsakes its Creator by sinning; in the other it is, by God's judgment, separated from its body as a penalty. The second death includes the death of the body and the everlasting punishment of the soul. The first death temporarily separates from their bodies the souls of good and bad alike. In the second death the wicked alone suffer torment in both body and soul for ever.

In the past all were subject to both deaths, for original sin made everyone liable to punishment. But the immortal and righteous Son of God came and took mortal flesh from us in order to die for us. In that flesh he bore the punishment for sin, but without any guilt, for there could be no sin in him. God's Son thus accepted on our behalf the second part of the first death, the death of the body alone, and by so doing rescued us from the control of sin and from the torment of everlasting punishment.

Christ now continues his merciful work: to those whom he encourages to live a good life he gives faith so that they may believe correctly, and charity so that they may readily devote themselves to good works. On the last day he will graciously raise them up in the body in order to give them everlasting blessedness. Therefore, beloved, now that our souls have been restored to life by faith, let us live uprightly so that we may rise to everlasting joy in our bodies as well. Let us be aware of the gift Christ has given us in the first resurrection, so that when we rise in the body we may deserve to reign with our Saviour for ever. Then death will be swallowed up in victory, and believers will be given true life and true joy. In return for their faith and good works they will receive the kingdom of heaven from their Saviour who is God Almighty, and who lives and reigns with the Father and the Holy Spirit through endless ages. Amen.

Mary, the Mother of God, was the pre-eminent saint of the Middle Ages. The special honour owed to Mary was described by Thomas Aquinas (d. 1274) as *hyperdoulia*, veneration greater than that paid to other saints, but infinitely below the adoration (*latria*) due to God alone. Mary's role in salvation and her work as protector of the Church were given special emphasis.

A Word in Season, pp. 161–162

From a sermon by Saint Peter Damian (d. 1072)

Beloved, the birthday of the pure and most blessed Mother of God brings us a special and indeed unparalleled joy, for the good reason that her birth marked the beginning of all human salvation.

In a way impossible to express, almighty God knew, even before human beings were created, that they would perish through the machinations of the devil, but, again before the ages began, his infinite love also formed a plan for their redemption. Not only did he decide, as part of this infinitely wise plan, the manner and order of redemption; he also determined beforehand the moment in time when he would carry out his plan.

Accordingly, just as the Son of God had to be born of the Virgin if the human race was to be redeemed, so also it was necessary for the Virgin to be born through whom the Word was to become flesh. The bridal chamber had first to be constructed that would receive the bridegroom as he came for his marriage with holy Church, the bridegroom for whom David with spiritual joy sang the wedding song that described the Lord as *a bridegroom coming from his wedding chamber*.

Rightly, then, is the whole earth filled with joyous exultation today; rightly does the entire holy Church sing songs of praise at the birth of the Mother of her Spouse. Let us therefore rejoice, beloved, on this day on which we pay homage to the birth of the blessed Virgin and celebrate the beginning of all the feasts of the New Covenant.

If Solomon and the Israelites celebrated with great solemnity such a rich and magnificent sacrifice for the dedication of a temple made of stone, how great and intense should be the joy of the Christian people at the birth of the Virgin Mary, into whose womb, as into the holiest of temples, God himself deigned to descend, there to take human nature from her and dwell visibly with human beings! For while we must believe that God indeed descended into Solomon's temple, in a far more wonderful and fruitful way did he deign to abide for our sake in this spiritual sanctuary, that is, the womb of the blessed Virgin, in which the Word became flesh and dwelt among us.

A Word in Season, pp. 162–163

Blessed Rabanus Maurus (d. 856)

This day we have been longing for, beloved, this day of Mary ever virgin, Mary blessed and venerable, has come. Let our earth, made illustrious by the birth of this great Virgin, exult with great rejoicing. By her childbearing the nature of creatures was changed and their sin blotted out. For in her God's woeful sentence, *In sorrow shall you bring forth children*, was rescinded, since she gave birth to the Lord in joy. Eve mourned, Mary rejoiced; Eve bore tears in her womb, Mary joy; for Eve gave birth to a sinner, Mary to one who was guiltless. Moreover, Mary gave birth as a virgin, and after bearing her Son she remained a virgin.

Hail, full of grace, the angel said to her; *the Lord is with you*. He is with you in your heart, in your womb, and in the assistance and support he gives you. Rejoice, blessed

Virgin: Christ the King has come from heaven into your womb. Blessed shall you be among women, for you have given birth to life for men and women alike. The mother of our race brought punishment upon the world; the mother of our Lord brought salvation to the world.

Eve killed, Mary gave life, since she replaced disobedience by obedience. In joy, therefore, does Mary bring forth her Child, in gladness she embraces her Son, carrying him who carries her. Listen to her as she says: *My soul proclaims the greatness of the Lord, my spirit rejoices in God my Saviour; for he has looked with favour on his lowly servant. From this day all generations will call me blessed, because the Almighty has done great things for me.*

Then, after the angel's prophecy of blessing, while the Virgin was silently asking herself what this greeting could mean, the heavenly messenger continued: *Do not be afraid, Mary, for you have found favour with God. You will conceive and bear a son, and you shall name him Jesus. How can this be, she said, since I am a virgin? The Holy Spirit will come upon you, the angel answered, and the power of the Most High will overshadow you; therefore the holy one to be born of you will be called the son of God.* Then, without delay, the messenger returned and Christ entered his virginal bridal chamber. Let us also rejoice on the special day of this great Virgin, who alone among women was found worthy to receive into her holy and chaste body, her virginal womb, the King whom neither the heavens, the earth, nor the sea can contain. May she lovingly intercede for us with her Son, who conducted her with great glory to his heavenly palace where she now lives and reigns with him for ever and ever. Amen.

S. J. Eales (trans.) and J. Mabillon (ed.) *The Life and Works of St. Bernard of Clairvaux* (1896) vol. III, pp. 293, 299, 315–316

Sermon on the Virgin Mary: St Bernard of Clairvaux (d. 1153)

5. To that city then was sent the Angel Gabriel by God; but to whom was he sent? *To a Virgin, espoused to a man whose name was Joseph.* Who is this virgin so worthy of reverence as to be saluted by an Angel: yet so humble, as to be betrothed to a carpenter? A beautiful combination is that of virginity with humility: and that soul singularly pleases God in which humility gives worth to virginity, and virginity throws a new lustre on humility. But of how great respect must she not be thought worthy, in whom maternity consecrates virginity, and the splendour of a Birth exalts humility? You hear her, a virgin, and humble: if you are not able to imitate the virginity of that humble soul, imitate at least her humility; Virginity is a praiseworthy virtue; but humility is more necessary. . . .

7. There is something still more admirable in Mary: namely, her maternity joined with virginity. For from the beginning was never such a thing heard, as that one should be at the same time Mother and Virgin. If you consider also of whom she is Mother, to what degree will not your admiration of such a marvellous advancement soar? Will you not feel that you can hardly admire it enough? Will not your judgment or rather that of the Truth, be, that she whose Son is God, is exalted even above the choirs of Angels? Is it not Mary who says boldly to God, the Lord of Angels, *Son, why hast thou thus dealt with us?* Who of the Angels would dare to speak thus? It is sufficient for them, and they count it for a great thing, that they are spirits by nature, that they were made and called Angels by His grace, as David testifies: *Who makes His Angels Spirits* (Ps. civ. 4). But Mary, knowing herself to be Mother, with confidence names Him Son, whom they obey with reverence. Nor does God disdain to be called by the name which He has deigned to

assume. For a little after the Evangelist adds: *And He was subject unto them* (Luke ii. 5I). Who, and to whom? God, to human beings; God, I say, to whom the Angels are subject, whom Principalities and Powers obey, was subject unto Mary; and to Joseph also for her sake. Admire then both the benign condescension of the Son and the most excellent dignity of the Mother; and choose whether of the two is the more admirable. Each is a wonder, each a miracle. God is obedient to a woman, an unexampled humility! a woman is in the place of ancestor to God, a distinction without a sharer! When the praises of virgins are sung, it is said, that they follow the Lamb whithersoever He goeth (Apoc. xiv. 4), of what praise shall she be thought worthy, who even goes before Him?

17. The verse of the Evangelist ends thus: *And the Virgin's name was Mary*. Let us say a few words upon this name also. The word Mary means *Star of the Sea*, which seems to have a wonderful fitness to the Virgin Mother. For she is fitly compared to a star; for just as a star sends forth its ray without injury to itself, so the Virgin, remaining a virgin, brought forth her Son. The ray does not diminish the clearness of the star, nor the Son of the Virgin her Virginity. She is even that noble star risen out of Jacob, whose ray enlightens the whole world, whose splendour both shines in the Heavens and penetrates into Hell: and as it traverses the lands, it causes minds to glow with virtues more than bodies with heat, while vices it burns up and consumes. She, I say, is that beautiful and admirable star, raised of necessity above this great and spacious sea of life, shining with virtues and affording an illustrious example. Whosoever thou art who knowest thyself to be tossed about among the storms and tempests of this troubled world rather than to be walking peacefully upon the shore, turn not thine eyes away from the shining of this star, if thou wouldst not be overwhelmed with the tempest. If the winds of temptation arise, if you are driving upon the rocks of tribulation, look to the star, invoke Mary. If you are tossed upon the waves of pride, of ambition, of envy, of rivalry, look to the star, invoke Mary. If wrath, avarice, temptations of the flesh assail the frail skiff of your mind, look to Mary. If you are troubled by the greatness of your crimes, confused by the foulness of your conscience, and desperate with the horror of judgment, you feel yourself drawn into the depth of sorrow and into the abyss of despair; in dangers, in difficulties, in perplexities: invoke and think of Mary. Let not the name depart from heart and from lips; and that you may obtain a part in the petitions of her prayer, do not desert the example of her life. If you think of and follow her you will not go wrong, nor despair if you beg of her. With her help you will not fall or be fatigued; if she is favourable you will be sure to arrive; and thus you will learn by your own experience how rightly it is said: *The Virgin's name was Mary*. But now let us stop for a little, that we may not have merely a passing glance at the lustre of the great light. For to use the words of the Apostles *It is good for us to be here*; it is a happiness to be able to contemplate in silence what a laboured discourse could not sufficiently explain. But in the meantime the pious contemplation of that brilliant star will give us new ardour for what remains to be said.

The martyrs of the Early Church were the pattern for subsequent saints. They died for the supremacy of the spiritual over the temporal either as victims of the Roman Empire or of paganism. Many of the martyrs were clerics, but a substantial and popular group were the virgin martyrs whose pure offering of their lives marked them for special devotion. Catherine of Alexandria, one of the most popular of these virgins, has a largely legendary life and her cult was developed in the ninth century, five centuries after her supposed existence.

E. C. E. Owen (trans.) *Some Authentic Acts of the Early Martyrs* (Oxford, 1927) pp. 95–99

The trials and execution of Cyprian (d. 258)

1.1. During the consulship of the emperors Valerian and Gallienus, Valerian being consul for the fourth and Gallienus for the third time, on August 30 at Carthage in his private room Paternus the proconsul said to Cyprian the bishop: 'The most sacred emperors Valerian and Gallienus have thought fit to send me a letter, in which they have commanded that those who do not observe the Roman religion must recognize the Roman rites. I have therefore made inquiries concerning yourself. What answer have you to give me?'

2. Cyprian the bishop said: 'I am a Christian and a bishop. I know no other God but the one true God, who "made heaven and earth, the sea, and all that in them is." This God we Christians serve, to him we pray day and night for ourselves, and for all men, and for the safety of the emperors themselves.'

3. The proconsul Paternus said: 'Is your will constant in this?'

Cyprian the bishop answered: 'A good will, which knows God, cannot be altered.'

4. The proconsul Paternus said: 'Can you then in accordance with the order of Valerius and Gallienus go into exile to the city of Curubis?'

Cyprian the bishop said: 'I will go.'

5. The proconsul Paternus said: 'They have thought fit to write to me not about bishops only, but also about priests. I would know therefore from you who the priests are, who reside in this city.'

Cyprian the bishop answered: 'It is an excellent and beneficial provision of your laws that informers are forbidden. They cannot therefore be revealed and reported by me. They will be found in their own cities.'

2.1. Then the proconsul Paternus ordered the blessed Cyprian to be banished. And as he stayed a long time in exile, the proconsul Aspasius Paternus was succeeded in the proconsulship by Galerius Maximus, who ordered the holy bishop Cyprian to be recalled from banishment and brought before him.

2. When Cyprian, the holy martyr chosen by God, had returned from the city [of] Curubis, which had been assigned as his place of banishment by command of Aspasius, then proconsul, by divine command he remained in his own gardens, whence he daily expected to be summoned, as had been shown him [in a vision, recorded in the account of his 'Life' by Pontius].

3. While he still lingered in that place, suddenly on September 13 in the consulship of Tuscus and Bassus there came to him two high officials, one an equerry of the staff of the proconsul Galerius Maximus, and the other a member of the same staff, an equerry of the bodyguard.

4. These lifted him into a carriage, placed him between them, and conveyed him to the house of Sextus, whither the proconsul Galerius Maximus had retired to recover his health.

5. And so the same Galerius Maximus the proconsul ordered Cyprian to be remanded till the morrow. For the time being blessed Cyprian withdrew under guard to the house of a high official, equerry on the same staff of the illustrious Galerius Maximus the proconsul, and remained with him at a house in the street which is called Saturn's between the temple of Venus and the temple of Public Welfare. There the whole congregation of the brethren gathered: when this came to holy Cyprian's knowledge he gave orders that charge should be kept of the young women, for all had remained in the street before the door of the official's house.

4.1. Galerius Maximus having conferred with the council gave sentence hardly and reluctantly in these terms: 'You have long lived in the holding of sacrilegious opinions, and have joined with yourself very many members of an abominable conspiracy, and have set yourself up as an enemy of the gods of Rome and religious ordinances, nor have the pious and most sacred emperors Valerian and Gallienus, the Augusti, and Valerian, the most noble Caesar, been able to recall you to the observance of their rites.

2. And therefore since you have been convicted as the contriver and standard-bearer in most atrocious crimes, you shall be an example to those whom by your wickedness you have joined with you: discipline shall be vindicated in your blood.'

3. With these words he read from his tablets the sentence: 'It is our pleasure that Thascius Cyprianus should be executed by the sword.'

Cyprian the bishop said: 'Thanks be to God!'

5.1. After this sentence the crowd of brethren cried: 'Let us also be beheaded with him.' Hence arose an uproar among the brethren, and a great crowd accompanied him.

2. So the same Cyprian was led forth on to the land of Sextus and there he divested himself of his mantle and kneeled upon the ground; and bowed in prayer to the Lord.

3. And when he had divested himself of his dalmatic and handed it to the deacons, he stood clad in his linen garment, and prepared to await the executioner.

4. When the executioner arrived he charged his friends that they should give to the same executioner twenty-five golden pieces. Napkins and handkerchiefs were strewn before him by the brethren.

5. Thereafter blessed Cyprian bound his eyes with his own hand, but, as he could not fasten the ends of the handkerchief for himself, the priest Julianus and the sub-deacon Julianus fastened them for him.

6. So the blessed Cyprian suffered, and his body was laid out hard by to content the curiosity of the heathen. Thence it was removed by night, and, accompanied by tapers and torches, was conducted with prayers in great triumph to the burial-ground of Macrobius Candidianus the procurator, which lies on the Mappalian way near the fish-ponds. A few days later Galerius Maximus the proconsul died.

The most blessed martyr Cyprian suffered on the 14th day of September under the emperors Valerian and Gallienus, in the reign of our Lord Jesus Christ, to whom belong honour and glory for ever and ever. Amen.

Conversion was a common theme in the lives of the saints and often led an individual to seek a radical pattern of religious life. Monks and other religious sought a lifetime search for God, and their holiness was expressed in miracle stories which showed both God's dealings with men and women, and the integration of the saints in the life of the world.

R. Hudleston (ed.) Sir Tobie Matthew, *The Confessions of Saint Augustine* (1927) pp. 200–203

St Augustine of Hippo (d. 430)

Book 8

CHAPTER XII: HOW BY A VOICE AND BY THE WORDS OF THE APOSTLE, HE WAS MIRACULOUSLY CONVERTED

So soon then as deep consideration had drawn up out of the secret depths of my heart the whole heap of my misery, and had piled it up before the sight of my mind, there rose a tempestuous storm which brought with it a huge shower of tears. And that I might pour them forth with cries unheard, I rose from Alipius – for solitude seemed to me more fit for such a business of weeping – and I withdrew so far off that his presence might not be a restraint to me. Thus was it with me at that moment and he perceived it; though I think I had said somewhat, whereby my voice betrayed my load of tears, and how gladly I would be delivered of them. In this sort I rose, and he remained where we had sat together, lost in amazement. I cast myself down, I know not how, under certain fig-tree, and gave full liberty to my tears, which brake like rivers from mine eyes, *an acceptable sacrifice unto thee, O Lord.* And I cried out at large to thee, not perhaps in these very words, but to this effect, *'And thou, O Lord, how long? How long, O Lord? Wilt thou be angry with me for ever? Remember not my iniquities of old times.'* For I felt myself to be still enthralled by them, and therefore did I cast forth these lamentable exclamations, 'How long, how long? To-morrow and to-morrow? Why not even now? Why not, even at this instant, make an end of my uncleanness?' Thus did I say, and I wept in the most bitter sorrow of my heart.

And lo, I heard a voice, as if it had been some boy or girl from a house not far off, uttering and often repeating in a sing-song manner, 'Take up and read. Take up and read.' And instantly, with changed countenance, I began to consider intently, whether children in some game of theirs were used to sing any such words; yet could I not find that I had ever heard the like. Then, stemming the course of my tears, I rose up, conceiving that I was required from heaven to read that chapter which the first opening of the book should lead me to. For I had heard how Antony, by reading of the Gospel – to the hearing of which he came once by accident – had held himself to be admonished, as if the passage read had been particularly meant for him: *'Go, sell all that thou hast, and give it to the poor, and thou shalt have treasure in heaven; and come thou, and follow me';* by which oracle he was instantly converted unto thee.

Hastily therefore I went back thither, to where Alipius was sitting, for there I had laid the book of the Apostle, when I had risen from thence. I took it quickly into my hand, I opened it, and I read in silence from that chapter, on which first mine eyes were cast: *'Not in rioting and drunkenness, not in chambering and wantonness, not in strife and envying; but put ye on the Lord Christ, and make no provision for the flesh and its concupiscences.'* No further would I read, nor was there cause why I should; for instantly with the end of this sentence, as by a clear and constant light infused into my heart, the darkness of all former doubts was driven away. Then shutting the book, and putting my finger or some other mark between the leaves, I declared unto Alipius all that had happened, with a quiet countenance. And he also, in like manner, revealed unto me that which had passed in his own heart, whereof I knew nothing. He then asked to see what I had read.

I showed it, and he read on further than I had done, for I was ignorant of what followed, which yet was this, '*Now him that is weak in the faith take with you;*' the which he applied unto himself, for so he told me. And by this admonition he was much strengthened and, without any troublesome delay, he united himself with me in that good purpose and resolution, the which was most agreeable to his disposition, wherein he did ever differ from me greatly, and greatly to the better.

From thence we went in unto my mother, we told her, and she rejoiced. Then did we declare to her in order in what manner the whole was done, whereon she did exult and triumph, and bless thee, O Lord, who *art able to do above that which we can either ask or think*; for now she saw that thou hadst given her more in my regard than she was wont to beg of thee in all her sad and tearful lamentations. For thou didst so convert me to thyself, as that I did no more desire a wife nor any other ambition of this world; setting my feet upon that Rule of Faith, whereon thou hadst revealed unto her, so many years before, that I should stand. Thus *didst thou turn her mourning into joy*, more plentiful than she had dared to wish for, and far more clear and purer than she could have found in the offspring of my flesh.

H. J. Coleridge (ed.) *The Dialogues of St. Gregory the Great* (1874) pp. 71–76

St Gregory the Great (d. 604)

Chapter VIII: How a loaf was poisoned, and carried far off by a crow

When as the aforesaid monasteries were zealous in the love of our Lord Jesus Christ, and their fame dispersed far and near, and many gave over the secular life, and subdued the passions of their soul under the light yoke of our Saviour, then, (as the manner of wicked people is to envy at that virtue which themselves desire not to follow,) one Florentius, priest of a church hard by, and grandfather to Florentius, our sub-deacon, possessed with diabolical malice, began to envy the holy man's virtues, to backbite his manner of living, and to withdraw as many as he could from going to visit him: and when he saw that he could not hinder his virtuous proceedings, but that, on the contrary, the fame of his holy life increased, and many daily, upon the very report of his sanctity, did betake themselves to a better state of life: burning more and more with the coals of envy, he became far worse; and though he desired not to imitate his commendable life, yet fain he would have had the reputation of his virtuous conversation. In conclusion, so much did malicious envy blind him, and so far did he wade in that sin, that he poisoned a loaf, and sent it to the servant of Almighty God, as it were for an holy present. The man of God received it with great thanks, yet not ignorant of that which was hidden within. At dinner time, a crow daily used to come unto him from the next wood, which took bread at his hands; coming that day, after his manner, the man of God threw him the loaf which the priest had sent him, giving him this charge: 'In the Name of Jesus Christ, our Lord, take up that loaf, and leave it in some such place where no man may find it.' Then the crow, opening his mouth, and lifting up his wings, began to hop up and down about the loaf, and after his manner to cry out, as though he would have said that he was willing to obey, and yet could not do what he was commanded. The man of God again and again bade him, saying 'Take it up without fear, and throw it where no man may find it.' At length, with much ado, the crow took it up and flew away; and after three hours, having despatched the loaf, he returned back again, and received his usual allowance from the man of God.

But the venerable father, perceiving the priest so wickedly bent against his life, was far more song for him than grieved for himself. And Florentius, seeing that he could not kill the body of the master, laboureth now what he can to destroy the souls of his disciples; and for that purpose he sent into the yard of the abbey before their eyes seven naked young women, which did there take hands together, play, and dance a long time before them: to the end that by this means they might inflame their minds to sinful lust: which damnable sight the holy man beholding out of his cell, and fearing the danger which thereby might ensue to his younger monks, and considering that all this was done only for the persecuting of himself, he gave place to envy; and therefore, after he had for those abbeys and oratories which he had there built appointed governors, and left some under their charge, himself, in the company of a few monks, removed to another place. And thus the man of God, upon humility, gave place to the other's malice; but yet Almighty God of justice did severely punish his wickedness. For when the aforesaid priest, being in his chamber, understood of the departure of holy Bennet [Benedict], and was very glad of that news, behold (the whole house besides continuing safe and sound) that chamber alone in which he was fell down, and so killed him: which strange accident the holy man's disciple, Maurus, understanding, sent him word, he being as yet scarce ten miles off, desiring him to return again, because the priest that did persecute him was slain; which thing when Bennet [Benedict] heard, he was passing sorrowful, and lamented much, both because his enemy died in such sort, and also for that one of his monks rejoiced thereat, and therefore he gave him penance for that, sending such news, he presumed to rejoice at his enemy's death.

PETER. The things you report be strange, and much to be wondered at: for in making the well to yield forth water, I see Moses; and in the iron which came from the bottom of the lake I behold Eliseus; in the walking of Maurus upon the water I perceive Peter; in the obedience of the crow I contemplate Elias; and in lamenting the death of his enemy I acknowledge David; and therefore, in mine opinion, this one man was full of the spirit of all good men.

GREGORY. The man of God, Bennet [Benedict], had the spirit of the One true God, Who, by the grace of our redemption, hath filled the hearts of His elect servants; of Whom St. John saith: 'He was the true Light, which doth lighten every man coming into this world.' Of whom again we find it written: 'Of His fullness we have all received.' For God's holy servants might receive virtues of our Lord, but to bestow them upon others they could not; and therefore it was He that gave the signs of miracles to His servants. Who promised to give the sign of Jonas to His enemies: so that He vouchsafed to die in the sight of the proud, and to rise again before the eyes of the humble: to the end that they might behold what they contemned, and those see that which they ought to worship and love: by reason of which mystery it cometh to pass that whereas the proud cast their eyes upon the contempt of His Death, the humble contrariwise, against death, lay hold of the glory of His power and might.

PETER. To what places, I pray you, after this, did the holy man go: and whether did he afterward in them work any miracles, or no?

GREGORY. The holy man, changing his place, did not, for all that, change his enemy. For afterwards he endured so much the more grievous battles, by how much he had now the Master of all wickedness fighting openly against him. For the town, which is called Cassino, standeth upon the side of an high mountain, which containeth, as it were, in the lap thereof, the aforesaid town, and afterward so riseth in height the space of three miles, that the top thereof seemeth to touch the very heavens: in this place there was an ancient chapel in which the foolish and simple country people, according to the custom of the old Gentiles, worshipped the god Apollo. Round about it likewise upon all sides there were woods for the service of the devils, in which, even to that very time, the mad multitude of infidels did offer most wicked sacrifice. The man of God coming thither, beat in pieces the idol, overthrew the altar, set fire on the woods, and in the temple of Apollo built the oratory of St. Martin: and where the altar of the same Apollo was he made an oratory of St. John: and by his continual preaching he brought the people dwelling in those parts to embrace the faith of Christ. The old enemy of mankind, not taking this in good part, did, not now privily or in a dream, but in open sight present himself to the eyes of that holy father, and with great outcries complained that he had offered him violence. The noise which he made the monks did hear, but himself they could not see: but as the venerable father told them he appeared visibly unto him most fell and cruel, and as though, with his fiery mouth and flaming eyes, he would have torn him in pieces: what the devil said unto him all the monks did hear; for first he would call him by his name, and because the man of God vouchsafed him not any answer, then would he fall a reviling and railing at him: for when he cried out, calling him 'Bennet,' and yet found that he gave him no answer, straightway he would turn his tune, and say: 'Cursed Bennet [Benedict], not blessed: what hast thou to do with me? And why dost thou thus persecute me?' Wherefore new battles of the old enemy against the servant of God are to be looked for, against whom willingly did he make war, but against his will did he give him occasion of many notable victories.

E. Brehaut (trans.) Gregory of Tours, *History of the Franks*, Records of Civilisation 2 (New York, 1916) pp. 260–262

Gregory of Tours (d. 594): The life of St Gall (d. c.630)

1. St. Gall was a servant of God from his youth up, loving the Lord with his whole heart, and he loved what he knew to be beloved by God. His father was named Georgius and his mother Leocadia a descendant of Vectius Epagatus who, as the history of Eusebius relates, was a martyr at Lyons. They belonged among the leading senators so that no family could be found in the Gauls better born or nobler. And although Gall's father wished to ask for a certain senator's daughter for him, he took a single attendant and went to the monastery at Cournon, six miles from Clermont, and besought the abbot to consent to give him the tonsure. The abbot noticed the good sense and fine bearing of the youth and inquired his name, his family and native place. He replied that he was called Gall and was a citizen of Auvergne, a son of the senator Georgius. When the abbot learned that he belonged to one of the first families he said: 'My son, what you wish is good, but you must first bring it to your father's attention and if he gives his consent, I will do what you ask.' Then the abbot sent messengers in regard to this matter to his father, asking what he wished to be done with the youth. The father was a little disappointed, but said: 'He is my oldest son and I therefore wished him to marry, but if the Lord deigns to receive him into His service, let His will

rather than mine be done.' And he added: 'Consent to the child's request which he made by God's inspiration.'

2. The abbot on receiving this message made him a clerk. He was very chaste and as if already old he had no wicked desires: he refrained from a young man's mirth; he had a voice wonderfully sweet and melodious; he devoted himself constantly to reading; he took pleasure in fasting and was very abstemious. When the blessed bishop Quintian came to this monastery and heard him sing, he did not allow him to stay there any longer, but took him to the city and, like the heavenly father, fed him on the sweetness of the spirit. On his father's death, when his voice was improving day by day and he was a great favourite among the people, they reported this to king Theodoric, who at once sent for him and showed him such affection that he loved him more than his own son; he was loved by the queen with a similar love, not only for his beautiful voice, but also for his chastity. At that time king Theodoric had taken many clerks from Auvergne whom he ordered to serve God in the church at Trèves; but he never allowed the blessed Gall to be separated from him. So it came that when the king went to Cologne, he went with him. There was there a heathen temple full of various articles of worship where the neighbouring barbarians used to make offerings and stuff themselves with food and drink until they vomited; there also they worshipped images as god, and carved limbs in wood, each one the limb in which he had suffered pain. When the holy Gall heard of this, he hastened to the place with only one clerk when none of the benighted pagans was present, and set it on fire. And they saw the smoke of the fire rolling up to the sky and searched for the one who had set it, and found him and pursued him sword in hand. He fled and took refuge in the king's court. But when the king had learned from the pagans' threats what had been done, he pacified them with agreeable words and so calmed their furious rage. The blessed man would often weep in telling this story, and say: 'Unhappy me that I did not stand my ground and let my life be ended in this affair.' He was deacon at the time. . . .

3. Later when the blessed bishop Quintian passed from this world by God's command, the holy Gall was living in Clermont, and the people of the city assembled at the house of the priest Inpetratus, Gall's uncle on his mother's side, lamenting at the bishop's death and asking who should be appointed in his place. After long debate they returned each to his own house. On their departure the holy Gall called one of the clerks and said, the holy spirit rushing into him: 'What are these people muttering about? Why are they running to and fro? What are they debating? They are wasting their time,' said he. 'I am going to be bishop; the Lord will deign to bestow this honour on me. Now when you hear that I am returning from the king's presence, take my predecessor's horse with the saddle on him and come and bring him to me. If you refuse to obey me, take care you are not sorry for it later.' As he said this, he was lying on his bed. The clerk was angry at him and abused him and struck him on the side, breaking the bed at the same time, and went off in a rage. On his departure the priest Inpetratus said to the blessed Gall: 'My son, hear my advice: don't waste a minute, but go to the king and tell him what has happened here, and if the Lord inspires him to bestow this holy office on you, I shall give thanks to God; otherwise you can at least recommend yourself to the man who is appointed.' He went and reported to the king what had happened. . . .

And the clerks of Clermont, with the choice of the foolish, went to the king with many gifts. Even then that seed of iniquity had begun to germinate, that bishoprics were sold by kings and bought by the clerks. Then they heard from the king that they were going to have St. Gall as bishop. He was ordained priest and the king gave orders to invite the citizens to a feast at the expense of the treasury and to make merry over the promotion of Gall the future bishop. This was done. He was in the habit of telling that he had given no more for the office of bishop than a third of a gold piece which he had given to the cook who prepared the feast. Then the king appointed two bishops to accompany him to Clermont. And the clerk, Viventius by name, who had struck him on the side when he was in bed, hastened to meet the bishop according to his command, but not without great shame, and he presented himself and the horse which Gall had ordered. When they had gone into the bath together, Gall gently reproached him for the pain in his side which he had incurred from the contemptuous violence of the clerk, and he caused him great shame, not in a spirit of anger, however, but only delighting in a pious joke. After that he was received into the city with much singing and was ordained bishop in his own church.

C. Garton (trans.) *The Metrical Life of St Hugh* (Lincoln, 1986) pp. 73–75

The miracle of the knight cured of cancer

The presence of so many persons of such high eminence taking part in Saint Hugh's funeral made plain in no uncertain manner what a man he was and the great rewards he was obtaining for the race he had run.

The bier was bedewed with a flood of tears by a knight of Lindsey, who was displaying to everyone the flesh, eaten away by cancer, of his putrefying arm. The bare bones were exposed, and the bone-wall was scarcely able to separate the tender marrow within from the voracious disease. For if a cancer has caused nature's normally hidden parts to lie open to view, it lives and devours: there is no art which can cure it. So the knight, weeping over his arm, consumed as it was by the wasting disease, touched the bishop's holy body and his uncovered face with the cancerous wound. As he did so, a wonderful and unprecedented thing suddenly happened. Medicine was dumbfounded at new causes of the effect at which it itself aims. When the dead body was touched the deadly wound was healed: bone was clothed with flesh, and flesh with skin in a marvellous way. Nowhere did traces of the disease remain, nowhere signs of a scar telling the tale of the old affliction.

Whether this skin along with the flesh was taken from the flesh of the arm, or whether it was conveyed or rather created there out of nothing, is a matter that hangs in doubt. Either eventuality appears difficult and unprecedented and seems impossible in the course of nature. For if it was taken from the flesh of the arm, this must have been by a motion either natural or violent. But if by nature, then a most pure fluid must by force of the gases have been drawn over the bare bones and condensed into flesh; and condensation into flesh does not take place except very gradually and by successive stages. But the flesh in question was condensed suddenly, and therefore not by motion of nature. If, however, it was by violent motion, it follows that what was inserted into this part was taken away from that; which is plainly false. It remains, therefore, that the flesh or the skin in question was not made from any source material. So it was simply created. It was therefore not made out of the elements or of abstract matter (hyle), and it will therefore not return into such matter. It will therefore be incorruptible. For anything that is generated out of abstract matter, tends when it is corrupted to turn back into abstract matter. Thus opinion ranges variously through a hundred arguments; the human mind vacillates via various reasoning to various goals, confronted as it is by the unprecedentedness of such a mind-boggling event.

At length the funeral ceremonies were solemnly completed by the lordships of the whole realm. The sacred body was reverently buried, and given an outstandingly honorific tomb.

Miracles became associated not only with the lives of saints but also with their relics. The cult of the saints was also a cult of the dead, and the relics of the saints concentrated saints' power to heal and inspire. Relics gave status to a church and brought in revenue and pilgrims, although even in the Middle Ages there were some critics of the more superstitious elements in the relic industry.

J. France (ed.) Radulf Glaber, *The Five Books of the Histories*, Oxford Medieval Texts (Oxford, 1989) book III, ch. vi, p. 19

The power of relics

vi. Holy relics found everywhere

19. When the whole world was, as we have said, clothed in a white mantle of new churches, a little later, in the eighth year after the millennium of the Saviour's Incarnation, the relics of many saints were revealed by various signs where they had long lain hidden. It was as though they had been waiting for a brilliant resurrection and were now by God's permission revealed to the gaze of the faithful; certainly they brought much comfort to men's minds. This revelation is known to have begun in the city of Sens in Gaul in the church of the holy martyr Stephen. The archbishop of that place was Lierri. Wonderful to relate, he discovered there many ancient and holy things which had long lain hidden, amongst them a fragment of the staff of Moses. News of this discovery brought numbers of the faithful, not just from the provinces of Gaul but from most of Italy and the lands beyond the sea; no small number of them were sick people who returned, cured by the intervention of the saints. But as so often happens when something occurs which at the start is good for men, the vice of greed flourishes and in the usual way disaster strikes. This city, to which such vast crowds resorted, as we have said, became immensely rich as a result of their piety, but its inhabitants conceived a terrible insolence because of this blessing. . . .

N. P. Tanner (ed. and trans.) *Decrees of the Ecumenical Councils* (Georgetown, 1990) vol. 1, p. 248

Instructions relating to relics

62. That saints' relics may not be exhibited outside reliquaries, nor may newly discovered relics be venerated without authorization from the Roman church

The Christian religion is frequently disparaged because certain people put saints' relics up for sale and display them indiscriminately. In order that it may not be disparaged in the future, we ordain by this present decree that henceforth ancient relics shall not be displayed outside a reliquary or be put up for sale. As for newly discovered relics, let no one presume to venerate them publicly unless they have previously been approved by the authority of the Roman Pontiff. Prelates, moreover, should not in future allow those who come to their churches, in order to venerate, to be deceived by lying stories or false documents, as has commonly happened in many places on account of the desire for profit. We also forbid the recognition of alms-collectors, some of whom deceive other people by proposing various errors in their preaching, unless they show authentic letters from the Apostolic See or from the diocesan bishop. Even then they shall not be permitted to put before the people anything beyond what is contained in the letters. . . .

Let those who are sent to seek alms be modest and discreet, and let them not stay in taverns or other unsuitable places or incur useless or excessive expenses, being careful above all not to wear the garb of false religion. Moreover, because the keys of the church are brought into contempt and satisfaction through penance loses its force through indiscriminate and excessive indulgences, which certain prelates of churches do not fear to grant, we therefore decree that when a basilica is dedicated, the indulgence shall not be for more than one year, whether it is dedicated by one bishop or by more than one, and for the anniversary of the dedication the remission of penances imposed is not to exceed forty days. We order that the letters of indulgence, which are granted for various reasons at different times, are to fix this number of days, since the Roman Pontiff himself, who possesses the plenitude of power is accustomed to observe this moderation in such things.

J. Scott (trans.) William of Malmesbury, *De Antiquitate Glastonie Ecclesie*, (Woodbridge, 1981) pp. 67, 71, 163

Glastonbury Abbey

18. On the sanctity and dignity of the church of Glastonbury

The church of Glastonbury, therefore, is the oldest of all those that I know of in England and hence the epithet applied to it. In it are preserved the bodily remains of many saints, besides Patrick and the others of whom I spoke above, and there is no part of the church that is without the ashes of the blessed. The stone-paved floor, the sides of the altar, the very altar itself, above and within, are filled with relics close-packed. Deservedly indeed is the repository of so many saints said to be a heavenly shrine on earth. How fortunate, good Lord, are those inhabitants who have been summoned to an upright life by reverence for that place. I cannot believe that any of these can fail of heaven, for their deaths are accompanied by the recommendation and advocacy of such great patrons. There one can observe all over the floor stones, artfully interlaced in the forms of triangles or squares and sealed with lead; I do no harm to religion if I believe some sacred mystery is contained beneath them. Its age and its multitude of saints have called forth such reverence for the place that at night scarcely anyone presumes to keep watch there, nor during the day to spit there; let anyone aware of displaying such foul contempt quake with bodily fear. No one has brought a hunting bird within the neighbouring cemetery or led a horse thither and left again without himself or his possessions being harmed. Within living memory everyone undergoing ordeal by iron or water who has offered a prayer there has, with one exception, rejoiced in his salvation. If anyone thought to place any building nearby which by its shade interfered with the light of the church that building became a ruin. It is quite clear that to the men of that province no oath was holier or more oft repeated than that 'by the old church', upon which they did anything rather than perjure themselves, out of fear of sudden retribution. The testimony of many absolutely truthful men throughout the ages upholds the truth, if it be doubtful, of the words we have set down.

22. *On the various relics deposited at Glastonbury*

Since the island of Glastonbury is remarkable in containing the ashes of so many saints besides those mentioned above it is a pleasure to record the names of a few out of the many whose bodily remains, we do not doubt, for the most part rest there. For to recount in detail the relics of saints collected there by kings and magnates would be to extend this volume immeasurably: besides, they are recorded in the Gospel-Books. I will pass over the ones mentioned before, namely the twelve disciples of St Philip, Phagan and Deruvian and their many disciples, Patrick, Benignus, Indract and his comrades, Gildas the wise, St David of Menevia and those whom the venerable Tyccea is said to have brought thither. Know that it is reliably said that resting there are St Paulinus, archbishop of Northumbria, two Innocents translated thither from Bethlehem by pious King Edgar, St Dunstan, our magnificent father an account of whose translation from Canterbury to Glastonbury we subjoin, as well as the bishops St Aidan and St Ultan, the brother of the blessed Fursey of whose wonderful deeds we read. There too are St Iltuit, so celebrated among the Welsh, and St Besilius, martyred at a tender age; also the relics of St Urban, pope and martyr, the bones of the martyrs St Anastasius, St Cesarius, St Benignus and St Melanus the bishop. There also rest St Aelflaed the queen and St Aelswitha, the virgin whose flesh and bones are still whole, as those who have seen them attest, and whose hair shirt and holy robe have not rotted. There too are the bones of the queen St Balthild and the virgin St Mamilla as well as the bodies of the saints Ursula, Daria, Crisanta, Udilia, Mary, Martha, Lucy, Luceus, Waleburga, Gertrude and Cecilia. In addition to the saints just mentioned there are innumerable relics of saints, the gifts of kings, princes, bishops and other noblemen, some of whose names are recorded in the old books of the church. Many relics too, carried from the kingdom of Northumbria at the time the Danes were waging war there. Others were brought from Wales, when it was being persecuted, to Glastonbury, as though to a storehouse of saints. And although we do not have complete knowledge of them, they themselves rejoice in their full knowledge and contemplation of God.

80. Customs

These were the customs observed in the time of Abbots Thurstan and Herluin. On some days of the week, namely Sunday, Tuesday, Thursday and Saturday, the brethren had three *generalia* and two *pitantiae* to eat but on the other three days, that is the second, fourth and sixth days, they had two *generalia* and three *pitantiae*. However, on holy days when the brethren were in copes they had cups of mead, fine wheaten cakes on the table, a measure of wine and three *generalia* and four or five *pitantiae*. On those days on which they wore albs they had a similar allowance of mead, fine wheaten cakes on their table and three *generalia* and three or four *pitantiae*. But on special festivals, that is Christmas, Easter, Pentecost, the Assumption and Nativity of the holy Mary and the Dedication of the church, there was a greater quantity for all, depending on the dignity of the festival. On the anniversaries of kings, bishops, abbots and ealdormen who helped build the church the brethren were obliged to celebrate mass for their souls at each altar, and, in particular, in the presence of the whole convent, to do so respectfully using the ornaments that they had given the church. At the same time 13 paupers were to be entertained on their behalves, after which they were to be served in the refectory as though it were a festival. This was the custom concerning dress: each of the brethren was to have two cowls, two frocks, two shirts of linsey-woolsey, two pairs of breeches, four pairs of stockings and a new pelisse every year, and on Maundy Thursday each was to have shoes for the day time and in winter for the night and two bed covers. They should also have ten pairs of slippers, two on the Festival of the Blessed Michael, four on the solemnity of All Saints, two on the Festival of St Martin and the other two when they considered it appropriate. And this is another ration: when they are to have wine in place of beer, each of them is to have two measures a day. For blood-letting see in the Gospel-book.

Saints in many monasteries were seen as part of the family and were included in monastic directories of signs.

D. Sherlock, *Signs for Silence: the sign language of the Monks of Ely in the Middle Ages* (Ely, ND) pp. 20–21

General signs for saints and martyrs

For an angel make the same sign as for alleluia.
Pro angelo fac idem signum quod pro alleluia.

For an Apostle draw the right hand downwards from the right side to the left and again from the left to the right for the pall which an archbishop wears. The same sign is for a bishop.
Pro apostolo trahe dexteram deorsum de dextero latere in sinistrum et iterum de sinistro in dexterum pro pallio quo archiepiscopus vestitur. Idem signum est episcopi.

For a Martyr place the right hand on the neck as if you want to cut something.
Pro martire inpone dexteram cervici quasi aliquid indicere velis.

For a Confessor if he is a bishop make the same sign as for an apostle; if he is an abbot make the sign for the Rule by taking hold of the hair.

Pro confessore si episcopus est fac idem signum quod pro apostolo; si abbas est fac signurn regule capillum comprehendendo.

For a Holy Virgin make the sign for a woman.
Pro sacra virgine fac signum femine.

For a festival make the sign for the first reading and bring forward all the fingers of each hand.
Pro festivitate fac signum primi lectionis et profer omnes digitos utriusque manus.

John F. Benton (ed.) and C. C. Swinton Bland (trans.) *Self and Society in Medieval France: the memoirs of Abbot Guibert of Nogent* (New York, 1970) pp. 196–197

Guibert of Nogent (d. 1125), The travelling relics of Laon Cathedral (1112)

Book III

CHAPTER 12

. . . Meanwhile, following the customary way, such as it is, of raising money, [the monks] began to carry around the feretories and relics of the saints. And so it came to pass that the gracious judge, who comforts with his pity in heaven those whom he reproves below, showed many miracles where they went. Now they were carrying, along with some box of undistinguished memory, a splendid little reliquary which contained parts of the robe of the Virgin Mother and of the sponge lifted to the lips of the Saviour and of his Cross. Whether it contained some of the hair of Our Lady, I do not know. It was made of gold and gems, and verses written on it in gold told of the wonders within.

On their second trip, coming to the district of Tours, they reached the town of Buzancais, which is held by a certain robber. There they preached to the people, among other things, about the disaster to their church. When our clergy saw that the lord and his garrison were listening to them with evil in their hearts and were planning to plunder them as they left the castle, the man who had the responsibility of speaking was placed in a difficult position. Although he did not believe his promises, he said to the people standing there, 'If there is an infirm soul among you, let him come to these holy relics, and, drinking the water which the relics have touched, he will assuredly by healed.'

Then the lord and the men of his castle were glad, thinking they must be caught for liars out of their own mouths, and they brought forward to him a servant about twenty years old, who was deaf and dumb. At that the danger and dismay of the clergy cannot be described. After they had prayed with deep sighs to the Lady of all and her only son, the Lord Jesus, the servant drank the holy water and the trembling priest asked him some question or other. He immediately replied, not with an answer to the question but with a repetition of the exact words which the priest had used. Since he had never before heard what was said to him, he was ignorant of any words but those just used. Why prolong the story? In that poor town their hearts suddenly became larger than their means. The lord of the town immediately gave the only horse he had, while the liberality of the rest went almost beyond their powers. And so the men who had planned to be their attackers became their advocates, with many tears praising God as their helper, and they freed the youth who had been cured so that he could stay with the holy relics forever. I saw this man in our church of Nogent, a person of dull intellect, awkward in speech and understanding, who faithfully carried round the tale of such a miracle and died not long afterward in the discharge of that duty.

In the city of Angers, there was a woman who had married as a little girl, and had worn the ring placed on her finger at that early age day and night, as she said, without ever taking it off. As years went by and the girl grew larger in body, the flesh rising up on each side of the ring had almost covered the metal, and consequently she had given up all hope of getting it off her finger. When the holy relics came there and she went with other women after the sermon to make her offering, as she held out her hand to place the money she had brought on the relics, the ring cracked and slipped from her hand before them. When the people, and especially the women, saw that the Virgin Mother had granted the woman such a favour, something she had not dared to ask for, the offerings of money by the people and of rings and necklaces by the women were beyond description. Touraine took much joy from the showering of the sweet odour of the merits of Our Lady, who is common to all, but the people of Anjou boasted that in a special sense they had the Mother of God at hand.

At another place – I cannot exactly say in what town it happened, but in the same diocese – at her own urgent prayer the relics were taken by the clergy to a certain honourable lady, who had long been in the grasp of a lasting and hopeless infirmity. And when she had adored the relics with all her heart and had drunk the holy water prepared from them, at once by Mary's healing she was restored to health. After she had done honour with due offerings to God's sacred relics and their bearer had left the threshold of her house, suddenly a boy came up on a horse, drawing a wagon which filled the middle of the narrow lane through which he had to pass. The cleric said to him, 'Halt, until the holy relics pass by'. And when the bearer had passed and the boy began to urge his horse forward, he was unable to continue his journey. The man who bore the relics then looked back that way and said, 'Go on, in the name of the Lord.' Once that was said, the horse and cart moved on. See what power you do grant in Mary and what respect she demands for herself!

In the third journey, they came to the castle of Nesle. Now Raoul, the lord of the castle, had in his house a deaf-and-dumb youth who supposedly knew the art of divination, learned no doubt from devils, and whom he was therefore said to love greatly. The relics were brought into the castle and honoured by the people with quite small gifts. The deaf-and-dumb man, who had been informed by signs of the curing of the other deaf-mute and who now actually saw him, gave his shoes to a poor man and, barefooted and with a penitent heart, followed the relics to the monastery of Lihons. As he lay during the day under the reliquary, it happened to be the hour for dinner: most of the clergy went to their meal and only a few remained to guard the relics. These men went for a short walk outside the church, and when they returned, they found the man stretched on the ground in great distress, with blood flowing from his mouth and ears with a great stench. When they saw this, the clerics called their companions who had gone to dinner to run to the scene of such a wonder. As the man came out of his fit, the clerics tried to ask him somehow or other if he could speak. Immediately he replied in the same words as he had heard his questioner use. They offered praise without limit and indescribable jubilation to God on high. At last by all sorts of prayers they were compelled to return to the town of Nesle, so that the poor first offering to the relics might be amply increased. And that was done to a wonderful degree. Here, too, Our Lady glorified herself, when her Divine Son made whole the gifts of nature which up to then he had held back.

CHAPTER 13

From here they sought lands overseas. When they had travelled to the Channel, they found certain wealthy merchants with ships for that voyage and were carried across calmly, as far as the winds were concerned. But suddenly they saw the galleys of pirates, whom they greatly feared, coming on directly against them. Steering toward them with oars sweeping the waters and their prows cutting through the waves, they were soon scarcely a furlong off. As the carriers of the relics were terribly afraid of those marine soldiers, one of our priests arose from their midst and lifted on high the reliquary in which the relics of the Queen of heaven were kept, forbidding their approach in the name of the Son and of the Mother. At that command the pirate craft immediately fell astern, driven off as speedily as they had with eagerness approached. Then there was thanksgiving among the delivered and much glorification, and the merchants with them offered many gifts in thanks to the gracious Mary.

They had a fair voyage then to England, and when they came to Winchester, many miracles done there brought renown. At Exeter similar events occurred and produced many gifts. Let me pass over the ordinary healing of sickness and touch only on exceptional cases. We are not writing their travel book – let them do that themselves – or what happened to each person. but are picking out examples useful for sermons. In almost all places, they were received with reverence, as was fitting, but when they came to a certain hamlet they were not admitted by the priest within the church, or by the peasants within their dwellings. They found two buildings without inhabitants and in one they bestowed themselves and their baggage and fitted up the other for the holy relics. Since that wicked crowd persisted in their obstinacy against the holy things, the next morning after the clergy left that place, suddenly, with a crash of thunder, a terrible bolt of lightning struck from the clouds and in its descent blasted their town, burning all the dwellings to ashes. But what a marvellous distinction God made! Although those two houses were in the midst of those that were burned, they remained as a manifest testimony by God that those unhappy men had suffered their fire because of the irreverence they had shown toward the Mother of God. The wicked priest, who had inflamed the cruelty of the barbarians instead of teaching them, gathered up the goods he was able to save from the heaven sent fire and carried them away, either to the river or the sea, intending to cross over. But there all the property he had gathered together to take across was destroyed on the spot by lightning. Thus these country people, uninstructed in the understanding of the mysteries of God, were taught by their own punishment.

They came to another town in which the great fervour of offerings to the sacred relics corresponded to their reputation and the evidence of the miracles. A certain Englishman standing in front of the church said to his companion, 'Let's go drink.' But the other said, 'I don't have the money.' Said the first, 'I will get some.' 'Where will you get it,' said he. 'I am thinking about those clerics,' said the first, 'who by their lying and their tricks get so much money out of the silly people. I will certainly manage in some sway or other to get out of them the expense of my entertainment.' After saying this, he entered the church and went to the platform on which the relics were placed, and, pretending that he wished to show his reverence for them by kissing them, he put his mouth against them with his lips open and sucked up some coins that had been offered. Then he went back to his companion and said, 'Come on, let's drink, for we have enough money now for our drinking bout.' 'Where did you get it,' said he, 'when you had none before?' 'I got it,' he said, 'by carrying away in my cheek some of the money given to those cheats in the church.' 'You have done something bad,' said the other, 'since you took it from the saints.' 'Be quiet,' replied he, 'and get along to the nearest tavern.' Why am I running on? They almost drank the sun down into the ocean. When evening came on, the man who had stolen the money from the holy altar mounted his horse and said he was going home. And when he had reached a nearby wood, he made a noose and hanged himself on a tree. Dying a miserable death, he paid the penalty for his sacrilegious lips. Out of the many things which the queenly Virgin did in England, it should be enough to have culled these instances.

After they had returned to Laon from collecting money, I have been told by a cleric of good character, who was given the job of carting wood for the repair of the roof of the church, that in ascending the mountain of Laon one of the oxen broke down from exhaustion. The cleric was exasperated, because he could not find another ox to put in its place, when suddenly an ox ran up to offer itself to him, coming as if it intended to help in the work. When he and the others had speedily drawn their carts right up to the church, the cleric was very anxious to know to whom he should return the strange ox. But as soon as the ox was unyoked, it did not wait for an oxherd or driver, but returned quickly to the place from which it came. . . .

C. E. McCracken (ed.) and A. Cabaniss (ed. and trans.) *Early Medieval Theology*, Library of Christian Classics 9 (Philadelphia, 1957) pp. 241–248

Criticism of the cult of relics: Claudius, Bishop of Turin (c. 816)

Your letter of chatter and dullness, together with the essay subjoined to it, I have received from the hands of the bumpkin who brought it to me. You declare that you have been troubled because a rumour about me has spread from Italy throughout all the regions of Gaul even to the frontiers of Spain as though I were announcing a new sect in opposition to the standard of catholic faith – an intolerable lie. It is not surprising, however, that they have spoken against me, those notorious members of the Devil who proclaimed our head Himself to be a diabolical seducer. It is not I who teach a sect, I who really hold the unity and preach the truth. On the contrary, as much as I have been able, I have suppressed, crushed, fought, and assaulted sects, schisms, superstitions, and heresies, and, as much as I am still able. I do not cease to do battle against them, relying wholeheartedly on the help of God. For which reason, of course, it came to pass that as soon as I was constrained to assume the burden of pastoral duty and to come to Italy to the city of Turin, sent there by our pious prince Louis, the son of the Lord's holy catholic church, I found all the churches filled, in defiance of the precept of truth, with those sluttish abominations – images. Since everyone was worshiping them, I undertook single-handedly to destroy them. Everyone thereupon opened his mouth to curse me, and had not God come to my aid, they would no doubt have swallowed me alive.

Since it is clearly enjoined that no representation should be made of anything in heaven, on earth, or under the earth, the commandment is to be understood, not only of likenesses of other gods, but also of heavenly creatures, and of those things which human conceit contrives in honour of the creator. To adore is to praise, revere, ask, entreat, implore, invoke, offer prayer. But to worship is to direct respect, be submissive, celebrate, venerate, love, esteem highly.

Those against whom we have undertaken to defend God's church say, 'We do not suppose that there is anything divine in the image which we adore. We adore it only to honour him whose likeness it is.' To whom we reply that if those who have abandoned the cult of demons now venerate the images of saints, they have not deserted their idols but have merely changed the name. For if you portray or depict on a wall representations of Peter and Paul, of Jupiter, Saturn, or Mercury, the latter representations are not gods and the former are not apostles, and neither the latter nor the former are men, although the word is used for that purpose. Nonetheless the selfsame error always persists both then and now. Surely if men may be venerated, it is the living rather than the dead who should be so esteemed, that is, where God's likeness is present, not where there is the likeness of cattle or (even worse) of stone or wood, all of which lack life, feeling, and reason. But if the works of God's hands must not be adored and worshiped, one should ponder carefully how much less are the works of men's hands to be adored and worshiped or held in honour of those whose likenesses they are. For if the image which one adores is not God, then in vain should it be venerated for honour of the saints who in vain arrogate to themselves divine dignities.

Above all, therefore, it should be perceived that not only he who worships visible figures and images, but also he who worships any creature, heavenly or earthly, spiritual or corporeal, in place of God's name, and who looks for the salvation of his soul from them (that salvation which is the prerogative of God alone), that it is he of whom the apostle speaks, 'They worshiped and served the creature rather than the Creator.'

Why do you humiliate yourselves and bow down to false images? Why do you bend your body like a captive before foolish likenesses and earthly structures? God made you upright, and although other animals face downward toward the earth, there is for you an upward posture and a countenance erect to heaven and to God. Look thither, lift your eyes thither, seek God in the heights, so that you can avoid those things which are below. Exalt your wavering heart to heavenly heights.

Why do you hurl yourself into the pit of death along with the insensate image which you worship? Why do you fall into the Devil's ruin through it and with it? Preserve the eminence which is yours by faith, continue to be what you were made by God.

But those adherents of false religion and superstition declare, 'It is to recall our Saviour that we worship, venerate, and adore a cross painted in his honour, bearing his likeness.' To them nothing seems good in our Saviour except what also seemed good to the unrighteous, namely the reproach of suffering and the mockery of death. They believe of him what even impious men, whether Jews or pagans, also believe who doubt that he rose again. They have not learned to think anything of him except that they believe and hold him in their heart as tortured and dead and always twisted in agony. They neither heed nor understand what the apostle says: 'Even though we once regarded Christ according to the flesh, we now regard him thus no longer.'

Against them we must reply that if they wish to adore all wood fashioned in the shape of a cross because Christ hung on a cross, then it is fitting for them to adore many other things which Christ did in the flesh. He hung on the cross scarcely six hours, but he was in the Virgin's womb nine lunar months and more than eleven days, a total of two hundred and seventy-six solar days, that is, nine months and more than six days. Let virgin girls therefore be adored, because a Virgin gave birth to Christ. Let mangers be adored, because as soon as he was born he was laid in a manger. Let old rags be adored, because immediately after he was born he was wrapped in old rags. Let boats be adored, because he often sailed in boats, taught the throngs from a small boat, slept in a boat, from a boat commanded the winds, and to the right of a fishing boat ordered them to cast the net when that great prophetic draught of fish was made. Let asses be adored, because he came to Jerusalem sitting on an ass. Let lambs be adored, because it was written of him, 'Behold, the Lamb of God, who takes away the sins of the world.' (But those infamous devotees of perverse doctrines prefer to eat the living lambs and adore only the ones painted on the wall!)

Still further, let lions be adored, because it was written of him. 'The Lion of the tribe of Judah, the Root of David, has conquered.' Let stones be adored, because when he was taken down from the Cross he was placed in a rock-hewn sepulchre, and because the apostle says of him, 'The Rock was Christ.' Yet Christ was called a rock, lamb and lion tropologically, not literally; in signification, not in substance. Let thorns of bramble-bushes be adored, because a crown of thorns was pressed upon his head at the time of his passion. Let reeds be adored, because with blows from them his head was struck by the soldiers. Finally, let lances be adored, because one of the soldiers at the Cross with a lance opened his side, whence flowed blood and water, the sacraments by which the church is formed.

All those things, of course, are facetious and should be lamented rather than recorded. But against fools we are compelled to propose foolish things, and against stony hearts to hurl, not verbal arrows and sentiments, but stony blows. 'Return to judgment, you liars,' you who have departed from the truth, who love vanity, and who have become vain; you who crucify the Son of God anew and hold him up for display and thereby cause the souls of wretched ones in disordered masses to become partners of demons. Estranging them through the impious sacrilege of idols, you cause them to be cast away by their own Creator and thrown into eternal damnation.

God commanded one thing; they do otherwise. God commanded them to bear the cross, not to adore it; they wish to adore what they are spiritually or corporally unwilling to bear. Yet thus to worship God is to depart from him, for he said, 'He who wishes to come after me, let him deny himself and take up his cross and follow me.' Unless one forsake himself, he does not approach the One who is above him; nor is he able to apprehend what is beyond himself if he does not know how to sacrifice what he is.

If you say that I forbid men to go to Rome for the sake of penance, you lie. I neither approve nor disapprove that journey, since I know that it does not injure, nor benefit, nor profit, nor harm anyone. If you believe that to go to Rome is to do penance, I ask you why you have lost so many souls in so much time, souls whom you have restrained in your monastery, or whom for the sake of penance you have received into your monastery and have not sent to Rome, but whom you have rather made to serve you. You say that you have a band of one hundred and forty monks who came to you for the sake of penance, surrendering themselves to the monastery. You have not permitted one of them to go to Rome. If these things are so (as you say, 'To go to Rome is to do penance'), what will you do about this statement of the Lord, 'Whoever causes one of these little ones who believe in me to stumble, it is expedient for him that a millstone be hung around his neck and that he be drowned in the deep, rather than cause one of these little ones who believe in me to stumble.' There is no greater scandal than to hinder a man from taking the road by which he can come to eternal joy.

We know, indeed, that the Evangelist's account of the Lord Saviour's words are not understood, where he says to the blessed apostle Peter 'You are Peter, and on this rock I will build my church, and I will give you the keys of the kingdom of heaven.' Because of these words of the Lord, the ignorant race of men, all spiritual understanding having been disregarded, wishes to go to Rome to secure eternal life. He who under-stands the keys of the kingdom in the manner stated above does not require the intercession of blessed Peter in a particular location, for if we consider carefully the proper meaning of the Lord's words, we find that he did not say to him, 'Whatever you shall loose in heaven shall be loosed on earth and whatever you shall bind in heaven shall be bound on earth.' One must know hereby that that ministry has been granted to bishops of the church just so long as they are pilgrims here in this mortal body. But when they have paid the debt of death, others who succeed in their place gain the same judicial authority, as it is written, 'Instead of your fathers, sons are born to you; you will appoint them princes over all the earth.'

Return, O you blind, to the true light that enlightens every man who comes into this world, because the light shines in darkness, and the darkness does not envelop it. By not looking at that light you are in the darkness. You walk in darkness and you do not know whither you are going, because the darkness has blinded your eyes.

Hear this also and be wise, you fools among the people, you who were formerly stupid, who seek the apostle's intercession by going to Rome; hear what the same oft-mentioned most blessed Augustine utters against you. In *On the Trinity*, book 8, he says, among other things, 'Come with me and let us consider why we should love the apostle. Is it because of the human form, which we hold to be quite ordinary, that we believe him to have been a man? By no means. Besides, does not he whom we love still live although that man no longer exists? His soul is indeed separated from the body, but we believe that even now there still lives what we love in him.'

Whoever is faithful ought to believe in God when he makes a promise, and by how much the more when he makes an oath. Why is it necessary to say, 'O that Noah, Daniel, and Job were present here.' Even if there were so much holiness, so much righ-teousness, so much merit, they, as great as they were, will not absolve son or daughter. He therefore says these things that no one may rely on the merit or intercession of the saints, for one cannot be saved unless he possess the same faith, righteousness, and truth which they possessed and by which they were pleasing to God.

Your fifth objection against me is that the apostolic lord was displeased with me (you state that I displease you as well). You said this of Paschal [I], bishop of the Roman church, who has departed from the present life [824]. An apostolic man is one who is guardian of the apostle or who exercises the office of an apostle. Surely that one should not be called an apostolic man who merely sits on an apostle's throne but the one who fulfils the apostolic function. Of those who hold the place but do not fulfil the function, the Lord once said, 'The scribes and pharisees sit on Moses' seat; so keep and perform whatever things they tell you. But be unwilling to act according to their works, for they talk but they do not practise.'

The miraculous was combined with the official in the formal proceedings which led to the canonisation of a saint. Edmund of Abingdon was an early Oxford master and was one of several English pastoral bishops canonised in the thirteenth century. The process for this canonisation was opened shortly after his death, beginning in April, 1244 at Pontigny and many of the documents relating to this early formal canonisation are preserved. St Edmund died at Soisy on 16 November 1240 and was buried at Pontigny Abbey. He was canonised in 1246.

H. Lawrence (trans.) *Documentary Sources for the Canonisation Process for Edmund of Abingdon, Archbishop of Canterbury, 1234* (1990) pp. 1–15

The canonisation process for Edmund of Abingdon

Translation of the letter of postulation from the University of Oxford (1241)

To their most gracious father and lord G(regory), by the grace of God Supreme Pontiff, his holiness's humble flock, the university of masters and scholars residing at Oxford, with the whole multitude of Friars Preachers and Friars Minor and other religious living in that place, offer a devoted kiss of his feet with their humble service and obedience.

We speak that which we know and we bear witness to that which we have seen of the life of our venerable father E[dmund] of good memory, recently archbishop of Canterbury, who resided no little time in our university as pupil and master.

The said father, then, was born of devout parents and was nurtured in religion from boyhood, so that under the instruction of his most Christian mother – whose life and reputation proclaimed her afterwards to have been the flower of widows – he began to fast and pray while he was still a small boy. When as a young man he embarked upon liberal studies, he proceeded of his own will along the path by which he had previously been led. For from that time he began willingly to sacrifice to God, of his own accord frequenting churches and avoiding the vain and frivolous things that occupy young men of that age. He earnestly applied himself to learning, and not merely fleeing the pleasures of the flesh, but continually bearing in his body the death of the cross of Christ, he zealously sought the Author of life with all the strength of his mind. For he seemed to have already understood that proverb which he had not yet read: 'a child in the way he should go, when he is old he will not depart from it.' In him this is really found to have been fulfilled. For from that time he was so habituated to fasting and keeping vigil and other hard works of penance that, as he himself admitted, in more advanced years they became easy and even delightful to him.

As the exercise of bodily mortification is useful to some extent, but piety is wholly valuable, we beg your holiness to hear with patience how grace increased with him as he grew in age. Thus when he was made a Master of Arts but not yet in holy orders nor under an obligation by reason of holding a benefice, but moved solely by love of God and religious zeal, he was accustomed to hear mass every day before he lectured. So as to do this more devoutly, he used the fees collected in his schools and such other resources as he could find to construct a chapel of the Blessed Virgin, whom he always loved with a particular devotion, in the parish where he was then residing, where solemn masses continue to be celebrated until now to her praise and glory. What he had left over, whether from the said fees or from other sources, he bestowed with great generosity upon the poor, and above all upon needy scholars.

Now after he had conducted a school in Arts for nearly six years, it pleased Him who had set him apart from his mother's womb that in him, and through him, He should reveal his Son, and he should be 'a chosen vessel'. While he was still giving cursory lectures on Arithmetic to some of his associates, his devout mother, who had died shortly before, appeared to him in a dream and said, 'My son, what are those figures to which you are giving such earnest attention?' When he replied, 'I am lecturing on such and such,' showing her the diagrams that are commonly used in that faculty, she seized his right hand and painted three circles in it, in which she wrote these three names one after the other: Father, Son, Holy Spirit. And doing this, she said, 'My dearest son, henceforth apply yourself to these figures and no others.' Instructed by this dream as if by a revelation, he immediately transferred to the study of theology, in which he quickly made such marvellous progress that after a few years he was persuaded by many to assume the master's chair.

When lecturing and disputing, and also when preaching, he was a powerful disseminator of the Word, pouring out words of divine wisdom for the instruction of others. For he was a zealous lecturer, acute in disputation, and a fervent preacher, and thus he was pleasing to the clergy, was appreciated by the laity, and was regarded with reverence even by princes. . . .

As 'it was fitting that we should have such a high priest, holy, blameless, unstained and separated from sinners', when after a time the see of Canterbury became vacant, he was by inspiration of divine grace elected archbishop. But having been made the pastor and illustrious leader of God's people, he did not lay aside his earlier humility, but by perpetual abstinence, rough clothing and constant vigils, he made the flesh serve the spirit and sensuality the rule of reason.

There are in fact some among us who were closely associated with him for a long period during his lifetime, namely Brother Robert Bacon, Master of Theology at Oxford, and Brother Richard of Dunstable, Prior of the Friars Preachers at that place. From their report we have learned, besides what we have stated above, also this: that the said holy man, from the time he was regent in Arts, never or only rarely got into bed, but restored his body with a little sleep, lying against the bed fully clothed. The rest of the night he spent in meditation and prayer. For he was constant in prayer, readily given to tears, and fervent in his zeal for souls. He was not remiss in times of prosperity, and was untroubled in adversity. . . .

Finally his laudable life won him a laudable end. For 'that the just man when dead should judge the impiety of the living' and that God, the author and reward of sanctity, should appear glorious in his saints, those whom he has first instructed by their merits and taught by their examples, he strengthens in their faith by evident and proven miracles. For, besides the holiness of his works and the signs of virtue that glorified him while still in the flesh, it is apparent what manner of spirit dwelt in the clod of his holy body from the many and various persons now cured of sickness and restored to their pristine health. In our times; when the whole Church seems overwhelmed by the darkness of tribulation and sin, the Lord has shone upon it as if with the outpourings of a new light through these miracles, for the conversion of un-believers, the repression of her enemies, and the comfort of the elect. Therefore, since there are so many agreed proofs of his sanctity, and there is so much testimony to the glory of his life, we humbly beseech your holiness that it please you to inscribe him, whom God has glorified in heaven and made the cause of marvels on earth, in the catalogue of the saints; so that, when called upon by many in memory of him, the Lord may succour the Church which is in much travail and the people of Christ may profit from his merits and example.

May the Lord preserve you for his Church for a long time to come.

Translation of the letter of postulation from the bishop, Robert Bingham and the chapter of Salisbury (1241)

To the most holy father and reverend lord by the grace of God Supreme Pontiff, his holiness's servants R(obert), by the divine mercy bishop of the church of Salisbury, and the dean and chapter of the same place, proffer a kiss of the feet with all submission and devotion.

We signify to your excellency in humble, truthful and plain speech, that which we have heard and which we, the chapter, have seen and as it were handled, concerning Edmund, formerly the venerable archbishop of Canterbury, who was translated from the bosom of our church to the eminence of the archbishopric.

May it please your holiness to know that he lived a distinguished and praiseworthy life in our church for nearly ten years, imitating him of whom it was written 'he was a burning and a shining light.' He was indeed burning with that fire of which the Truth said, 'I am come to set fire on the earth'. For in all his works he showed to the limit of his power a shining zeal for souls, a burning charity and love of religion. Despising the world, in lecturing and preaching he did the work of an evangelist. So catholic and clear was his teaching that throughout the land of England men said of him his 'tongue is the pen of a ready writer.' For he knew how, according to his human capacity, to bring forth from the treasury of holy Scripture 'things new and old', so that when he lectured or preached, it seemed to his audience that what he spoke had been written upon his heart by the finger of God. Appointed a general preacher, he preached moving words of exhortation, tirelessly and effectively to crowds of people, tax-collectors and knights, people great and small of either sex, religious and clergy. He emulated, in fact, the precursor of Our Lord in his amazing abstinence from food and drink, the harshness of his garments of hair, and the paucity of his sleep (he never or rarely rested his limbs in a bed), continually bearing in his body the death of the Cross. And not to weary your serene holiness with a long speech, occupied as you are with great business, it seems to us that he was a most true worshipper of God, mighty in work and speech, who worked tirelessly in the Lord's vineyard, watchful and awaiting the blessed calling of the Lord. Therefore, since he has been called by the Lord and since the divine mercy has demonstrated the merit of his life by frequent miracles at his tomb and elsewhere when his name has been invoked, prostrating ourselves at the feet of your holiness, we humbly and devoutly beseech you to have so great a light placed upon a candlestick and to count him in the catalogue of the saints.

May the most High preserve your life and keep you safely for us and his Church for a long time to come. (The bishop's seal is attached.)

(The omission of the pope's name suggests that news of the death of Gregory IX, on 22 August 1241, had reached England, but that the name of his successor was not yet known when this letter was written.)

Letter from the abbot and convent of Westminster postulating the canonisation of St Edmund (1241–1242)

To the most holy father and lord in Christ, the most beloved Lord . . . by the grace of God Supreme Pontiff of the universal Church, his holiness's devoted sons, Ricardus by divine permission the humble minister of the church of Westminster, and the convent of the same place, proffer a kiss of the blessed feet.

Pointless though it is to help the material sun to shine brighter by the use of torches, it is nevertheless fitting that those who are counted as Christians should proclaim the Sun of righteousness, rising for the salvation of those who fear him and sending his rays upon both the good and evil, to preach and glorify the mighty works of Christ and his saints etc.

Holy father, reverend father, a lamp should not be hidden under a bushel but should by declaration of the truth be raised in the midst upon a candlestick, to give light to all who are in the house of the Lord, that the regions of the world may be illuminated by his light. Indeed we call Edmund, the venerable archbishop of Canterbury a lamp with good reason, who is blessed, according to the meaning of his name, for he has, as we believe, obtained eternal beatitude through his purity . . . etc.

Therefore, lest the Lord's treasure be any longer hidden under a bushel, prostrating ourselves at the feet of your gracious goodness, we present our special prayers, humbly and devoutly beseeching you to condescend by your apostolic authority to make glorious the said confessor of the Lord, whom the Lord has already long since named in virtue of his sanctity. As he is proclaimed by divers miracles, please decree that he is to be inscribed in the catalogue of holy confessors and, as he was venerable in this life, pronounce that he be venerated and made the subject of cult in the Church of God. May your holiness ever enjoy health in the Lord.

Letter from Prior Robert and the brethren of Merton Priory postulating the canonisation of St Edmund (27 February 1242)

To their most gracious father and reverend lord by the grace of God Supreme Pontiff, Robert, humble minister of the brethren of the monastery of Merton of the Order of St Augustine, and the convent of the same place, humbly proffer a devoted kiss of the blessed feet.

Although we believe your holiness is not unaware, thanks to the declaration of all the faithful, of the blessed life, the more blessed death, and the acts and merits of the venerable father Edmund of happy memory, formerly archbishop of Canterbury, who was truly a lamp not hidden under a bushel but placed upon a candlestick, shining with refulgent light upon all who were in the house; yet, as it is written, 'cry aloud, spare not', we are not adequate to commend him fully; the reward of his merits is what commends him. So that we should, however, venerate him on earth, who was glorious in faith and works, Our Lord has, as we believe, deigned to set him in glory among the saints in heaven. Not only have we heard and firmly believe the divers kinds of miracles which the Lord has performed for him after his departure from this world, but we bear witness to what we know as fact and to what we have seen with our own eyes.

For this same venerable father, before he taught theology publicly in the schools, stayed continuously for a year and more in our house, and afterwards for a long time he frequently came and went as if he was one of us. Indeed certain of our brethren took great delight in his holy conversation and were encouraged by his counsel, marvelling beyond words at his manner of life. For, while living in the world, he trampled the world under foot, and though young in age, he surpassed old men in faith, learning, knowledge and judgement and, wonderful to relate, while moving among seculars, amongst us he seemed to be not merely a religious but even a model of the whole religious life. For he was assiduous in reading and meditation, most devout in prayer, always fasting and constantly keeping vigil; he never missed the hour of matins through sleep, but came to all the hours as if he was a vowed member of our community. Nor did he perform merely the exterior acts of religion, but practised even those that are most private, which he had learned from the Holy Spirit, having the key to all religious life. For he had 'made a covenant with his eyes', so much so that he did not recognise at all a brother who had served him for a year at table.

Truly, not only we, but everyone knew how he grew in heavenly virtue that he might 'see the God of Gods in Syon'. Therefore we have spoken briefly about his holy life, omitting the inexpressible goodness which many of the brethren observed in secret and received at his hands, and we are mentioning only briefly the manner in which the Lord has acted through his merits since his death, whom we loved on earth. For after this holy man had quitted the prison of the flesh, it happened that a canon named John, one of our brethren, was struck down by a grave illness and paralysed. He was utterly deprived of the power to move his limbs, so that the doctors who came to treat him considered him to be incurable. And when some of our brethren who were in the infirmary with him heard how the Lord had glorified his saint in heaven and made him wonderful on earth, they prayed God for him through the merits of the said glorious archbishop. And because God is attentive to the desires of his poor, their craving was satisfied, for after a few days that same brother completely recovered his health.

Since therefore the said saint lived a most holy life among us, and his shining merits have been illuminated by so great a miracle and by many others, may it please your holiness to number him in the catalogue of the saints, to the honour and glory of the holy Church of God and of the glorious Virgin Mary, that we may be bound to venerate on earth him whom God has glorified in heaven, to the glory and honour of Our Lord and of the universal Church.

May the Almighty long preserve you as a pastor of his holy Church. Given in the year of grace one thousand, twelve hundred and forty one, on the Thursday following the feast of St Mathias.

(The conventual seal of Merton Priory in brown wax is attached.)

Procès-verbal of the inquiry in the process of St Edmund (1244)

. . . Bernard of Perrons, having been sworn and questioned, said that while he was sleeping in a field minding four oxen, he felt a stab in his back and did not know what this was. He returned home, feeling no pain, but then he began to feel pain in his back. He followed his oxen [i.e. at the plough], however, for eight days, and he then began to use a staff when he wanted to walk, and he was not otherwise able to walk for fifteen days. After this he lay in bed, but he could not leave his bed without using two crutches, without which he could neither stand nor walk, and he felt as though he was completely broken in his back and from his back right down to his right foot. And he was in this condition for nearly a year. At the end of that year, about the following Easter, having made confession of his sins, he made a vow to Saint Edmund, and he then began to improve, so much so that on the holy day of Pentecost he set off after lunch to make the journey to the said saint, and on the morrow he entered the monastery in which Saint Edmund had been buried. And when he was praying at the tomb and Vespers were being sung, he raised himself without the staffs, and he discarded them there and began to walk through the monastery without any support, and on the morrow he walked from the said monastery to the ville of Perrons, which is eleven leagues away, in a single day.

(The next three entries record the testimony of Edelma de Perrons, Johanna de Perrons, and Leodegar de Perrons, confirming Bernard's statement.)

Translation of the letter from Richard, Bishop of Chichester (November 1245)

To the most holy father and lord Innocent, by the grace of God Supreme Pontiff, his ever devoted Richard, by divine permission humble minister of the church of Chichester, . . . prior of Canon's Ashby of the Order of St Augustine, and Brother Robert Bacon of the Order of Preachers, regent master in the Sacred Page at Oxford, offer, with all submission, honour and reverence, a devoted kiss of the blessed feet.

We have recently received with due devotion the letters of your holiness concerning the examination of four or five miracles that God has deigned to perform through the merits of Edmund of holy memory, formerly archbishop of Canterbury, as is commonly alleged and preached in our country. After holding careful discussions with men of discretion, we announced fixed days and suitable locations in those areas where greater knowledge of the matter was available and where fuller certainty of the truth could be obtained, and we had the Ordinaries of the places summon to our presence those who were said to have been favoured with cures through his merits; so that they could come and bear witness to the truth, together with persons who had knowledge of the occurrence whether by seeing, hearing, report of it, by proof or personal experience, with the testimony of their prelates. And we published this order in various dioceses by the authority under which we were acting.

Coming in person, therefore, to these places, we administered legally binding oaths relating to telling the truth without any falsehood, and set out specific articles of inquiry. We subjected witnesses to what we consider was a careful scrutiny and to the best of our ability extracted the forms of miracle and proceeded with the business of examination, observing all the rules that should be observed in such cases, applying to it all the diligence and carefulness we could. In fact, although we were offered many widely reported miracles, we were careful to examine mainly those that seemed more to the point, according to the tenor of the original letter sent us, namely those for which a number of witnesses was to be had and in which the power of nature was unavailing, but where the suddenness of the cure clearly displayed the hand of the divine mercy. We are sufficiently convinced that this appears in the particular miracles we have committed to writing. In accordance with your command, we submit to the feet of your holiness transcripts containing the words of witnesses, enclosed under our seals.

Dated the month of November, the year of Our Lord twelve hundred and forty-five. May the Most High preserve your life and health for himself and his holy Church for a long time to come.

The papal bull

Innocent, bishop, servant of the servants of God, to our beloved sons the nobles, all earls, barons and other noblemen throughout the kingdom of England, greetings and apostolic blessing.

With great gladness we report the new joy of mother Church as she celebrates a new saint. With exultation of spirit we proclaim a great festival that is being kept by the company of heaven which has gained a new member. The Church indeed rejoices to have produced so great a son, to guide others by the example of his holy life and to give them a sure hope of salvation by having himself won the prize of blessedness. . . . Rejoice with immense joy because you have gained a new patron with the Lord, because there stands in His presence a gentle intercessor for our salvation. See with what loving zeal the blessed archbishop Edmund, wisely reflecting that the creature is directed by natural affection towards its creator and that fallen nature ought to acknowledge its restorer, sought his own creator and redeemer. . . .

Allow us therefore to relate something of his acts; the more fully his life is described, the more it enchants the narrator and the more pleasure it gives to those who hear it. He loved the Son of God from his tender years and did not cease later to keep Him in his heart, for the stilus of contemplation inscribed Him upon the soft tablet of his mind. Rather, indeed, the more he advanced in age, the fuller the knowledge that fired his love. And lest the fervour of his spirit should be extinguished by the heat of the flesh but rather fired by its mortification, he tamed it harshly by constant use of a hairshirt, binding its desires with the bonds of strict abstinence. . . . For he afflicted his body with severe fasting: to the observance of the ancients he added a new austerity that he imposed upon himself; despising the delights of delicate food and content with the meals of humble people, at the periods of general fasting, he chose to abstain even from the foods that were permitted, and on other days of the week he abstained still more. He also hated excessive sleep, was given to prolonged vigils, and subjected his body to the discipline of constant prayer . . . wherefore, like a man of the spirit untouched by the contagion of the flesh, when he was dying Edmund uttered these marvellous words, words that we should note with the utmost attention, when the body of Christ was brought to him: 'Thou art he whom I have believed, whom I have preached, of whom I have taught. And thou art my witness, Lord, that I have sought nothing on earth except thee; as thou knowest, I want nothing except that which is thy will. Thy will be done.' Truly, having in his lifetime illuminated the Church of God by his shining merits, in death he has not deprived her of the rays of his glory. For it was not the will of the Lord that the holiness of so great a man should be lost to the world, but that it should be made manifest by divers miracles as it had been by his numerous merits. For he restored sight to the blind and, which is more glorious, he has infused clear sight and banished the darkness of one who was born blind. He cleansed a leper with a sudden and wonderful ablution that caused the scales of leprosy to fall off. He has fortified the trembling limbs of one paralysed by giving him solid sinews. . . . The flame of his brightness has shown itself in these and many other manifest miracles, the list of which we did not consider it proper to include in these letters. . . . Let the church of Canterbury, therefore, sing a song of praise to the Lord. . . . Let the monastery of Pontigny rejoice that she merited the honour of having the presence of such great fathers, one of whom long resided there and ennobled her by the manner of his life, and the other on coming there, after rendering his soul to heaven, has endowed her with the treasure of his body.

Furthermore, since it is fitting that those whom God has magnified in heaven with a crown of unending glory should be venerated by men on earth with the utmost zeal and devotion, so that by solemnly commemorating the saints the faithful may be more deserving of their patronage, we therefore, after careful and solemn inquiry and strict examination, have reached full certainty regarding the holiness of life and the truth of the miracles of the same saint Edmund: and with the common counsel and assent of our brethren and of all the prelates then present at the Apostolic See, on the Sunday of Advent on which *Gaudete in Domino semper* is sung, we thought it our duty to inscribe him in the catalogue of the saints, or rather to proclaim that he was already so inscribed. Therefore we advise and earnestly exhort your excellences, and by apostolic letters we command you, to devoutly and solemnly celebrate his feast on the 16th November, the day when his happy soul, freed from the prison of the flesh, ascended the skies and came to the halls of heaven, there to enjoy the bliss of paradise.

But in order that Christian people may come in greater numbers and with greater fervour to his venerable tomb and that the solemn festival of the saint may be observed with greater magnificence, to all those truly penitent and confessed, who come thither annually on the feast day to seek his intercession, we, trusting in the mercy of Almighty God and in the authority of the Blessed Peter and Paul his apostles, remit a year and forty days of the penance enjoined on them, and forty days to those coming each year to the said tomb within the octave of the said festival.

Given at Lyons on the 10th January in the 4th year of our pontificate.

(The leaden bulla of Pope Innocent IV is attached by silk strings of crimson and gold – the customary method of sealing a solemn privilege.)

Further Reading

P. R. L. Brown, *The Cult of the Saints* (London, 1981).
—— *Society and the Holy in Late Antiquity* (London, 1982).
P. Geary, *Living with the Dead in the Middle Ages* (Ithaca, 1994).
T. Head (ed.) *Medieval Hagiography: an anthology* (London, 1991).
J. Pelikan, *Mary through the Centuries* (New Haven, 1996).
S. J. E. Riches and S. Salih (eds) *Gender and Holiness: Men, Women, and Saints in Late Medieval Europe* (London, 2002).
A. Thacker and R. Sharpe (eds) *Local Saints and Local Churches in the Early Medieval West* (Oxford, 2002).
A. Vauchez, *Sainthood in the Late Middle Ages* (Cambridge, 1997).
B. Ward, *Miracles and the Medieval Mind* (Aldershot, 1982).

2 Monks and nuns

Individual conversion in adult live could follow the infant baptism which made a person a member of the Church and could lead to a calling from God to spend a lifetime in the Lord's service. In a developing tradition men and women became 'professional' religious attempting, either as solitaries or as groups, to live the Christian life of prayer and community demanded by the Gospel. The whole purpose of the life was to provide the necessary conditions for a life of contemplation.

J. B. McLaughlin (trans.) *St. Antony the Hermit, by St. Athanasius* (1924) pp. 121–122

St Athanasius (d. 373) on St Antony the Hermit (d. 356)

Book 2: Antony's teachings on the monk's vocation and the assaults of demons

5. When he had to cross the canal of Arsenoe (the need was his visitation of the brethren), the canal was full of crocodiles. And simply praying, he entered – with all his companions; and they passed through unhurt.

He returned to the monastery and continued the same holy and generous labours. He preached constantly, increasing the zeal of those who were already monks, and stirring many others to the love of the religious life; and soon, as the word drew men, the number of monasteries became very great; and to all he was a guide and a father.

One day, when he had gone out and all the monks came to him asking to hear [a] discourse, he spoke to them as follows in the Egyptian tongue:

'The scriptures are enough for our instruction. Yet it is well that we should encourage each other in the faith, and stimulate each other with words. Do you, therefore, bring what you know and tell it like children to your father; while I, as your elder, share with you what I know and have experienced. First of all, let one same zeal be common to all, not to give up what we have begun, not to be faint-hearted in our labours, not to say we have lived long in this service, but rather as beginners to have greater zeal each day. For the whole life of a man is very short, measured beside the ages to come, so that all our time is nothing compared to eternal life. And in the world, every merchandise is sold at its worth, and men barter like value for like. But the promise of eternal life is bought for a trifle. For it is written, "The days of our life have seventy years in them; and in the mighty they are eighty years and more, they are a labour and a burden." If, then, we spend the whole eighty years in the religious life, or even a hundred, we shall not reign in heaven for the same space of a hundred years, but in return for the hundred we shall reign through ages of ages.

And if our striving is on earth, our inheritance shall not be on earth; but in heaven is our promised reward. Our body, too, we give up corruptible; we receive it back incorruptible.

Therefore, children, let us not faint, nor weary, nor think we are doing much, "For the sufferings of this present time are not worthy to be compared to the glory that shall be revealed to us." Neither let us look back to the world thinking that we have renounced much. For the whole earth is but a narrow thing compared to all heaven. If, then, we were lords of the whole earth, and renounced the whole earth, that, too, would be worth nothing beside the kingdom of heaven. As though a man should make light of one bronze coin to gain a hundred pieces of gold; so he that owns all the earth and renounces it, gives up but little, and receives a hundredfold. If, then, the whole earth is no price for heaven, surely he who has given up a few acres must not boast nor grow careless; for what he forsakes is as nothing even if he leaves a home and much wealth.

There is another thing to consider: if we do not forsake these things for virtue's sake, still we leave them later on when we die; and often, as Ecclesiastes reminds us, to those whom we would not. Then why not leave them for virtue's sake, and to inherit a kingdom?

Therefore let none of us have even the wish to possess. For what profit is it to possess these things which yet we cannot take with us? Why not rather possess those things which we can take away with us – prudence, justice, fortitude, understanding, charity, love of the poor, gentleness, hospitality? For if we gain these possessions, we shall find them going beforehand, to make a welcome for us in the land of the meek.

With these thoughts let a man urge himself not to grow careless; especially if he considers that he is one of God's servants, and owes service to his master. Now as a servant would not dare to say, "Today I do not work, because I worked yesterday," nor would count up the time that is past and rest in the coming days; but each day, as is written in the Gospel, he shows the same willingness, in order to keep his Lord's favour and avoid danger; so let us too daily abide in our service, knowing that if we are slovenly for one day he will not pardon us for the sake of past times, but will be angry with us for slighting him. So have we heard in Ezechiel; so, too, Judas in one night destroyed all his past toil.

Therefore, children, let us hold fast to the religious life, and not grow careless. For in this we have the Lord working with us, as it is written, "God co-operates unto good with everyone that chooseth the good." And to prevent negligence, it is well for us to ponder on the apostle's saying, 'I die daily.' For if we also so live as dying daily, we shall not sin. What is meant is this: that when we wake each day, we should think we shall not live till evening; and again when we go to sleep we should think we shall not wake, for our life is of its nature uncertain, and is measured out to us daily by Providence.

So thinking, and so living from day to day, we shall not sin, nor shall we have any longing for anything, nor cherish wrath against anyone, nor lay up treasure on the earth; but as men who each day expect to die, we shall be poor, we shall forgive everything to all men. The desire of women and of evil pleasure we shall not meet and master but we shall turn away from it as a fleeting thing, striving always and always looking to the day of judgment. For the greater fear and the danger of torment always breaks the delight of pleasure and steadies the wavering mind.

Having made a beginning, and set out on the way of virtue, let us stretch out yet more to reach the things that are before us. Let none turn back like Lot's wife, especially as the Lord has said, "No man setting his hand to the plough and turning back is fit for the kingdom of heaven." Turning back simply means changing one's mind and caring again for worldly things. And when you hear of virtue, do not fear nor feel the word strange; for it is not afar from us, not something that stands without; no, the thing is within us, and the doing is easy, if only we have the will. The Greeks go abroad and cross the sea to study letters; but we have no need to go abroad for the kingdom of heaven, nor to cross the sea after virtue. For the Lord has told us beforehand, "The kingdom of heaven is within you." Virtue, therefore, needs only our will, since it is within us, and grows from us. For virtue grows when the soul keeps the understanding according to nature. It is according to nature when it remains as it was made. Now it was made beautiful, and perfectly straight. For this reason Joshua, the son of Nun, commanded the people, "Make straight your hearts to your ways." For the straightness of the soul consists in the mind's being according to nature, as it was made; as, on the other hand, the soul is said to be evil when it bends and gets twisted away from what is according to nature. So the task is not difficult; if we remain as God made us, we are in virtue; if we give our minds to evil, we are accounted wicked. If, then, it were a thing that must be sought from without, the task would indeed be hard; but if it be within us, let us guard ourselves from evil thoughts and keep our soul for the Lord, as a trust we have received from him; that he may recognize his work, finding it as it was when he made it.

Let us fight also not to be mastered by anger, nor enslaved by concupiscence. For it is written that "the anger of man worketh not the justice of God." And "concupiscence having conceived bringeth forth sin, and sin when it is completed bringeth forth death." '

A Word in Season, pp. 27–28

Monastic constitutions attributed to Saint Basil the Great (d. 379)

Martha acted as hostess to the Lord: Mary sat at his feet. Though shown in different ways, the zeal of both sisters was praiseworthy. Martha employed herself in service, preparing something to satisfy the Lord's bodily needs: Mary sat at his feet concentrating on his words. The one offered refreshment to the nature she could see, the other served what was unseen. For in fact their guest was both man and God, and as Lord of both women he accepted their goodwill.

Martha, however, finding the work too much for her and wanting her sister's help, begged the Lord to intervene: Tell her to get up and help me she said. But the Lord replied: Martha, Martha, you worry and fret over so many things, but only one is necessary. Mary's choice is a good one: it shall not be taken away from her. We are not here to recline on couches and feed our bodies: we are here to feed you with the word of truth and the contemplation of mysteries. And so he did not take Martha away from her work, but he commended Mary for her attention.

Let us then take a closer look at the two ways of life which these two women represent: the one extremely useful but less important, since it is concerned with the needs of the body; the other a higher because more spiritual way, which rises to mystical contemplation. As you listen to these words understand them spiritually, and choose which path you will follow. If you wish to serve, do so in the name of Christ, for he himself said: Whatever you did for the least of these my brothers and sisters, you did for me. Whether you take in strangers, relieve the poor, show compassion for the suffering, offer a helping hand to those in distress and misfortune, or minister to the sick, Christ receives it all as done for himself.

And so, beloved, you have your models and my explanation. Follow whichever you will: either serve the poor or devote yourself to the teaching of Christ. But if you can imitate both models you will obtain the fruit of salvation from both, although spiritual teaching ranks first, and everything else is of secondary importance. As scripture says: *Mary's choice is a good one.*

A Word in Season, pp. 25–26

From a conference by John Cassian (d. 433)

This should be our chief effort, this the steadfast aim and constant desire of our heart: always to cling in spirit to God and to whatever is Godlike. Anything else, however excellent, should be given second place in our scale of values, or even regarded as of no consequence and possibly harmful. This is the attitude and way of life that the gospel puts before us so well in the figures of Martha and Mary.

Martha's work was indeed a holy one, since it was directed to the Lord himself and his disciples, while Mary sat at his feet, intent only upon Jesus' spiritual teaching. Yet the Lord put her service first, because she had chosen that better part which could not be taken away from her. Martha, entirely taken up by the duties of a good hostess, saw that she had more to do than she could manage alone. She said to the Lord: *Do you not care that my sister has left all the serving to me? Tell her to come and help me.* It was certainly to no unworthy service but to a noble one that Martha was calling her sister, yet what did she hear from the Lord? *Martha, Martha, you worry and fret over so many things, but only a few are needed, or just one. Mary has chosen that good part which shall not be taken away from her.*

You see then that the Lord placed the sovereign good in the contemplation of divine things. Therefore we hold that the other virtues, good, necessary, and useful though they be, are to be given second place, since they are all exercised with a view to this alone. By his words, *You worry and fret over so many things, but only a few are needed, or just one*, the Lord was saying that the sovereign good lies not in activity however praiseworthy and fruitful, but in the simple and undivided contemplation of himself. By his assertion that few things are needed for perfect blessedness, he meant that the first level of contemplation is one in which we meditate on the lives of a small number of saints. From this contemplation whoever is still on the way will rise to what is called 'the One' – that is, he or she will attain, by the help of God, to the contemplation of God alone. Passing beyond even the wonderful deeds and ministries of the saints, such a person will be nourished solely by the knowledge and beauty of God.

Mary has chosen that good part which shall not be taken away from her. Consider this too very carefully. When the Lord says, *Mary has chosen that good part* he does not mention Martha, and in no sense seems to blame her. Nevertheless, by praising the one he makes it clear that the other's is a lesser good. Again, when he says, *which shall not be taken away from her*, he means that whereas Martha's work will cease (for no physical service can last for ever) Mary's occupation will never come to an end.

The first monks and nuns, 'desert fathers and mothers', responded directly to the Gospel but gradually rules of life emerged often following the teaching of a charismatic founder. The most influential rules in the Western Church were those of St Augustine of Hippo (d. 430) and St Benedict of Nursia (d. c.550), both deeply influenced by the earlier and predominantly Eastern tradition.

Augustine of Hippo, *The Monastic Rules*, with a commentary by G. Bonner (New York, 2004) pp. 106–108

III The *Ordo Monasterii*

1. Before all else, dearest brothers, let God be loved and then your neighbour, because these are the chief commandments which have been given us.

2. We now set down how we ought to pray and recite the psalms. At morning prayer let three psalms be said: the sixty-second, the fifth, and the eighty-ninth. At the third hour let one psalm first be said responsorially, then two antiphons, a reading, and then the closing prayer. Let prayers be said in a similar fashion at the sixth and ninth hours. At lamplighting (*lucernarium*) a responsorial psalm, four antiphons, another responsorial psalm, a reading, and then the closing prayer. And at a suitable time after lamplighting, once all [the congregation] have been seated, there are to be readings, and afterwards the customary psalms before sleeping. Now for the night prayers: in the month of November, December, January and February, twelve antiphons, six psalms, and three readings. In March, April, September and October, ten antiphons, five psalms, and three readings. In May, June, July and August, eight antiphons, four psalms, and two readings.

3. [The monks] are to work from early morning to the sixth hour and then let them have time for reading from the sixth hour to the ninth. At the ninth hour they are to hand back their books, and after they have eaten let them do some work in the garden or wherever it may be necessary until the time for lamplighting.

4. No one should claim anything as his own (Acts 4:32), whether in clothing or in anything else, since we choose to lead a life on the apostolic pattern.

5. Let no one grumble at whatever he has to do, lest he incur the judgement inflicted on grumblers.

6. Let them obey faithfully. Let them honour their [spiritual] father next to God and submit to their superior as becomes saints (Eph 5:3).

7. Let them keep silence when they sit at table and listen to the reading. If anything is needed, their superior should take care of it. On Saturdays and Sundays, wine is to be provided for those who wish to have it, in accordance with the regulations.

8. If it is necessary for someone to be sent out from the monastery on some essential business, a pair should go together. No one is to eat or drink outside the monastery without permission, for such behaviour does not accord with monastic discipline. If any brothers are sent to sell the produce of the monastery, let them take good care to do nothing contrary to their instructions, knowing that this would move God to anger against his servants. Again, if they buy anything needed by the monastery, let them act carefully and faithfully, as becomes the servants of God.

9. Let there be no idle talk among them. From break of day they are to sit at their various tasks, and after the prayers of the third hour let them go to work in similar fashion. They should not stand about telling stories [*fabulas contestant*] unless it concerns

something useful to the soul. Sitting at their tasks they are to keep silence unless by chance the needs of their work require someone to speak.

10. If anyone does not strive to carry out these things with all his strength, aided by the Lord's mercy, but stubbornly refuses to respect them and, after being warned once and again, does not amend his ways, let him know himself to be subject to the monastic discipline as may be fitting. If however his age shall be such [as to make it appropriate], he may even be whipped.

11. By faithfully and prayerfully observing these things in Christ's name you, on the one hand, will make progress and we, on the other, will have no small joy in your salvation. Amen.

J. McCann (ed. and trans.) *The Rule of St Benedict* (1952) pp. 129–135

The Rule of St Benedict (d. c.550)

The order for the reception of brethren

When anyone newly cometh to be a monk, let him not be granted an easy admittance; but, as the apostle saith: Test the spirits, to see whether they come from God. If such a one, therefore, persevere in his knocking, and if it be seen after four or five days that he bears patiently his harsh treatment and the difficulty of admission and persists in his petition, then let admittance be granted to him, and let him stay in the guest-house for a few days. After that let him dwell in the noviciate, where the novices work, eat, and sleep. And let a senior be assigned to them who is skilled in winning souls that he may watch over them with the utmost care. Let him examine whether the novice truly seeks God, and whether he is zealous for the Work of God, for obedience, and for humiliations. Let him be told all the hardships and trials through which we travel to God.

If he promise to persevere in his purpose, then at the end of two months let this Rule be read through to him, and let him be addressed thus: 'Behold the law under which you wish to serve; if you can observe it, enter; if you cannot, freely depart.' If he still abide, then let him be led back into the aforesaid noviciate and again tested in all patience. After the lapse of six months let the Rule be read to him, so that he may know on what he is entering. And, if he still abide, after four months let the Rule be read to him again. And if, upon mature deliberation, he promise to observe all things and to obey all the commands that are given him, then let him be received into the community. But let him understand that according to the law of the Rule he is no longer free to leave the monastery, or to withdraw his neck from under the yoke of the Rule, which it was open to him, during that prolonged deliberation, either to refuse or to accept.

Now this shall be the manner of his reception. In the oratory, in the presence of all, he shall promise stability, conversion of his life, and obedience; and this before God and his Saints, so that he may know that should he ever do otherwise he will be condemned by him whom he mocks.

He shall embody this promise of his in a petition, drawn up in the names of the Saints whose relics are there and of the abbot who is present. Let him write this document with his own hand; or, if he cannot write, let another do it at his request, and let the novice put his mark to it and place it on the altar with his own hand. When he has placed it there, let the novice himself at once intone this verse: *Suscipe me, Domine, secundum eloquium tuum, et vivam: et ne confundas me ab exspectatione mea.* Let the whole community repeat this after him three times, adding at the end of all the *Gloria Patri.* Then let the novice prostrate himself before the feet of each monk, asking them to pray for him; and from that day let him be counted as one of the community. If he possess any property, let him either give it beforehand to the poor, or make a formal donation bestowing it on the monastery. Let him keep back nothing at all for himself, as knowing that thenceforward he will not have the disposition even of his own body. So let him, there and then in the oratory, be stripped of his own clothes which he is wearing and dressed in the clothes of the monastery. But let those clothes, which have been taken off him, be put aside in the clothes-room and kept there. Then, should he ever listen to the persuasions of the devil and decide to leave the monastery (which God forbid), let them take off him the clothes of the monastery and so dismiss him. But his petition, which the abbot took from off the altar, shall not be returned to him, but shall be preserved in the monastery.

A Word in Season, pp. 22–23

From an ancient rule for nuns

Here I stand knocking at the door. If anyone opens it for me I will come in and we shall have a meal together.

Whenever our Lord graciously allows us to take part in the Divine Office, we must be alert both in body and soul, so that when he knocks our hearts may be ready to receive him. They should be aflame with the fire of the Holy Spirit, and their dispositions such as will draw our Creator in his mercy to come to our supper and invite us to his. Whoever partakes of the supper of the Lord feasts on the abundance of his house and drinks from the torrent of his delights, because in Christ is the source of life, and in his light we see light. He extends his mercy to those who know him, and he justifies the upright of heart.

Let there be always on our lips such words as befit the service of God, in accordance with the Psalmist's exhortation: *Serve the Lord with reverence, and praise him with fear and trembling.* We serve our Creator with reverence when we join good works to the singing of his praises, for we then carry out that other counsel of the Psalmist: *Sing to the Lord wisely.*

To sing wisely is to allow no sinful deeds to contradict our words of praise, and earnestly to strive to render fitting service to almighty God by good monastic observance. We should come with minds not distracted by worldly interests or darkened by sins, but intent upon the sacred psalmody and prepared to pray. Absorbed by the things of heaven, we should reach out toward our eternal reward with humility, purity, and eager devotion, our hearts so filled with sorrow for our sins that our merciful Creator will be moved to clemency. Let each of us believe that she will not be heard for her wordiness but for her purity of heart and her many tears. The pity of our merciful Judge will not be aroused by the length of our prayers, but only by the dispositions of our will.

Let us then pray unceasingly for sinners to him who by his passion and cross brought healing to a sick world, Jesus Christ, the world's eternal salvation, who with the Father and the Holy Spirit lives and reigns for ever and ever. Amen.

The basic rules were supplemented by more precise legislation, often in the form of constitutions or commentaries on the foundation documents. Discussion on the nature of the monastic life could be much more contentious than it might at first appear, and this is revealed particularly strongly in the conflict in the twelfth century between the Cluniacs and the Cistercians, who both claimed to be disciples of St Benedict. The Cluniacs were monks who owed their obedience to the Abbey of Cluny, in Burgundy, founded in the tenth century and famous for its liturgical observance and its elaborate architecture. The Cistercians, who sought a return to what they considered to be the pure simplicity of monastic life, owed their inspiration to the new monastery of Citeaux, also in Burgundy, consolidated in the early years of the twelfth century.

Idung of Prüfening, *Cistercians and Cluniacs, the Case for Citeaux. A dialogue between two monks, an argument on four questions* (Kalamazoo, 1977) pp. 33–45

Cistercians and Cluniacs: the case for Citeaux

CISTERCIAN. Here you have the answer to your question. You tell me in what treatise he [Bernard] praised your Order, which follows not the Rule but man-made traditions instead? I find it hard to believe that an abbot so cautious, so holy, and so judicious in his written works and spoken words could have contradicted himself so completely.

[I, 14.1] CLUNIAC. In the treatise which he wrote to the monks of our Order at Chartres, and in the long letter which he wrote to William of St Thierry, also of our Order. Read them both and you will find in both outspoken praise of our Order.

[I, 14.] CISTERCIAN. I have read and re-read them both and have given them a great deal of thought. My impression was not unlike yours when I read them for the first time. That should not surprise anybody, because he uses in each that genre of speech which deceives the simple-witted and those who merely skim over what they read.

[I, 16.] CLUNIAC. What is this genre of speech which obscures the minds of its hearers when they hear it and the minds of the readers when they read it?

[I, 17.] CISTERCIAN. Rhetoricians call this 'veiled illusion'; it is to be used as part of the legal defence of a defendant whom the case examiners dislike so much that they have no desire whatever to listen to the defence counsel's pleas. At that stage, the defendant's advocate begins his statement of rebuttal of charges by calling the hostile witnesses to testify by accusing the accusers of the person whose release he intends ultimately to obtain. Then later on, by the marvellous artfulness of words, he sets about weakening what he has made strong, exculpating whom he has accused, thereby turning a lawsuit which was headed in one way in the opposite direction.

Do not be one whit surprised if a man of learned holiness and eloquent wisdom used the method of veiled illusion practised by a meticulous orator in writing to you at the time when your monks hated our monks with intemperate hatred, calling them slanderers and manglers of the Order, and thinking them to be esteemed more lowly and contemptible in the eyes of the world [than themselves] because they seemed to be a singular and new kind of monk living in your midst. This is what Archbishop Hugh of Lyons said when in one of his letters he used the very words which I have just quoted. That holy man wrote as a holy man should write, that is, as one whom St Jerome described in expounding the words of the book of the prophet Daniel: 'They who are learned shall shine as the brightness of the firmament, and they who instruct many to justice are as stars for all eternity.' When explaining the differences between holy men, he says: 'You can see how great the difference is between learned holiness and holy crudeness. The difference is as great as that between one star and the whole firmament.'

[I, 18.] CLUNIAC. Though we have both this treatise and this letter in almost all our monasteries, and though in our Order there are many learned and liberally-educated men, not one of them has ever understood them as you do – as glorifying your Order and degrading ours. Furthermore, monks and abbots of your Order who have been our guests and whom we know quite well have never put the interpretation on these writings that you do, but they have agreed with ours. And if by any chance both Orders were ever mentioned, as it were in one and the same breath, all praised and paid respect to our Order and said that the transfer made by many from our to your Order was made without profit, without need, and that it was done more out of empty-headed inquisitiveness and instability than out of necessity and advantage.

[I, 19.] CISTERCIAN. Among his store of maxims the ordinary man usually has one to suit the occasion, such as: 'I must sing the song of the man whose bread I eat.' Many of our monks, being less than perfect while they were your guests, heeded that same proverb even without uttering it. Although they are possessed of knowledge, they are not possessed of the fervent love of God. (Again, there are those who possess a fervent love of God but haven't much knowledge.) If there are those who possess both, that is zeal for God based on knowledge, they are sparing in the time they spend as guests. As Solomon says: 'All things have their season, a time for silence and a time to speak.'

I am firmly convinced that they kept silent longer than they chatted about the customs of your Order. Nor do I believe that they are to be blamed for their silence during that time. Hence, as Augustine says in commenting on psalm five: 'Clearly one must not be blamed whenever it is clear that he is keeping silence about the truth.'

[I, 20.] CLUNIAC. According to Ambrose and according to the truth of the matter, it is much safer to be silent than to speak, because many sin when they speak, few do so by remaining silent. Hence Jerome in his *Commentary on the Letter to the Ephesians* says: 'As often as we speak, be the time appropriate or not, be the place appropriate or not, and be what we are saying suitable for our listeners to hear or not, so often does evil speech proceed from our mouths to the ruination of those who hear us. We must pay close attention to what we say because at the day of judgement we shall have to render account for our every idle word. Even though we do no harm, we do not edify the listeners and we will have to pay the penalty for evil speech.' This opinion, promulgated widely by blessed Jerome, can strike terror to all who are quick and prone to speech, especially to monks whose profession demands that, in accordance with the precepts of the Rule, they should be zealous at all times in observing silence.

[I, 21.] CISTERCIAN. Truth, who produced human speech through the mouth of a donkey – irrational animal – has now wrenched from your mouth the great condemnation of your Order. Because you do not realize what you were saying, you are not unlike that donkey.

[I, 22.] CLUNIAC. Because I am very eager to hear what constitutes this condemnation [of my Order], I am meanwhile putting up patiently with being impudently called a jackass.

[I, 23.] CISTERCIAN. Not impudently, but in that manner of charity which, in accordance with the words of the wise man, 'is wont to vent in its anger tenderness,' for the correction of the transgressor. It is for this reason that the Apostle called the Galatians 'senseless.' I do not see how you can utter a harsher denunciation of your Order than by dragging front and centre that terrifying sentence of Jerome and that precept of the Rule about the zealous observance of silence at all times. If monks must at all times be zealous in observing silence that means a forceful application of the mind to maintaining it because a forceful application of the mind to the maintenance of silence and to being zealous about its maintenance are equated, just as decree and the matter decreed are equated – then they should be zealous about keeping it then and after Chapter. But at those times [after Chapter] they eagerly gossip and chatter back and forth by permission of the Order – if indeed it is of the order and not more of the disorder. They sit because the time is so drawn-out and extended that they cannot stand, and each chatters on about whatever he chooses with anybody he chooses. To take a seat is itself the signal for such application. Rumours fly from the loftiest to the lowliest and contrariwise from the lowliest to the loftiest. And because each speaks with those sitting near him there arises a kind of confused din, with a sound akin to what one would hear in an inn or in a tavern full of sots where all the men are talking with their fellow souses and all the women drinkers talking with their drinking companions. Sometimes they reproach each other so bitterly and so harshly in conversation that they do all their accusing there rather than in Chapter. From this permission to chatter idly arises the wherewithal for brawling. From the brawl come threats and acrimony, so much so that at times it is necessary to recall the Chapter by striking the wooden clappers [used for summoning Chapter].

Is this that 'holy leisure' you were talking about a little while ago when you said: 'Our Order is contemplative because of its holy leisure and yours is active because of its prescribed measure of manual labour,' – as if you were ignorant of what really constitutes the active and contemplative life? This is the reason I answered you as I did above: 'Brother, you err, because you do not know the Scriptures.'

CLUNIAC. You have expressed yourself in sufficiently mordant strictures about our Order's dispensations [from the rule].

[I, 24.] CISTERCIAN. Actually, I have not been talking about the Order's dispensation, but its dissipation. Dispensation should not and cannot be given except for some great need, so that when the need has come to an end that also should end which was done for necessity's sake or for some compensatory good of great utility. Nor may he grant dispensations who lives under the very precept which is to be dispensed. A dispensation is nothing more than a permitted discontinuation of what has been ordered. And who can give himself permission to discontinue unless he does so with the most absurd presumption? According to the wise man's saying: 'It is not yours to dispense; it is yours to be dispensed.'

[I, 25.] CLUNIAC. Do you mean that abbots cannot dispense from precept of the Rule?

CISTERCIAN. They cannot, except as the Rule provides. They too are subject to the Rule, which teaches that the abbot is to do everything in accordance with the Rule. If I may put it more forcefully – with all due respect to abbots – it is more necessary for them to obey the teachings in the Rule than it is for their subjects who are only monks. Abbots, in fact, profess the Rule twice: the first time at their profession as a monk; the second at their installation as abbot. I ask you, what dispensation is necessary from those precepts which are remarkable for their discretion.

CLUNIAC. None that I know of, because if a dispensation is necessary the precepts are not remarkable for their discretion.

CISTERCIAN. You agree with me! What is our Rule but certain legal precepts regulating the monastic way of life and forming the conduct of monks?

[I, 26.] CLUNIAC. Nothing else. As St James demonstrates when he says in his Epistle: 'He who offends in one point' – here he has in mind the precept of the law – 'is guilty of all' – here he has in mind the breaking of the law, because the law is nothing other than the sum of all its precepts and, conversely, all its precepts are nothing other than the law. The same St James said to this point: 'He who offends in one, offends in all.' And he added a careful and proper gloss when he said: 'He who said 'You shall not commit adultery,' also said 'You shall not kill.' If you do not commit adultery but do kill, then are you become a transgressor of the law.' Here you have what we mean by a transgressor of the law and what we understand by a culprit in all.

CISTERCIAN. I find that what you say pleases me, but what I am about to say will displease you.

[I, 27.] CLUNIAC. By and large, everything you have so far said has displeased me. Why wonder if what you are about to say will also be displeasing? But tell me what else there is, for I want to listen with an open mind to such things and I want to be wrought up by them.

CISTERCIAN. The confession of your own lips and the concession in your statement incontestably prove that the Customs of Cluny are a deviation from the law given us by God, that is, from the Rule. And thereby they bring dishonour on the giver of the law, that is, on God, and on the expounder of that law, that is, on St Benedict.

CLUNIAC. Far be such a confession from my mouth and from my thoughts such a concession.

[I, 28.] CISTERCIAN. Pay heed in patience and think carefully and you will understand the truth of what I say. Your mouth did confess and your statement did concede that precepts of remarkable discretion in no way lend themselves readily to dispensation.

CLUNIAC. I don't deny it.

[I, 29.] CISTERCIAN. But the precepts of the Rule are remarkable for their discretion, as the Holy Spirit bears witness when, using blessed Gregory as his instrument, he said: 'Peter, I do not wish to conceal from you that that man of God, Benedict, was renowned in this world by reason of the miracles he performed and, in addition, he was equally famous for his teaching. He wrote a Rule for Monks remarkable in its discretion and rich in its clarity of expression.' You have heard one witness, and an extremely reliable one, Gregory, on the remarkable discretion of the Rule. Now listen to another, even to St Benedict himself and to his words in the Prologue [to the Rule]: 'Therefore we must establish a school for the Lord's service, in whose founding we hope to ordain nothing harsh or burdensome. But if for a good reason, for the amendment of evil habits or the preservation of charity, there is some strictness of discipline, do not be at once dismayed and run away from the way of salvation, the entrance to which must needs be narrow.' He himself implies that his Rule is a dispensation from other monastic rules when he says: 'We do, indeed, read that wine is no drink for monks. But since monks nowadays cannot be persuaded of this, let us agree at least upon this, to drink temperately and not to satiety.'

[I, 30.] CLUNIAC. What are these Rules which are so harsh and rigid that our Rule dispenses them?

CISTERCIAN. The Rule of Augustine, which ordered that the flesh be beaten into submission 'by abstinence in eating and drinking insofar as one's state of health allows'; the Rule of St Pachomius, written by an angel, forbade monks the use of wine and fish sauce. Gather from its own words the great austerity of the Rule of Macarius, which says: 'The wise man works with his hands, thereby obtaining his own daily food and increasing his prayers and fastings. If he should accept food from another, what good does it do him to pray and keep watch? Like the hired labourer, he went forth naked.'

CLUNIAC. This language is indeed harsh. Who can heed it?

[I, 31.] CISTERCIAN. The language is harsh and we monks are its hardened listeners, because it is of no matter to us. We are always ready to receive but never will we say 'That is enough,' because each one's greed is his own. Tell me if you ever heard of a monastery which had sufficient – and more than sufficient – revenues and whose monks would accept nothing from those who had made offerings to them?

CLUNIAC. Why put that question to me when you already know full well that even the rich monks had made for themselves a law to accept gifts from every giver, even from the wicked?

[I, 32.] CISTERCIAN. Nowhere is this found either in natural or in written law. As a matter of fact, Jerome says the contrary in expounding the words of the Psalmist, 'He who gives food to the hungry'. He says to monks: 'Monk, pay attention you who give food to the hungry and not to the regurgitating; you who are surfeited, take your food but do not take the bread of the hungry. Take what you can put into your stomach not what you can put in a bag. Take what you can put on your back, not what you can put into a chest.' Prosper [of Aquitaine] in his Rule for Canons agrees with St Jerome when he says: 'To give something to those who already have is nothing other than to lose it.' I hold with Prosper's opinion – but I do not hold with his exact words that alms should be given only to those poor who are so ill and weak in body that they are unable to make a living by working. When poor man of sound body accepts alms, he is, so to say, stealing the portion of alms which should be allotted to the poor sick man.

[I, 33.] CLUNIAC. It seems to me that this language is no less harsh than the language used by St Macarius. I do not see why we monks who are healthy in body and rich in revenues should accept alms.

CISTERCIAN. Neither do I. Alms and mercy mean one and the same thing. The former is Greek in etymology, the latter is Latin. Mercy and misery mutually complement each other. Therefore, where there is no misery, there is no room for mercy, that is, for alms. If the donation of a wicked man is accepted by those who already have enough of their own [without it] the misdeed is twofold; if prayers are said for him after his death – and he had not repented – the misdeed is threefold.

[I, 34.] CLUNIAC. Because I do not completely understand, please give me a clearer explanation of what you have just been saying.

CISTERCIAN. You do not understand that the first misdeed lies in accepting the donation, the second in accepting it from a wicked man, the third in praying for this unrepentant donor after his death. Dom Rubert, abbot of Deutz and our contemporary, bears witness that a wicked man's donation is not to be accepted. He says: 'A donation accepted from a wicked man is not only of no profit to the donor, but it also makes a colluder of him who receives it, because the first sins obstinately and the second continues to eat the product of his sins.' It is for this reason that the apostle John bears witness that we should not pray for him who dies in his sins when he ordered: 'There is a sin unto death: I do not say that you should pray for him.' Read, besides, Bede's *Life of Abbot Fursey*, and you will discover that monks accept donations from the wicked to their great peril.

[I, 35.] CLUNIAC. What are you implying when you speak this way, when you call what the wicked man gives not alms but a donation?

CISTERCIAN. Alms not properly directed [toward their appointed end] are not alms, that is, mercy.

CLUNIAC. How should they be directed?

CISTERCIAN. The person who wishes to give alms must begin with himself. This means that he has first to have mercy on himself, that is, he must repent of his sins, because it is written: 'Have pity on your soul' etcetera. Again: 'He who is evil to himself, to whom will he be good?' According to the Gospel this is what Truth said to the Pharisees about the frequency with which they gave alms: 'You Pharisees make clean the outside of the cup, not the inside. . . . Give alms, however, of what remains and all will be clean with you,' as much as to say: before anything else, give yourselves by believing in me, and give your goods afterwards.

CLUNIAC. I like what you say.

[I, 36.] CISTERCIAN. Your Order, because it, unlike our Order, did not cut off at the roots the delights of the five senses, receives more because it wants more – not because it needs, but merely because it wants, more.

CLUNIAC. What are these [delights]?

CISTERCIAN. Beautiful paintings, beautiful basreliefs, carved [in ivory usually] and each embossed with gold, beautiful and costly cloaks, beautiful hanging tapestries painted in different colours, beautiful and costly [stained glass] windows, blue-collared sheet glass, copes and chasubles with golden orphreys, chalices of gold and precious stones, books illuminated with gold leaf. Necessity and utility do not require all these things, only the lust of the eyes does.

[I, 37.] CLUNIAC. So that I may hold my tongue about the other items, I ask what more becoming thing can be done than to pay honour to the most holy sacrament of Christ by using the most precious metals?

CISTERCIAN. In his treatise *On the Duties* [*of the Clergy*] St Ambrose has Christ make a case against a bishop in these words: 'Why do you allow my poor to perish of hunger?' The bishop answered: 'I have given what I have to the poor.' Christ said to him: 'Do you have gold?' 'Only in your chalice,' replied the bishop. And Christ answered: 'My sacraments do not require gold.'

St Jerome in his Letter to Nepotian says: 'Either we reject gold together with other superstitions of the Jews, or if the gold is pleasing, the Jews must also be pleasing.' In that very letter in which you say he praised your Order, the abbot of Clairvaux casts aspersions on the same order when he says with great irony: 'Ask the poor [monks], if they are poor, what gold is doing in their sanctuary.'

[I, 38.] CLUNIAC. Yes, that's true. I have read it myself and I have marvelled why he [the abbot of Clairvaux] would so criticize outward expressions of our devotion to God as to rake up satirical censure on us.

CISTERCIAN. Did the founding fathers of your Order, who are unknown, think that at the Last Judgement Christ would say, among other things, to his elect: 'Come, you blessed of my Father, because you have fashioned for me a golden cup and a chasuble emblazoned in gold,' and that he would say the exact opposite to the wicked?

CLUNIAC. Why did you say the founding fathers 'who are unknown', when Saints Odilo and Maieul drew up our Customary?

[I, 39.] CISTERCIAN. Where did you read that? You do not find that in Cluny's Book of Customs, but you do discover that St Odilo instituted one rather strange custom, and that was that a monk who has fallen into the crime both base and vile [sodomy] is to be punished in secret if there is any way to keep it hidden. I heard, when I was a member of that Order seeking information [about this custom] from my seniors, that the Cluniacs had borrowed it from some insignificant monastery which later on they took under their jurisdiction. The monks still argue about who authored this particular constitution and to this very day it is an unresolved legal argument among them. Who does not wonder, and in wondering does not become incensed, that the institutes of the Rule, whose author was filled with the spirit of all the just and who had the spirit of prophecy, are by you placed second to institutes whose authority is in doubt and which are contrary to all canons?

[I, 40.] CLUNIAC. Tell me, I pray, in what particulars are our customs contrary to the canons?

CISTERCIAN. In many.

CLUNIAC. Of the many, enumerate at least a few. But before you do, take up again and finish what you were saying about the [remaining] four delights of the senses in which, according to you, we take pleasure. You have already said enough about [the fifth sense] sight.

CISTERCIAN. Necessity and utility do not, but itching ears do, require many large bells of different tones and of such ponderous weight that two monks can barely ring one. Some monks – as they themselves have told me – have worked so strenuously at pulling the ropes that the great weight caused them injury. This is the use to which is put the great expense and the great effort of manufacturing bells.

Those high-pitched and gelded voices to which you have given the name and which are usually sharpened by a drink made from liquorice and choice electuaries – what are they but delights to the ear forbidden by the precepts of the Rule?

CLUNIAC. Where does the Rule forbid them?

CISTERCIAN. Where it orders that we read and chant 'with humility and dignity'. St Ambrose in his book *On the Duties* [*of the Clergy*] also forbids them in the following words: 'Let the voice be full with manliness and not pitched like a woman's.' Contrary to the respected canonical decrees, you make use of such voices in new and frolicsome songs on your new and unauthorised feast days.

CLUNIAC. What are these new and unauthorized feast days of ours?

[I, 42.] CISTERCIAN. The Feast of the Transfiguration and the Feast of the Holy Trinity which should have no special feast day since we praise and venerate the Holy Trinity in hymns, psalms, responsories and masses every day when we say 'Glory be to the Father, Son and Holy Spirit'.

And since the opportunity has presented itself, I cannot keep quiet about one great and ridiculous incongruity of yours: you celebrate the solemn office of the Lord's circumcision and you sing the office hymn *Vultum tuum* of St Martina, Virgin and Martyr, but you make no commemoration of her. Nor should we overlook the fact that while your deacon is reading the Gospel he turns toward the East. In this custom of yours, you are acting contrary not only to holy authority but also to your own mother churches and to yourselves.

[I, 43.] CLUNIAC. According to what Solomon said, 'a man who keeps not a guard over what he says shall meet with evil' and I have no doubt that man who has no guard over what he does shall also meet with evil. Our heed for ourselves would be of little or no avail if we acted contrary to our own interests. It could even be said that not only would we be heedless of our own future good, but that our actions would be wilfully illegal.

CISTERCIAN. In your private Masses, which way do you turn when you read the Gospel?

CLUNIAC. To the north.

[I, 44.] CISTERCIAN. As it should be. Augustine says so in one of his Letters: 'The reader of the Gospel faces northward because the Lord said to the Prophet: "Proclaim these words to the north." In the book which bears the title *Sacramentary* one reads: 'While the deacon is reading he is so positioned that he stands facing northward because the Gospel is being preached to those whose faith has become chilled. But in Rome where the men stand facing south and the women toward the north, the deacon turns in the direction of the worthier sex.' Here you are! Contrary to sacred authority, contrary to the roman way, contrary to your own way in private masses, you read the Gospel facing eastward when celebrating public masses. Tell me, I ask you, do you know of any reason for this strange custom of yours?

CLUNIAC. I cannot tell you of one for the simple reason that I know of none, nor do our superiors give any other than the authority of our own Customary.

[I, 45.] CISTERCIAN. Usage which goes contrary to reason and sacred authority is abuse rather than use. St Ambrose in his book on the Duties [of the Clergy] orders: 'Do nothing if you cannot give an unqualified reason and one that will withstand proof for what you do.'

CLUNIAC. Does St Ambrose want me to disobey my superiors?

CISTERCIAN. Most certainly he wants you to obey, but not in matters which are contrary to reason and sacred authority.

CLUNIAC. Our abbots do not agree with St Ambrose's opinion.

CISTERCIAN. Our abbots, because they are human beings, can make mistakes. The Holy Spirit who speaks through Scripture cannot make a mistake because he is God. To whom do you owe greater obedience, God or man?

CLUNIAC. I answer in the words of the Apostle: 'We should obey God rather than man.'

CISTERCIAN. St Basil in his Rule for Monks used the same evidence drawn from sacred Scripture. In this Rule he delineated the obedience due respectively to sacred Scripture and to man.

CLUNIAC. I should like to hear his conclusions. If you remember it, please quote it.

The call to solitude as well as total community remained persistent throughout the period and the Carthusians were both the most austere and the most eremetical of the major religious orders. The Carthusians owed their origin to St Bruno (d. 1101) and their name to the location of their first monastery in the Chartreuse, in the Diocese of Grenoble. The Carthusian cell was a monastery in miniature.

E. Selway (trans.) *Coutumes de Chartreuse* (Paris, 1984) cited in D. A. Bellenger, *The Carthusians of Somerset* (Bath, 2003) pp. 222–225

Guigo I (d. 1136): the cell

1. The inhabitant of the cell receives, therefore, for the straw bed with strong cover, a pillow, a quilt or blanket made of two large sheepskins and covered with a piece of rough wool. For clothing, two hair-shirts, two gowns, two capes, one more used, the other better, and of the same two cowls, two pairs of stockings, four pairs of slipper skins, a hood, shoes for night and day, some grease to oil the shoes, two waist cords, a belt – these last objects of coarse hemp. And the hermit will have no care as to the coarseness or colour of anything regarding the bed or clothing. Because to all monks, and above all to us, it is assuredly necessary to wear poor worn clothes and to use all things valueless, poor and mean. There are also two needles, thread and scissors, a comb, a razor for the head, one stone and one strap to whet.

2. And to write, a desk, pens, chalk, two pumice stones, two inkwells, a pocket knife, two razors to level the surface of the parchments, an awl, a bradawl, a lead thread, a ruler, a small board for adjusting the page, tablets [covered in wax to take notes, with a stylus, which could be erased afterwards] and a stylus. And if a brother devotes himself to another art – which happens very rarely with us because we teach copy work to nearly all those whom we receive, if that is possible – he will have the tools appropriate to his art.

3. Then the inhabitant of the cell receives also from the library two books to read. He has the duty to bring all diligence and care possible that the books are not soiled by smoke, dust or any other stain, because we wish that the books be made with the most application and kept with very great care, as a perpetual food of our souls, in order to preach by our hands the word of God, since we cannot do so with the mouth.

4. For this purpose, as many books as we copy, as many times we seem to make in our place heralds of the truth and we hope from our Saviour Lord a reward – for all those who by these books will have been cured from error, or will progress in the Catholic truth, for all those also who will have repented their sins and vices and who will have been enflamed with desire for the celestial home.

5. And since, as with other necessary tasks which are proper to abjectness and humility, we also do our own cooking, to the hermit is given two saucepans, two bowls, a third for bread or instead, a napkin. A fourth basin, quite big, will serve for washing, two spoons, a knife for the bread, a jug, a cup, a receptacle for the water, a salt cellar, a small platter, two small bags for vegetables, a hand-towel. For the fire, sticks, kindling, a flint, a store of wood, an axe and for work, a hatchet. We ask those who will have read this not to scoff or blame those who have lived previously rather a long time in a cell among the great snows and such dreadful cold.

6. Because if we allow so many objects to each it is so that he will not be obliged to leave his cell, which we consider as unlawful. In effect that is never permitted except when the community unites in the cloister or church, which we are accustomed to do in observing the rules.

The Carthusians represented the dominance of contemplation within the monastic tradition, but there was also a place for action. Many of the earlier monks had been active missionaries. In the latter years of the sixth century Gregory the Great sent Augustine, prior of St Gregory's monastery in Rome, to England.

A. M. Sellar (trans.) *Bede's Ecclesiastical History of England* (1907) pp. 42–43

St Augustine (of Canterbury) (d. c.604) sent to England

Ch. XXIII. How the holy Pope Gregory sent Augustine, with other monks, to preach to the English nation, and encouraged them by a letter of exhortation, not to desist from their labour [596]

IN the year of our Lord 582, Maurice, the fifty-fourth from Augustus, ascended the throne, and reigned twenty-one years. In the tenth year of his reign, Gregory, a man eminent in learning and the conduct of affairs, was promoted to the Apostolic see of Rome, and presided over it thirteen years, six months and ten days. He, being moved by Divine inspiration, in the fourteenth year of the same emperor, and about the one hundred and fiftieth after the coming of the English into Britain, sent the servant of God, Augustine, and with him divers other monks, who feared the Lord, to preach the Word of God to the English nation. They having, in obedience to the pope's commands, undertaken that work, when they had gone but a little way on their journey, were seized with craven terror, and began to think of returning home, rather than proceed to a barbarous, fierce, and unbelieving nation, to whose very language they were strangers; and by common consent they decided that this was the safer course. At once Augustine, who had been appointed to be consecrated bishop, if they should be received by the English, was sent back, that he might, by humble entreaty, obtain of the blessed Gregory, that they should not be compelled to undertake so dangerous, toilsome, and uncertain a journey. The pope, in reply, sent them a letter of exhortation, persuading them to set forth to the work of the Divine Word, and rely on the help of God. The purport of which letter was as follows:

Gregory, the servant of the servants of God, to the servants of our Lord. Forasmuch as it had been better not to begin a good work, than to think of desisting from one which has been begun, it behoves you, my beloved sons, to fulfil with all diligence the good work, which, by the help of the Lord, you have undertaken. Let not, therefore, the toil of the journey, nor the tongues of evilspeaking men, discourage you; but with all earnestness and zeal perform, by God's guidance, that which you have set about; being assured, that great labour is followed by the greater glory of an eternal reward. When Augustine, your Superior, returns, whom we also constitute your abbot, humbly obey him in all things; knowing, that whatsoever you shall do by his direction, will, in all respects, be profitable to your souls. Almighty God protect you with His grace, and grant that I may, in the heavenly country, see the fruits of your labour, inasmuch as, though I cannot labour with you, I shall partake in the joy of the reward, because I am willing to labour. God keep you in safety, my most beloved sons. Given the 23rd of July, in the fourteenth year of the reign of our most religious lord, Mauritius Tiberius Augustus, the thirteenth year after the consulship of our lord aforesaid, and the fourteenth indiction.

With the advent of lay brothers in the Cistercian and Carthusian traditions there was a significant body of religious dedicated to hard work and the economic development of the monastic order without the distraction of Church services.

C. Waddell, *Cistercian Lay Brothers: twelfth-century usages with related texts* (Citeaux, 2000) *Studia et Documenta*, vol. X, pp. 204–209

The Clairvaux Breve et Memoriale Scriptum

Chapter IX. About the guestmaster at the grange

The guestmaster at the grange, should any of the brothers make him a sign for permission to speak, has a place assigned in which he can speak to him. But if the Master is outside the grange enclosure, the guestmaster will be able to speak throughout the entire court, and with everyone. If the Master is present, he may speak with those attached to the grange (*familia*) and the guests. The grange master does not have a horse at his disposal; but when he comes to the abbey, he goes on foot as one of the others.

Chapter X. The brother herdsmen

From the feast of the Holy Cross until the feast of Saint Martin, as soon as Matins is over all the brothers put on their hoods and occupy themselves until day with various tasks, so that they are not idle. But from the feast of Saint Martin until the Purification, they use that interval for husking and shelling field produce. At all seasons the brother herdsmen, after Prime has been said, harness the oxen for the day's field-work, speaking in pairs in the same place. They observe silence as they go a further distance, until they start plowing. Once they have begun, they can speak until they reach the point where the furrows reverse direction, where it is customary to observe silence. Similarly, too, when they meet others in their plowing they stop speaking, to avoid scandalising those listening to them. But after they stop work, they return to their stables in silence. There they have a place assigned where the Master speaks with them, but standing. During the mowing and harvesting seasons, they speak with each other as, in twos, they go from and return to their wagon-loads; but they are nevertheless silent, as was said, and interrupt their exchange when others coming from the opposite direction meet them. They take their meal where they are plowing; each has his own cooked portion. From the time the oxen are put out to pasture, each of the herdsmen takes his turn, individually or in pairs, looking after the oxen by night in the pastures, keeping night watch over them. But for all that, they go out the next day to the field-work.

Chapter XI. About the sheep herders

When the brothers who are sheep herders leave the grange during non fasting seasons, each receives bread in his wallet; and goes off to the pastures, leading the sheep. They eat at the proper hour. If they have any bread left over, they bring it back home. They are to presume to eat nothing else, even if someone sends it to them, unless they find woodland fruits, which they are permitted to eat. Going and returning they observe silence with each other and with everyone else, unless perhaps they point out the right direction to someone, or provide information about a stray animal, or inquire briefly about their own strays. But when they arrive at the pastures, they speak with one another in twos, but silently, so that others may not understand. When they are back home, they have no place assigned for speaking; but they do have a place somewhere or another for speaking with their Master even as the necessity of obedience demands.

Chapter XIII. About cobblers, skinners, and weavers

Cobblers, skinners, and weavers observe practically the same order. However, they speak to absolutely no one other than to abbot or prior. If at times one of the brothers does not know what to do or how to do it, he goes outside, calls the Master with a sign, and diligently inquires from him how something is to be done. But the brothers stand as they speak about their necessities with their Master, who is also standing; and this they do briefly and silently. But if another brother wishes to speak, let him wait patiently until the matter has been completed or rejected, and the other brother has returned. The Master, however, is to speak outside with those serving him, standing or sitting. Outside their own house, however, the lay brothers observe silence, with the exception of their Master, who necessarily may speak about the work.

Chapter XIV. About the bakers

But the bakers speak with their Master, standing, in front of the mill and at the entrance to the house, to the right or to the left. In the place where the bread is weighed out, however, only the Master speaks.

Chapter XV. About the cloth-fullers

The cloth-fullers, too, because of the noise made by the water, may speak privately with their Master within their own house.

Chapter XVI. About the blacksmiths

The blacksmiths are to have forges assigned them with the [other] blacksmiths. But should one brother go to the forge of another blacksmith for reasons of work, he is to ask for what he needs only by sign; and he thus leaves without saying anything. The Master, however, is to inspect all the forges frequently, to see what work is being done by each of the blacksmiths.

The monastic ideal was both an elite aspiration and an inclusive one. The lay brothers revealed the fact that the religious orders were open not only to the literate but also to the labouring peasant stratum of society. The military orders, including the Templars and the Hospitallers, opened the way for those who had pursued a military life to integrate their knightly virtues with the monastic ideal. For women the pursuit of the contemplative life could provide a genuine alternative to marriage and the demands of procreation.

C. H. Talbot (ed. and trans.) *The Life of Christina of Markyate: a twelfth century recluse* (Oxford, 1959) pp. 183–189

Christina of Markyate (twelfth century)

It happened once that a certain pilgrim, quite unknown but of reverend mien, came to the virgin Christina's cell. She welcomed him hospitably as she did everyone, not asking him who he was nor being told by him at that time who he was. So he went on his way, leaving on her memory a deep impression. After a while he returned a second time: first he offered prayers to the Lord and then he settled down to enjoy Christina's conversation. Whilst they were talking, she felt a divine fervour which made her recognize him as being far beyond ordinary men or man's deserts. Greatly delighted at this, she urged him with kindly hospitality to take food. He sat down whilst she and her sister Margaret prepared the repast. Christina paid more attention to the man, whilst Margaret was busily moving about concerned with the preparations of the meal, so that if it had been possible to see Jesus sitting down you would recognize another Mary and another Martha. And so, when the table was prepared, he raised bread to his mouth and seemed to eat. But if you had been present, you would have noticed that he tasted rather than ate. And when he was invited to taste a little of the fish that was set before him, he replied that there was no need to take more than would keep body and soul together. And whilst both sisters were admiring his well shaped features, his handsome beard, his grave appearance, and his well-weighed words, they were filled with such spiritual joy that they felt they had before them an angel rather than a man, and, if their virginal modesty had allowed, they would have asked him to stay. But he, after imparting a blessing, and taking his leave of them, went on his way, still known to the sisters only by sight. On the other hand so deep an impression did his manner leave on their hearts, so much sweetness did he instil into them, that often when they were talking together they would say, with sighs that showed their feelings: 'If only our pilgrim would return. If only we could enjoy his company once more. If only we could gaze upon him and learn more from his grave and beautiful example.' With these yearnings for the man they often stimulated each other's desire. Christina, (thinking over) these things, prepared herself for the coming of the feast of Christmas, uncertain however where her yearnings would lead her. On the day preceding the vigil of the feast, she was confined to bed with an illness, and so strong was her weakness that she was unable to go to church on the vigil. Two monks, religiously inclined, hearing this decided to visit her out of courtesy. And whilst they were chanting the hours of the Christmas vigil to the sick virgin, she heard, and retained in her mind along with the rest the versicle of the hour of None, that special joy of that singular feast: Today ye shall know that the Lord will come and tomorrow ye shall see His glory. Realizing the significance of the verse, she was so moved with joy that for the rest of the day and the following night thoughts of this kind kept running through her mind: 'O at what hour will the Lord come? How will He come? Who shall see Him when He comes? Who will deserve to see His glory? What will that glory be like? and how great? What and how great will be the joy of those who see it?' Fixing her mind on holy desires of this kind, confined as she was to bed with a severe illness, she prepared herself, with great joy for the hours of Matins. And as she heard the [anthem] proper to the feast, Christ is born, she understood that she had been invited to the joy of His birth. Her illness disappeared and she was filled with such spiritual happiness that her mind could dwell on nothing but divine things. And when the others sang the hymn *Te Deum laudamus*, she looked up and felt as if she had been borne into the church of St. Albans and stood on the steps of the lectern where the lessons of Matins are read out. And looking down on the choir, she saw a person in the middle of the choir looking approvingly at the reverent behaviour of the monks singing. His beauty exceeded the power and capacity of man to describe. On his head he bore a golden crown thickly encrusted with precious stones which seemed to excel any work of human skill. On the top was a cross of gold of marvellous craftsmanship, not so much man-made as divine. Hanging over his face, one on either side, were two bands or fillets attached to the crown, delicate and shining, and on the tops of the gems there were seen as it were drops of dew. In this guise appeared the man whose beauty had only to be seen to be loved, for He is the fairest of the children of men. And when she had gazed on this beauty, she felt herself rapt in some way to another world. But whether she saw these things in the body or out of the body (God is her witness), she never knew. On the morrow of Christmas day, when the time for the procession was near, a message was brought to her that her beloved pilgrim had arrived. When she heard this, her joy was unbounded, and added fire to the flames of her desire. For she hoped to reap no little benefit by entertaining in the person of this pilgrim Him whose presence had brought her such sweet relief. She ordered the doors, therefore, [to be closed.]

Therefore the pilgrim followed the procession of chanting virgins: his modesty in gait, his grave expression, his mature appearance, were closely observed, setting as it did the virgin's choir an example of grave deportment, as it says in Scripture: 'I will give Thee thanks in the great congregation.' In the procession and the Mass and the other parts of the service the pilgrim took part. And when they were over, the virgin of Christ, preceding the rest (for she could not have too much of her pilgrim), left the church so that she should be the first to greet him as he came out. For there was no other place of exit except where Christina was. As he stayed awhile, the virgin became impatient with waiting. And when they had all come out, she said: 'Where is the pilgrim?' 'He is praying in the church', they answered. Impatient of delay, she sent some of the nuns to call him. But they returned to say that he could not be found anywhere. The virgin, rather surprised and disturbed, said: 'Where is the key of the door?' 'Here it is', said the one who had charge of it. 'From the moment that Mass began no one could come out, since the door had been closed and I have guarded the key.' Nor was there anyone else who had even seen him come out of the Church. Who else could we say he was, except an angel or the Lord Jesus? For He who appeared that night in such a guise showed Himself in some sort of way as He will be seen in glory. For this is how that glory appears to us in this present life, since we see it only through a glass. Hence God is said to dwell in darkness; not that He dwells in darkness, but His light because of its brightness blinds us who are weighed down by the body. On that day He wished to appear under the guise of a pilgrim, of a grown-up man because, as . . . [rest missing].

In the thirteenth century the religious life was revolutionised by the emergence of the friars who emphasised the importance of evangelical poverty and the active promotion of the Gospel. The friars often lived in the towns and lacked the gracious spaciousness of the monk's surroundings. As preachers and teachers they brought the religious life into the market place and revealed the possibility of the cloister and the world co-existing.

R. J. Armstrong, J. A. Wayne Hellmann and W. J. Short (eds) *Francis of Assisi: early documents*, vol. 1: *The Saint* (New York, 1999) pp. 61–62, 99–106

A rule for hermitages (1217–1221)

1. Let those who wish to stay in hermitages in a religious way be three brothers or, at the most, four; let two of these be 'the mother' and have two 'sons' or at least one.
2. Let the two who are 'mothers' keep the life of Martha and the two 'sons' the life of Mary and let one have one enclosure in which each one may have his cell in which he may pray and sleep.
3. And let them always recite Compline of the day immediately after sunset and strive to maintain silence, recite their Hours, rise for Matins, and seek first the kingdom of God and His justice.
4. And let them recite Prime at the proper hour and, after Terce, they may end their silence, speak with and go to their mothers.
5. And when it pleases them, they can beg alms from them as poor little ones out of love of the Lord God.
6. And afterwards let them recite Sext, None and, at the proper hour, Vespers.
7. And they may not permit anyone to enter or eat in the enclosure where they dwell.
8. Let those brothers who are the 'mothers' strive to stay far from everyone and, because of obedience to their minister, protect their 'sons' from everyone so that no one can speak with them.
9. And those 'sons' may not talk with anyone except with their 'mothers' and with the minister and his custodian when it pleases them to visit with the Lord's blessing.
10. The 'sons,' however, may periodically assume the role of the 'mothers,' taking turns for a time as they have mutually decided. Let them strive to observe conscientiously and eagerly everything mentioned above.

The earlier rule of St Francis had its origins in the statement presented to and approved by Pope Innocent III in 1209/10.

The later rule (1223)

Bull of Pope Honorius III

Honorius,
Bishop, Servant of the servants of God,
to His Beloved Sons,
Brother Francis and the other brothers
of the Order of the Lesser Brothers,
Health and Apostolic Benediction.

The Apostolic See is accustomed to grant the pious requests and favourably to accede to the laudable desires of its petitioners. Therefore, beloved sons in the Lord, attentive to your pious prayers, We confirm with Our Apostolic Authority, and by these words ratify, the Rule of your Order, herein outlined and approved by Our predecessor, Pope Innocent of happy memory, which is as follows:

CHAPTER I. IN THE NAME OF THE LORD! THE LIFE OF THE LESSER BROTHERS BEGINS

1. The Rule and Life of the Lesser Brothers is this: to observe the Holy Gospel of Our Lord Jesus Christ by living in obedience, without anything of one's own, and in chastity.

2. Brother Francis promises obedience and reverence to our Lord Pope Honorius and his successors canonically elected and to the Roman Church.

3. Let the other brothers be bound to obey Brother Francis and his successors.

CHAPTER II. THOSE WHO WISH TO ADOPT THIS LIFE, AND HOW THEY SHOULD BE RECEIVED

1. If there are any who wish to accept this life and come to our brothers, let them send them to their provincial ministers, to whom alone and not to others is permission granted to receive the brothers.

2. Let the ministers examine them carefully concerning the Catholic faith and the sacraments of the Church.

3. If they believe all these things, will faithfully profess them, and steadfastly observe them to the end;

4. and if they have no wives, or if they have wives who have already taken a vow of continence and are of such an age that suspicion cannot be raised about them, and who have already entered a monastery or have given their husbands permission by the authority of the bishop of the diocese,

5. let the ministers speak to them the words of the holy Gospel that they go and sell all they have and take care to give it to the poor.

6. If they cannot do this, their good will may suffice.

7. Let the brothers and the minister be careful not to interfere with their temporal goods that they may dispose of their belongings as the Lord inspires them.

8. If, however, counsel is sought, the minister may send them to some God-fearing persons according to whose advice their goods may be distributed to the poor.

9. Then they may be given the clothes of probation, namely, two tunics without a hood, a cord, short trousers, and a little cape reaching to the cord,

10. unless, at times, it seems good to these same ministers, before God, to act otherwise.

11. When the year of probation has come to an end, they may be received to obedience promising always to observe this rule and life.

12. On no account shall it be lawful for them to leave this Order, according to the decree of our Lord the Pope,

13. for, according to the Gospel: *no one who puts a hand to the plough and looks to what was left behind is fit for the kingdom of God.*

14. Those who have already promised obedience may have one tunic with a hood and another, if they wish, without a hood.

15. And those who are compelled by necessity may wear shoes.

16. Let all the brothers wear poor clothes and they may mend them with pieces of sackcloth or other material with the blessing of God.

17. I admonish and exhort them not to look down upon or judge those whom they see dressed in soft and fine clothes and enjoying the choicest food and drink, but rather let everyone judge and look down upon himself.

CHAPTER III. THE DIVINE OFFICE, FASTING AND HOW THE BROTHERS SHOULD GO ABOUT IN THE WORLD

1. Let the clerical [brothers] recite the Divine Office according to the rite of the holy Roman Church excepting the psalter,
2. for which reason they may have breviaries.
3. The lay [brothers], however, may say twenty-four *Our Fathers* for Matins, and five for Lauds; seven for each of the Hours of Prime, Terce, Sext, and None, twelve for Vespers, and seven for Compline.
4. Let them pray for the dead.
5. Let them fast from the feast of All Saints until the Lord's Nativity.
6. May those be blessed by the Lord who fast voluntarily during that holy Lent that begins at the Epiphany and lasts during the forty days which our Lord consecrated by His own fast; but those who do not wish to keep it will not be obliged.
7. Let them fast, however, during the other [Lent] until the Lord's Resurrection.
8. At other times they may not be bound to fast except on Fridays.
9. During a time of obvious need, however, the brothers may not be bound by corporal fast.
10. I counsel, admonish and exhort my brothers in the Lord Jesus Christ not to quarrel or argue or judge others when they go about in the world;
11. but let them be meek, peaceful, modest, gentle, and humble, speaking courteously to everyone, as is becoming.
12. They should not ride horseback unless they are compelled by an obvious need or an infirmity.
13. Into whatever house they enter, let them first say: 'Peace be to this house!'
14. According to the holy Gospel, let them eat whatever food is set before them.

CHAPTER IV. LET THE BROTHERS NEVER RECEIVE MONEY

1. I strictly command all my brothers not to receive coins or money in any form, either personally or through intermediaries.
2. Nevertheless, the ministers and custodians alone may take special care through their spiritual friends to provide for the needs of the sick and the clothing of the others according to places, seasons and cold climates, as they judge necessary,
3. saving always that, as stated above, they do not receive coins or money.

CHAPTER V. THE MANNER OF WORKING

1. Those brothers to whom the Lord has given the grace of working may work faithfully and devotedly;
2. so that, while avoiding idleness, the enemy of the soul, they do not extinguish the Spirit of holy prayer and devotion to which all temporal things must contribute.
3. In payment for their work they may receive whatever is necessary for the bodily support of themselves and their brothers, excepting coin or money,
4. and let them do this humbly as is becoming for servants of God and followers of most holy poverty.

CHAPTER VI. LET THE BROTHERS NOT MAKE ANYTHING THEIR OWN; BEGGING ALMS, THE SICK BROTHERS

1. Let the brothers not make anything their own, neither house, nor place, nor anything at all.

2. As pilgrims and strangers in this world, serving the Lord in poverty and humility, let them go seeking alms with confidence,

3. and they should not be ashamed because, for our sakes, our Lord made Himself poor in this world.

4. This is that sublime height of most exalted poverty which has made you, my most beloved brothers, heirs and kings of the Kingdom of Heaven, poor in temporal things but exalted in virtue.

5. Let this be your portion which leads into the land of the living.

6. Giving yourselves totally to this, beloved brothers, never seek anything else under heaven for the name of our Lord Jesus Christ.

7. Wherever the brothers may be and meet one another, let them show that they are members of the same family.

8. Let each one confidently make known his need to the other, for if a mother loves and cares for her son according to the flesh, how much more diligently must someone love and care for his brother according to the Spirit!

9. When any brother falls sick, the other brothers must serve him as they would wish to be served themselves.

CHAPTER VII. THE PENANCE TO BE IMPOSED ON THE BROTHERS WHO SIN

1. If any brother, at the instigation of the enemy, sins mortally in regard to those sins concerning which it has been decreed among the brothers to have recourse only to the provincial ministers, let him have recourse as quickly as possible and without delay.

2. If these ministers are priests, with a heart full of mercy let them impose on him a penance; but, if the ministers are not priests, let them have it imposed by others who are priests of the Order, as in the sight of God appears to them more expedient.

3. They must be careful not to be angry or disturbed at the sin of another, for anger and disturbance impede charity in themselves and in others.

CHAPTER VIII. THE ELECTION OF THE GENERAL MINISTER OF THIS FRATERNITY AND THE CHAPTER OF PENTECOST

1. Let all the brothers always be bound to have one of the brothers of this Order as general minister and servant of the whole fraternity and let them be strictly bound to obey him.

2. When he dies, let the election of his successor be made by the provincial ministers and custodians in the Chapter of Pentecost, at which all the provincial ministers are bound to assemble in whatever place the general minister may have designated.

3. Let them do this once in every three years, or at other longer or shorter intervals, as determined by the aforesaid minister.

4. If, at any time, it appears to the body of the provincial ministers and custodians that the aforesaid general minister is not qualified for the service and general welfare of the brothers, let the aforesaid brothers, to whom the election is committed, be bound to elect another as custodian in the name of the Lord.

5. Moreover, after the Chapter of Pentecost, the provincial ministers and custodians may each, if they wish and it seems expedient to them, convoke a Chapter of the brothers in their custodies once in the same year.

CHAPTER IX. PREACHERS

1. The brothers may not preach in the diocese of any bishop when he has opposed their doing so.

2. And let none of the brothers dare to preach in any way to the people unless he has been examined and approved by the general minister of this fraternity and the office of preacher has been conferred upon him.

3. Moreover, I admonish and exhort those brothers that when they preach their *language be well-considered and chaste* for the benefit and edification of the people, announcing to them vices and virtues, punishment and glory, with brevity, because our Lord when on earth kept his word brief.

CHAPTER X. THE ADMONITION AND CORRECTION OF THE BROTHERS

1. Let the brothers who are the ministers and servants of the others visit and admonish their brothers and humbly and charitably correct them, not commanding them anything that is against their soul and our rule.

2. Let the brothers who are subject, however, remember that, for God's sake, they have renounced their own wills.

3. Therefore, I strictly command them to obey their ministers in everything they have promised the Lord to observe and which is not against their soul or our Rule.

4. Wherever the brothers may be who know and feel they cannot observe the Rule spiritually, they can and should have recourse to their ministers.

5. Let the ministers, moreover, receive them charitably and kindly and have such familiarity with them that these same brothers may speak and deal with them as masters with their servants,

6. for so it must be that the ministers are the servants of all the brothers.

7. Moreover, I admonish and exhort the brothers in the Lord Jesus Christ to beware of all pride, vainglory, envy and greed, of care and solicitude for the things of this world, of detraction and murmuring. Let those who are illiterate not be anxious to learn,

8. but let them pay attention to what they must desire above all else: to have the Spirit of the Lord and Its holy activity,

9. to pray always to Him with a pure heart, to have humility and patience in persecution and infirmity,

10. and to love those who persecute, rebuke and find fault with us, because the Lord says: *Love your enemies and pray for those who persecute and calumniate you.*

11. *Blessed are those who suffer persecution for the sake of justice, for theirs is the kingdom of heaven.*

12. *But whoever perseveres to the end will be saved.*

CHAPTER XI. THE BROTHERS MAY NOT ENTER THE MONASTERIES OF NUNS

1. I strictly command all the brothers not to have any suspicious dealings or conversations with women,

2. and they may not enter the monasteries of nuns, excepting those brothers to whom special permission has been granted by the Apostolic See;

3. and they may not be godfathers to men or women, so that scandal may not arise among the brothers or concerning them on account of this.

CHAPTER XII. THOSE GOING AMONG THE SARACENS AND OTHER NON-BELIEVERS

1. Let those brothers who wish by divine inspiration to go among the Saracens or other non-believers ask permission to go from their provincial ministers.

2. The ministers, however, may not grant permission except to those whom they see fit to be sent.

3. In addition to these points, I command the ministers through obedience to petition from our Lord the Pope for one of the Cardinals of the Holy Roman Church, who would be the governor, protector and corrector of this fraternity,

4. so that, being always submissive and subject at the feet of the same Holy Church and steadfast in the Catholic Faith, we may observe poverty, humility, and the Holy Gospel of our Lord Jesus Christ as we have firmly promised.

It is forbidden, therefore, for anyone to tamper with this decree which we have confirmed, or rashly dare to oppose it. If anyone presume to attempt this, let him know that he shall incur the anger of Almighty God and of His blessed Apostles Peter and Paul.

Given at the Lateran, the twenty-ninth day of November, in the eighth year of Our pontificate.

Further reading

J. Burton, *Monastic and Religious Orders in Britain, 1000–1300* (Cambridge, 1994).

G. Constable, *The Reformation of the Twelfth Century* (Cambridge, 1996).

—— *Monks, Hermits and Crusaders in Medieval Europe* (Aldershot, 2002).

G. Coppack and M. Aston, *Christ's Poor Men: the Carthusians in England* (Stroud, 2002).

D. Knowles, *The Monastic Order in England* (Cambridge, 1940).

C. H. Laurence, *The Friars: the impact of the early mendicant movement on Western society* (London, 1994).

—— *Medieval Monasticism* (London, 2003).

3   The hierarchical Church

The Catholic Church in the Middle Ages had a structure of government and ministry based on an ordained body of clergy. This body consisted of three grades which were seen as being of divine institution; bishops, priests and deacons, and the subdiaconate and minor orders instituted by the Church itself. The bishops, as the chief pastors of the Church, formed a centre of unity in their dioceses, or local church, and were seen as the successors of the Apostles and the principal preachers of the Gospel. They were entrusted with the power to confer holy orders on their associates. The title bishop means 'an overseer' and the English word bishop is an Anglo-Saxon corruption of the Latin *episcopus*. The power of the bishop beyond his diocese was a matter of intense debate and differing emphases. A metropolitan, sometimes referred to as an archbishop, in the Western Church, presides as principal bishop of a region designated as his province, and, with his dependent or suffragan bishops was largely autonomous. The title primate, given to some archbishops, is largely one of honour often, as with Canterbury, based on historical precedence.

J. Barmby, *The Book of Pastoral Rule and Selected Epistles of Gregory the Great*, Nicene and Post-Nicene Fathers, vol. XII (New York, 1895) pp. 1–2, 9–14, 20–25, 29, 71–72

St Gregory the Great: the pastoral rule

Part I

CHAPTER I

No one presumes to teach an art till he has first, with intent meditation, learnt it. What rashness is it, then, for the unskilful to assume pastoral authority, since the government of souls is the art of arts! For who can be ignorant that the sores of the thoughts of men are more occult than the sores of the bowels? And yet how often do men who have no knowledge whatever of spiritual precepts fearlessly profess themselves physicians of the heart, though those who are ignorant of the effect of drugs blush to appear as physicians of the flesh! But because, through the ordering of God, all the highest in rank of this present age are inclined to reverence religion, there are some who, through the outward show of rule within the holy Church, affect the glory of distinction. They desire to appear as teachers, they covet superiority to others, and, as the Truth attests, they seek the first salutations in the marketplace, the first rooms at feasts, the first seats in assemblies (Matt. xxiii. 6,7), being all the less able to administer worthily the office they have undertaken of pastoral care, as they have reached the magisterial position of humility out of elation only. For, indeed, in a magisterial position language itself is confounded when one thing is learnt and another taught. Against such the Lord complains by the prophet, saying, 'They have reigned, and not by Me; they have been set up as princes, and I knew it not' (Hos. viii. 4). For those reign of themselves, and not by the Will of the Supreme Ruler, who, supported by no virtues, and in no way divinely called, but inflamed by their own desire, seize rather than attain supreme rule. . . . And therefore the Truth complains of not being known of them, and protests that He knows not the principality of those who know not Him; because in truth these who know not the things of the Lord are unknown to the Lord; as Paul attests, who says, 'But if any man knoweth not, he shall not be known' (I Cor. xiv. 38). Yet this unskillfulness of the shepherds doubtless suits often the deserts of those who are subject to them, because, though it is their own fault that they have not the light of knowledge, yet it is in the dealing of strict judgment that through their ignorance those also who follow them should stumble. Hence it is that, in the Gospel, the Truth in person says, 'If the blind lead the blind, both fall into the ditch' (Matt. xv. 14). Hence the Psalmist (not expressing his own desire, but in his ministry as a prophet) denounces such, when he says, 'Let their eyes be blinded that they see not, and ever bow thou down their back' (Ps. lxviii. 24). For, indeed, those persons are eyes who, placed in the very face of the highest dignity, have undertaken the office of spying out the road; while those who are attached to them and follow them are denominated backs. And so, when the eyes are blinded the back is bent, because, when those who go before lose the light of knowledge, those who follow are bowed down to carry the burden of their sins. . . .

Part II. Of the life of the pastor

CHAPTER I

The conduct of a prelate ought so far to transcend the conduct of the people as the life of a shepherd is wont to exalt him above the flock. For one whose estimation is such that the people are called his flock is bound anxiously to consider what great necessity is laid upon him to maintain rectitude. It is necessary, then, that in thought he should be pure, in action chief; discreet in keeping silence, profitable in speech; a near neighbour to every one in sympathy, exalted above all in contemplation; a familiar friend of good livers through humility, unbending against the vices of evildoers through zeal for righteousness; not relaxing in his care for what is inward from being occupied in outward things, nor neglecting to provide for outward things in his solicitude for what is inward. But the things which we have thus briefly touched on let us now unfold and discuss more at length.

CHAPTER II

The ruler should always be pure in thought, inasmuch as no impurity ought to pollute him who has undertaken the office of wiping away the stains of pollution in the hearts of others also; for the hand that would cleanse from dirt must needs be clean, lest, being itself sordid with clinging mire, it soil whatever it touches all the more. For on this account it is said through the prophet, 'Be ye clean that bear the vessels of the Lord' (Isai. lii. 11). For they bear the vessels of the Lord who undertake, on the surety of their own conversation, to conduct the souls of their neighbours to the eternal sanctuary. Let them therefore perceive within themselves how purified they ought to be who carry in the bosom of their own personal responsibility living vessels to the temple of eternity. . . .

CHAPTER III

The ruler should always be chief in action, that by his living he may point out the way of life to those that are put under him, and that the flock, which follows the voice and manners of the shepherd, may learn how to walk better through example than through words. For he who is required by the necessity of his position to speak the highest things is compelled by the same necessity to exhibit the highest things. For that voice more readily penetrates the hearer's heart, which the speaker's life commends, since what he commands by speaking he helps the doing of by shewing. Hence it is said through the prophet, 'Get thee up into the high mountain, thou that bringest good tidings to Sion' (Isai. xl. 9) which means that he who is engaged in heavenly preaching should already have forsaken the low level of earthly works, and appear as standing on the summit of things, and by so much the more easily should draw those who are under him to better things as by the merit of his life he cries aloud from heights above. . . .

CHAPTER IV

The ruler should be discreet in keeping silence, profitable in speech; lest he either utter what ought to be suppressed or suppress what he ought to utter. For, as incautious speaking leads into error, so indiscreet silence leaves in error those who might have been instructed. For often improvident rulers, fearing to lose human favour, shrink timidly from speaking freely the things that are right; and, according to the voice of the Truth (John x. 12) serve unto the custody of the flock by no means with the zeal of shepherds, but in the way of hirelings; since they fly when the wolf cometh if they hide themselves under silence. For hence it is that the Lord through the prophet upbraids them, saying, 'Dumb dogs, that cannot bark' (Isai. lvi. 10). Hence again He complains, saying, 'Ye have not gone up against the enemy, neither opposed a wall for the house of Israel, to stand in the battle in the day of the Lord' (Ezek. xiii. 5). Now to go up against the enemy is to go with free voice against the powers of this world for defence of the flock; and to stand in the battle in the day of the Lord is out of love of justice to resist bad men when they contend against us. For, for a shepherd to have feared to say what is right, what else is it but to have turned his back in keeping silence? But surely, if he puts himself in front for the flock, he opposes a wall against the enemy for the house of Israel. . . .

But, when the ruler prepares himself for speaking, let him bear in mind with what studious caution he ought to speak, lest, if he be hurried inordinately into speaking, the hearts of hearers be smitten with the wound of error, and, while he perchance desires to seem wise, he unwisely sever the bond of unity. For on this account the Truth says, 'Have salt in yourselves, and have peace one with another' (Mark ix. 49).

Now by salt is denoted the word of wisdom. Let him, therefore, who strives to speak wisely fear greatly, lest by his eloquence the unity of his hearers be disturbed. Hence Paul says, 'Not to be more wise than behoveth to be wise, but to be wise unto sobriety' (Rom. xii. 3). . . .

CHAPTER V

The ruler should be a near neighbour to every one in sympathy, and exalted above all in contemplation, so that through the bowels of loving-kindness he may transfer the infirmities of others to himself, and by loftiness of speculation transcend even himself in his aspiration after the invisible; lest either in seeking high things he despise the weak things of his neighbours, or in suiting himself to the weak things of his neighbours he relinquish his aspiration after high things. . . . And for the most part it comes to pass that, while the ruler's mind becomes aware, through conde-scension, of the trials of others, it is itself also attacked by the temptations whereof it hears; since the same water of the laver in which a multitude of people is cleansed is undoubtedly itself defiled. For, in receiving the pollutions of those who wash, it loses, as it were, the calmness of its own purity. But of this the pastor ought by no means to be afraid, since, under God, who nicely balances all things, he is the more easily rescued from his own temptations as he is more compassionately distressed by those of others. . . .

CHAPTER X

It should be known too that the vices of subjects ought sometimes to be prudently connived at; but indicated in that they are connived at; that things, even though openly known, ought sometimes to be seasonably tolerated, but sometimes, though hidden, be closely investigated; that they ought sometimes to be gently reproved, but sometimes vehemently censured. For, indeed, some things, as we have said, ought to be prudently connived at, but indicated in that they are connived at, so that, when the delinquent is aware that he is discovered and borne with, he may blush to augment those faults which he considers in himself are tolerated in silence, and may punish himself in his own judgment as being one whom the patience of his ruler in his own mind mercifully excuses. By such connivance the Lord well reproves Judah, when He says through the prophet, 'Thou hast lied, and hast not remembered Me, nor laid it to thy heart, because I have held My peace and been as one that saw not' (Isai. lvii. 11). Thus He both connived at faults and made them known, since He both held His peace against the sinner, and nevertheless declared this very thing, that He had held His peace. But some things, even though openly known, ought to be seasonably tolerated; that is, when circumstances afford no suitable opportunity for openly correcting them. For sores by being reasonably cut are the worse inflamed; and, if medicaments suit not the time, it is undoubtedly evident that they lose their medic-inal function. But, while a fitting time for the correction of subordinates is being sought, the patience of the prelate is exercised under the very weight of their offences. Whence it is well said by the Psalmist, 'Sinners have built upon my back' (Ps. cxxviii. 3). For on the back we support burdens; and therefore he complains that sinners had built upon his back, as if to say plainly, Those whom I am unable to correct I carry as a burden laid upon me.

Some hidden things, however, ought to be closely investigated, that, by the breaking out of certain symptoms, the ruler may discover all that lies closely hidden in the minds of his subordinates, and, by reproof intervening at the nick of time, from very small things become aware of greater ones. . . .

Some things, however, ought to be gently reproved: for, when fault is committed, not of malice, but only from ignorance or infirmity, it is certainly necessary that the very censure of it be tempered with great moderation. For it is true that all of us, so long as we subsist in this mortal flesh, are subject to the infirmities of our corruption. Every one, therefore, ought to gather from himself how it behoves him to pity another's weakness, lest, if he be too fervently hurried to words of reprehension against a neighbour's infirmity, he should seem to be forgetful of his own. Whence Paul admonishes well, when he says, 'If a man be overtaken in any fault, ye which are spiritual restore such an one in the spirit of meekness, considering thyself, lest thou also be tempted' (Galat. vi. 1); as if to say plainly, When what thou seest of the infirmity of another displeases thee, consider what thou art; that so the spirit may moderate itself in the zeal of reprehension, while for itself also it fears what it reprehends.

Some things, however, ought to be vehemently reproved, that, when a fault is not recognised by him who has committed it, he may be made sensible of its gravity from the mouth of the reprover; and that, when any one smooths over to himself the evil that he has perpetrated, he may be led by the asperity of his censurer to entertain grave fears of its effects against himself. For indeed it is the duty of a ruler to shew by the voice of preaching the glory of the supernal country, to disclose what great temptations of the old enemy are lurking in this life's journey, and to correct with great asperity of zeal such evils among those who are under his sway as ought not to be gently borne with; lest, in being too little incensed against faults, of all faults he be himself held guilty. . . .

CHAPTER XI

But all this is duly executed by a ruler, if inspired by the spirit of heavenly fear and love, he meditate daily on the precepts of Sacred Writ, that the words of Divine admonition may restore in him the power of solicitude and of provident circumspection with regard to the celestial life, which familiar intercourse with men continually destroys; and that one who is drawn to oldness of life by secular society may by the aspiration of compunction be ever renewed to love of the spiritual country. For the heart runs greatly to waste in the midst of human talk; and, since it is undoubtedly evident that, when driven by the tumults of external occupations, it loses its balance and falls, one ought incessantly to take care that through keen pursuit of instruction it may rise again. For hence it is that Paul admonishes his disciple who had been put over the flock, saying, 'Till I come, give attendance to reading' (i Tim. iv. 13). Hence David says, 'How have I loved Thy Law, O Lord! It is my meditation all the day' (Ps. cix. 97). . . .

Part III. How the ruler, while living well, ought to teach and admonish those that are put under him

PROLOGUE

Since, then, we have shewn what manner of man the pastor ought to be, let us now set forth after what manner he should teach. For as long before us Gregory Nazianzen of reverend memory has taught, one and the same exhortation does not suit all, inasmuch as neither are all bound together by similarity of character. For the things that profit some often hurt others; seeing that also for the most part herbs which nourish some animals are fatal to others; and the gentle hissing that quiets horses incites whelps; and the medicine which abates one disease aggravates another; and the bread which invigorates the life of the strong kills little children. Therefore according to the quality of the hearers ought the discourse of teachers to be fashioned, so as to suit all and each for their several needs, and yet never deviate from the art of common edification. For what are the intent minds of hearers but, so to speak, a kind of tight tensions of strings in a harp, which the skilful player, that he may produce a tune not at variance with itself, strikes variously? And for this reason the strings render back a consonant modulation, that they are struck indeed with one quill, but not with one kind of stroke. Whence every teacher also, that he may edify all in the one virtue of charity, ought to touch the hearts of his hearers out of one doctrine, but not with one and the same exhortation.

CHAPTER I

Differently to be admonished are these that follow:
　　Men and women.
　　The poor and the rich.
　　The joyful and the sad.
　　Prelates and subordinates.
　　Servants and masters.
　　The wise of this world and the dull.
　　The impudent and the bashful.
　　The forward and the fainthearted.
　　The impatient and the patient.
　　The kindly disposed and the envious.
　　The simple and the insincere.
　　The whole and the sick.
　　Those who fear scourges, and therefore live innocently; and those who have grown so hard in iniquity as not to be corrected even by scourges.
　　The too silent, and those who spend time in much speaking.
　　The slothful and the hasty.
　　The meek and the passionate.
　　The humble and the haughty.
　　The obstinate and the fickle.
　　The gluttonous and the abstinent.
　　Those who mercifully give of their own, and those who would fain seize what belongs to others.

Those who neither seize the things of others nor are bountiful with their own; and those who both give away the things they have, and yet cease not to seize what belongs to others.

Those that are at variance, and those that are at peace.

Lovers of strifes and peacemakers.

Those that understand not aright the words of sacred law; and those who understand them indeed aright, but speak them without humility.

Those who, though able to preach worthily, are afraid through excessive humility; and those whom imperfection or age debars from preaching, and yet rashness impels to it.

Those who prosper in what they desire in temporal matters; and those who covet indeed the things that are of the world, and yet are wearied with the toils of adversity.

Those who are bound by wedlock, and those who are free from the ties of wedlock.

Those who have had experience of carnal intercourse, and those who are ignorant of it.

Those who deplore sins of deed, and those who deplore sins of thought.

Those who bewail misdeeds, yet forsake them not; and those who forsake them, yet bewail them not.

Those who even praise the unlawful things they do; and those who censure what is wrong, yet avoid it not.

Those who are overcome by sudden passion, and those who are bound in guilt of set purpose.

Those who, though their unlawful deeds are trivial, yet do them frequently; and those who keep themselves from small sins, but are occasionally whelmed in graver ones.

Those who do not even begin what is good, and those who fail entirely to complete the good begun.

Those who do evil secretly and good publicly; and those who conceal the good they do, and yet in some things done publicly allow evil to be thought of them.

But of what profit is it for us to run through all these things collected together in a list, unless we also set forth, with all possible brevity, the modes of admonition for each?

(Admonition 1.) Differently, then, to be admonished are men and women; because on the former heavier injunctions, on the latter lighter are to be laid, that those may be exercised by great things, but these winningly converted by light ones.

(Admonition 2.) Differently to be admonished are young men and old; because for the most part severity of admonition directs the former to improvement, while kind remonstrance disposes the latter to better deeds. For it is written, 'Rebuke not an elder, but entreat him as a father' (i Tim. v. i). . . .

CHAPTER VIII

(Admonition 9.) Differently to be admonished are the forward and the faint-hearted. For the former, presuming on themselves too much, disdain all others when reproved by them; but the latter, while too conscious of their own infirmity, for the most part fall into despondency. Those count all they do to be singularly eminent; these think what they do to be exceedingly despised, and so are broken down to despondency. Therefore the works of the forward are to be finely sifted by the reprover, that wherein they please themselves they may be shewn to displease God.

For we then best correct the forward, when what they believe themselves to have done well we shew to have been ill done; that whence glory is believed to have been gained, thence wholesome confusion may ensue. . . .

But on the other hand we more fitly bring back the faint-hearted to the way of well-doing, if we search collaterally for some good points about them, so that, while some things in them we attack with our reproof, others we may embrace with our praise; to the end that the hearing of praise may nourish their tenderness, which the rebuking of their fault chastises. And for the most part we make more way with them for their profit, if we also make mention of their good deeds; and, in case of some wrong things having been done by them, if we find not fault with them as though they were already perpetrated, but, as it were, prohibit them as what ought not to be perpetrated; that so both the favour shewn may increase the things which we approve, and our modest exhortation avail more with the faint-hearted against the things which we blame. Whence the same Paul, when he came to know that the Thessalonians, who stood fast in the preaching which they had received, were troubled with a certain faint-heartedness as though the end of the world were nigh at hand, first praises that wherein he sees them to be strong, and afterwards, with cautious admonition, strengthens what was weak. For he says, 'We are bound to thank God always for you, brethren, as it is meet, because that your faith groweth exceedingly, and the charity of every one of you all toward each other aboundeth; so that we ourselves too glory in you in the churches of God for your patience and faith' (2 Thess. i. 3, 4). But, having premised these flattering encomiums of their life, a little while after he subjoined, 'Now we beseech you, brethren, by the coming of our Lord Jesus Christ, and our gathering together unto Him, that ye be not soon shaken in mind, or be troubled, neither by spirit, nor by word, nor by letter as sent by us, as that the day of the Lord is at hand' (Ibid. ii. 1). For the true teacher so proceeded that they should first hear, in being praised, what they might thankfully acknowledge, and afterwards, in being exhorted, what they should follow; to the end that the precedent praise should settle their mind, lest the subjoined admonition should shake it; and, though he knew that they had been disquieted by suspicion of the end being near, he did not yet reprove them as having been so, but, as if ignorant of the past, forbade them to be disquieted in future; so that, while they believed themselves to be unknown to their preacher with respect even to the levity of their disquietude, they might be as much afraid of being open to blame as they were of being known by him to be so.

Part IV

HOW THE PREACHER, WHEN HE HAS ACCOMPLISHED ALL ARIGHT, SHOULD RETURN TO HIMSELF, LEST EITHER HIS LIFE OR HIS PREACHING LIFT HIM UP

But since often, when preaching is abundantly poured forth in fitting ways, the mind of the speaker is elevated in itself by a hidden delight in self-display, great care is needed that he may gnaw himself with the laceration of fear, lest he who recalls the diseases of others to health by remedies should himself swell through neglect of his own health; lest in helping others he desert himself, lest in lifting up others he fall. For to some the greatness of their virtue has often been the occasion of their perdition; causing them, while inordinately secure in confidence of strength, to die unexpectedly through negligence. For virtue strives with vices; the mind flatters itself with a certain delight in it; and it comes to pass that the soul of a well-doer casts aside the fear of its circumspection, and rests secure in self-confidence; and to it, now torpid, the cunning seducer enumerates all things that it has done well, and exalts it in swelling thoughts as though superexcellent beyond all beside. Whence it is brought about, that before the eyes of the just judge the memory of virtue is a pitfall of the soul; because, in calling to mind what it has done well, while it lifts itself up in its own eyes, it falls before the author of humility. . . . Whence it is needful that, when abundance of virtues flatters us, the eye of the soul should return to its own weaknesses, and salubriously depress itself; that it should look, not at the right things that it has done, but those that it has left undone; so that, while the heart is bruised by recollection of infirmity, it may be the more strongly confirmed in virtue before the author of humility. For it is generally for this purpose that Almighty God, though perfecting in great part the minds of rulers, still in some small part leaves them imperfect; in order that, when they shine with wonderful virtues, they may pine with disgust at their own imperfection, and by no means lift themselves up for great things, while still labouring in their struggle against the least; but that, since they are not strong enough to overcome in what is last and lowest, they may not dare to glory in their chief performances.

See now, good man, how, compelled by the necessity laid upon me by thy reproof, being intent on shewing what a Pastor ought to be, I have been as an ill-favoured painter portraying a handsome man; and how I direct others to the shore of perfection, while myself still tossed among the waves of transgressions. But in the shipwreck of this present life sustain me, I beseech thee, by the plank of thy prayer, that, since my own weight sinks me down, the hand of thy merit may raise me up.

The institution of the papacy became a centre of unity in the Western Church from an early date. Conflict over the precise authority and jurisdiction of the Bishop of Rome was related to two main issues: one, the relationship with other Church leaders, especially those in the Eastern Church, and secondly, the relationship between the papacy and the emerging secular state. The Bishop of Rome became the presiding bishop of the Western Church and was accorded the title of Pope or Father. The role of the Pope, as Vicar of Christ and successor of St Peter, was gradually enhanced by the great popes of the Patristic period including St Leo the Great (d. 461) and St Gregory the Great (d. 604). The conversion of Constantine at the beginning of the fourth century was the beginning of the process by which Christianity became the principal religion in the West. The early Church Fathers attempted to work out what the role of the papacy was using as their foundation text the commission by Christ to St Peter in St Matthew's Gospel.

A Word in Season: monastic lectionary for the divine office, pt iv, Santoral (1991) pp. 28–29

From a homily by Saint John Chrysostom, Archbishop of Constantinople (d. 407)

The Lord said: *It is by your love for one another that everyone will know you are my disciples.* You see, the mark of disciples is their way of life, not their miracles. *Peter, do you love me more than these others do?* There is another sign of discipleship, again a question of the kind of life one lives. A third indication is to be found in the command: *Do not rejoice because the spirits obey you; rejoice rather that your names are written in heaven.* This also concerns the perfection of Christian behaviour. Would you have a fourth proof of discipleship? The Lord says: *Let your light shine before other people so that they may see your good works and praise your Father in heaven.* Once again, it is deeds that are noticed. And when he says elsewhere: *Whoever has left a house, or brothers or sisters for my sake shall be repaid a hundred times over, and also inherit eternal life,* he is praising personal behaviour, and a life brought to perfection.

You see then that disciples were known by their love for one another; he whose love for Christ was greater than that of the other apostles was distinguished by being given the pastoral care of his brothers and sisters; disciples were to rejoice not because they cast out devils, but because their names were written in heaven; those who give glory to God are recognized by the nobility of their deeds; and those who attain life and receive a hundredfold do so because of their contempt for everything belonging only to this present world. Peter himself received that name not for performing miracles, but for his zeal and sincere love; he did not win it by raising the dead or healing the lame, but by the genuine faith manifested in his confession. *You are Peter, and upon this rock I shall build my Church.* Why did the Lord say this? Not because Peter worked miracles, but because he said: *You are the Christ, the Son of the living God.*

But speaking of Peter reminds me of a second Peter, our father and teacher, our bishop, who succeeded to the other's virtue and inherited his episcopal chair. For it is the special privilege of this city of Antioch to have had in the beginning the leader of the apostles as its teacher. It was indeed fitting that the city that was the first to be honoured with the name of Christian should have the first of the apostles as its shepherd. But although we had him as our teacher, we did not keep him, but surrendered him to imperial Rome. But no, I should rather say that we have kept him; we have not kept his body but we have kept his faith as though it were Peter himself: in possessing Peter's faith we possess Peter. So it is that we seem to see Peter in the person of the one who patterns his life on his. Christ called John Elijah not because he really was Elijah, but because he came in the spirit and power of Elijah. Therefore as John, having come in the spirit and power of Elijah, was called Elijah, so when this man came with the same profession of faith as Peter, he was rightly thought worthy of the name of Peter. The same name follows from the same faith and manner of life.

A Word in Season, pp. 30–31

From a letter of Theodoret of Cyrrhus to Saint Leo the Great (d. 461)

When a dispute arose at Antioch regarding the obligation of living according to the law, Paul, that herald of truth and trumpet of the most Holy Spirit, hastened to the great Peter for a solution to the problem. With much more reason then do we, poor and insignificant as we are, hasten to your apostolic see to receive from you a remedy for the wounds of the churches.

For countless reasons it is right for you to hold the primacy, since your see is distinguished by many advantages. Other cities, indeed, are far-famed for their size, or their beauty, or their large populations; some, lacking in these respects, are renowned for certain spiritual endowments. But upon your city the great Provider has lavished an abundance of blessings. The greatest and most splendid of all cities, it is the capital of the world, and overflows with the multitude of its inhabitants. Having won a sovereignty which endures to this day, it confers its name upon its subjects. But above all it is honoured for its faith. The divine Apostle bears witness to this when he exclaims: *Your faith is spoken of throughout the whole world.* If, then, from the moment it received the seeds of the message of salvation, your city bore an abundance of such admirable fruits, what words can fitly praise the piety found in it today?

Furthermore, it possesses those tombs which shed light on the souls of believers, the tombs of Peter and Paul, our common fathers and teachers of the truth. That thrice-blessed pair rose in the East and sent out their rays in all directions; but it is from the West, where they gladly welcomed the setting of their earthly lives, that they now illuminate the world. It is they who made your see so illustrious; they are your crowning grace. Yet in our day also their God has adorned their throne by placing upon it your holiness, for you radiate the splendour of orthodoxy.

A Word in Season, pp. 94–95

From a sermon by Saint Leo the Great (d. 461)

Every holy festival, dearly beloved, is shared in by the whole world. Loyalty to the one faith demands that whatever is recorded as having been done for the salvation of all should be celebrated everywhere with common rejoicing. But in addition to the veneration which today's feast has gained throughout the world, it should be honoured with particular exultation by our city of Rome. On the day when the chief apostles were martyred the joy should be greatest in the place where they met their glorious end. These are the men through whom the light of Christ's gospel shone upon you, O Rome, so that you who were a teacher of error became a disciple of truth.

When the twelve apostles had received from the Holy Spirit the ability to speak in every language, they divided the world among themselves and undertook to instruct it in the gospel. The most blessed Peter, the chief of the apostles, was then chosen to go to the citadel of the Roman empire, so that from its very head the light of truth, which was being revealed for the salvation of all nations, might spread abroad more easily throughout the body of the world.

To this city you did not fear to come, most blessed apostle Peter. While your companion in glory, the apostle Paul, was still occupied in the regulation of other churches, you entered this forest of raging beasts, this ocean of stormy depths, with firmer step than when you walked upon the sea. You had already instructed the Jewish believers; you had already founded the church at Antioch where the honourable name of Christian originated: you had already taught Pontus, Cappadocia, Asia, and Bithynia the laws proclaimed by the gospel. Then, without doubt as to the success of your work and with full knowledge of how short your life would be, you carried the sign of Christ's cross into the citadel of Rome, where by decree of divine providence both the honour of supreme authority and the glory of suffering awaited you.

To this city came also your blessed fellow apostle Paul, the chosen vessel and special teacher of the Gentiles, and was associated with you at a time when all innocence, all decency, and all liberty were in jeopardy under the rule of Nero. His fury, inflamed by excess in every vice, hurled him into such a torrent of madness that he was the first to attack the Christian name in a general persecution – as if God's grace could be destroyed by the slaughter of his saints, whose greatest gain was to win eternal happiness by contempt for this fleeting life!

Precious, then, in *the sight of the Lord is the death of his saints.* No form of cruelty can destroy the religion founded on the mystery of the cross of Christ. Persecution does not weaken the Church, but strengthens it. The grains which fall singly spring up and are multiplied a hundredfold, clothing the Lord's field with an ever more abundant harvest.

In the centuries following Gregory the Great, the prestige of the city of Rome went into a steep decline, but theologians continued to proclaim the importance of the role of the Pope as the successor to St Peter.

A Word in Season, pp. 159–160

From a homily by Saint Bede (d. 735)

Today's reading from the holy gospel urges upon us the virtue of perfect love. Perfect love is defined in the command to love the Lord with our whole heart and soul and strength and our neighbour as ourselves. Neither of these two loves can be complete without the other, for no one can truly love God without loving his neighbour, nor can anyone love his neighbour truly without loving God. Therefore, each time the Lord asked Peter whether he loved him and Peter replied that the Lord knew he loved him, the Lord ended with the words: *Feed my sheep* or *Feed my lambs.* It is as if he had said in so many words that the only real proof of wholehearted love of God is to show concern for one's brothers and sisters by devoted work for them.

With prudent kindness the Lord asked Peter three times whether he loved him, in order that this triple profession might undo the fetters in which his triple denial had shackled him. As often as Peter, terrified by the Lord's sufferings, had denied all knowledge of him, so often he declared his wholehearted love for him once he had been reborn through the Lord's resurrection. By a provident dispensation the Lord three times committed the feeding of his sheep to the one who had three times declared his love; for once Peter had renewed his faith in him it was fitting for the shepherd to entrust him with the care of his members as many times as his faith in him had previously wavered.

The words *Feed my sheep* repeat what the Lord had said more plainly to Peter before the passion: *But I have prayed for you that your faith may not fail, and once you have turned back to me, strengthen your brothers and sisters.* To feed Christ's sheep, then, is to strengthen those who believe in Christ so that they may not lose their faith, and to devote constant effort to helping them make continual progress in faith.

The words *Feed my sheep* spoken to Peter were spoken to all, for what Peter was the other apostles also were. Primacy, however, was given to Peter in order to emphasize the unity of the Church. All of them were pastors, but there was to be only one flock fed by all the apostles in harmony and now fed by their successors who share solicitude for it. Of these, many have been called to glorify their Creator by their death; all have been called to glorify him by their life.

Not only those great luminaries of the Church but the rest of the throng of chosen ones have in their time each glorified their God by their lives or by their deaths. We too, in our time, must follow in their footsteps by so ordering our lives as to give examples of good deeds, and by persevering until death in the ideal of moral rectitude that we have set ourselves. Then, having shared the apostles' way of life, we may deserve to share their reward as well.

We shall reach this goal if, in keeping with this holy gospel reading, we give our Redeemer the love we owe him, and if we watch with fraternal concern over the salvation of our neighbours, with the help of him who bids us act in this way and promises to reward us for so acting, Jesus Christ our Lord, who lives and reigns with the Father as God in the unity of the Holy Spirit through endless ages. Amen.

Gregory VII was confronted with a series of conflicts with the German king, the Emperor Henry IV (d. 1106). Gregory's ideal was to free the papacy from secular interference and especially from the power of the Germans, who had become too dominant in the power vacuum that was the Italy of the time. The documentation on what is often called the Investiture Contest because it centred on the origin of Church office, whether it came from royal power or from priestly power, is vast, and includes contemporary letters, papal statements, sermons and commentaries.

E. F. Henderson (trans.) *Select Historical Documents of the Middle Ages* (1910) pp. 372–373

Letter from Henry IV to Gregory VII condemning the Pope as a usurper (24 January 1076)

Henry, king not through usurpation but through the holy ordination of God, to Hildebrand, at present not pope but false monk.

Such greeting as this hast thou merited through thy disturbances, inasmuch as there is no grade in the church which thou hast omitted to make a partaker not of honour but of confusion, not of benediction but of malediction. For, to mention few and especial cases out of many, not only hast thou not feared to lay hands upon the rulers of the holy church, the anointed of the Lord – the archbishops, namely, bishops and priests – but thou hast trodden them under foot like slaves ignorant of what their master is doing. Thou hast won favour from the common herd by crushing them; thou hast looked upon all of them as knowing nothing, upon thy sole self, moreover, as knowing all things. This knowledge, however, thou hast used not for edification but for destruction; so that with reason we believe that St. Gregory, whose name thou has usurped for thyself, was prophesying concerning thee when he said: 'The pride of him who is in power increases the more, the greater the number of those subject to him; and he thinks that he himself can do more than all.' And we, indeed, have endured all this, being eager to guard the honour of the apostolic see; thou, however, has understood our humility to be fear, and hast not, accordingly, shunned to rise up against the royal power conferred upon us by God, daring to threaten to divest us of it. As if we had received our kingdom from thee! As if the kingdom and the empire were in thine and not in God's hand! And this although our Lord Jesus Christ did call us to the kingdom, did not, however, call thee to the priesthood. For thou has ascended by the following steps. By wiles, namely, which the profession of monk abhors, thou has achieved money; by money, favour; by the sword, the throne of peace. And from the throne of peace thou hast disturbed peace, inasmuch as thou hast armed subjects against those in authority over them; inasmuch as thou, who wert not called, hast taught that our bishops called of God are to be despised; inasmuch as thou hast usurped for laymen and the ministry over their priests, allowing them to depose or condemn those whom they themselves had received as teachers from the hand of God through the laying on of hands of the bishops. On me also who, although unworthy to be among the anointed, have nevertheless been anointed to the kingdom, thou hast lain thy hand; me who as the tradition of the holy Fathers teaches, declaring that I am not to be deposed for any crime unless, which God forbid, I should have strayed from the faith – am subject to the judgment of God alone. For the wisdom of the holy fathers committed even Julian the apostate not to themselves, but to God alone, to be judged and to be deposed. For himself the true pope, Peter, also exclaims: 'Fear God, honour the king.' But thou who does not fear God, dost dishonour in me his appointed one. Wherefore St. Paul, when he has not spared an angel of Heaven if he shall have preached other-wise, has not excepted thee also who dost teach other-wise upon earth. For he says: 'If any one, either I or an angel from Heaven, should preach a gospel other than that which has been preached to you, he shall be damned.' Thou, therefore, damned by this curse and by the judgment of all our bishops and by our own, descend and relinquish the apostolic chair which thou has usurped. Let another ascend the throne of St. Peter, who shall not practise violence under the cloak of religion, but shall teach the sound doctrine of St. Peter. I Henry, king by the grace of God, do say unto thee, together with all our bishops: Descend, descend, to be damned throughout the ages.

E. F. Henderson (trans.) *Select Historical Documents of the Middle Ages* (1910) pp. 376–377

Gregory VII: first deposition and banning of Henry IV (22 February 1076)

O St. Peter, chief of the apostles, incline to us, I beg, thy holy ears, and hear me thy servant whom thou has nourished from infancy, and whom, until this day, thou hast freed from the hand of the wicked, who have hated and do hate me for my faithfulness to thee. Thou, and my mistress the mother of God, and thy brother St. Paul are witnesses for me among all the saints that thy holy Roman church drew me to its helm against my will; that I had no thought of ascending thy chair through force, and that I would rather have ended my life as a pilgrim than, by secular means, to have seized thy throne for the sake of earthly glory. And therefore I believe it to be through thy grace and not through my own deeds that it has pleased and does please thee that the Christian people, who have been especially committed to thee, should obey me. And especially to me, as thy representative and by thy favour, has the power been granted by God of binding and loosing in Heaven and on earth. On the strength of this belief therefore, for the honour and security of thy church, in the name of Almighty God, Father, Son and Holy Ghost, I withdraw, through thy power and authority, from Henry the king, son of Henry the emperor, who has risen against thy church with unheard of insolence, the rule over the whole kingdom of the Germans and over Italy. And I absolve all Christians from the bonds of the oath which they have made or shall make to him; and I forbid any one to serve him as king. For it is fitting that he who strives to lessen the honour of thy church should himself lose the honour which belongs to him. And since he has scorned to obey as a Christian, and has not returned to God whom he had deserted – holding intercourse with the excommunicated; practising manifold iniquities; spurning my commands which, as thou dost bear witness, I issued to him for his own salvation; separating himself from thy church and striving to rend it – I bind him in thy stead with the chain of the anathema. And, leaning on thee, I so bind him that the people may know and have proof that thou art Peter, and above thy rock the Son of the living God hath built His church, and the gates of Hell shall not prevail against it.

E. F. Henderson (trans.) *Select Historical Documents of the Middle Ages* (1910) pp. 365–366

Ban on lay investitures

Decree of 19 November 1078

Inasmuch as we have learned that, contrary to the establishments of the holy fathers, the investiture with churches is, in many places, performed by lay persons; and that from this cause many disturbances arise in the church by which the Christian religion is trodden underfoot: we decree that no one of the clergy shall receive the investiture with a bishopric or abbey or church from the hand of an emperor or king or of any lay person, male or female. But if he shall presume to do so he shall clearly know that such investiture is bereft of apostolic authority, and that he himself shall lie under excommunication until fitting satisfaction shall have been rendered.

Decree of 7 March 1080

Following the statutes of the holy fathers, as, in the former councils which by the mercy of God we have held, we decreed concerning the ordering of ecclesiastical dignities, so also now we decree and confirm: that, if any one henceforth shall receive a bishopric or abbey from the hand of any lay person, he shall by no means be considered as among the number of the bishops or abbots; nor shall any hearing be granted him as bishop or abbot. Moreover do we further deny to him the favour of St. Peter and the entry to the Church until, coming to his senses, he shall desert the place that he has taken by the crime of ambition as well as by that of disobedience – which is the sin of idolatry. In a like manner also we decree concerning the inferior ecclesiastical dignities.

Likewise if any emperor, king, duke, margrave, count or any one at all of the secular powers or persons shall presume to perform the investiture with bishoprics or with any ecclesiastical dignity, – he shall be bound by the bonds of the same condemnation. And, moreover, unless he come to his senses and relinquish to the Church her own prerogative, he shall feel in this present life, the divine displeasure as well with regard to his body as to his other belongings: in order that, at the coming of the Lord, his soul may be saved.

The Church/state conflict was more than merely a political movement. The freedom of the Church, especially of the Roman See, was seen as both a protector of Church reform and as a guarantee of tradition. The cult of the two great Apostles, Peter and Paul, was seen as verification of the unique apostolic witness of the papacy.

A Word in Season, pp. 95–96

From a sermon by Saint Aelred (d. 1167)

You know, brethren, that of all our Lord's apostles and martyrs the two whose feast we celebrate today seem to possess a special grandeur. Nor is this surprising, since to these two men the Lord entrusted his Church in a special way. For when Saint Peter proclaimed that the Lord was the Son of God, the Lord told him: *You are Peter, and on this rock I will build my Church. And I will give you the keys of the kingdom of heaven.* But in a way the Lord put Saint Paul on the same level, as Paul himself said: *He who worked through Peter in the apostolate also worked through me among the Gentiles.*

These are the men whom the Lord promised to the Church when he said through the prophet: *In place of your fathers, sons are born to you.* The fathers of the Church are the holy patriarchs and prophets who first taught the law of God and foretold the coming of our Lord. Our Lord came, and to replace the prophets he chose the holy apostles, thus fulfilling what the prophet had said: *In place of your fathers, sons are born to you.* See, moreover, how he shows the responsibility of the apostles to be greater than that of the prophets. The prophets were leaders of a single people and lived in a single nation and one part of the world, whereas he said of the apostles: *You will make them princes over all the earth.* And indeed, brethren, is there any place on earth that has not seen the power and grandeur of these apostles?

These are the pillars that support the Church by their teaching, their prayers, their example of patience. Our Lord strengthened these pillars. In the beginning they were very weak and could not support either themselves or others. This had been wonderfully arranged by our Lord, for if they had always been strong, one might have thought their strength was their own. Our Lord wished to show first what they were of themselves and only afterwards to strengthen them, so that all would know that their strength was entirely from God. Again, these men were to be fathers of the Church and physicians who would heal the weak. But they would be unable to pity the weaknesses of others unless they had first experienced their own weakness.

And so our Lord strengthened these pillars of the world, that is, of the Church. One pillar, Saint Peter, was very weak indeed, to be overthrown by the words of a single maidservant. Afterwards the Lord strengthened this pillar. He did so first when he asked him three times: 'Peter, do you love me?' and Peter three times answered, 'I love you.' For when he had three times denied the Lord, his love for him was to some extent lessened and this pillar became weak and broke, but by three times confessing his love for him it was strengthened. This strengthening was followed by another when the Holy Spirit was sent. Then this pillar became so strong that he could not be moved by being flogged, stoned, threatened, and at last even by being put to death.

Again, that other pillar, Paul, was undoubtedly weak at first, but hear how strong he became afterwards. *I am certain,* he said, *that neither death nor life, nor angels nor anything else in all creation will be able to separate me from the love of God.*

A Word in Season, pp. 97–98

From a sermon by Peter of Blois (d. c.1212)

'I saw men united, and an angel of the Lord spoke, saying: These are holy men who have become friends of God.'

Who are these men who are united? Surely they are the venerable princes of the earth and of the Church, Peter and Paul. The same faith united them; the same city, the same way of life, the same day made them equal in martyrdom under the same tyrant. Since then they have been united in so many ways, it is right that they share the same feast.

Christ changed Saul into Paul, and Simon into Peter: for it is of these that the prophet had once foretold: *And he will call his servants by a new name. You are Peter*, Christ said, *and on this rock I will build my church.* The rock was Christ, and Christ gave Peter his own name, so that Peter might be a rock. For as, in the desert, water flowed from the rock for the thirsty people, so too there flowed from Peter a saving confession of faith for others who were thirsty for faith.

When Christ was about to ascend to heaven, he entrusted to Peter the feeding of his sheep and lambs. Peter had been used to steering a small boat, but now Christ put him at the helm of a great ship: he made him head of the whole Church. To Peter, as the best steward, he handed over the keys of his house. Peter's righteousness made him such a powerful judge that the judgment of heaven depends on his decision; not even an angel would presume to challenge his sentence.

When the Lord asked him who people were saying he was, in a brief confession of faith Peter proclaimed the mystery of the divine majesty in Christ. It was not flesh and blood that revealed this to you, Peter (for it is not flesh and blood that will possess the kingdom of God), but the Spirit of God the Father, who is in heaven. The admirable fisherman, who once searched the depths of the sea, faithfully confessed the inscrutable mystery of the godhead in Christ. In answer to the Lord's question: 'Peter, do you love me?' Peter blotted out his triple denial with a triple confession of faith.

Peter fell, Paul was thrown to the ground; both were made weak that they might rise again strong and perfect. When Peter relied on his own strength, the intrepidity of his promise to stand firm was matched by the gravity of his fall. Yet after that detestable sin of apostasy, Peter obtained the highest place among the teachers of the faith and in the Church. Paul, who was struck blind and thrown to the ground, was raised to the third heaven to contemplate, with purified mental eye, the heavenly court's inexpressible glory.

I believe that by remembering the glorious death of these two, we honour all the apostles and martyrs; for we venerate them as martyrs and as the most outstanding of the apostles. How blessed is the martyrdom, how glorious the death that makes those who die with Christ immortal, so that united with him in a death like his they now reign with him! *To the eyes of the foolish they appeared to die, and their death was thought an afflic-tion; but blessed are those who die in the Lord.* They fell asleep in Christ to become co-heirs with Christ.

The power of the hierarchical Church was most immediately exercised by those who worked as parish priests and those who imparted the faith through teaching. The Fourth

Council of the Lateran (1215) codified the tasks of the local clergy and identified some of the problems of the clerical life.

N. P. Tanner (ed. and trans.) *Decrees of the Ecumenical Councils* (Georgetown, 1990) vol. 1, pp. 240, 242–245, 248

Decrees of the Fourth Lateran Council

11. On schoolmasters

Zeal for learning and the opportunity to make progress is denied to some through lack of means. The Lateran council therefore dutifully decreed that in each cathedral church there should be provided a suitable benefice for a master who shall instruct without charge the clerics of the cathedral church and other poor scholars, thus at once satisfying the teacher's needs and opening up the way of knowledge to learners. This decree, however, is very little observed in many churches. We therefore confirm it and add that not only in every cathedral church but also in other churches with sufficient resources, a suitable master, elected by the chapter or by the greater and sounder part of it, shall be appointed by the prelate to teach grammar and other branches of study, as far as is possible, to the clerics of those and other churches. The metropolitan church shall have a theologian to teach scripture to priests and others and especially to instruct them in matters which are recognized as pertaining to the cure of souls. The income of one prebend shall be assigned by the chapter to each master, and as much shall be assigned by the metropolitan to the theologian. The incumbent does not by this become a canon but he receives the income of one as long as he continues to teach. If the metropolitan church finds providing for two masters a burden, let it provide for the theologian in the aforesaid way but get adequate provision made for the grammarian in another church of the city or diocese. . . .

14. On punishing clerical incontinence

In order that the morals and conduct of clerics may be reformed for the better, let all of them strive to live in a continent and chaste way, especially those in holy orders. Let them beware of every vice involving lust, especially that on account of which the wrath of God came down from heaven upon the sons of disobedience, so that they may be worthy to minister in the sight of Almighty God with a pure heart and an unsullied body. Lest the ease of receiving pardon prove an incentive to sin, we decree that those who are caught giving way to the vice of incontinence are to be punished according to canonical sanctions, in proportion to the seriousness of their sins. We order such sanctions to be effectively and strictly observed, in order that those whom the fear of God does not hold back from evil may at least be restrained from sin by temporal punishment. Therefore anyone who has been suspended for this reason and presumes to celebrate divine services, shall not only be deprived of his ecclesiastical benefices but shall also, on account of his twofold fault, be deposed in perpetuity. Prelates who dare to support such persons in their wickedness, especially if they do it for money or for some other temporal advantage, are to be subject to like punishment. Those clerics who have not renounced the marriage bond, following the custom of their region, shall be punished even more severely if they fall into sin, since for them it is possible to make lawful use of matrimony.

15. *On preventing drunkenness among the clergy*

All clerics should carefully abstain from gluttony and drunkenness. They should temper the wine to themselves and themselves to the wine. Let no one be urged to drink, since drunkenness obscures the intellect and stirs up lust. Accordingly we decree that that abuse is to be entirely abolished whereby in some places drinkers bind themselves to drink equal amounts, and that man is most praised who makes the most people drunk and himself drains the deepest cups. If anyone shows himself worthy of blame in these matters, let him be suspended from his benefice or office, unless after being warned by his superior he makes suitable satisfaction. We forbid all clerics to hunt or to fowl, so let them not presume to have dogs or birds for fowling.

16. *On the dress of clerics*

Clerics should not practice callings or business of a secular nature, especially those that are dishonourable. They should not watch mimes, entertainers and actors. Let them avoid taverns altogether, unless by chance they are obliged by necessity on a journey. They should not play at games of chance or of dice, nor be present at such games. They should have a suitable crown and tonsure, and let them diligently apply them- selves to the divine services and other good pursuits. Their outer garments should be closed and neither too short nor too long. Let them not indulge in red or green cloths, long sleeves or shoes with embroidery or pointed toes, or in bridles, saddles, breast- plates and spurs that are gilded or have other superfluous ornamentation. Let them not wear cloaks with sleeves at divine services in a church, nor even elsewhere, if they are priests or parsons, unless a justifiable fear requires a change of dress. They are not to wear buckles or belts ornamented with gold or silver, or even rings except for those whose dignity it befits to have them. All bishops should wear outer garments of linen in public and in church, unless they have been monks, in which case they should wear the monastic habit; and let them not wear their cloaks loose in public but rather fastened together behind the neck or across the chest. . . .

18. *On sentences involving either the shedding of blood or a duel being forbidden to clerics*

No cleric may decree or pronounce a sentence involving the shedding of blood, or carry out a punishment involving the same, or be present when such punishment is carried out. If anyone, however, under cover of this statute, dares to inflict injury on churches or ecclesiastical persons, let him be restrained by ecclesiastical censure. A cleric may not write or dictate letters which require punishments involving the shedding of blood; in the courts of princes this responsibility should be entrusted to laymen and not to clerics. Moreover no cleric may be put in command of mercenaries or cross- bowmen or suchlike men of blood; nor may a subdeacon, deacon or priest practise the art of surgery, which involves cauterizing and making incisions; nor may anyone confer a rite of blessing or consecration on a purgation by ordeal of boiling or cold water or of the red-hot iron saving nevertheless the previously promulgated prohibitions regarding single combats and duels. . . .

27. *On the instruction of ordinands*

To guide souls is a supreme art. We therefore strictly order bishops carefully to prepare those who are to be promoted to the priesthood and to instruct them, either by themselves or through other suitable persons, in the divine services and the sacraments of the church, so that they may be able to celebrate them correctly. But if they presume henceforth to ordain the ignorant and unformed, which can indeed easily be detected, we decree that both the ordainers and those ordained are to be subject to severe punishment. For it is preferable, especially in the ordination of priests, to have a few good ministers than many bad ones, for if a blind man leads another blind man, both will fall into the pit. . . .

63. *On simony*

As we have certainly learnt, shameful and wicked exactions and extortions are levied in many places and by many persons, who are like the sellers of doves in the temple for the consecration of bishops, the blessing of abbots and the ordination of clerics. There is fixed how much is to be paid for this or that and for yet another thing. Some even strive to defend this disgrace and wickedness on the grounds of long-established custom, thereby heaping up for themselves still further damnation. Wishing therefore to abolish so great an abuse, we altogether reject such a custom which should rather be termed a corruption. We firmly decree that nobody shall dare to demand or extort anything under any pretext for the conferring of such things or for their having been conferred. Otherwise both he who receives and he who gives such an absolutely condemned payment shall be condemned with Gehazi and Simon. . . .

66. *On the same with regard to the avarice of clerics*

It has frequently been reported to the Apostolic See that certain clerics demand and extort payments for funeral rites for the dead, the blessing of those marrying, and the like; and if it happens that their greed is not satisfied, they deceitfully set up false impediments. On the other hand some lay people, stirred by a ferment of heretical wickedness, strive to infringe a praiseworthy custom of Holy Church, introduced by the pious devotion of the faithful, under the pretext of canonical scruples. We therefore both forbid wicked exactions to be made in these matters and order pious customs to be observed, ordaining that the church's sacraments are to be given freely but also that those who maliciously try to change a praiseworthy custom are to be restrained when the truth is known, by the bishop of the place. . . .

The hierarchy included many much less exalted individuals than bishops. The great cathedrals, other great churches and collegiate corporations had their own complexity of administrative and liturgical practice which paralleled the monasteries.

C. Wordsworth and D. MacLeane (eds) *Statutes and Customs of the Cathedral Church of the Blessed Virgin Mary of Salisbury* (1915) pp. 26–39, 56–69

The institution charter [the constitution or] ordinances of St Osmund (d. 1099)

These be the privileges and customs of the Church of Salisbury, which I, Osmund, Bishop of the same church, in the name of the Holy Trinity in the 1091st year after the Incarnation of our Lord have instituted, and have at the same time granted, to Personages and Canons of the same church, having myself taken advice from my lords the Archbishop and other our brother Bishops, whose names are written below, and with the assent of our lord King William which came to us at the time (*interveniente*); to wit:

That a Dean and a Chanter [or precentor], Chancellor and Treasurer be resident assiduously in Salisbury church, any sort of excuse being removed.

Let the Archdeacons fulfil the office of Archdeaconship, with this reservation, that two of their number shall always keep residence in the church of Salisbury, unless a pressing and clear reason may exempt them.

The Canons, however, nothing can exempt from being resident themselves in Salisbury church unless it be the reason of attendance at schools of learning, or the service of our lord the King, who may employ one Canon in his chapel; the Archbishop also, one; the Bishop, three.

Howbeit, if a Canon is required to be absent [on business] for the common benefit of the church or that of his prebend, and this be obviously the case, he may be so for the third part of a year.

It is the Dean's privilege, and that of all the Canons to make answer to the Bishop in no matter unless it be in Chapter, and to comply with the judgement of the Chapter only.

They have also their own court in all their prebends, and the privilege of an Archdeacon wheresoever their prebends shall have been assigned within our diocese (*parochia*), whether such prebends consist in churches or in tithes or in lands, in such sort that neither the Bishop nor any other shall make any demand of them in their prebends in the form of presents or assize or any customary duty whatsoever, but they enjoy fully and unmolested all those same liberties and privileges which either I myself, Osmund the Bishop, or any other beside me, have enjoyed in those prebends, while we retained them in our own domain.

When anyone is constituted a Canon, it is his duty to make oath before the brethren in Chapter, in presence of the Gospel, that he will observe inviolably the privileges and customs of the church of Salisbury.

The Dean is superior to all Canons and all Vicars as regards the regimen of souls and the correction of behaviour.

The Chanter's duty is to rule the choir in respect of song; and he has power to raise and lower the singing.

The Treasurer is supreme as chief custodian of treasures and ornaments, and in serving out of lights.

The Chancellor, in like manner, in ruling schools, and as corrector of the books.

The Archdeacons are vigorous in thoughtful care of parishes, and in cure of souls.

Dean, Chanter, Treasurer, and Chancellor, receive double commons; the other Canons single commons; nevertheless none participates in commons unless he have been resident in the church.

If a Canon have attended a [church] dedication, he takes a share of the offerings equally with the chaplains of the Bishop.

If my lord Bishop shall have been dedicating churches or chapels pertaining to prebends, neither the Bishop's chaplains nor any other receive a share, save only the Canon to whom the prebend in each case belongs.

The Subdean receives in possession from the Dean the archdeaconry of the city and its suburban district.

The Succentor receives in possession from the Chanter the appurtenances of chantry.

In case the Dean is lacking to the church, let the Subdean supply his place. Similarly, in the Chanter's case, let the Succentor do the like for him.

The School Rector's (*Archiscola*) duty is to hear the lessons read, and to determine their length; he is to carry the seal of the church, to compose letters and documents, and to mark the readers' names upon the board [or 'wax brede'], and the Chanter's duty is to do the like for the singers.

The elders are to be besought like brethren. Howbeit, if they are found wanting too often, and without reasonable cause, at the daily sacrifice or at the canonical hours, and if, after correction by the Dean, they have not reformed this fault, it is their duty to receive punishment (*veniam*) in Chapter prostrate in presence of the Dean and brethren.

And if they have been found guilty of disobedience or insubordination or any other notorious misdemeanour, they ought to be deposed from their stall, and to do penance at the choir door, behind the Dean, or in the choir at the bottom of the boys' row, according to the measure of their misbehaviour. If they take no account of this correction and show themselves to be incorrigible, let them submit to vengeance more austere.

Now of this constitution graciously made and granted on my part these be the witnesses

William, King of the English
Thomas [of York] archbishop
Walkelin [of Winchester] bishop
Maurice [of London] bishop
John [of Bath] bishop,
Hoel of Le Mans, bishop
Robert [? of Hereford or of Lichfield] bishop
Herbert [of Norwich] bishop
Remigius [of Lincoln] bishop
Ralf [of Chichester] bishop
Gundulf [of Rochester] bishop
Robert the chancellor
and many clerks and laymen besides, being persons of great name and worth.

You shall find this record written in a little worn-out gospel-text of mean value.

The Persons and their duties and privileges, and the customs whereby the Church of Salisbury is regulated according to the constitution of Bishop Osmund of happy memory, its founder, the present Treatise explains.

There are then four Principal Persons in the Church of Salisbury: the Dean, Precentor, Chancellor and Treasurer, and four Archdeacons – to wit, the Archdeacon of Dorset, of Berks, and two of Wilts; a Subdean besides, and a Succentor.

The tenor of a NOTE of the ORNAMENTS and JEWELS which the said OSMUND gave to his Church of Salisbury.

Herein is contained a memorandum of the ornaments which Osmund, Bishop of Salisbury, gave to the Church of St. Mary Sarum, viz.: 6 shrines silver gilt; 10 texts silver gilt; 2 boxes, ditto; 3 crosses, ditto; 6 candlesticks, ditto; one bucket, ditto; 2 basons, ditto; 1 chalice of gold of 4 marks, and 7 chalices silver gilt with patens; 4 altars silver gilt; 1 silver vessel to carry wine; 1 silver phial (?), to carry water in the service of the mass; the arm of St. Aldhelm silver gilt; 3 vessels, whereof two are of silver, with 2 silver spoons, and the third vessel of precious pearl, to put frankincense in; a bishop's crismatory, and 2 silver flasks to carry the cream and the oil in; a silver-gilt front before the altar; 2 horns (tusks) of ivory; 27 reliquaries, silver gilt, whereof nine have golden chains, two are of crystal, and one of jet (agate); 17 dossal hangings of cloth and 4 of wool and 2 of linen; 7 curtains; 4 cloths fitted for the altar; 8 Spanish leather hangings; 3 embroidered cloths of silk for the service of the altars; an embroidered ciborium for the service of the dead; 9 bench cloths of wool; 6 carpets; 34 copes, whereof seven and twenty are of cloth, and the rest of purple: nine also have the adornment of gold thread orphreys reaching down to the foot, and twelve are adorned with tassels and golden thread; 3 cloaks for the service of acolytes, whereof one has two pieces of gold embroidery attached; 20 chasubles: of this number eighteen are of cloth, and nine have orphreys of gold thread, and two of purple; 13 dalmatics, whereof two are of cloth, and all the rest of purple; 13 stoles with 17 fanons, one [stole] with its fanon being most precious; 40 albes: of these four are of purple and three of coarse silk, 30 and three are apparelled down to the feet with cloth; 43 amices: twelve of these are apparelled with orphreys of gold thread; 8 girdles of cloth, and sandals with buskins; 3 mass [-books?] and 11 tunicles, whereof three are of cloth, and all the rest of purple.

The duties and dignities of the persons

THE *Personæ* and their duties, the dignities and the customs by which the Church of Salisbury is ordered and regulated according to the Institution of Bishop Osmund, its founder of blessed memory, the present treatise explains.

Of the Personæ established in the church of Salisbury

The Principal Persons then in the Church of Salisbury are four: Dean, Chanter, Chancellor, and Treasurer.

There are also four Archdeacons, viz. Archdeacon of Dorset, Berkshire, and two of Wiltshire. Besides these there is a Subdean. A Succentor.

Of the duties of the several persons

I:

The duty of the DEAN it is, seeing that he is pre-eminent 'over all the Canons and Vicars in spiritual rule and correction of manners,' to hear all causes which relate to the Chapter, and by the judgement of the Chapter to determine them; to correct the trangressions of the clerics, and to visit with due punishment the persons of offenders, according to the measure of the fault and with consideration of their personal standing.

Moreover, the Canons receive from the Bishop institution, and from the Dean possession of their prebends.

It belongs also to the Dean to bestow upon the Canons after they are instituted the common distribution of the Church in his own right, and to assign them a stall in the choir and a place in the Chapter.

To provide with suitable clerks, any vacant vicarages on presentations made by the Canons either present in person, or else, if they be absent, provided that such absence is excused by a just or reasonable cause for which permission is given by the Dean and Chapter. But if any vicarship is vacant while the Canon is absent beyond seas for any cause, the Dean may confer it upon any suitable clerk he pleases, on his own authority, independently of consent from the absent Canon himself.

Furthermore, no one of the clerks of the higher step, or of the second form, is admitted in choir, except by the Dean's authority.

Furthermore, on every double feast, in the Bishop's absence, and on the first Sunday of Advent, and on Palm Sunday, and on Ash-Wednesday, and on the three days before Easter, and on Whitsun Eve, and on anniversaries of Bishops and Deans of the Church, he is bound to perform Divine service [and to celebrate].

Of the chanter [or precentor]'s duty.

The duty of the Chanter is 'to rule the choir in respect of raising or lowering the pitch of the chants,' and 'to set down in order on the table of services the singers' and minis-trants of the altar. To him also belongs the instruction and discipline of the boys, as well as their admission and ordering in the choir.

Furthermore, he is bound to be present on greater double feasts, and to take his part at ruling the choir, at the mass only, with the other rulers of the choir. And further, on every double feast he is bound to instruct the other rulers of the choir respecting the setting and beginning of the chants. Also, in his own person to indicate to the Bishop all chants which it is the Bishop's duty to begin.

Of the chancellor's duty

I:

It is the duty of the Chancellor to give his attention to 'ruling the schools and correcting the books, to hear the lessons read and bring them to an ending,' 'to keep the seal of the church,' to compose letters and documents, 'to read such letters as have to be read in Chapter,' 'to mark down the names of readers on the table of services,' and to notify (or set, *iniungere*) those lessons at mass which are not written on the table of services.

Of the treasurer's duty

I:

It is the Treasurer's duty to keep [or attend to] the ornaments and 'treasures' of the church.

To furnish lights that is to say, on the first Sunday in Advent 4 candles at both evensongs and at mattins and at mass: viz. on the superaltar, 2 more on the step before the altar. So also let it be done on Palm Sunday. But on all other Sundays throughout the year and whenever the choir has rulers and the invitatory is sung by two persons only, he ought to find 2 candles at the least at first and second evensong, at mattins, and at mass, but on [all] the Sundays 4 candles at mass. On Christmas Day he must provide for both evensongs and for mass 8 candles, each of them of a pound weight at least, about the altar, and 2 candles before the image of the Blessed Mary; at mattins, the same number. And 6 others besides, high up (in *eminencia*) before the relics and the crucifix and images set in that place. And on the crown (*corona*) before the altar [*al.* before the choir-step] 6 (*al.* 5), each of them of half a pound weight at least, and 6 (*al.* 5) above the wall behind the pulpit where lections are read.

Let the same directions be observed on all double feasts which have a procession.

It is also the Treasurer's duty to provide 7 candles for the brasen candlestick from Pentecost to the Nativity of B. Mary and on [her] Nativity itself [Sept. 8th], but on other lesser double feasts, 4 about the altar and 2 before the image of B. Mary at both evensongs and at mass; at mattins 3 besides in the crown (*corona*), and 3 behind the lectern (*pulpitum*).

Whenever the invitatory is said by three persons, as well as on Thursday, Friday, and Saturday in Easter week and Whitsun week, the same service in respect of candles is demanded as on the first Sunday in Advent. On Maundy Thursday, as on Sunday at mass. On Good Friday and on every feast of three lessons when the invitatory is double, it is his duty to set out 2 candles for mass. On every weekday (*feria*) throughout the year, 1 candle only at mattins, viz. at the choir-step; but 2 candles for mass. On Easter Eve and Whitsun Eve as many at mass as on greater double feasts.

Furthermore, on Good Friday, after the Lord's Body has been laid in the sepulchre, two candles of half a pound at least from the treasury shall burn all the day before the sepulchre. On the night which follows and so onwards until the procession which takes place on Easter Day before Mattins, one of those 2 candles only shall be kept alight.

Also the great paschal candle [he shall provide].

Furthermore, the Treasurer is bound to provide a mortar-light every night in the year before St. Martin's altar.

Also another before the doors of the western gate of the choir while mattins service is fully done.

The Treasurer is bound also to furnish forth the sacrists at his proper cost. Also to manage the bell ringing in a manner befitting the church; to keep them hung in fitting condition, and to provide things needful for their use. To repair the ornaments of the church at his own cost. To provide bread, wine, water, and candles (*candelas*) for each of the altars of the church, except the parish altar. To get incense, charcoal, straw, rushes, and reed-mats (*nattas*) for all the year: viz. rushes for Ascension Day, Pentecost, St. John Baptist's Nativity, and the Assumption and Nativity B. Mary; straw for All Saints' Day, Christmas Day, and the Purification of the B. Virgin, and on Easter Day; reed-mats for All Saints' Day.

The archdeacons' duty

Archdeacons are officials of the Lord Bishop, and their office consists in administration external [to the Church and Chapter of Sarum].

The subdean's duty

I:

The Subdean's duty it is, 'if the Dean is not forthcoming to the church, to supply his place'; [and] to exercise the care 'of an archdeaconship in the city [of Salisbury] and its suburbs.'

The succentor's duty

I:

The Succentor's duty it is ' to supply the place of the Chanter when he is absent,' [and] to manage the songschool through his official.

Of the privilege of personages and canons in the church of Salisbury

The privilege of the Dean it is, that none of the Canons or of the other clerks of the church may be let blood without his permission, nor leave Salisbury with the intention of staying a night away. Furthermore, when the Dean comes into the quire or the Chapter [house], or passes across the place, all clerks are bound to rise, and those who enter the quire from the west entrance, or go out by it, are bound to make a bow to him.

'It is the Dean's privilege . . . [his] own domain'.

Furthermore, each Canon who obtains a prebend is bound to pay one ounce of gold to the Dean, and forty shillings, or a day's provision to the Canons, for love's sake.

'And if any of the Canons shall be in attendance. . . . for the space of one year.' (St. Osmund's *Foundation Charter*.)

In addition thereto, all burial dues 'with the offerings which are brought to the Bishop when celebrating mass in the church of Salisbury, excepting one moiety of the gold.'

'If my lord Bishop shall have been dedicating . . . prebend in each case belongs.' (St. Osmund's *Institution*.)

Furthermore, if the Dean or any Canon is passing through a prebend, the Canon who holds that prebend, whether he be himself present there or not, ought to provide him of right and privilege, so as to make honourable provision for him for one night. And if, owing to the fault of this Canon or his servant, the Dean or his servant, the Dean or the Canon aforesaid be not received with suitable attention as a guest, let the expenses of that night be repaid in full to the Canon who makes complaint about it, as the Chapter shall decide. A Canon shall be bound also to exercise the grace of hospitality towards his brother Canon for one or more nights; and, if there is manifest reason, he shall find him horses as far as Sarum.

Of the residence of the personages and canons; and other customs of the church of Salisbury

'That a Dean and a Chanter . . . the third part of a year' (as in St. Osmund's *Institution Charter*).

'When any one is constituted a Canon . . . make oath . . . customs of the Church of S.'.

When a Canon dies all the proceeds (*exitus*) and obventions and incomings of his prebend for the whole term in which his death has occurred are due to him. Likewise, the rents of the term next following, and the obventions of the first day of that next term.

There are four terms, viz. Michaelmas term, Christmas, Easter, and that of the Nativity of St. John Baptist.

Furthermore, when the term in which the Canon died is past, he receives one-third of the entire prebend for the ensuing year; but from this third the stipend of the Vicar of the prebend is due for the year following. Let the residue be disbursed for the use of the poor, or in some other manner according to the directions of the deceased. Furthermore, for a Canon deceased it is decreed that service of thirty days be done in the community (*in conventu*), and that each of the presbyters severally should celebrate a trental. That the others, of whatsoever order they be, should sing 20 psalters severally, and that the year's mind (*anniversarium*) be celebrated by each privately in his own week of duty.

Of the punishment [al. penance] of delinquents

I:

'The elders are to be besought . . . more austere' (as in St. Osmund's *Institution Charter*).

Of the stalls of personages in the choir of Sarum church

The stalls of the four principal persons of the choir of Salisbury Church are at the extreme ends (*sunt terminalia*). At the entrance of the choir on the west, the Dean's stall is on the right, the Chanter's on the left. At the east end, the Chancellor's stall is on the right hand, and the Treasurer's is opposite. Next to the Dean's stall in choir stands the Archdeacon of Dorset; after him, the Subdean; next to the Chancellor, is the Archdeacon of Wiltshire. In the middle space, stand the Canons nearest to the dignitaries. Then the Vicars in Priest's order, and just a few in Deacon's order who are allowed to be in the upper row by dispensation in consideration of their age and character. Next the Chanter the Archdeacon of Berkshire stands in choir; then the

Succentor. Next to the Treasurer the [other] Archdeacon of Wiltshire; then the other Canons and the Clergy arranged in the manner aforesaid.

In the second bench let the junior Canons be placed, then Deacons, and after them the other boys [*al.* clergy].

In the first [or front] bench, Boy Canons are placed, and after them the other Boys according as their age requires.

Of the clergy entering and leaving the choir

Let clergy entering the choir so comport themselves that when they enter at the east end they bow first towards the altar, and afterwards to the Bishop if he is present. When they enter at the west, they bow first towards the altar, and then to the Dean. With the same reverential behaviour let them leave the choir.

At what point it is lawful to come into quire at various hours of service

I:

Clergy may come into choir until the hymn is done at Mattins or any other Hour of Service for which an office hymn is appointed at the opening.

But at Evensong they may come in down to the third or fourth verse of the first psalm, and at Compline likewise:– i.e. such clerks as have been at the Evensong preceding it. Under other circumstances they must not come into choir at Compline or at the Vigils of the Dead.

In Lent, however, they may come in at Compline on the same condition as at Evensong at the other seasons of the year.

At the Vigil of the Dead and at Collation, at any time. At mass they may come in up to the first collect. At the other Hours which follow mass immediately no one may come in who has not been at mass. In Lent, however, those who have attended at the Hours of the day (though they may not have been at mass) on ferial days when the service is of the feria, may come into choir for Evensong; and on feasts of nine lessons they may do so notwithstanding that they may not have been previously at any of the Hours of the day. And any one may join the procession at any season of the year, although he may not have been present at any hour previously that day.

Of the crossing of the clerks from one side of the choir to the other

I:

Furthermore, if a clerk passes from one side of the choir to the other, let him bow to the altar in going and returning. And when they come in let the clergy betake themselves in orderly manner to their places, not leaping over the benches disorderly. Let them observe the same order when they go out of the choir.

Let no sound be made in choir by the clerks nor let there be any talking between them, save what is necessary.

On Christmas Day, the Epiphany, Easter Day, Whitsunday, Ascension Day, Trinity Sunday, the feasts of Relics [Sunday next after July 7th], Assumption [August 15th], the Dedication [September 30th], and All Hallows [November 1st], the rulers of the choir use the most sumptuous copes (*capis solemnioribus*) of colours medley. The attendant ministers of the altar use in like manner the (best) dalmatics and tunicles; excepting that on the Epiphany it matters not of what colour dalmatic and tunic be, provided that they have stars upon them.

Also for the three days immediately following Christmas Day, and on the Monday and Tuesday both of Easter week and of Whitsun week, they use the next most sumptuous copes. However, on St. Stephen's Day and Innocents' Day, and their octaves, they wear red dalmatics and tunicles. And on the feast of St. John the Evangelist in Christmas week they wear white (*albis*) dalmatics and tunicles, and on the octave they wear dalmatics and tunicles of the same colour with white copes. And on Monday of Easter week, and Monday of Whitsun week white dalmatics and tunicles must be worn.

On the feasts of the Circumcision, Purification, and Annunciation, and from Wednesday in Easter week and Whitsun week, and for the remaining days of those weeks, and through Ascension octave and on the octave day of the same, on all Sundays and other feast days in Eastertide [i.e. to Whitsun Eve], excepting only the Invention of the Cross [3 May], also on the Nativity of St. John Baptist [24 June], within the octaves and on the octave day of the Assumption [16–21 August] and Nativity [9–15 September] of Blessed Mary, and on her Conception [8 December] and on her Commemoration [usually on Saturday], 2 on both festivals of St. Michael [Dedication, 19 September, and in *monte tumba*, 16 October] and on the octave of the Dedication and also on feasts of virgins and of St. Mary Magdalen [22 July] the rulers of the choir and the ministers of the altar wear white (*candidis*) vestments.

Within the octave of the Epiphany and on the octave day itself [7–13 January], and on both feasts of Holy Cross, Invention [3 May]; Exaltation [14 September], and on all others of Apostles or Evangelists, or Martyrs out of Easter-tide, and on all Sundays of that tide whenever the service is of the Sunday, and while tracts are sung, they wear red copes, dalmatics, and tunicles.

At masses of the dead, at times when ministers of the altar wear dalmatics and tunicles, they wear black ones only.

On Easter eve and Whitsun eve, and when the genealogies are sung, they wear dalmatics and tunicles striped across (*ex transverso stragulatas*).

On Wednesday in Whitsun week they wear green dalmatics and tunicles.

On the arrangement of the list for Sundays

The list (*tabula*) for Sundays should be thus arranged

1   Rulers of the choir; viz. Canons, according to their order, as their names are entered in the roll (*matricula*) of the church; in pairs; for 15 days.
2   Clerics to read the lections and sing the responds (to lessons), to be entered as placed on the list by the Precentor himself.
3   The boy to read in Chapter for the week; viz. one of the bigger boys (*pueri maiores*).
4   Who are told off to take the candlesticks; viz. two smaller boys (*pueri minores*).

5   The censers; viz. two acolytes.
6   The water; viz. a smaller boy.
7   The cross; viz. an acolyte.
8   For mass:– two boys to sing the grail.
9   The Alleluya, two of the top step.
10   To sing mass [the priest].
11   To read the Epistle (the 'sub-deacon').
12   To read the Gospel (the 'deacon').

The foregoing arrangement takes place (*locum habet*) on all Sundays, and on simple feasts of nine lessons not falling within an octave. On Palm Sunday some additional entries must be made, viz., two of the second bench to carry the reliques in the procession; three of the said bench for *En Rex venit*; seven boys for *Gloria, laws et honor*; three priests for *Unus autem*.

Further Reading

A. Bellenger and S. Fletcher, *Princes of the Church: the English cardinals* (Stroud, 2001).
E. Duffy, *Saints and Sinners: a history of the popes* (London, 1997).
J. N. D. Kelly, *The Oxford Dictionary of Popes* (Oxford, 1986).
C. Morris, *The Papal Monarchy: the Western Church from 1050–1250* (Oxford, 1989).
I. S. Robinson, *The Papacy 1073–1198* (Cambridge, 1990).

4 Pilgrimage

The image of the journey from life to death and from death to eternity was reflected in the medieval idea of pilgrimage. A pilgrimage was important both for its destination and for its journey. Holy places were given increased force by the necessity of long, and often perilous, voyages by land and sea. Pilgrims were men and women who took their Christian life so seriously that they were prepared to travel far from home. Pilgrimages could often have their enjoyable and convivial side but they were religious in their origins. The pilgrim who attempted to reach the Holy Land was seen as taking the Cross and following in the footsteps of Christ. The crusading movement began as an attempt to keep the pilgrim paths open and was seen by many as an armed pilgrimage. The most favoured destination of the ambitious pilgrim was the holy city of Jerusalem, which always appeared at the centre of the medieval map of the world.

M. L. McClure and C. L. Feltoe (eds and trans.) *The Pilgrimage of Etheria* (1919) pp. 32–33, 45–52

Etheria, Travelogue *(c. 380)*

Then, journeying through certain stations, I came to a city whose name we read recorded in the Scriptures, Batanis, which city exists today: it has a church with a truly holy bishop, both monk and confessor, and certain martyr memorials. The city has a teeming population, and the soldiery with their tribune are stationed there. Departing thence, we arrived at Edessa in the Name of Christ our God, and, on our arrival, we straightway repaired to the church and memorial of saint Thomas. There, according to custom, prayers were made and the other things that were customary in the holy places were done; we read also some things concerning saint Thomas himself. The church there is very great, very beautiful and of new construction, well worthy to be the house of God, and as there was much that I desired to see, it was necessary for me to make a three days' stay there. Thus I saw in that city many memorials, together with holy monks, some dwelling at the memorials, while other had their cells in more secluded spots farther from the city. Moreover, the holy bishop of the city, a truly devout man, both monk and confessor, received me willingly and said: 'As I see, daughter, that for the sake of devotion you have undertaken so great a labour in coming to these places from far distant lands, if you are willing, we will show you all the places that are pleasant to the sight of Christians.' Then, first thanking God, I besought the bishop much that he would deign to do as he said. He thereupon led me first to the palace of King Abgar, where he showed me a great marble statue of him very much like him, as they said having a sheen as if made of pearl. From the face of Abgar it seemed that he was a very wise and honourable man. Then the holy bishop said to me: 'Behold King Abgar, who before he saw the Lord believed in Him that He was in truth the Son of God.' There was another statue near, made of the same marble, which he said was that of his son Magnus; this also had something gracious in the face. Then we entered the inner part of the palace, and there were fountains full of fish such as I never saw before, of so great size, so bright and of so good a flavour were they. The city has no water at all other than that which comes out of the palace, which is like a great silver river.

Jerusalem

II. SUNDAY OFFICES: 1. VIGIL

But on the seventh day, that is on the Lord's Day, the whole multitude assembles before cockcrow, in as great numbers as the place can hold, as at Easter, in the basilica which is near the Anastasis, but outside the doors, where lights are hanging for the purpose. And for fear that they should not be there at cockcrow they come beforehand and sit down there. Hymns as well as antiphons are said, and prayers are made between the several hymns and antiphons, for at the vigils there are always both priests and deacons ready there for the assembling of the multitude, the custom being that the holy places are not opened before cockcrow. Now as soon as the first cock has crowed, the bishop arrives and enters the cave at the Anastasis; all the doors are opened and the whole multitude enters the Anastasis, where countless lights are already burning. And when the people have entered, one of the priests says a psalm to which all respond, and after-wards prayer is made; then one of the deacons says a psalm and prayer is again made, a third psalm is said by one of the clergy, prayer is made for the third time and there is a commemoration of all. After these three psalms and three prayers are ended, lo! censers are brought into the cave of the Anastasis so that the whole basilica of the Anastasis is filled with odours. And then the bishop, standing within the rails, takes the book of the Gospel, and proceeding to the door, himself reads the (narrative of the) Resurrection of the Lord. And when the reading is begun, there is so great a moaning and groaning among all, with so many tears, that the hardest of heart might be moved to tears for that the Lord had borne such things for us. After the reading of the Gospel the bishop goes out, and is accompanied to the Cross by all the people with hymns, there again a psalm is said and prayer is made, after which he blesses the faithful and the dismissal takes place, and as he comes out all approach to his hand. And forthwith the bishop betakes himself to his house, and from that hour all the monks return to the Anastasis, where psalms and antiphons, with prayer after each psalm or antiphon, are said until daylight; the priests and deacons also keep watch in turn daily at the Anastasis with the people, but of the lay people, whether men or women, those who are so minded, remain in the place until daybreak, and those who are not, return to their houses and betake themselves to sleep.

2. MORNING SERVICES

Now at daybreak because it is the Lord's Day every one proceeds to the greater church, built by Constantine, which is situated in Golgotha behind the Cross, where all things are done which are customary everywhere on the Lord's Day. But the custom here is that of all the priests who take their seats, as many as are willing, preach, and after them all the bishop preaches, and these sermons are always on the Lord's Day, in order that the people may always be instructed in the Scriptures and in the love of God. The delivery of these sermons greatly delays the dismissal from the church, so that the dismissal does [not] take place before the fourth or perhaps the fifth hour. But when the dismissal from the church is made in the manner that is customary everywhere, the monks accompany the bishop with hymns from the church to the Anastasis, and as he approaches with hymns all the doors of the basilica of the Anastasis are opened, and the people, that is the faithful, enter, but not the catechumens. And after the people the bishop enters, and goes at once within the rails of the cave of the martyrium. Thanks are first given to God, then prayer is made for all, after which the deacon bids all bow their heads, where they stand, and the bishop standing within the inner rails blesses them and goes out, each one drawing near to his hand as he makes his exit. Thus the dismissal is delayed until nearly the fifth or sixth hour. And in like manner it is done at *lucernare*, according to daily custom.

This then is the custom observed every day throughout the whole year except on solemn days, to the keeping of which we will refer later on. But among all things it is a special feature that they arrange that suitable psalms and antiphons are said on every occasion, both those said by night, or in the morning, as well as those throughout the day, at the sixth hour, the ninth hour, or at *lucernare*, all being so appropriate and so reasonable as to bear on the matter in hand. And they proceed to the greater church, which was built by Constantine, and which is situated in Golgotha, that is behind the Cross, on every Lord's Day throughout the year except on the one Sunday of Pentecost, when they proceed to Sion, as you will find mentioned below; but even then they go to Sion before the third hour, the dismissal having been first made in the greater church.

W. Butler-Bowdon (ed.) *The Book of Margery Kempe, 1436* (1936) pp. 106–108

Pilgrimage to Jerusalem

So they went forth into the Holy Land till they could see Jerusalem. And when this creature saw Jerusalem, riding on an ass, she thanked God with all her heart, praying Him for His mercy that, as He had brought her to see His earthly city of Jerusalem, He would grant her grace to see the blissful city of Jerusalem above, the city of Heaven. Our Lord Jesus Christ, answering her thought, granted her to have her desire.

Then for the joy she had, and the sweetness she felt in the dalliance with Our Lord, she was on the point of falling off her ass, for she could not bear the sweetness and grace that God wrought in her soul. Then two pilgrims, Duchemen, went to her, and kept her from falling; one of whom was a priest, and he put spices in her mouth to comfort her, thinking she had been sick. And so they helped her on to Jerusalem, and when she came there, she said:

'Sirs, I pray you be not displeased though I weep sore in this holy place where Our Lord Jesus Christ was quick and dead.'

Then went they to the temple in Jerusalem and they were let in on the same day at evensong time, and abode there till the next day at evensong time. Then the friars lifted up a cross and led the pilgrims about from one place to another where Our Lord suffered His [word missing] and His Passion, every man and woman bearing a wax candle in one hand. And the friars always, as they went about, told them what Our Lord suffered in every place. The aforesaid creature wept and sobbed as plenteously as though she had seen Our Lord with her bodily eye, suffering His Passion at that time. Before her in her soul she saw Him verily by contemplation, and that caused her to have compassion. And when they came up on to the Mount of Calvary, she fell down because she could not stand or kneel, and rolled and wrested with her body, spreading her arms abroad, and cried with a loud voice as though her heart burst asunder; for, in the city of her soul, she saw verily and clearly how Our Lord was crucified. Before her face, she heard and saw, in her ghostly sight, the mourning of Our Lady, of Saint John, and Mary Magdalene and of many others that loved Our Lord.

And she had such great compassion and such great pain, at seeing Our Lord's pain that she could not keep herself from crying and roaring though she should have died for it. And this was the first cry that ever she cried in any contemplation. And this manner of crying endured many years after this time, for aught any man might do, and therefore, suffered she much despite and much reproof. The crying was so loud and so wonderful that it made the people astounded unless they had heard it before, or unless they knew the cause of the crying. And she had them so often that they made her right weak in her bodily might, and especially if she heard of Our Lord's Passion.

And sometimes, when she saw the crucifix, or if she saw a man with a wound, or a beast, whichever it were, or if a man beat a child before her, or smote a horse or other beast with a whip, if she saw it or heard it, she thought she saw Our Lord being beaten or wounded, just as she saw it in the man or the beast either in the field or the town, and by herself alone as well as amongst the people.

First when she had her cryings in Jerusalem, she had them often, and in Rome also. And when she came home to England, first at her coming home, it came but seldom, as it were once a month, then once a week, afterwards daily, and once she had fourteen in one day, and another day she had seven, and so on, as God would visit her, sometimes in church, sometimes in the street, sometimes in her chamber, sometimes in the fields, whenever God would send them, for she never knew the time nor the hour when they would come. And they never came without passing great sweetness of devotion and high contemplation. And as soon as she perceived that she would cry, she would keep it in as much as she might that the people should not hear it, to their annoyance. For some said that a wicked spirit vexed her; some said it was a sickness; some said she had drunk too much wine; some banned her; some wished she was in the harbour; some wished she was on the sea in a bottomless boat; and thus each man as he thought. Other ghostly men loved her and favoured her the more. Some great clerks said Our Lady cried never so, nor any saint in Heaven, but they knew full little what she felt, nor would they believe that she could not stop crying if she wished.

Jerusalem and the Holy Land were closely associated with Jesus Christ himself, but other pilgrimage centres gained popularity through less exalted figures who had a strong local cult. The Spanish pilgrimage centre of Santiago de Compostela had the shrine of the Apostle James and became one of the most favoured pilgrimage destinations, with pilgrims coming from all over Europe. Those who travelled to Jerusalem were often called palmers because they brought back palms but those who went to Compostela identified themselves with a scallop shell, the sign of St James, and like all pilgrims carried a staff for both support and protection.

The *Pilgrim's Guide,* attributed to Aymery Picaud, a French monk who lived in the twelfth century, is the fifth book of the *Codex Calixtinus* and the earliest known description of the pilgrimage to Santiago.

The *Song of the Pilgrims*, written in the *langue d'oc* of southern France, is similar in structure and content to a French *grande chanson*, on the same subject. It probably dates from the early fourteenth century and concerns a group of pilgrims from Aurillac in the Auvergne. The monks from the abbey of St Gerald of Aurillac, who is invoked in the song, administered the hospital, or pilgrim hostel, at El Cebrero from 1072 until it was taken over by the Benedictine monks of Cluny.

James Hogarth (trans.) *The Pilgrim's Guide* (1992) pp. 87–88

A pilgrim's guide

> A weaver in Nantua, a town between Geneva and Lyons, refused bread to a pilgrim of St James who asked for it; and at once he saw his cloth fall to the ground, rent asunder. At Villeneuve a poor pilgrim of St James asked for alms, for the love of God and the blessed James, from a woman who was keeping bread under hot ashes. She told him that she had no bread: whereupon the pilgrim said, 'May the bread that you have turn into stone!' The pilgrim had left the house and gone some distance on his way when the wicked woman went to take her bread out of the ashes and found a round stone in the place where the bread had been. Struck with remorse, she set out to look for the pilgrim, but could not find him.

P. Henderson (ed.) *A Pilgrim Anthology* (1994) p. 117

A conversation with a returning pilgrim: Erasmus, from the Colloquies

> 'What country has sent you safely back to us, covered with shells, laden with tin and leaden images, and adorned with straw necklaces, while your arms display a row of serpents' eggs?'
>
> 'I have been to St James of Compostella.'
>
> 'What answer did St James give to your professions?'
>
> 'None, but he was seen to smile, and nod his head, when I offered my presents, and held out to me this imbricated shell.'
>
> 'Why that shell rather than any other kind?' 'Because the adjacent sea abounds in them.'

P. Henderson (ed.) *A Pilgrim Anthology* (1994) p. 17

Dante Alighieri, from the Vita Nuova

> These pilgrims seem to me to be from a far country and I believe that they have not even heard speak of my lady and know naught of her; rather their thoughts are of

other things than of these here; for perchance they are thinking of their distant friends whom we know not. ... In the wide sense, whoever is outside his fatherland is a pilgrim; in the narrow sense, none is called a pilgrim save he who is journeying towards the sanctuary of St James, or is returning. They are called palmers, in so far as they Journey over the sea, there, whence many times they bring back palm branches; they are called pilgrims in so far as they journey to the sanctuary of Galicia, because the tomb of St James was farther from his own country than that of any other apostle.

Pilgrims had their own songs and hymns which talked of the holy places they would visit and begged aid from the patron of the shrine.

P. Henderson (ed.) *A Pilgrim Anthology* (1994) pp. 36–39

The song of the pilgrims of Saint James

We are pilgrims from the town called Aurillac near Jordanne.
We have left our parents, our wives and all our relations
to travel in a great band to see St James of Compostella.
May Christ who rights all wrongs much embellish my verse!
From our lane and house, next to the chapel of St Gerald,
we all went to the parish church and took our scallops there.
We prayed to Our Lady the Virgin to send us to Paradise,
and to exempt us from tolls in order to make the holy journey easily.
When we were near here, in Bordeaux,
we had to risk our lives in the water.
'God, what unfortunates! What will happen to us if St Gerald does not protect us?'
When we were down there, in Bayonne, very near to the Spanish lands,
we had to change good money for escudos and debased coins.
When we were at Vitoria, we saw the greenery in flower;
joyfully, we picked lavender, thyme in a meadow, and rosemary.
When we were on the little bridges, how they trembled at our passage!
We thought we would die: 'Peace, oh peace! Save the pilgrims, St James!'
Before the judge we told them that we came to worship God,
not to do harm or damage.
The judge said: 'Peace! A safe journey!'
We are in Galicia.
Oh St James, protect the pilgrims against sin
and give them wheat and cheese because they cost a great deal of money.
Let us pray for our lord the Abbot who has succoured us all in his house on the mountain with bread, wine and provisions.

J. M. Neale (trans.) in P. Dearmer, R. V. Williams and M. Shaw, *Songs of Praise* (Oxford, 1925) no. 198

Bernard of Cluny, 'Jerusalem the Golden' (twelfth century)

JERUSALEM the golden,
With milk and honey blest,

Beneath thy contemplation
Sink heart and voice opprest.
I know not, O I know not,
What social joys are there,
What radiancy of glory,
What light beyond compare.
They stand, those halls of Sion,
Conjubilant with song,
And bright with many an angel,
And all the martyr throng;
The Prince is ever with them,
The daylight is serene,
The pastures of the blessed
Are decked in glorious sheen.

Pilgrimage could become a way of life and the *perigrinatio* or continuous pilgrimage, favoured by Celtic monks, was replicated throughout the period. Most religious orders made provision for pilgrims and the Church authorities provided them with appropriate services and prayers.

J. McCann (ed. and trans.) *The Rule of St Benedict* (1952) pp. 139–141

The Rule of St Benedict

How pilgrim monks are to be received

If a pilgrim monk come from a distant region and desire to dwell in the monastery as a guest, let him be received for as long a time as he wishes, provided that he is content with the customs of the place as they are, and does not disturb the monastery by exorbitant wants, but is simply content with what he finds. Should he reasonably, modestly, and charitably censure or remark upon any defect, let the abbot consider the matter prudently, lest perchance the Lord have sent him for this very end. And if later on he should wish to bind himself to stability, let not his desire be denied him, especially as the character of his life could be discerned during the time that he was a guest.

But if during that time he be found exacting or depraved, not only should he not be made a member of the community, but he should be told politely to depart, lest others should be corrupted by his lamentable life. If, however, he do not deserve to be dismissed, not only should he be received on his asking as a member of the community, but he should even be urged to stay, so that others may be instructed by his example, and because wherever we are we serve the same Lord and fight for the same King. And the abbot may even give him a higher place in the community, if he consider him worthy of it. And so also, not only with a monk, but also with the aforesaid orders of priests and clerics: the abbot may give them a rank higher than is theirs by their entry, if he see that their life deserves it. But let the abbot beware lest he ever receive a monk of some other known monastery as a member of his community without the consent of his abbot and a letter of recommendation, because it is written *Do not thou to another what thou wouldst not have done to thyself.*

F. E. Warren (trans.) *The Sarum Missal in English* (1913) part 2, pp. 166–173

Order of service for pilgrims

First, the following Psalms are said over them prostrate in front of the altar, after they have made their confessions, beginning thus

Psalm

Unto thee, O Lord, will I lift up etc. [Ps. xxv.]

Psalm

Have mercy upon me, O God etc. [Ps. li.]

Psalm

Whoso dwelleth under the defence etc. [Ps. xci.]
with Glory be to the Father etc. *after each Psalm.*
Lord, have mercy [upon us.]
Christ, have mercy [upon us.]
Lord, have mercy [upon us.]
Our Father etc.
V. And lead us not into temptation,
R. But deliver us from evil.
V. I said, Lord, be merciful unto me;
R. Heal my soul, for I have sinned against thee.
V. The Lord show thee his ways;
R. And teach thee his paths.
V. The Lord direct thy steps according to his word;
R. That no unrighteousness get the dominion over thee.
V. O that thy ways were made so direct;
R. That thou mightest keep the statutes of the Lord.
V. The Lord uphold thy goings in his paths;
R. That thy footsteps slip not.
V. Blessed be the Lord God daily;
R. The God of our salvation prosper thy way before thee.
V. The good angel of the Lord accompany thee;
R. And dispose thy way and thine actions aright, that thou mayest return again to thine own place with joy.
V. Blessed are those that are undefiled in the way;
R. And walk in the law of the Lord.
V. Let the enemy have no advantage against thee;
R. And let not the son of wickedness approach to hurt thee.
V. O Lord, arise, help us,
R. And deliver us for thy name's sake.
V. Turn us again, O Lord God of hosts;
R. And show the light of thy countenance upon us, and we shall be whole.
V. Lord, hear my prayer;
R. And let my crying come unto thee.

V. The Lord be with you.
R. And with thy spirit.

Let us pray.

Collect

Assist us, O Lord, in these our supplications, and dispose the way of thy 'servant N. towards the attainment of thy salvation, that among all the changes and chances of the journey through life, he may ever be defended by thy help. Through etc.
Let us pray.

Collect

O God, who leadest unto life, and guardest with thy fatherly protection them that trust in thee, we beseech thee that thou wouldest grant unto these thy servants N. here present, going forth from amongst us, an escort of angels; that they, being protected by thy aid, may be shaken by no fear of evil, nor be depressed by any lingering adversity, nor be troubled by any enemy lying in wait to assail them; but that having prosperously accomplished the course of their appointed journey, they may return unto their own homes; and having been received back in safety, may pay due thanks unto thy name. Through etc.
Let us pray.

Collect

O God, who ever bestowest thy pity upon them that love thee, and who art in no place far distant from them that serve thee; direct the way of this thy servant N. according to thy will, that thou being his protector and guide, he may walk without stumbling in the paths of righteousness. Through etc.

Here shall the pilgrims rise from their prostration, and the blessing of the scrip and staff shall follow, thus:

V. The Lord be with you.
R. And with thy spirit.

Let us pray.
O Lord Jesu Christ, who of thy unspeakable mercy, and at the bidding of the Father, and with the co-operation of the Holy Ghost, didst will to come down from heaven, and to seek the sheep that was lost through the wiles of the devil, and to bear it back on thine own shoulders to the flock of the heavenly country, and didst command the sons of mother Church by prayer to ask, by holy living to seek, and by knocking to persevere, that they may be able to find more quickly the rewards of saving life; we humbly beseech thee that thou wouldest vouchsafe to sanctify and bless these scrips (or this scrip), and these staves (or this staff); that whosoever, for love of thy name, shall desire to wear the same, like the armour of humility, at his side, or to hang it from his neck, or to carry it in his hands, and so on his pilgrimage to seek the prayers of the saints, with the accompaniment of humble devotion, may be found worthy, through the protecting defence of thy right hand, to attain unto the joys of the everlasting vision, through thee, O Saviour of the world. Who livest etc.

Here the priest shall sprinkle the scrip with holy water, and place it on the neck of the pilgrim, saying:

In the name of our Lord Jesus Christ receive this scrip, the habit of thy pilgrimage; that after being well chastened thou mayest be found worthy both to reach in safety the thresholds of the saints, whither thou desirest to go; and that when thy journey is finished thou mayest return to us in safety. Through etc.

Let it thus be done to each person, if there be more than one.

Then shall the priest deliver the staff to each one, saying:

Receive this staff for the support of thy journey, and for the labour of thy pilgrimage; that thou mayest be able to overcome all the hosts of the enemy, and to arrive in safety at the thresholds of the saints, whither thou desirest to go; and that when thy journey hath been obediently accomplished, thou mayest again return to us with joy. Through etc.
And thus let him say to others, if there be more than one.

Blessing of a cross for one on a pilgrimage to Jerusalem

V. The Lord be with you.
R. And with thy spirit.

Let us pray.
O God of unconquered power, and boundless pity, the entire aid and consolation of pilgrims, who givest to thy servants most invincible armour; we pray thee that thou vouchsafe to bless this cross, which is humbly dedicated to thee; that the banner of the venerated cross, the figure whereof hath been depicted upon it, may be a most invincible strength to thy servant against the wickedest temptation of the ancient enemy; that it may be a defence by the way, a guard in thy house, and a protection to us everywhere. Through etc.

Here shall holy water be sprinkled upon the dress. Then if any of those present be about to journey to Jerusalem, a vestment shall be given to him marked with the cross, the priest saying thus

Receive this vestment, marked with the cross of our Lord and Saviour, that through it there may accompany thee safety, blessing, and strength for a prosperous journey to the sepulchre of him, who with God the Father etc.

And thus shall it be done to the rest, if there be more than one present.

The branding of a cross upon the flesh of pilgrims going to Jerusalem has been forbidden by canon law under pain of the greater excommunication. This done, there shall be said a

Mass for travellers

after the manner of a simple feast of nine lessons.

Office

Be thou my strong rock, and house of defence: that thou mayest save me. For thou art my strong rock and my castle: be thou also my guide, and lead me for thy name's sake.[Ps. xxxi. 3, 4.]

In Easter-tide, Alleluya, alleluya.

Ps. In thee, O Lord, have I put my trust; let me never be put to confusion, deliver me in thy righteousness. [Ps. xxxi. 3, 1.]

Collect

Assist us, O Lord, in these our supplications, and dispose the way of thy servants N. and N. towards the attainment of thy salvation; that among all the changes and the chances of their journey through this life, they may ever be defended by thy help. Through etc.

Lesson. Gen. xxiv. 7.

The Lord God . . . angel before thee.

Gradual

Be thou my strong rock and house of defence: that thou mayest save me.
V. In thee, O Lord, have I put my trust: let me never be put to confusion.

The Gradual shall be repeated.

Alleluya. V. Ye that fear the Lord, put your trust in the Lord: he is their helper and defender.

If this service happen to be used in Easter-tide, then the second Alleluya *will be one of those which are written down after the Office*, As new-born babes etc.

Gospel. St. Matt. x. 7–15

And as ye go . . . for that city.

Offertory

And all they that know thy name will put their trust in thee for thou, Lord, hast never failed them that seek thee. O praise the Lord which dwelleth in Sion. For he forgetteth not the complaint of the poor.

In Easter-tide, Alleluya.

Here shall the pilgrims make their offering.

Secret

Be favourable, we beseech thee, O Lord, to our supplications, and graciously receive these offerings which we present unto thee on behalf of thy servants; that thou wouldest direct their way by thy preventing grace, and accompany and follow them, so that we may rejoice in their safe performance of their journey by thy merciful protection. Through etc.

Communion

Thou hast charged: that we shall diligently keep thy commandments: O that my ways were made so direct: that I might keep thy statutes!

In Easter-tide, Alleluya, alleluya.

Postcommunion

We beseech thee, O Lord, that the reception of the sacrament of the heavenly mystery may further the good success of thy servants' journey, and bring them to all things profitable to their salvation. Through etc.

After mass the priest shall say these prayers following over the pilgrims prostrate before the altar, whether they shall be travelling to Jerusalem, or to the threshold of St. James, [the shrine of St. James of Compostela] or on any other pilgrimage.

V. The Lord be with you.
R. And with thy spirit.
Let us pray.
O God of infinite mercy and boundless majesty, whom neither space nor time separate from those whom thou defendest, be present with thy servant (or thy servants) who everywhere putteth his trust (or their trust) in thee, and vouchsafe to be his (or their) leader and companion in every way in which he (or they) shall go: let no adversity harm him (or them), no difficulty hinder him (or them); let all things be healthful, and all things be prosperous for him (or them); that whatsoever he (or they) shall rightly ask, he (or they) may speedily and effectually obtain by the aid of thy right hand. Through etc.
Let us pray.

Collect

May the almighty and everlasting God, who is the way, the truth, and the life, dispose thy (or your) journey according to his good pleasure; may he send his angel Raphael to be thy (or your) guardian in thy (or your) pilgrimage; to conduct thee on thy way, in peace, to the place whither thou wouldest go, and to bring thee back again in safety on thy return to us. May Mary, the blessed mother of God, intervene for thee (or you), together with all angels and archangels, and patriarchs, and prophets. May the holy apostles Peter and Paul intercede for thee (or you), together with the rest of the apostles, martyrs, confessors, and virgins; and may the saints, whose prayers thou askest (or ye ask), together with all the saints, obtain for thee (or for you) just desires, and prosperity, and remission of all sins, and life everlasting. Through etc.

Then shall the pilgrims be communicated, and so depart in the name of the Lord.

Local pilgrimages were also encouraged by the Church and most parts of Christian Europe had shrines of varying popularity which were often seen as places of physical, as well as spiritual, healing.

J. Bertram (trans.) St Aelred of Rievaulx, *Life of St. Edward the Confessor* (1997) book 2, ch. 35, pp. 110–112

The miracles of St Edward the Confessor

Of a girl, cured at his tomb

There was in the city a noblewoman, Matilda by name, very skilled in embroidery. She used to enhance the robes of royalty and the rich with gold, stud them with jewels and adorn them in needlework with scenes and flowers. She was commissioned for some expensive work by a certain noble lady, who was very rich, and being engaged to the Earl of Gloucester, ranked not far below the queen. She was determined to excel the other countesses of England in the splendour of her wardrobe, as she already did in her wealth. She came daily to insist that everything should be got ready not only with the greatest skill but with haste as well.

There arrived the principal feast of Saint Edward, King and Martyr, the uncle of our sovereign: he was the one who was blameless but slain by the wicked, and is believed to have been crowned with the martyrdom of innocence. The sagacious woman was undecided: she knew that she would incur the wrath of the haughty lady for delaying the task, but feared she would be liable to divine vengeance for violating the sacred festival with prohibited work. She turned therefore to her associate, a young woman: 'What do you decide between the urgency of this work and the festival of the holy King Edward? It seems to me that to be idle would be profitless, but to work would be dangerous on such a solemnity.'

The girl laughed: 'Is that the Edward which the common herd venerate as a king at Westminster? What have I to do with him? Let others be idle and mourn the dead with their singing, or honour him indeed: I'm not going to abandon the work I have begun, not for him, no more than for a peasant, even if you do tell me to!'

The mistress was afraid and grew indignant: thinking it over, her wrath eventually burst out with loud and shocked rebuke: she castigated the blasphemer as if she had been possessed by the devil, with severe reproaches. But the apprentice sneered, mocking her mistress' foolishness. She piled mockery on mockery, till suddenly, in front of many, she was seized by a paralytic stroke: her blaspheming mouth was twisted up to her right ear, and she was deprived of the use of the tongue she had misused. Her lips writhed, she gnashed her teeth and they grew dry; her whole body went into painful convulsions.

When the girl's mistress saw that this had come about by the just judgment of God, her wrath gave way to grief, her anger to tears. She wept, and her whole household with her. The one that she had reviled as a blasphemer she now pitied for suffering so much intolerable pain. The matter was noised in the city, and many came to console the mistress or to gape at the apprentice.

While she was debating what to do, a personage of considerable dignity appeared, and instructed her to place the poor girl on a boat, and take her to the holy relics that she had blasphemed, and that she would receive relief by the merits of him whom she had offended and so suffered such a dire punishment.

It was done as he said: the unfortunate woman was taken to the saintly king's tomb, a candle was lit as long as herself, and her mistress was diligent in prayer and vigil. There was a great lamentation around her, for the terrible illness she suffered seemed incurable. The only hope they all had was in the piety of Edward, who had learnt from the Lord Jesus to repay evil with good, hatred with love.

She remained in pain all that night, while the others wept and prayed. The brothers of the monastery prayed for her as well, and their superior conducted a solemn litany for her with great devotion. In the sight of the holy king competed prayer and sickness, the wickedness of the sinful servant and the faith of her merciful mistress, the greatness of the crime and the amount of her grief.

At length that pardon which so often prevails, through the merits of the saintly king prevailed over Jesus: soon mild mercy moderated the sentence which justice had decreed, overruling right in the case of the sick girl. And so it was that she continued in pain for a night and a day, but at the hour when the sacred duties of that day were being concluded with vespers, suddenly she found herself restored to wholeness, among the chanting voices and sobbing prayers.

She gazed at the company, puzzled by their tears: her speech returned and she asked where she was, what had happened, how had she come there, and what was the reason for such grief. Her mouth, which the disease had twisted, had returned to its proper form: she recovered her former beauty along with her sanity. When she heard all that had happened she burst into tears: her mouth, tongue, mind and intelligence proclaimed her repentance, and heavy sighs betrayed her inner contrition.

Then those who stood by sang of the mercy and justice of the Lord, who strikes and also heals, he gives death and also life, he leads down to hell and brings up again. The girl, giving thanks to God and his holy servant Edward, returned unharmed home with her mistress. From then on, whenever she heard the name of the glorious king, she was so shaken by fear that her face would go pale and shuddering overtake her whole body.

The most famous of the English pilgrimage centres was Canterbury. This was not on account of its place in the origins of Christianity in England, or its many saintly arch-bishops, but because of the miracle-working tomb of Thomas of Canterbury, murdered in his own cathedral in 1170.

The late medieval *Canterbury Tales*, written by Geoffrey Chaucer (d. 1400), present a mirror of a pilgrimage group and the stories they told each other on the journey from London to Canterbury. This work of imagination presents the most vivid surviving evocation of pilgrimage.

D. Wright (trans.) Geoffrey Chaucer, *The Canterbury Tales* (Oxford, 1986) pp. 19–22

The Canterbury Tales, *General prologue*

And now I've told you truly and concisely
The rank, and dress, and number of us all,
And why we gathered in a company
In Southwark, at that noble hostelry
Known as the Tabard, that's hard by the Bell.
But now the time has come for me to tell

What passed among us, what was said and done
The night of our arrival at the inn;
And afterwards I'll tell you how we journeyed,
And all the remainder of our pilgrimage.
But first I beg you, not to put it down
To my ill-breeding if my speech be plain
When telling what they looked like, what they said,
Or if I use the exact words they used.
For, as you all must know as well as I,
To tell a tale told by another man
You must repeat as nearly as you can
Each word, if that's the task you've undertaken,
However coarse or broad his language is;
Or, in the telling, you'll have to distort it
Or make things up, or find new words for it.
You can't hold back, even if he's your brother:
Whatever word is used, you must use also.
Christ Himself spoke out plain in Holy Writ,
And well you know there's nothing wrong with that.
Plato, as those who read him know, has said,
'The word must be related to the deed.'
Also I beg you to forgive it me
If I overlooked all standing and degree
As regards the order in which people come
Here in this tally, as I set them down:
My wits are none too bright, as you can see.
Our host gave each and all a warm welcome,
And set us down to supper there and then.
The eatables he served were of the best;
Strong was the wine; we matched it with our thirst.
A handsome man our host, handsome indeed,
And a fit master of ceremonies.
He was a big man with protruding eyes
– You'll find no better burgess in Cheapside
Racy in talk, well-schooled and shrewd was he;
Also a proper man in every way.
And moreover he was a right good sort,
And after supper he began to joke,
And, when we had all paid our reckonings,
He spoke of pleasure, among other things:
'Truly,' said he, 'ladies and gentlemen,
Here you are all most heartily welcome.
Upon my word – I'm telling you no lie
All year I've seen no jollier company
At one time in this inn, than I have now.
I'd make some fun for you, if I knew how.
And, as it happens, I have just now thought
Of something that will please you, at no cost.

'You're off to Canterbury – so Godspeed!
The blessed martyr give you your reward!
And I'll be bound, that while you're on your way,
You'll be telling tales, and making holiday;
It makes no sense, and really it's no fun
To ride along the road dumb as a stone.
And therefore I'll devise a game for you,
To give you pleasure, as I said I'd do.
And if with one accord you all consent
To abide by my decision and judgement,
And if you'll do exactly as I say,
Tomorrow, when you're riding on your way,
Then, by my father's soul – for he is dead
If you don't find it fun, why, here's my head!
Now not another word! Hold up your hands!'
We were not long in making up our minds.
It seemed not worth deliberating, so
We gave our consent without more ado,
Told him to give us what commands he wished.
'Ladies and gentlemen,' began our host,
'Do yourselves a good turn, and hear me out:
But please don't turn your noses up at it.
I'll put it in a nutshell: here's the nub:
It's that you each, to shorten the long journey,
Shall tell two tales en route to Canterbury,
And, coming homeward, tell another two,
Stories of things that happened long ago.
Whoever best acquits himself, and tells
The most amusing and instructive tale,
Shall have a dinner, paid for by us all,
Here in this inn, and under this roof-tree,
When we come back again from Canterbury.
To make it the more fun, I'll gladly ride
With you at my own cost, and be your guide.
And anyone who disputes what I say
Must pay all our expenses on the way!
And if this plan appeals to all of you,
Tell me at once, and with no more ado,
And I'll make my arrangements here and now.'
To this we all agreed, and gladly swore
To keep our promises; and furthermore
We asked him if he would consent to do
As he had said, and come and be our leader,
And judge our tales, and act as arbiter,
Set up our dinner too, at a fixed price;
And we'd obey whatever he might decide
In everything. And so, with one consent,

We bound ourselves to bow to his judgement.
And thereupon wine was at once brought in.
We drank; and not long after, everyone
Went off to bed, and that without delay.
Next morning our host rose at break of day:
He was our cockcrow; so we all awoke.
He gathered us together in a flock,
And we rode, at little more than walking-pace
Till we had reached St Thomas' watering-place,
Where our host began reining in his horse.
'Ladies and gentlemen, attention please!'
Said he. 'All of you know what we agreed,
And I'm reminding you. If evensong
And matins are in harmony – that's to say,
If you are still of the same mind today
Let's see who'll tell the first tale, and begin.
And whosoever baulks at my decision
Must pay for all we spend upon the way,
Or may I never touch a drop again!
And now let's draw lots before going on.
The one who draws the short straw must begin.
Sir Knight, my lord and master,' said our host,
'Now let's draw lots, for such is my request.
Come near,' said he, 'my lady Prioress,
And, Mister Scholar, lay by bashfulness,
Stop dreaming! Hands to drawing, everyone!'
To cut the story short, the draw began,
And, whether it was luck, or chance, or fate,
The truth is this: the lot fell to the knight,
Much to the content of the company.
Now, as was only right and proper, he
Must tell his tale, according to the bargain
Which, as you know, he'd made. What more to say?
And when the good man saw it must be so,
Being sensible, and accustomed to obey
And keep a promise he had freely given,
He said, 'Well, since I must begin the game,
Then welcome to the short straw, in God's name!
Now let's ride on, and listen to what I say.'
And at these words we rode off on our way,
And he at once began, with cheerful face, His tale.

Pilgrimage became an essential part of the Islamic faith where the pilgrimage to the holy city of Mecca became the lifetime ambition of many Muslims. The centre of that pilgrimage is the Ka'ba, the House of God, believed by Muslims to have been built by Abraham and his son, Ishmael. The experience of the pilgrimage to Mecca makes an interesting parallel to the Christian pilgrimages to Jerusalem and Rome.

T. Mackintosh-Smith, *The Travels of Ibn Battutah* (2003) pp. 43–57

A pilgrimage to Mecca (1325)

When the new moon of Shawwal appeared in the above-mentioned year [1 September 1326], the Hijaz caravan went out to the outskirts of Damascus and encamped at the village called al-Kiswah, and I set out on the move with them. We marched to the town of Bosra, and thence to the castle of al-Karak.

Al-Karak is one of the most marvellous, inaccessible, and celebrated of fortresses, and it is called 'the Castle of the Raven'. The river bed encircles it on all sides, and it has but one gate, the entrance to which is hewn in the living rock, as also is the entrance to its vestibule. The caravan stopped outside al-Karak for four days, at a place called al-Thaniyah, and made preparations for entering the wilderness. Thence we travelled to Ma'an, which is the last town in Syria, and descended through the Pass of al-Sawan into the desert, of which the saying goes: 'He who enters it is lost, and he who leaves it is born.' After a march of two days we halted at Dhat Hajj, a place of subterranean waterbeds with no habitations, then on to Wadi Baldah (but there is no water in it), and then to Tabuk. This is the place which was raided by the Apostle of God (God bless and give him peace). It has a spring which used to yield a scanty supply of water, but when the Apostle of God (God bless and give him peace) went down to it and used it for his ablutions it gave an abundant flow of running water and continues to do so to this day, through the blessed power of the Apostle of God (God bless and give him peace). It is the custom of the Syrian pilgrims, on reaching the camping ground of Tabuk, to take their weapons and unsheath their swords, charge upon the camp and strike the palms with their swords, saying, 'Thus did the Apostle of God (God bless and give him peace) enter it.'

The huge caravan encamps near the spring referred to, and every one of them slakes his thirst from it. They remain here for four days to rest themselves and to water the camels and lay in supplies of water for the fearsome wilderness between Tabuk and al-Ula. It is the practice of the water-carriers to take up their positions at the sides of this spring, and they have tanks made of buffalo hides, like great reservoirs, from which they water the camels and fill the large waterbags and ordinary waterskins. Each amir or person of rank has a private tank from which his camels and those of his retinue are watered, and their waterbags filled; the rest of the people arrange with the water-carriers to water the camel and fill the waterskin of each person for a fixed sum of money.

The caravan then sets out from Tabuk and pushes on speedily night and day, for fear of this wilderness. Halfway through is the valley of al-Ukhaidir, which might well be the valley of Hell (God preserve us from it). One year the pilgrims suffered severe distress in this place, by reason of the samum-wind which blows there, their water supplies dried up, and the price of a drink of water rose to a thousand dinars, but both seller and buyer perished. The story of this is inscribed on one of the rocks in the valley. Going on from there, the caravan halts at the Pool of al-Mu'azzam, a vast basin, called after al-Malik al-Mu'azzam of the house of Ayyub, in which the rainwater collects in certain years, but which is generally dry in others.

On the fifth day after leaving Tabuk, they reach the well of al-Hijr – the Hijr of Thamud – which has an abundance of water, but not one of the pilgrims draws of it, however violent their thirst, following the example set by the Apostle of God (God bless and give him peace), when he passed it by on the expedition to Tabuk. For he drove on his riding camel, giving orders that none should water from it, and those who had used it to make dough fed their camels with it. At this place are the dwellings of Thamud, in some hills of red rock. They are hewn out and have carved thresholds, such that anyone seeing them would take them to be of recent construction. Their bones lie crumbling inside these houses – 'verily, in that is a warning example'. The place of kneeling of the she-camel of Salih (on him be peace) is between two hills there, and in the space between them are the traces of a mosque, in which the pilgrims perform a prayer.

From al-Hijr to al-Ula is half a day's journey or less. Al-Ula is a large and pleasant village with palm gardens and watersprings at which the pilgrims halt for the space of four nights. They provision themselves and wash their clothes, and also deposit here any surplus of provisions they may have, taking on with them only the amount of their strict necessities. The inhabitants of this village are trustworthy persons. This is the limit to which the Christian merchants of Syria may come, and beyond which they may not pass, and they trade in provisions and other goods with the pilgrims here.

The caravan then sets out from al-Ula and encamps on the day following the resumption of the journey in the valley known as al-Itas. It is a place of violent heat, in which the fatal samoom-wind blows. It blew up one year on the caravan, and none but a few of the pilgrims escaped with their lives; that year is known as the year of the Amir al-Jaligi. After this they encamp at Hadiyah, which is a place of subterranean waterbeds in a valley; they dig pits in it and the water comes up, but brackish. On the third day they alight outside the sanctified city of al-Madinah, the holy and illustrious.

Taibah, the city of the Apostle of God (God bless and give him peace, exalt and ennoble him!)

On the evening of the same day, after sunset, we entered the holy sanctuary and reached at length the illustrious mosque. We halted at the Gate of Peace to pay our respects, and prayed at the noble Garden between the tomb of the Apostle and the noble pulpit. We kissed the fragment that remains of the palm trunk that whimpered for the Apostle of God (God bless and give him peace), which is now attached to a pillar standing between the tomb and the mimbar, on the right as one faces the giblah. We paid the meed of salutation to the lord of men, first and last, the intercessor for sinners and transgressors, the apostle-prophet of the tribe of Hashim from the Vale of Mecca, Muhammad (God bless and give him peace, exalt and ennoble him), and the meed of salutation to his two companions who share his tomb, Abu Bakr al-Siddiq and Abu Hafs Umar al-Faruq (God be pleased with them). We then retired to our camp, rejoicing at this most signal favour, with hearts cheered at obtaining this most great bounty, praising God Most High for our safe arrival at the sacred abodes of His Apostle and his glorious and sublime sanctuaries, and praying Him to grant that this be not our last association with them and that we might be of those whose visitation is accepted and whose journey upon the path of God has been ordained.

Our stay at al-Madinah the Illustrious on this journey lasted four days. We spent each night in the holy mosque, where everyone engaged in pious exercises; some, having formed circles in the court and lit a quantity of candles, and with book-rests in their midst on which were placed volumes of the Holy Qur'an, were reciting from it; some were intoning hymns of praise to God; others were occupied in contemplation of the Immaculate Tomb (God increase it in sweetness); while on every side were singers chanting in eulogy of the Apostle of God (God bless and give him peace). This is the custom observed by all visitors to al-Madinah during those blessed nights, and they also bestow large sums in alms upon the 'sojourners' and the needy.

Then came our departure from al-Madinah to go to Mecca (God Most High ennoble her). We halted near the mosque of Dhu'l-Hulaifah, where the Apostle of God (God bless and give him peace) assumed the pilgrim garb. It is at a distance of five miles from al-Madinah, of whose sacred territory it forms the limit, and not far from it is the wadi of al-Aqiq. Here I divested myself of my tailored clothes, bathed, put on the garment of my consecration, and made a prayer of two bowings. I entered the pilgrim state and in my enthusiasm I did not cease crying *Labbaika Allahumma* through every valley and hill and rise and descent.

Thus prepared for the Pilgrimage, we marched for a further eight days until at last we encamped in the Bottom of Mart, a fertile valley with numerous date-palms and a gushing spring of flowing water which serves for the irrigation of that district. From this valley fruit and vegetables are brought to Mecca (God Most High ennoble her). We set out again at night from this blessed valley, with hearts full of gladness at reaching the goal of their hopes, rejoicing in their present condition and future state, and arrived in the morning at the City of Surety, Mecca (God Most High ennoble her).

Of the wondrous doings of God Most High is this, that He has created the hearts of men with an instinctive desire to seek these sublime sanctuaries, and yearning to present themselves at their illustrious sites, and has given the love of them such power over men's hearts that none alights in them but they seize his whole heart, nor quits them but with grief at separation from them, sorrowing at his journey away from them, filled with longing for them, and purposing to repeat his visitation to them. For their blessed soil is the focus of all eyes, and love of it the marrow of all hearts, in virtue of a wise disposition of God which achieves its sublime purpose, and in fulfilment of the prayer of His Friend [Abraham] (upon him be peace). Intensity of yearning brings them near while yet far off, presents them to the eye while yet unseen, and makes of little account to him who seeks them the fatigues which he meets and the distress which he endures. How many a weak-ling sees death before reaching them, and beholds destruction on their road, yet when God brings him safely to them he welcomes them with joy and gladness, as though he had not tasted bitterness, nor suffered torment and affliction for their sakes! Truly this is a divine thing and a God-given benefit, a proof uncontaminated by ambiguity, unob-scured by dubiety, and inaccessible to deception, which is of compelling cogency in the perception of men of understanding, and shatters the rationalism of the intellectuals. He whose soul God Most High hath sustained by granting him to alight in those regions and to present himself in that court, upon him hath God bestowed the greatest of all favours and possession of the best of both abodes, that of his present world and the other of the world to come. It is meet for him, therefore, that he should abundantly give thanks for what He has bestowed upon him. May God Most High number us amongst those whose visitation is accepted, whose merchandises in seeking to perform it brings him gain in the world to come, whose actions in the cause of God are written in the Book of Life, and whose burdens of sin are effaced by the acceptance of the merit earned by Pilgrimage, through His loving kindness and graciousness.

The venerable city of Mecca

Mecca is a large town, compactly built and oblong in shape, situated in the hollow of a valley which is so shut in by hills that the visitor to her sees nothing of her until he actu-ally reaches her. These hills that overlook her are of no exceeding elevation. She lies, as

God has related in His glorious Book, 'in a valley bare of corn', but the blessed prayer of Abraham has anticipated her needs, so that every delicacy is brought to her, and fruits of every kind are gathered for her. I myself have eaten there fruits, such as grapes, figs, peaches, and fresh dates, that have not their equal in the world; likewise the melons which are transported to her have none to compare with them for flavour and sweetness. The flesh-meats in Mecca are fat and exceedingly delicious in taste. All the commodities that are dispersed in different countries find assembly in her.

The Meccans: their good qualities

The citizens of Mecca are given to well-doing, of consummate generosity and good disposition, liberal to the poor and to those who have renounced the world, and kindly towards strangers. One of their generous customs is that when any of them makes a feast, he begins by giving food to the poor brethren who have devoted themselves to the religious life and are sojourning at the Sanctuary, first inviting them with courtesy, kindness and delicacy, and then giving them to eat. The majority of these destitute devotees are to be found by the public ovens, where the people bake their bread. When anyone has his bread baked and takes it away to his house, the destitute follow him up and he gives each one of them whatever he assigns to him, sending none away disappointed. Even if he has but a single loaf, he gives away a third or a half of it, conceding it cheerfully and without grudgingness.

Another good habit of theirs is that orphan children make a practice of sitting in the bazaar, each with two baskets, one large and one small. A man of the townsfolk of Mecca comes to the bazaar, where he buys grain, meat and vegetables, and passes these to a boy, who puts the grain in one of his baskets and the meat and vegetables in the other, and takes them to the man's house, so that his meal may be prepared from them. Meanwhile the man goes about his devotions and his business. There is no instance related of any of the boys having ever abused their trust in this matter – on the contrary he delivers what he has been given to carry, with the most scrupulous honesty. They receive for this a fixed fee of a few coppers.

The Meccans are elegant and clean in their dress, and as they mostly wear white their garments always appear spotless and snowy. They use perfume freely, paint their eyes with kohl, and are constantly polishing their teeth with twigs of green arak-wood. The Meccan women are of rare and surpassing beauty, pious and chaste. They too make much use of perfumes, to such a degree that a woman will spend the night hungry and buy perfume with the price of her food. They make a practice of performing the circuit of the House on the eve of each Friday, and come in their finest apparel, and the Sanctuary is saturated with the smell of their perfume. When one of these women goes away, the odour of the perfume clings as an effluvium to the place after she has gone.

Anecdote of blessed import

I had a dream in the days of my residence in Mecca (God ennoble her), while I was living in the Muzaffariyah college there, that the Apostle of God (God bless and give him peace) was sitting in the classroom of this college, beside the window from which one looks out upon the illustrious Ka'bah, and the people were taking his hand and swearing allegiance to him. I saw in my dream that the Shaikh Abu Abdallah called

Khalil came in, squatted before the Apostle of God (God bless and give him peace), and placing his hand in the hand of the Apostle of God (God bless and give him peace) he said, 'I give thee my allegiance to do thus and thus', and enumerated a number of things including 'never to turn away a destitute man from my house disappointed'. This was the last phrase of his oath, and I was surprised to hear him saying it, and thought to myself: 'How can he say this and carry out his word, seeing the multitude of the poor of Mecca itself and those who come hither from the Yaman, Zaila, al-Iraq, Persia, Egypt and Syria?' As I saw him in my dream, he was wearing a short white tunic of the cotton fabric called fushtan, which he used sometimes to put on. Next morning, after performing the dawn prayer, I went to him and told him of my dream. It gave him great pleasure and he wept and said to me: 'This tunic was given by one of the saints to my grandfather and for that reason I put it on sometimes for the sake of the blessing.' I never saw him after that turn away a suppliant disappointed. He used to bid his servants bake bread and cook food and bring it to me after the afternoon prayer every day. The people of Mecca eat only once in the day, after the afternoon prayer, and content themselves with that until the same time on the following day. If anyone wishes to eat at any other time of day, he eats dried dates, and it is for that reason that their bodies are healthy and that diseases and infirmities are rarely found amongst them.

There lived in Mecca in the days of my sojourn there Hasan the Maghribi, the demoniac, a man of strange life and remarkable character. He had formerly been sound in mind and a servitor of the saint Najm al-Din al-Isbahani during the lifetime of the latter.

His story

Hasan the demoniac was assiduous in making circuits of the Ka'bah by night, and he used to see during his nightly circuits a faqir busily circuiting whom he never saw by day. This faqir came up to him one night, asked him how he was, and said to him, 'O Hasan, your mother is weeping for you and longing to see you.' (She was one of the handmaidens of God.) 'Would you like to see her?' 'Yes,' he replied, 'but I have no means of doing that.' The faqir said to him, 'We shall meet here tomorrow night, if God Most High will.' The following night, which was the eve of Friday, Hasan found him at the spot which he had appointed for their meeting, and they made the circuit of the House together many times. The faqir then went out of the Sanctuary, Hasan following close behind him, to the Ma'la Gate; when they arrived there he bade him shut his eyes and hold fast to his garment. Hasan did so. After a time the faqir asked: 'Would you recognize your own town?' 'Yes,' said Hasan. 'Well, here it is,' he said. Hasan opened his eyes and lo! he was at the gate of his mother's house. So he went in to her, without telling her anything of what had happened, and stayed with her for a fortnight – I think his town was the city of Asafi. He then went out to the cemetery where he found his friend the faqir, who said to him, 'How are you?' He replied: 'O sir, I have been longing to see Shaikh Najm al-Din, for I went out of his house in my usual way and have been away from him all these days, and I should like you to take me back to him.' The faqir, saying, 'Yes certainly,' made an appointment to meet him at the cemetery by night. When Hasan came to him there, he bade him do as he had done at Mecca (God ennoble her), that is, close his eyes and grip his skirt. He did so, and lo! he was in Mecca (God ennoble her)! The faqir charged him to speak no word to Najm al-

Din of what had happened, nor to speak of it to any other person, but when he came into Najm al-Din the saint said to him, 'Where have you been, Hasan, during your absence?' Hasan at first would not tell him, but when Najm al-Din pressed him, he told him the story. The shaikh then said, 'Show me the man,' and came with him by night. The man came according to his usual custom, and when he passed them Hasan said to his master, 'Sir, this is he.' The man heard him and struck him on the mouth with his hand saying, 'Be silent, God make thee silent.' Immediately his tongue became tied, and his reason went. So he remained in the Sanctuary, a demented man, making circuits night and day without either ablutions or prayers, while the people looked upon him as a means of blessing and clothed him. When he felt hungry he went out to the market which is between al-Safa and Marwa, where he would make for one of the booths and eat what he liked from it; nobody would drive him off or hinder him – on the contrary, everyone from whose stock he ate anything was rejoiced, and it procured for that person blessing and increase in his sales and profits. Whenever he came into the market, the stallkeepers would crane their necks towards him, on account of the experience they had gained of the blessing which he conferred. He did exactly the same with the watercarriers when he wished to drink. This continued to be his way of living until the year seven hundred and twenty-eight, when the Amir Saif al-Din Yalmalak came on pilgrimage and took him back with him to Egypt. From that time no further news of him was heard – God Most High profit us by him!

The departure from Mecca (God Most High ennoble her)

Having performed the rites of Pilgrimage, on the twentieth day precisely of Dhu 'l-Hijjah I went out of Mecca in company with the commander of the caravan of al-Iraq. He hired for me the half of a double litter as far as Baghdad, paying its cost from his own purse, and took me under his protection. We went out to the Bottom of Man, after performing the Farewell Circuit with a host of men of al-Iraq, Khurasan, Fars and other eastern lands, of uncountable multitude, so many that the earth surged with them as the sea surges with dashing waves and their advance was like the march of high-piled clouds. Anyone who left the caravan for a natural want and had no mark by which to guide himself to his place could not find it again for the vast number of people. Included in this caravan were many watercarrying camels for the poorer pilgrims, who could obtain drinking water from them, and other camels to carry provisions for issue as alms and to carry medicines, potions and sugar for those who should be attacked by illness. Whenever the caravan halted food was cooked in great brass cauldrons, and supplied from them to the poorer pilgrims and those who had no provisions. With the caravan also was a number of spare camels for the carriage of those who were unable to walk. All of this was due to the benefactions and generosity of the Sultan Abu Sa'id.

This caravan contained also animated bazaars and great supplies of luxuries and all kinds of food and fruit. They used to march during the night and light torches in front of the file of camels and litters, so that you saw the countryside gleaming with light and the darkness turned into radiant day.

We at length reached Taibah, the City of the Apostle of God (God bless and give him peace), and were privileged to visit once again the tomb of the Apostle of God (God bless and give him peace).

We stayed at al-Madinah (God Most High glorify her) for six days, and taking with us from there water for a three nights' journey, we set out from her. On the third night we encamped at Wadi 'l-Arus, where we provided ourselves with water from underground waterbeds. They dig holes above them in the ground, and procure sweet flowing water. We then left Wadi 'l-Arus and entered the land of the Najd, which is a level stretch of country extending as far as eye can see, and inhaled its sweet-scented air. We halted after covering four stages at a water-point known as al-Usailah, and going on from there halted at a water-point known as al-Nagirah, where there are the remains of cisterns like vast reservoirs. Thence we marched to a waterpoint known as al-Qarurah, being certain tanks filled with rainwater, of those which were constructed by order of Zubaidah, daughter of Ja'far (God's mercy and favour upon her). This place is the centre of the land of Najd, spacious, with sweet air and healthy climate, clean-soiled, and temperate in every season of the year. Then, leaving al-Qarurah, we stopped at al-Hajir, where there are tanks for water, but as they often dry up water has to be procured by digging temporary wells, and going on from there stopped next at Samirah, which is a patch of low-lying ground situated in a plain where there is a kind of an inhabited enceinte. The water at Samirah is plentiful and drawn from cased wells, but it is brackish. The bedouins of that district bring sheep, melted butter and curdled milk, and sell these to the pilgrims for pieces of coarse cotton cloth, and they will not exchange them for anything but this. We resumed our journey and halted at the 'Hill with the Hole', which lies in a tract of desert land and has at its summit a perforation from side to side through which the wind blows. We proceeded from there to Wadi 'l-Kurush, which is waterless in spite of its name, and after marching on through the night came in the morning to the fort of Faid.

Faid is a large fortified enceinte on a level plain and surrounded by a wall, with a suburb outside it. Its inhabitants are Arabs, who make a living off the pilgrims by selling and trading. At that point the pilgrims leave some part of their provisions at the time of their arrival from al-Iraq on the way to Mecca (God Most High ennoble her), and on the return journey they pick them up again. It lies halfway between Mecca and Baghdad, and from it to Kufah is a twelve days' journey by an easy road furnished with supplies of water in tanks. It is the practice of the caravan to enter this place in military formation and warlike array, in order to overawe the Arabs who are assembled there in considerable numbers and to cut short their hopes of despoiling the caravan. We met there in two amirs of the Arabs, Fayyad and Hiyar, sons of the Amir Muhanna b. Isa, accompanied by a body of Arab horsemen and foot soldiers not to be reckoned for multitude; both of them displayed zeal for the safety and protection of the pilgrims and their possessions. The Arabs brought camels and sheep for sale and the pilgrims bought from them what they could afford.

We set out again and halted at the place known as al-Ajfur and made famous through the romantic lovers Jamil and Buthainah. Then travelling on we halted in the open desert, and again marching through the night halted at Zarud, a level plain, in which there are extensive sands. The place itself has some small dwellings, which they have surrounded by a sort of fortified enceinte, and there are wells of water there but they are unpalatable. Proceeding, we halted at al-Tha'labiyah, where there is a ruined fort, opposite which is an enormous reservoir reached by a stairway and containing a quantity of rainwater enough to meet the needs of the whole caravan. A great host of bedouin Arabs assemble at this place and they sell camels, sheep, melted butter and milk. From there to al-Kufah are three marches. We continued our journey and halted at Birkat al-

Marjum ('The Pool of the Stoned'), the latter being a tomb in the roadway with a great heap of stones upon it, and everyone who passes by throws a stone at it. It is related that the person who is thus stoned was a Rafidi; he set out with the caravan to make the Pilgrimage, but a dispute broke out between him and some Turks, followers of the Sunnah, in the course of which he reviled one of the Companions of the Prophet, so they killed him by throwing stones. At this place there are many tents of the bedouins, who come to the caravan bringing melted butter, curdled milk and so on, and there is also a large reservoir enough to supply the needs of the entire caravan. This too is one of those constructed by Zubaidah (God's mercy upon her); indeed, every reservoir, pool or well on this road which goes from Mecca to Baghdad is due to her munificent bounty – God give her goodly reward and recompense her for them in full; for, had it not been for her concern on behalf of this road, it would not be usable by anyone.

Continuing our journey, we halted at a place known as al-Mashquq ['the Cleft'], where there are two reservoirs containing fresh sweet water. Everyone emptied out what water was still in his possession and took a fresh supply from them. Then we went on and after halting at a place called al-Tananir ['the Ovens'], where there is a reservoir filled with water, we made a night march from there and sometime after sunrise arrived before Zumalah, an inhabited village with a fortified grange belonging to some Arabs, two reservoirs of water and many wells. This place is one of the natural watering-places on this road. We set out again and halted at al-Haithaman, where there are two reservoirs of water; then continuing on our way halted below the defile known as Aqabat al-Shaitan ['Devil's Pass']. We climbed the defile on the following day. There is no steep place on that road except this, and even it is neither difficult nor considerable. We halted next at a place called Waqisah, where there is a large fortified grange and reservoirs of water. It is inhabited by bedouin Arabs, and is the last of the natural watering-places on this road, for thereafter until al-Kufah there is no conspicuous watering-place except the watercourses derived from the Euphrates. At this point many of the people of al-Kufah come out to meet the pilgrim caravan, bringing flour, bread, dried dates and fruit, and the travellers congratulate one another on their safe journey. We then halted at a place known as Lawrah, where there is a large reservoir for water; then at a place known as al-Masajid ['the Mosques'], where there are three reservoirs; then at a place known as Manarat al-Quinn ['the Tower of Horns'], this being a tower in a desert locality, conspicuous in height and decorated on top with horns of gazelles, with no habitation around it. We halted next at a place known as al-Udhaib, which is a fruitful valley covered with dwellings and cultivation and surrounded by a plain abounding in pasture and affording a pleasant prospect to the eyes. Thereafter we halted at al-Qadisiyah, where the famous battle was fought against the Persians, in which God manifested the triumph of the Faith of Islam, and subdued the Magians, the fire worshippers, so that after it no foot was left for them to stand on and God extirpated their root. The commander of the Muslims at that time was Sa'd b. Abi Waqqas (God be pleased with him), and al-Qadisiyah was a great city which Sa'd took by force, but it fell into ruins so that nothing now remains of it except as much as constitutes a large village. The place contains some palm groves and at it there are water courses of Euphrates water.

We went on from there and halted at the town of Mashhad Ali b. Abi Talib (God be pleased with him) at al-Najaf. It is a fine city, situated in a wide rocky plain – one of the finest, most populous, and most substantially built cities of al-Iraq, and it has beautiful clean bazaars. We entered it by the outer Bab al-Hadrah and made our way through the bazaar of the greengrocers, cooks, and butchers, then through the fruit-market, then the bazaar of the tailors and the qaisariyah, then the perfumers' bazaar, and so came to the inner Bab al-Hadrah, where is the tomb which they claim to be the tomb of Ali (peace be upon him). Fronting it are a number of colleges, religious houses and convents, most beautifully adorned, their walls being faced with gashani, tiles, which resemble the *zalij* in our country but are more lustrous in colour and more finely decorated.

The mausoleum and tombs contained in it

One enters through the Bab al-Hadrah into a vast college, inhabited by students and sufis belonging to the Shi'ah. Everyone who visits it receives hospitality for three days – namely, bread, meat, and dried dates twice daily. From this college one gains access to the gateway of the domed shrine, which is guarded by a number of doorkeepers, chamberlains and eunuchs. As the visitor to the tomb approaches, one of them rises to meet him or all of them do, this being regulated by the visitor's rank. They stand beside him on the threshold and ask permission for him to enter, saying: 'By your leave, O Commander of the Faithful, this feeble creature asks permission for his entry to the sublime mausoleum. If ye grant it to him so be it, but if not, he will turn back; and though he be not worthy of this favour, ye are the possessor of generous qualities and of dignity.' They then bid him kiss the threshold, which is of silver, as also are the doorposts. Having done so, he enters the shrine, which is carpeted with various sorts of carpets of silk and other materials, and contains candelabra of gold and silver, large and small. In the centre of the space beneath the dome is a square platform, faced with wood, upon which are carved golden plaques of excellent workmanship, hammered on with silver nails, which have so completely masked the wood that none of it is visible. The height of the platform is less than the stature of a man, and on top of it are three tombs, of which they assert that one is the tomb of Adam (upon him be blessing and peace), the second the tomb of Noah (upon him be blessing and peace), and the third the tomb of Ali (God be pleased with him). Between the tombs are dishes of gold and silver, containing rose-water, musk and various kinds of perfumes. The visitor dips his hand in this and anoints his face with it for a blessing. The shrine has another door the threshold of which is likewise of silver, and with hangings of coloured silk over it. This leads to a mosque laid with beautiful carpets, its walls and ceiling concealed by silken hangings, and having four doorways with thresholds of silver and covered by silken hangings.

The inhabitants of this city are all of them Rafidis, and at this mausoleum certain miracles are operated, whereby it is established, so they claim, that the mausoleum does indeed contain the grave of Ali (God be pleased with him). One of these miracles is that on the eve of the twenty-seventh of Rajab, which is called by them 'the night of life', all the crippled are brought to this mausoleum from the two Iraqs, Khurasan, and the countries of Fars and Rum, so that there are assembled some thirty or forty of them. After the last ritual prayer of the night, they are placed upon the sanctified tomb, while the people wait in expectation of their rising and pass the time, some in praying, others in reciting liturgies, or reading the Qur'an, or in contemplation of the mausoleum. When the night is half over, or two-thirds or so, the whole company arise sound in body, with no trace of disease, and saying: 'There is no God but God; Muhammad is the Apostle of God; Ali is the Friend of God.' This is a thing much spoken of among them; I heard of it from trustworthy persons, but I was not actually present on any such night. I saw, however, in the Guests' College three men, one from the land of Rum, the second from Isfahan and the third from Khurasan, who were cripples, and when I asked them about themselves they told me that they had missed the 'Night of Life' and were waiting for its time to come round next year. This night serves as occasion for a gathering of the people from the district, and they hold a great fair lasting for ten days.

In this town there is no tax, no farmer of market or *octroi* dues, and no royal governor, but the government over them is exercised solely by the marshal of the Sharifs. Its inhabitants are merchants, who travel far and wide; they are courageous and open-handed, and their protege suffers no wrong on his journeyings with them, so that their company is highly commended. But they are fanatical about Ali (God be pleased with him). There are some people in the land of al-Iraq and other lands who, if attacked by illness, vow to make a votive offering to the mausoleum when they recover. In other cases a man suffering from illness in the head will make a head of gold or silver and bring it to the mausoleum, and the marshal puts it into the treasury; likewise with hand or foot, or any other member. The treasury of the mausoleum is enormous, and contains such a quantity of riches as defies exact computation.

Jerusalem was at the heart of Jewish religious culture and despite the destruction of the Temple the Holy City remained a place of pilgrimage alongside other sites of religious importance in Palestine and other parts of the Near East. In 1166 a rabbi, Benjamin, from Tuledo, took a journey through Europe and the Near East in which he visited the Jewish holy sites. His descriptions of Jerusalem and the tomb of Ezekiel demonstrate the importance he placed on visiting these sites and, for us, act as a reminder that in every faith, even a small site may be the focal point not only for locals but also for pilgrims from further afield.

M. N. Adler, *The Itinerary of Benjamin of Tuledo: critical text, translation and commentary* (New York, 1907) pp. 22–24, 43–45

Jerusalem

From there it is three parasangs to Jerusalem, which is a small city, fortified by three walls. It is full of people whom the Mohammedans call Jacobites, Syrians, Greeks, Georgians and Franks, and of people of all tongues. It contains a dyeing-house, for which the Jews pay a small rent annually to the king, on condition that besides the Jews no other dyers be allowed in Jerusalem. There are about 200 who dwell under the Tower of David in one corner of the city. The lower portion of the wall of the Tower of David, to the extent of about ten cubits, is part of the ancient foundation set up by our ancestors, the remaining portion having been built by the Mohammedans. There is no structure in the whole city stronger than the Tower of David. The city also contains two buildings from one of which – the hospital – there issue forth four hundred knights; and therein all the sick who come thither are lodged and cared for in life and in death. The other building is called the Temple of Solomon; it is the palace built by Solomon the king of Israel. Three hundred knights are quartered there, and issue therefrom every day for military exercise, besides those who come from the land of the Franks and the other parts of Christendom, having taken upon themselves to serve there a year or two until their vow is fulfilled. In Jerusalem is the great church called the Sepulchre, and here is the burial-place of Jesus, unto which the Christians make pilgrimages.

Jerusalem has four gates – the gate of Abraham, the gate of David, the gate of Zion, and the gate of Gushpat, which is the gate of Jehoshaphat, facing our ancient Temple, now called Templum Domini. Upon the site of the sanctuary Omar ben al Khataab erected an edifice with a very large and magnificent cupola, into which the Gentiles do not bring any image or effigy, but they merely come there to pray. In front of this place is the western wall, which is one of the walls of the Holy of Holies. This is called the Gate of Mercy, and thither come all the Jews to pray before the walls of the court of the Temple. In Jerusalem, attached to the palace which belonged to Solomon, are the stables built by him, forming a very substantial structure, composed of large stones, and the like of which is not to be seen anywhere in the world. There is also visible up to this day the pool used by the priests before offering their sacrifices, and the Jews coming thither write their names upon the wall. The gate of Jehoshaphat leads to the valley of Jehoshaphat, which is the gatheringplace of the nations. Here is the pillar called Absolam's Hand, and the sepulchre of King Uzziah.

In the neighbourhood is also a great spring, called the Waters of Siloam, connected with the brook of Kidron. Over the spring is a large structure dating from the time of our ancestors, but little water is found, and the people of Jerusalem for the most part drink the rain-water, which they collect in cisterns in their houses. From the valley of Jehoshaphat one ascends the Mount of Olives; it is the valley only which separates Jerusalem from the Mount of Olives. From the Mount of Olives one can see the Sea of Sodom, and at a distance of two parasangs from the Sea of Sodom is the Pillar of Salt into which Lot's wife was turned; the sheep lick it continually, but afterwards it regains its original shape. The whole land of the plain and the valley of Shittim as far as Mount Nebo are visible from here.

In front of Jerusalem is Mount Zion, on which there is no building, except a place of worship belonging to the Christians. Facing Jerusalem for a distance of three miles are the cemeteries belong to the Israelites, who in the days of old buried their dead in caves, and upon each sepulchre is a dated inscription, but the Christians destroy the sepulchres, employing the stones thereof in building their houses. These sepulchres reach as far as Zelzah in the territory of Benjamin. Around Jerusalem are high mountains.

On Mount Zion are the sepulchres of the House of David, and the sepulchres of the kings that ruled after him. The exact place cannot be identified, inasmuch as fifteen years ago a wall of the church of Mount Zion fell in.

Tomb of Ezekiel in Iraq

Thence it is three parasangs to the Synagogue of Ezekiel, the prophet of blessed memory, which is by the river Euphrates. It is fronted by sixty turrets, and between each turret there is a minor Synagogue, and in the court of the Synagogue is the ark, and at the back of the Synagogue is the sepulchre of Ezekiel. It is surmounted by a large cupola, and it is a very handsome structure. It was built of old by King Jeconiah, king of Judah, and the 35,000 Jews who came with him, when Evil-merodach brought him forth out of prison. This place is by the river Chebar on the one side, and by the river Euphrates on the other, and the name of Jeconiah and those that accompanied him are engraved on the wall: Jeconiah at the top, and Ezekiel at the bottom. This place is held sacred by Israel as a lesser sanctuary unto this day, and people come from a distance to pray there from the time of the New Year until the Day of Atonement. The Israelites have great rejoicings on these occasions. Thither also come the Head of the Captivity, and the Head of the Academies from Bagdad. Their camp occupies a space of about two miles, and Arab merchants come there as well. A great gathering like a fair takes place, which is called Fera, and they bring forth a scroll of the Law written on parchment by Ezekiel the Prophet, and read from it on the Day of Atonement. A lamp burns day and night over the sepulchre of Ezekiel; the light thereof has been kept burning from the day that he lighted it himself, and they continually renew the wick thereof, and replenish the oil until the present day. A large house belonging to the sanctuary is filled with books, some of them from the time of the first temple, and some from the time of the second temple. And he who has no sons consecrates his books to its use. The Jews that come thither to pray from the land of Persia and Media bring the money which their country men have offered to the Synagogue of Ezekiel the Prophet. The Synagogue owns property, lands and villages, which belonged to King Jeconiah, and when Mohammed came he confirmed all these rights to the Synagogue of Ezekiel. Distinguished Mohammedans also come hither to pray, so great is their love for Ezekiel the Prophet; and they call it Bar (Dar) Melicha (the Dwelling of Beauty). All the Arabs come there to pray.

Further reading

R. Barber, *Pilgrimages* (Woodbridge, 1991).
A. Elad, *Medieval Jerusalem and Islamic Worship: holy places, ceremonies, pilgrimage* (Leiden, 1999).
R. C. Finucane, *Miracles and Pilgrims: popular beliefs in medieval England* (London, 1977).
R. Fletcher, *St James's Catapult: the life and times of Diego Gelmirez of Santiago de Compostela* (Oxford, 1984).
S. Hopper, *To Be a Pilgrim: the medieval pilgrimage experience* (Stroud, 2002).
J. Stopford (ed.) *Pilgrimage Explored* (Woodbridge, 1999).
J. Sumption, *Pilgrimage: an image of medieval religion* (London, 1975).
D. Webb, *Pilgrims and Pilgrimage in the Medieval West* (London, 1999).
—— *Pilgrimage in Medieval England* (London, 2000).
—— *Medieval European Pilgrimage, c.700–c.1500* (Basingstoke, 2002).

Plates

Sacraments

Seven steps in the Christian life. Through Baptism the person is admitted to the Church and through the other sacraments the whole of life is made holy.

Plate 1 Font, East Meon, Hampshire. This black Tournai marble font of c.1130 has carvings of the Creation of Adam and Eve. Through baptism men and women become part of Christ's new creation.

Plate 2 Seven sacrament font, Cley, Norfolk. There are forty of these fonts in England; twenty-five are
found in Norfolk. They date, like this one, mainly from the fifteenth century. Baptism (left) and
confirmation are depicted.

Monastic buildings

A monastery is a place for Christian lives in which the buildings reflect a total community. Centred on the church, the place of prayer, and arranged around the cloister, the link building of the complex, every part of the common life is served.

Plate 3 Choir stalls, Winchester Cathedral, Hampshire, early fourteenth century. The *opus Dei*, especially the choral recitation of the psalms, was the chief work of the monks.

Plate 4 Cloister, Norwich Cathedral, Norfolk. Rebuilt from 1297, the great cloister at Norwich has nearly 400 carved roof bosses which provide a mirror of the Christian life of the Middle Ages.

Plate 5 Cloister walk, Gloucester Cathedral, Gloucestershire, c.1400. The south walk of the cloister contains twenty carrels, or small studies, where the Benedictine monks read and meditated.

Plate 6 Chapter house, Worcester Cathedral, Worcestershire, c.1120. The meeting place of the monastic community where elections were held and the Rule enforced. This was the first of what became the characteristic round English chapter house with a column in the middle.

Plate 7 Dorter or dormitory, Fontenay Abbey, Burgundy, c.1150. A spacious and airy chamber for a
night interrupted by prayer reflecting the austere grandeur of the early Cistercians.

Plate 8 Lavatorium, Gloucester Cathedral, Gloucestershire, c.1400. A washing place, revealing an extensive drainage system, surmounted by a fan-vault.

Plate 9 Kitchen, Glastonbury Abbey, Somerset, c.1350. An octagonal interior allows for four fireplaces in a kitchen where industrial quantities of food could be cooked, the fumes released through an elegant lantern.

Plate 10 Refectory or frater, Dover Priory, c.1139. The frater or refectory, still in use in this case, as a dining room for a public school, was a formal space where the monks ate in silence. This refectory was once dominated by a wall painting of the Last Supper, now almost faded away.

Plate 11 Undercroft, Fountains Abbey, Yorkshire, c.1150. This 300 foot long space, supported on a central row of nineteen pillars, was a versatile area for storage and accommodation.

Plate 12 Prior's chapel, Castle Acre Priory, Norfolk, twelfth century. The private chapel of this
Cluniac monastery became part, in the early sixteenth century, of an extensive range of
private rooms for the superior.

Plate 13 Reredorter, Fountains Abbey, Yorkshire, twelfth century. The monks' lavatories showed the drainage skills of the Cistercians.

Shrines

All the baptised aspired to sanctity and those who were publicly venerated as holy, the saints, attracted devotion, patronage and pilgrimage.

Plate 14 Holy Sepulchre, Church of the Holy Sepulchre, Jerusalem. The climax of medieval pilgrimage, a much rebuilt and embellished structure, above Christ's tomb, within the rotunda of the twelfth-century crusader church.

Plate 15 Shrine of St Alban, St Alban's Cathedral, Hertfordshire. Erected in c.1305 on the site of the martyrdom of St Alban, who died as early as 209. Reconstructed from fragments in the twentieth century, and accompanied by a fifteenth-century watching loft.

Plate 16 Pavement, Canterbury Cathedral, Kent, c.1220. The site of the shrine of St Thomas of Canterbury, who died in 1170. The tomb was destroyed in 1538 but the complicated geometrical pavement survived.

Plate 17 Stained glass window, Trinity Chapel ambulatory, Canterbury Cathedral, Kent, c.1220–1230. The miracles of St Thomas are depicted in these windows which overlooked his tomb.

Plate 18 St Foy, Conques, Aveyron, France, a Benedictine abbey on the road to Santiago de
Compostela, was the shrine of St Foy, a virgin martyr (d. 303). The gold and bejewelled reliquary was commissioned in 949.

Plate 19 Santiago de Compostela, Spain. The thirteenth-century statue of St James above the high
altar and burial place of the apostle James, the end of the pilgrim road.

Plate 20 Pilgrim, Chester Cathedral, Chester, late fourteenth century. The pilgrim, pattern of the quest for God in the medieval Church, stands on a stall, part of perhaps the first set of surviving choir stalls.

5   Magic and heresy

Medieval magic is difficult to define and we must be wary of calling medieval religious practices magic, since medieval Christianity had its own definition of magic as something adverse to true religion. The word magic comes from the Greek word for witchcraft.

Much of our information relating to medieval magic comes from the law, penitentials, and sermons of the Church condemning magic and its practitioners. Within Western Christendom, magic was defined by those who were in a position to make that definition: the bishops and theologians of the Church. In that sense, medieval magic was whatever practices the Church condemned as being not of God and, as such, they associated magic with the devil, paganism, and witchcraft or sorcery.

Some have traditionally differentiated magic from religion by stipulating that magic manipulates natural or supernatural forces, whilst religion involves supplication of a deity. In this view magicians, therefore, have the power to compel, whereas suppliants humbly beg. Simon Magus is the prototypical magician of the New Testament who attempted to purchase the gift of the Holy Spirit from the Disciples, giving us the expression 'simony' for the offence of buying and selling spiritual offices.

Acts of the Apostles, New Revised Standard Version (1993)

Acts 8:9–11, 18–20: Simon Magus

> But there was a man named Simon who had previously practiced magic in the city and amazed the nation of Samaria, saying that he himself was somebody great. They all gave heed to him, from the least to the greatest, saying, 'This man is that power of God which is called Great.' And they gave heed to him, because for a long time he had amazed them with his magic.
>
> Now when Simon saw that the Spirit was given through the laying on of the apostles' hands, he offered them money, saying, 'Give me also this power, that any one on whom I lay my hands may receive the Holy Spirit.' But Peter said to him, 'Your silver perish with you, because you thought you could obtain the gift of God with money!'

The Church authorities saw popular superstition as an undermining influence on Christian life, and 'folk' practices, which may have predated Christianity, were looked on with particular disfavour.

D. Ayerst and A. Fisher, *Records of Christianity, vol. II: Christendom* (Oxford, 1977) pp. 218–219

Witchcraft

One woman baptises a waxen image, another a piece of wood, another a dead man's bone, all for working some charm. One bewitches with herbs, another with holy chrism, another with God's body. . . . She conjures to get a husband, she conjures when she has got him; she conjures before her child is born, conjures before it is baptized, conjures after its baptism.

Translations and Reprints from the Original Sources of European History (Pennsylvania, 1907?) vol. III, no. 4, pp. 6–7

Johannes Nider, 'The Ant Hill' (c.1437)

I will relate to you some examples, which I have gained in part from the teachers of our faculty, in part from the experience of a certain upright secular judge, worthy of all faith, who from the torture and confession of witches and from his experiences in public and private has learned many things of this sort – a man with whom I have often discussed this subject broadly and deeply – to wit, Peter, a citizen of Bern, in the diocese of Lausanne, who has burned many witches of both sexes, and has driven others out of the territory of the Bernese. I have moreover conferred with one Benedict, a monk of the Benedictine order, who, although now a very devout cleric in a reformed monastery at Vienna, was a decade ago, while still in the world, a necromancer, juggler, buffoon, and strolling player, well-known as an expert among the secular nobility. I have likewise heard certain of the following things from the Inquisitor of Heretical Pravity at Autun, who was a devoted reformer of our order in the convent at Lyons, and has convicted many of witchcraft in the diocese of Autun.

The same procedure was more clearly described by another young man, arrested and burned as a witch, although as I believe, truly, penitent, who had earlier, together with his wife, a witch invincible to persuasion, escaped the clutches of the aforesaid judge, Peter. The aforesaid youth, being again indicted at Bern, with his wife, and placed in a different prison from hers, declared: 'If I can obtain absolution for my sins, I will freely lay bare all I know about witchcraft, for I see that I have death to expect.' And when he had been assured by the scholars that, if he should truly repent, he would certainly be able to gain absolution for his sins, then he gladly offered himself to death, and disclosed the methods of the primeval infection.

The ceremony, he said, of my seduction was as follows: First, on a Sunday, before the holy water is consecrated, the future disciple with his masters must go into the church, and there in their presence must renounce Christ and his faith, baptism, and the church universal. Then he must do homage to the magisterulus, that is, to the little master (for so, and not otherwise, they call the Devil). Afterward he drinks from the aforesaid flask: and, this done, he forthwith feels himself to conceive and hold within himself an image of our art and the chief rites of this sect. After this fashion was I seduced; and my wife also, whom I believe of so great pertinacity that she will endure the flames rather than confess the least whit of the truth; but, alas, we are both guilty.

What the young man had said was found in all respects the truth. For, after confession, the young man was seen to die in great contrition. His wife, however, though convicted by the testimony of witnesses, would not confess the truth even under the torture or in death; but when the fire was prepared for her by the executioner, uttered in most evil words a curse upon him, and so was burned.

Magical potions and charms used in conjunction with prayers mixed superstition with religion and attempted to invest non-sacramental acts with the power of the sacrament. Mixing professional religious activities with folk remedies was seen as particularly malicious.

K. L. Jolly, *Popular Religion in Late Saxon England: elf charms in context* (Chapel Hill, 1996) pp. 6–8

Aecerbot (field remedy) ritual (late tenth or early eleventh century)

Here is the remedy, how you may better your land, if it will not grow well or if some harmful thing has been done to it by a sorcerer [dry] or by a poisoner [*lyblace*].

Take then at night, before dawn, four sods from four sides of the land, and mark where they were before.

Then take oil and honey and yeast, and milk of each animal that is on the land, and a piece of each type of tree that grows on the land, except hard beams, and a piece of each herb known by name, except burdock [glappan] only, and put then holy water thereon, and drip it three times on the base of the sods, and say then these words:

Crescite, grow, *et multiplicamini*, and multiply, *et replete*, and fill, *terre*, the earth. *In nomine patris et filii et spiritus sancti sit benedicti.* [In the name of the father and the son and the holy spirit be blessed.] And the *Pater noster* [Our Father] as often as the other.

And then bear the sods into church, and let a masspriest sing four masses over the sods, and let someone turn the green [sides] to the altar, and after that let someone bring the sods to where they were before, before the sun sets.

And have made for them four signs of Christ [crosses] of quickbeam and write on each end: Matthew and Mark, Luke, and John. Lay that sign of Christ in the bottom of the pit [where each sod had been cut out], saying then: *crux Matheus, crux Marcus, crux Lucas, crux sanctus Iohannes.*

Take then the sods and set them down there on [the crosses], and say then nine times these words, *Crescite* [grow], and as often the *Pater noster*, and turn then to the east, and bow nine times humbly, and speak then these words:

Eastwards I stand, for mercies I pray,
I pray the great *domine* [Lord], I pray the powerful lord,
I pray the holy guardian of heaven-kingdom,
earth I pray and sky
and the true *sancta* Mary
and heaven's might and high hall,
that I may this charm by the gift of the lord
open with [my] teeth through firm thought,
to call forth these plants for our worldly use,

to fill this land with firm belief,
to beautify this grassy turf, as the wiseman said
that he would have riches on earth who alms
gave with justice by the grace of the lord.

Then turn thrice with the sun's course, stretch then out lengthwise and enumerate there the litanies and say then: *Sanctus, sanctus, sanctus* to the end. Sing then *Benedicite* with outstretched arms and *Magnificat* and *Pater noster* thrice, and commend it [the land] to Christ and saint Mary and the holy cross for praise and for worship and for the benefit of the one who owns that land and all those who are serving under him. When all that is done, then let a man take unknown seed from beggars and give them twice as much as he took from them, and let him gather all his plough tools together; then let him bore a hole in the beam [of the plough, putting in] incense and fennel and hallowed soap and hallowed salt. Take then that seed, set it on the plough's body, say then:

Erce, Erce, Erce, earth's mother,
May the all-ruler grant you, the eternal lord,
fields growing and flourishing,
propagating and strengthening,
tall shafts, bright crops,
and broad barley crops,
and white wheat crops,
and all earth's crops.
May the eternal lord grant him,
and his holy ones, who are in heaven,
that his produce be guarded against any enemies whatsoever,
and that it be safe against any harm at all,
from poisons [*lyblaca*] sown around the land.
Now I bid the Master, who shaped this world,
that there be no speaking-woman [*cwidol wif*] nor artful man [*craeftig* man]
that can overturn these words thus spoken.
Then let a man drive forth the plough and the first furrow cuts, say then:
Whole may you be [Be well] earth, mother of men!
May you be growing in God's embrace,
with food filled for the needs of men.

Take then each kind of flour and have someone bake a loaf [the size of] a hand's palm and knead it with milk and with holy water and lay it under the first furrow. Say then:

Field full of food for mankind,
bright-blooming, you are blessed
in the holy name of the one who shaped heaven
and the earth on which we live;
the God, the one who made the ground, grant us the gift of growing,
that for us each grain might come to use.
Say then thrice *Crescite in nomine patris, sit benedicti* [Grow in the name of the father, be blessed]. Amen and *Pater noster* three times.

Medieval sermon stories exemplify the power of the host and their purpose is often to thwart demonic magic with Christian miracle, to arouse interest and to convey moral truths. As Jacques de Vitry (d. 1240) said, 'It is necessary to employ a great many proverbs, historical stories and anecdotes, especially when the audience is tired and begins to get sleepy.' Caesarius of Heisterbach (d. c.1250), master of novices and prior of the Cistercian monastery of Heisterbach, was one of the greatest sources of sermon-stories.

C. G. Coulton (ed.) *Life in the Middle Ages* (New York, 1910) vol. 1, pp. 70–72

Caesarius of Heisterbach: the Eucharist as a charm

Monk: I think it is less than two years now since a certain priest who doubted of the Sacrament of Christ's Body celebrated mass in the town of Wildenburg. As he was reciting the canon of the mass, with some hesitation concerning so marvellous a conversion of bread into Christ's Body, the Lord showed him raw flesh in the host. This was seen also by Widekind, a noble standing behind his back, who drew the priest aside after mass and enquired diligently what he had done or thought during the canon; he, therefore, terrified both by the vision and by the question, confessed and denied not how at that hour he had doubted of the sacrament. And each told the other how he had seen raw flesh in the host. This same Widekind had to wife the daughter of Siegfried of Runkel, a niece of the abbess of Rheindorf, who told me this vision last year. Would you also know what the Lord shows to priests of evil life, for that He is crucified by them? . . . A certain lecherous priest wooed a woman; and, unable to obtain her consent, he kept the most pure Body of the Lord in his mouth after mass, hoping that, if he thus kissed her, her will would be bent to his desire by the force of the Sacrament. But the Lord, (who complains through the mouth of the Prophet Zachariah, saying 'You crucify me daily, even the whole nation of you' [a misquote of Zach. 3:9]) thus hindered his evildoing. When he would fain have gone forth from the church door, he seemed to himself to grow so huge that he struck his head against the ceiling of the sacred building. The wretched man was so startled that he drew the host from his mouth, and buried it, not knowing what he did, in a corner of the church [*note*: churches were commonly unpaved at this date]. But, fearing the swift vengeance of God, he confessed the sacrilege to a priest his familiar friend. So they went together to the place and threw back the dust, where they found not the appearance of bread, but the shape, though small, of a man hanging on the cross, fleshy and blood-stained. What was afterwards done with it or what the priest did, I forget, for it is long since this was told me by Hermann our Cantor, to whom the story was well-known.

Novice: If all priests heard such stories, and believed in them, I think that they would honour Divine Sacraments more than they do now.

Monk: It is somewhat pitiful that we men, for whose salvation this sacrament was instituted, should be so lukewarm about it; while brute beasts, worms, and reptiles recognize in it their Creator. . . . A certain woman kept many bees, which throve not but died in great numbers; and, as she sought everywhere for a remedy, it was told her that if she placed the Lord's Body among them, this plague would soon cease. She therefore went to church and, making as though she would communicate, took the Lord's Body, which she took from her mouth as soon as the priest had departed, and laid it in one of her hives. Mark the marvellous power of God! These little worms, recognizing the might of their Creator, built their sweetest Guest, out of their sweetest honeycombs, a chapel of marvellous workmanship, wherein they set up a tiny altar of the same material and laid thereon this most holy Body: and God blessed their labours. In process of time the woman opened this hive, and was aware of the afore-said chapel whereupon she hastened and confessed to the priest all that she had done and seen. Then he took with him his parishioners and came to the hive, where they drove away the bees that hovered round and buzzed in Praise of their creator; and, marvelling at the little chapel with its walls and windows, roof and tower, door and altar, they brought back the Lord's Body with praise and glory to the church. For though God be marvellous in the saints, yet these His smallest creatures preached Him yet more marvellously.

Translations and Reprints from the Original Sources of European History, (Pennsylvania, 1907?) vol. II, no. 4, pp. 18–20

Caesarius of Heisterbach: Christ seen in the hands of a priest

In Himmerode an aged priest, Henry by name, died a few years ago. He was a holy and just man, and had been for very many years sacristan in that monastery. When he was reading the mass one day at the altar of St. John the Baptist, in the choir of the lay brethren, a certain one of the lay-brethren standing near, saw, in the hands of the priest, the Saviour in the form of a man. Nevertheless the priest himself did not see it. This was told to me by one of the elders in that convent.

Caesarius of Heisterbach: woman punished for scattering the host upon her vegetables

On the same island a maiden, not a nun, whom I saw there, was possessed. When the devil was asked by a priest why he had so long and so cruelly tortured Hartdyfa de Cogheme, he replied through the mouth of the girl. 'Why? She has most certainly deserved it. She scattered the Most High upon her vegetables.'

Since he did not at all understand the saying and the devil was unwilling to explain, the priest went to the woman and told her what the devil had said about her, advising her not to deny if she understood. She immediately confessed her guilt, saying, 'I understand the saying well, although I have never told any man of it. When I was a young girl and had a garden to cultivate, I received a wandering woman as a guest one night. When I told her of the losses in my garden, saying that all the vegetables were being devoured by caterpillars, she replied, "I will tell you a good remedy. Receive the body of the Lord, break it in pieces, scatter it over your vegetables, and the plague will cease at once." I, wretched one! who cared more for my garden than for the sacrament, when I had received the body of our Lord at Easter, took it out of my mouth and did with it as I had been taught. What I had intended as a remedy for my vegetables, became a source of torment to me, as the devil is my witness.'

NOVICE: This woman was more cruel than the attendants of Pilate, who spared Jesus after His death and did not break His bones.

MONK: Therefore, up to the present day she atones for that heinous sin and suffers unheard-of tortures. Let those who employ the divine sacrament for temporal gain, or what is more execrable, for evil-doing, give heed to this punishment, even if they do not consider the sinfulness. Also if vermin neglect the reverence due to this sacrament, they sometimes suffer punishment.

In the early decades of the eleventh century (c.1020), Burchardt, bishop of Worms, produced a lengthy list of questions which were to be asked of penitents to find out how far they indulged in magical practices.

D. Ayerst and A. Fisher, *Records of Christianity, vol. II: Christendom* (Oxford, 1977) pp. 218–219

1   Have you kept the New Year's Day with pagan rites by doing anything more on that day than you usually do on the day before or after?
2   Have you sat on the roof of your house, having drawn a circle round you with a sword, so that you might see and know what was going to happen to you in the coming year?
3   Have you sat on a bull's hide at the cross-roads, so that there too you may learn your future?
4   Have you caused loaves to be made in your name on New Year's Eve, so that you might foresee a year of prosperity for yourself, if the loaves rose high and were close-textured?
5   Have you done what some do on the first of January, the octave of Christmas Day, spin, weave, and sew on that holy night so that whatever task they begin on that New Year is begun on the devil's instigation?
6   Have you done as some women do at certain times of the year, prepared a table in your house with food and drink and three extra knives, so that those three sisters whom ancient ignorance and folly called the Fates should get refreshment there?
7   Have you taken the power and Name of divine piety and handed it over to the devil? I mean, have you believed that those you call the sisters can be of any help to you now or in the future?

'Heresy' means 'wrong belief', that is the holding of ideas incompatible with the accepted doctrines of the Church. In the medieval period, it was seen as a deviation from orthodoxy and was therefore defined in relation to orthodoxy – that is the orthodoxy of the teaching Church, the arbiter of Christian belief. Schism was defined as formal separation from the unity of the Church. Heresy, in whatever form it might take, was the outcome of official condemnation by the Church.

C. G. Coulton (ed.) *Life in the Middle Ages* (New York, c.1910) vol. 1, pp. 1–7

Ralph Glaber: on the first millennium, from Miracles De Saint Benoit

The first millennium

Warned by the prophecy of Holy Writ, we see clearer than daylight that in the process of the Last Days, as love waxed cold and iniquity abounded among mankind,

We pay for him, and he pays for us! If we weep, he soothes us! I would that all the convent could see him at this very moment just as I do, even if I had to fast for it till dusk! Not one would there be, methinks, who would be able to restrain his laughter if that he witnessed the tumbling of this fellow, who thus kills himself, and who so excites him by tumbling, that he has no pity on himself. God counts it unto him for penance, for he does it without evil intent, and, certes, I hold it not to be ill, for, as I believe, he does it, according to his lights, in good faith, for he wishes not to be idle.'

And the monk saw how that he laboured without ceasing all the day long. And he laughed much, and made merry over the matter, but it caused him sorrow as well as merriment. And he went to the abbot, and rehearsed unto him, from beginning to end, all that he had learnt, even as you have heard it.

And the abbot arose, and said to the monk, 'On your vow of obedience, I command that you keep silence, and noise this not abroad, and that you so well observe this command, that you speak not of this matter save to me alone, and we will both go thither, and we shall see if this can be, and we will beseech the heavenly King, and His very gentle and dear Mother, who is so precious, and of so great renown, that she, of her sweetness, will go pray of her Son, her Father, and her Lord, that if it so pleases Him, He will this day suffer me to witness this service in such sort that God may be the more loved on account of this, and that, if thus it pleases Him, the good man may not be found worthy of blame for it.'

And then they went thither quite quietly, and without delay they hid themselves in a covert nook unto the altar, so that he saw them not. And the abbot, watching there, observed all the service of the novice, and the divers somersaults the [*sic*] which he turned, and how that he capered, and danced, and bowed before the image, and jumped, and leaped, until that he was nigh fainting. And so greatly was he overcome of fatigue, that he fell heavily to the ground, and so exhausted was he, that he sweated all over from his efforts, so that the sweat ran all down the middle of the crypt. But in a little, the Mother of God, whom he served all without guile, came to his succour, and well knew she how to aid him.

And anon the abbot looked, and he saw descend from the vaulting so glorious a lady, that never had he seen one so fair or so richly crowned, and never had another so beautiful been created. Her vesture was all wrought with gold and precious stones, and with her were the angels and the archangels from the heavens above, who came around the tumbler, and solaced and sustained him. And when that they were ranged around him, he was wholly comforted, and they made ready to tend him, for they desired to make recompense unto him for the services the which he had rendered unto their Lady, who is so precious a gem. And the sweet and noble Queen took a white cloth, and with it she very gently fanned her minstrel before the altar. And the noble and gracious Lady fanned his neck and body and face to cool him, and greatly did she concern herself to aid him, and gave herself up to the care of him; but of this the good man took no heed, for he neither perceived, nor did he know, that he was in such fair company.

And the holy angels who remained with him, paid him much honour, but the Lady no longer sojourned there, and she made the sign of the cross as she turned away, and the holy angels, who greatly rejoiced to keep watch over their companion, took charge over him, and they did but await the hour when God would take him from this life, and they might bear away his soul.

And full four times did the abbot and the monk witness, without hindrance, how that each hour he went there, and how the Mother of God came there to aid her liegeman, for well knows she how to protect her own. And the abbot had much joy of it, for very desirous had he been to know the truth concerning it. Now had God verily shown unto him that the services the which this poor man rendered were pleasing unto Him. And the monk was quite bewildered by it, and from anguish he glowed like fire. 'Your mercy, Sire!' said he to the abbot, 'this is a holy man whom I see here. If that I have said aught concerning him that is evil, it is right that my body should make amends for it. Therefore ordain me a penance, for without doubt he is altogether an upright man. Verily have we seen all, and no longer can we be mistaken.'

And the abbot said, 'You speak truly. God has indeed made us to know that He loves him with a very great love. And now I straightway give command unto you that, in virtue of obedience, and so that you fall not under condemnation, you speak to no one of that which you have seen, save to God or to me.'

'Sire,' said he, 'to this do I assent.'

And at these words they departed, and no longer did they stay in the crypt, and the good man did not remain, but when that he had done all his service, he clothed himself again in his garments, and went direct himself in the monastery.

And thus passed the time, until that, a little while, it came to pass that the abbot sent for him who was so good. And when he heard that he was sent for, and that it was the abbot who made enquiry for him, so greatly was he troubled, that he knew not what he should say. 'Alas,' said he, 'I am found out. Never a day passes without distress, or without toil or disgrace, for my service counts for naught. Methinks it is not pleasing unto God. Alas, as the truth has been found out, I bethink me that it is displeasing unto Him. Can I conceive that these tricks, which I do, could give pleasure to the Supreme God if that I did them openly? No pleasure would they give Him. Alas! I never do right. What shall I do, and what shall I say? Blessed and very dear God, what will become of me? Now shall I be rebuked and put to shame, and I shall be banished hence, and shall again become like unto a target for all the ill-treatment of the world without. Gentle Lady, Holy Mary, how troubled is my mind! I know not, Lady, from whom to get counsel, so come now to mine aid. Very dear God, help me now. Tarry not, but hasten, and bring with you your Mother. Of your mercy, come not without her, and do you both come to aid me, for verily I know not of myself how to plead my cause. And at the first word, anon will they say, Away with you! Woe is I! How shall I be able to make answer when I know not one single word with the which to make explanation? But what avails this? It behoves me to go.'

And weeping, so that his face was all wet, he came before the abbot, and he knelt before him in tears. 'Sire,' said he, 'for God's sake, have mercy! Would you drive me hence? Tell me all your behests, and all your bidding will I do.'

Then said the abbot, 'This would I know, and I would that you answer me truly. Longwhiles have you been here, both winter and summer, and I would know by what services, and in what manner, you earn your bread.'

'Alas,' said he, 'well knew I that all would become known, and that when all my doings were known, no longer would any one have to do with me. Sire,' said he, 'now will I depart hence. Miserable am I, and miserable shall I be, for I never do aught that is right.'

Then the abbot made answer, 'Never have I said this, but I pray and demand of you, and further I command you, that, in virtue of obedience, you wholly reveal unto me your thoughts, and tell unto me in what manner you serve us in our monastery.'

'Sire,' said he, 'this will be my death! This command will kill me.'

Then he straightway unfolded unto him, howsoever grievous it was, his whole life, from beginning to end, in such sort that he left naught unsaid, just as I have told it unto you. And with clasped hands, and weeping, he told and rehearsed unto him everything, and, sighing, he kissed his feet.

And the holy abbot turned to him, and, all weeping, raised him up. And he kissed both his eyes. 'Brother,' said he, 'be silent now, for truly do I promise unto you that you shall be at peace with us. God grant that we may have your fellowship so long as we are deserving of it. Good friends shall we be. Fair, gentle brother, pray for me, and I will pray in return for you. And so I beseech and command of you, my sweet friend, that *you* forthwith render this service openly, just as you have done it, and still better even, if that you know how.'

'Sire,' said he, 'are you in good earnest?'

'Yea, truly,' said the abbot, 'and I charge you, on pain of penance, that you no longer doubt it.'

Then was the good man so *very* joyous, so the story relates, that he scarce knew what he did. But despite himself, he was constrained to rest, for he had become all pale. And when that he was come to himself again, he was so overcome of joy, that he was seized with a sickness, of the which in a short space he died. But very cheerfully did he perform his service without ceasing, morning and evening, by night and by day, so that not an hour did he miss, until that he fell ill. Then verily such great sickness laid hold upon him, that he could not move from his bed. But that which distressed him the most, since never did he make complaint of his sufferings, was that he could not pay for his sustenance, for the which he was much troubled in mind, and moreover he feared that his penance would be in vain, for that he did not busy himself with such service as was his wont, and *very* deserving of blame did he seem unto himself to be.

And the good man, who was so filled with anguish, besought of God that He would receive him before that more shame came unto him. For so much grieved was he that his doings were become known, that he could not endure it. And he was constrained to lie down forthwith.

And greatly did the holy abbot hold him in honour, and he and his monks went each hour to chant beside his bed, and such great delight had he in that which was sung to him of God, that in nowise did he long for Poitou, so much did it pleasure him to learn that all would be pardoned unto him. And he made a good confession and repentance, but nevertheless he was fearful. And, as I have told unto you, at last it came to pass that he died.

And the abbot was there, and all his monks, and the novices and good folk, who kept watch over him very humbly, and quite clearly did they see a right wondrous miracle. Of a truth they saw how that, at his death, the angels, and the Mother of God, and the archangels, were ranged around him. And there, also, were the very evil and cruel and violent devils, for to possess them of his soul, and no fancy is this. But to no purpose had they so long lain in wait for him, and striven so earnestly for him and pursued him, for now no power had they over his soul. And forthwith his soul quitted his body, but in nowise was it lost, for the Mother of God received it. And the holy angels who were there, sang for joy, and then they departed, and bare it to heaven, and this was seen of all the monks, and of all the others who were there.

Now they wholly knew and perceived that God willed it that the love of His good servant should no longer be hid, and that all should know and perceive his goodness, and they had great joy and great wonderment of it, and much honour did they pay to his body, and they carried it into the Church, and heartily did they celebrate the service of God. And they buried him with honour in the choir of the mother-church.

With great honour did they bury him, and then, like some saintly body, they kept watch over him. And anon, without concealing aught, the abbot told unto them all his doings, and his whole life, and all that he had seen in the crypt, even as you have heard it. And eagerly did the monks listen unto him. 'Certes,' said they, 'well may it be believed. It cannot be misdoubted, for the truth bears witness to it. Fully is the matter proven, and certain is it that he has done his penance.' And greatly did they rejoice together there.

Thus died the minstrel. Cheerfully did he tumble, and cheerfully did he serve, for the which he merited great honour, and none was there to compare unto him.

And the holy Fathers have related unto us that it thus befel this minstrel. Now let us pray God, without ceasing, that He may grant unto us so worthily to serve Him, that we may be deserving of His love. The story of the Tumbler is set forth.

Here endeth The Tumbler of Our Lady.

A sacrament is an outward sign of inward grace, and signs were particularly powerful for the medieval Church. Seven sacraments were identified as authoritative in the Western Church by the twelfth century: baptism, confirmation, penance, Holy Communion, holy orders, matrimony, and the anointing of the sick or dying.

E. F. Rogers, *Peter Lombard and the Sacramental System* (New York, 1917) pp. 79, 119, 134

Peter Lombard on the sacraments

II. What a sacrament is

'A sacrament is the sign of a sacred thing (res).' However, a sacred mystery is also called a sacrament, as the sacrament of divinity, so that a sacrament may be the sign of something sacred, and the sacred thing signified; but now we are considering a sacrament as a sign. – So, 'A sacrament is the visible form of an invisible grace.'

III. What a sign is

'But a sign, is the thing (res) behind the form which it wears to the senses, which brings by means of itself something else to our minds.'

I. Of the sacrament of the altar

'After the sacrament of baptism and of confirmation, follows the sacrament of the Eucharist. Through baptism we are cleansed, through the Eucharist, we are perfected in what is good.' Baptism extinguishes the fire of sins, the Eucharist restores us spiritually. Wherefore it is well called the Eucharist, that is, good grace, because in this sacrament not only is there increase of virtue and grace, but he who is the fount and source of all grace is received entire.

I. Of the manner of conversion

But if anyone asks what the nature of that conversion is, whether of form, or of substance, or of some other sort; I am not able to define. I know however that it is not of form, because the appearances of the things remain what they were before, and the taste and the weight. To some it seems to be a change of substance, for they say that substance is so converted into substance, that the latter becomes the former in essence. With this opinion the foregoing authorities seem to agree.

But others make the following objection to this opinion: if the substance of bread, they say, or of wine is converted in substance into the body or blood of Christ, a substance is daily made the body or blood of Christ, which previously was not; and today there is a body of Christ, which yesterday was not; and daily the body of Christ is increased and formed of material, of which at its conception it was not made. – To these we can reply as follows: that the body of Christ is not said to be made by the divine words in the sense that the very body formed when the Virgin conceived is formed again, but that the substance of bread or wine which formerly was not the body or blood of Christ, is, by the divine words, made his body and blood. And therefore priests are said to make the body and blood of Christ, because by their ministry the substance of bread is made the flesh, and the substance of wine is made the blood of Christ; yet nothing is added to his body or blood, nor is the body or blood of Christ increased.

Baptism was the sacrament of initiation into the Church; confirmation, generally administered by a bishop, completed an individual's adult relationship with the Church as infant baptism was the medieval norm.

D. Ayerst and A. Fisher, *Records of Christianity, vol. II: Christendom* (Oxford, 1977) pp. 215–216

Baptism: John Myrc, Instructions for Parish Priests in English (c.fourteenth century)

If any child mischance at home
And is baptised and given his name,
When it is brought to church to thee,
As it later ought to be,
Then must thou full subtilly
Ask of them that were thereby
How they did then in that case
When the child baptised was,
Whether the words were said aright
And not disordered in that plight . . .
English or Latin, whichever is saith,
It is sufficient to the faith
If the words are said in order.
'I christen thee or baptise thee
In the name of the Father, and the Son, and the Holy Spirit,
In nomine patris et filii et spiritus sancti.'

And though, I say, they often use
Sorry Latin in this wise:
'*In nomina patria et filia spiritus sanctia*'
Of these words take thou no heed;
The christening is good, no dread,
If their intention and their wit Was for to baptise it.
So that they hold the first syllable
The baptism is good, no fable.
Pa of patris, fi of filii, spi of spiritus sancti . . .
But if they said the words amiss –
In nomine filii et patris
Et spiritus sancti –
Then must thou, to make it true,
Say the service all anew.

D. Ayerst and A. Fisher, *Records of Christianity, vol. II: Christendom* (Oxford, 1977) pp. 216–217

Confirmation: John Myrc, Instructions for Parish Priests in English (c.fourteenth century)

The second sacrament is Confirming.
That the bishop gives to them that are baptised,
Gives through his power to them that take it
The grace and the gifts of the Holy Ghost,
To make them more stalwart than they were before
To stand against the fiend and deadly sin,
Which none has power to do but the bishop alone,
Who has the state and the stead of Christ's apostles.

Thomas Aquinas: on confirmation, from Summa Theologica, 3a, 62

The sacraments of the New Law are instituted to produce special effects of grace. Accordingly, where a special occasion occurs, there a special sacrament is provided. Things of sense bear the likeness of things of mind, and turning points in the life of the body have their equivalents in the life of the spirit. Coming of age ends a definite period; after that a man is capable of acting for himself: 'When I was a child, I spoke as a child, I understood as a child, I thought as a child; but when I became a man I put away childish things' (1 Cor. 13, 11). By the process of being born we receive bodily life, by the process of growing up we become adult. So it is in the life of the spirit. Born by baptism, we reach our full stature by confirmation.

Penance or confession began as a public act, but by the time of the Crusades the formal forgiving of sins was seen as a private moment between God and the penitent with the priest as intermediary. An elaborate literature of penitentials existed which helped or sometimes complicated the life of both priests and penitents.

J. T. McNeill and H. M. Gamer, *Medieval Handbooks of Penance: a translation of the principal libri poenitentiales and selections from related documents* (New York, 1938) pp. 397–398

Letter of Alcuin of York (d. 804) to the Goths of Septimania in which he urges confession to priests, which he has learned is neglected in the Gothic province (c.798)

If thou sayest: 'It is good to confess to the Lord': yet it is good to have a witness of this confession. . . . Greatly hast thou offended thy Lord, and wilt thou not have another reconciler except thyself? . . . Ought we not in sacred baptism to give to the priests of Christ confession of our faith and renunciation of Satan and so be washed from all sins through the priestly ministry, by the operation of divine grace? Why then in the second baptism of penance also ought we not to be absolved likewise with priestly help, the same divine grace being pitiful, from all the sins committed after the first baptism.

If sins are not exposed to the priests, why are the prayers of reconciliation written in the sacramentary? How shall the priest reconcile one whom he does not know to be a sinner?

From Alcuin's letter to the Irish, c.792–804

And no one, senior or junior, secular or monastic, man or woman shall hesitate to confess his sins and to make amends by penance for whatever he has done against God's will. It is better to have one man a witness of his sins unto the salvation of his soul than to look for the accusation of devilish deceit before the judge of all the ages and before the choirs of angels and the multitude of the whole human race. Indeed, while a man lives in this world confession and penance are fruitful; in the judgment that is to come there will forsooth be penance, but one that is not fruitful, since everyone shall be judged according to his works.

J. T. McNeill and H. M. Gamer, *Medieval Handbooks of Penance: a translation of the principal libri poenitentiales and selections from related documents* (New York, 1938) pp. 413–414

From the Council of Westminster, held under Hubert Walter, Archbishop of Canterbury (c.1200)

IV. Of penance

Since the more carefulness is to be applied to penance, which is the second plank after shipwreck, as reparation is the more necessary after fall, we, following the provisions of the sacred canons, command that priests diligently give heed in penance to the circumstances, the condition of the person, the magnitude of the fault, the time, the place, the cause, the delay made in [a state of] sin, the devotion of mind of the penitent. And let penance be so enjoined on the wife that she may [not] be placed under her husband's suspicion for any secret and heinous sin: the same is to be observed in the case of the husband. And let no priest after a lapse and before he confesses presume to approach the altar in order to celebrate. This we add to cure the covetousness of priests: that in penance masses be not enjoined on those who are not [themselves] priests. Saving in all things [the honour and privilege of the most Holy Roman Church].

D. Ayerst and A. Fisher, *Records of Christianity*, vol. II: *Christendom* (Oxford, 1977) pp. 217–218

Penance: John Myrc, Instructions for Parish Priests in English (c.fourteenth century)

> The third sacrament is called penance,
> That is soothfast forethinking we have of our sin,
> Without will or thought to turn again to it.
> And this must have three things if it be steadfast:
> One is sorrow of heart that we have sinned;
> Another is open shrift of our mouth, how we have sinned;
> And the third is right making amends for what we have sinned.
> These three with good will to forsake our sin,
> Cleanses and washes us of all kinds of sin.

Confession: John Myrc, Instructions for Parish Priests in English (c.fourteenth century)

> When a man hath done a sin,
> Look he lie not long therein,
> But anon that he him shrive
> Be it husband, be it wife,
> Lest he forget by Easter Day
> And out of mind it go away.
> Women that be with child also,
> Thou must teach them what to do.
> When their time is nearly come,
> Bid them do thus, all and some.
> Teach them to come and shrive them clean
> And also housel [receive Communion] themselves at e'en,
> For dread of peril that may befall
> In their travailing that come shall . . .
> And first when any shriven would be,
> Teach him to kneel down on his knee.
> The first thing thou must ask him then
> Is whether he be thy parishen.
> And if he answer and say nay
> Teach him to fare home on his way
> Unless he hath leave of his priest
> To be a-shriven where he list . . .
> For causes such as these, no nay,
> He may have leave to go his way: [i.e. go to a priest outside his parish]
> If he knew by ready token

That his shrift would be made open,
Or if himself had done a sin
With the priest's own sibling kin . . .
Their shrift lawfully you may hear
Of scholar, sailor, or passenger . . .
Teach him to kneel down on his knee,
Poor man or rich man whether he be;
Over your eyes then pull your hood,
And hear his shrift with mild mood.
But when a woman cometh to thee
Be sure her face thou dost not see,
But teach her to kneel down thee by,
And thy face somewhat from her wry.
Still as stone do thou sit,
And be careful not to spit
Nor cough at hearing of the sins,
Nor twist about with thy shins,
Lest she suppose you make that stir
For loathing what you hear from her . . .

N. P. Tanner (ed. and trans.) *Decrees of the Ecumenical Councils* (Georgetown, 1990) vol. 1, p. 245

Confession

21. On confession being made, and not revealed by the priest, and on communicating at least at Easter

All the faithful of either sex, after they have reached the age of discernment, should individually confess all their sins in a faithful manner to their own priest at least once a year, and let them take care to do what they can to perform the penance imposed on them. Let them reverently receive the sacrament of the eucharist at least at Easter unless they think, for a good reason and on the advice of their own priest, that they should abstain from receiving it for a time. Otherwise they shall be barred from entering a church during their lifetime and they shall be denied a Christian burial at death. Let this salutary decree be frequently published in churches, so that nobody may find the presence of an excuse in the blindness of ignorance. If any persons wish, for good reasons, to confess their sins to another priest let them first ask and obtain the permission of their own priest; for otherwise the other priest will not have the power to absolve or to bind them. The priest shall be discerning and prudent, so that like a skilled doctor he may pour wine and oil over the wounds of the injured one. Let him carefully inquire about the circumstances of both the sinner and the sin, so that he may prudently discern what sort of advice he ought to give and what remedy to apply, using various means to heal the sick person. Let him take the utmost care, however, not to betray the sinner at all by word or sign or in any other way. If the priest needs wise advice, let him seek it cautiously without any mention of the person concerned. For if anyone presumes to reveal a sin disclosed to him in confession, we decree that he is not only to be deposed from his priestly office but also to be confined to a strict monastery to do perpetual penance. . . .

D. Ayerst and A. Fisher, *Records of Christianity, vol. II: Christendom* (Oxford, 1977) pp. 219–220

Peter Abelard: advice to penitents

There are doctors so unskilled that it is dangerous or useless to entrust sick people to them. Similarly many priests may be found who, without faith or discretion, will lightly reveal sins confessed to them. To confess to such men is not only useless: it may be dangerous.

They do not pray with intention and are not worthy to have their petitions heard. They do not know the canon law and prescribe excessive penances. They often promise, as a consequence of those penances, a false security. The hopes they instil are disappointed. To quote the scriptures they are blind leading the blind and both will fall into a pit (Matt. 15, 14). Also, as we said, by turning confidences into gossip they arouse the indignation of their penitents. Instead of healing sin they cause it to break out afresh and those who hear them blabbing resolve to abstain from confession. The priest's betrayals of his vows, whether from anger or frivolity, is a serious sin against the Church. It also causes serious danger to the penitents.

On account of these dangers some penitents decide to go to others whom they consider better fitted to deal with their case, and you cannot blame them. Their resort to an abler physician is entirely reasonable. And if they can get their own priests to agree to the change it is even more commendable, for they make the change in a spirit of humble obedience. On the other hand arrogant priests may forbid it, feeling that it is an insult to their own competence if a better physician is asked for. But let the sick man who cares for his health insist on receiving the medicine he believes is the best, and the wiser counsel. If one is given a guide who turns out to be blind, one is not obliged to follow him into the pit. It is far better to choose a guide who can see.

J. T. McNeill and H. M. Gamer, *Medieval Handbooks of Penance: a translation of the principal libri poenitentiales and selections from related documents* (New York, 1938) pp. 353–354

From the penitential of Robert of Flamesbury (c.1207–1215)

(1) Penance is either public, or solemn, or private. Solemn penance is that which takes place at the beginning of the [Lenten] fast since the penitents are expelled from the church with solemnity, in ashes and sackcloth. This is also public because it takes place publicly. Public penance which is not solemn is that which takes place before the church without the above-mentioned solemnity, such as a pilgrimage. Private penance is that which is done privately every day in the presence of a priest. No one but a bishop or one authorized by him may enjoin solemn penance, except under necessity: in that case even a layman shall have power to reconcile the penitent. An ordinary priest enjoins public, just as [he enjoins] private, penance, and at any time.

(2) [The priest is warned against any negligence, favouritism, or irregularity in penance. If he cannot induce the confessant to undertake canonical penance he is to say to him]: Brother, it is necessary for thee to be punished in this life or in purgatory: but incomparably more severe will be the penalty of purgatory than any in this life. Behold, thy soul is in thy hands. Choose therefore for thyself whether to be sufficiently

punished in this life according to canonical or authentic penances or to await purgatory.

(3) Concerning remissions which consist in the building of churches or of bridges or in other matters, different men have different opinions as to how much value they have and for whom. But we, whatever is said, commend such remissions to all, especially to those who are burdened and weighed down with sins and penances.

The sacrament of Holy Communion, the Mass, presided over by a bishop or priest, was the central rite of the Christian Church in which the divine presence was brought to the people. An elaborate and stylised ritual emerged in the Latin language which had local variations with a common core.

P. Robinson (trans.) *The Writings of Saint Francis of Assisi* (Philadelphia, 1905; 1906) pp. 98–103

St Francis of Assisi

15. Confession and communion

We ought indeed to confess all our sins to a priest and receive from him the Body and Blood of our Lord Jesus Christ. He who does not eat His Flesh and does not drink His Blood cannot enter into the Kingdom of God. Let him, however, eat and drink worthily, because he who receives unworthily 'eateth and drinketh judgment to himself, not discerning the Body of the Lord' (I Cor. 11:29), – that is, not discerning it from other foods.

16. Reverence for Catholic life, the body and blood of Christ, and for priests

We ought also to fast and to abstain from vices and sins and from superfluity of food and drink, and to be Catholics. We ought also to visit Churches frequently and to reverence clerics not only for themselves, if they are sinners, but on account of their office and administration of the most holy Body and Blood of our Lord Jesus Christ, which they sacrifice on the altar and receive and administer to others. And let us all know for certain that no one can be saved except by the Blood of our Lord Jesus Christ and by the holy words of the Lord which clerics say and announce and distribute and they alone administer and not others. But religious especially, who have renounced the world, are bound to do more and greater things, but 'not to leave the other undone' (Luke 11:42)

J. Johnson, *A Collection of the Laws and Canons of the Church of England* (Oxford, 1850) vol. I, pp. 452–453.

Theodulf of Orleans (760–821): bishops, mass-priests, and the government of souls

1. Ye ought to know and always to bear in mind that the care of God's people is without doubt intrusted with us and the government of their souls; that we shall justly be punished at dooms-day for all those that perish through our neglect; and that we are

to receive the reward of eternal life for them that we have gained to God with our example and doctrine. To us it is said by our Lord, 'ye are the salt of the earth.' If then Christian people are God's meat, and we the salt; then shall the people by the divine assistance by our means be with pleasure enjoyed by God. And ye ought to know, that your order is the second after ours and the next to us. As the bishops are in the stead of the Apostles in the assembly of the saints; so are the mass-priests in the stead of Christ's disciples. The bishops have the order of Aaron, the mass-priests the order of his sons; for it behoves you always to be mindful how high the dignity of the order [is,] and the consecration, and the anointing of your hand, which ye received from the bishop when ye took orders; that ye may never forfeit so high a favour, and never defile, by sinning, the hands that have been anointed with so holy an unction; but that ye keep your heart and body in purity, give all people an example to live well, and teach those over whom ye are, the right way to the kingdom of heaven.

D. N. Orlandi and H. J. Robinson (eds and trans.) *Sermons* (Siena, 1920) pp. 5ff.

Bernardine of Siena (1380–1444) on preaching and the Mass

O how many of you here present this morning will say: I knew not what I did, I thought I did well while rather I was doing evil; and remembering this sermon they will say to themselves: O now am I enlightened as to what I should do, addressing these words to God: '*Verbum tuum lucerna mea est* Thy word is my enlightenment' (Ps. 119:105; D. 118:105). And when thou art about to make some contract in thy business, thou wilt pause first to think, saying: what said Friar Bernardine of such matters? He told me, in such matters you must do thus or thus; that is evil, that is not commendable, but this is good, and this I wish to do. And in this wise it will befall thee merely because of the words which thou hast heard preached to thee. But tell me: what would become of this world, I mean of the Christian faith, if there were no preaching? Within a very little our faith would have perished, for we should believe nothing of that which we now believe. And because of this Holy Church hath ordered that every Sunday there shall be preaching, much or little, but some preaching. And she hath ordered thee to go to hear Mass, and if of these two duties thou canst perform but one, that is either hear Mass or hear the preaching, thou shouldst rather lose Mass and hear the preaching; since the reason for this doth appear plainly, thou dost not so endanger thy soul by not hearing Mass as by not listening to the preaching. Canst thou not perceive and understand without further argument? For tell me, should you believe in the Blessed Sacrament of the Altar if this had not been preached in holy sermons? Thou hast learned to believe in the Mass only from preaching. More than this, how ever shouldst thou have known what sin is, if not from preaching? What wouldst thou know of hell, if there were no preaching? What wouldst thou know of any good work, or how thou shouldst perform it, if not from preaching, or what wouldst thou know of the glories of Heaven? All these things that thou knowest came to thee through the words heard by thine ears, and it is in this wise that thou comest by knowledge to faith, and that which thou knowest and which thou hast hath come all through the word of God. And this is a sovereign rule, that which we have of the faith of Jesus Christ hath come merely through preaching. And this faith will never perish while it shall be preached.

D. Ayerst and A. Fisher, *Records of Christianity, vol. II: Christendom* (Oxford, 1977) pp. 222–223

Thomas Aquinas: the body and blood of Christ, from Summa Theologica, III, Q. 75, Articles 4, 5 (c.1270)

On whether bread can be converted into the body of Christ: I reply that this conversion is not like natural conversions, but is wholly supernatural, effected solely by the power of God. All conversion which takes place according to the laws of nature is a change in form. . . . But God can produce not only a formal conversion, i.e. the superseding of one form by another in the same subject, but the conversion of the whole being, i.e. the conversion of the whole 'substance' of A into the whole 'substance' of B. And this is done in this sacrament by the power of God, for the whole 'substance' of bread is converted into the whole 'substance' of Christ's body. . . . Hence this conversion is properly called transubstantiation.

On whether in this sacrament the 'accidents' of bread and wine remain after the conversion: I reply that it is apparent to sense that after consecration all the 'accidents' of bread and wine remain. And this indeed happens with reason, by divine providence. First, because it is not customary but abhorrent for men to eat man's flesh and to drink man's blood. Therefore Christ's flesh and blood are set before us to be taken under the appearances of those things which are of frequent use, namely bread and wine. Secondly, lest this sacrament should be mocked at by the infidels, if we ate our Lord under his proper appearance. Thirdly, in order that, while we take the Lord's body and blood invisibly, this fact may avail towards the merit of faith.

Rites of passage were made solemn in sacramental form and the sacrament of marriage was seen as a making holy of the sexual relationship between men and women. Marriage was seen as a lifelong commitment and a public affirmation of a couple's desire to live together.

D. Ayerst and A. Fisher, *Records of Christianity, vol. II: Christendom* (Oxford, 1977) pp. 230–232

Thomas Aquinas: marriage

Married friendship is useful, delightful, and honourable. It serves to provide for domestic life. It brings the delight of sex, and the physical pleasure animals have. And if husband and wife are fair to one another, their friendship is expressed in virtue proper to them both, rendering it mutually agreeable.

Peter Abelard: the virtue and delight of sex, from Ethics

The mere desire to do something immoral is never to be called a sin, but only the consent to it is sinful. We consent to the immorality when we do not draw ourselves back from such a deed, and are prepared to complete it should opportunity offer. He who is discovered in this intention, though he has not completed the deed, is already guilty in the eyes of God, for he is trying hard to sin and, as the blessed Augustine reminds us, he performs as much in his own mind as if he were caught in the act.

Some are highly indignant when we assert that the act of sinning adds no further to the guilt in God's eyes. They argue that in this act a certain delight accrues which increases the sin, as in sexual intercourse or indulgence in food. Their statement is absurd unless they can prove that physical pleasure of this kind is a sin in itself, and that such pleasure cannot be taken without committing a sin. If it is as they say, then no one is permitted to enjoy physical pleasure. Married couples do not avoid sin when they take their physical rights, nor does a man who eats his own fruits with relish. . . .

God, the creator of food and of the bodies that receive it, would be guilty for having instilled flavours which must involve the ignorant tasters in sin. Yet why did he supply such things for our consumption or let them be consumed, if it is impossible for us to eat them without sinning? How can there be sin in doing what is allowed? If things which were once unlawful and forbidden are later made lawful and allowed, they can be done entirely without sin. For instance, eating pork and much else which was once forbidden to Jews are now allowed to Christians. When Jews become Christians they gladly eat of these foods their law had prohibited, and we can only defend the rightness of their act by affirming that this freedom has been given to them by God. . . . Who then shall say that a man sins in a matter which has been made lawful for him by divine permission? If the marriage-bed or the eating of delicious foods was permitted from the first day of our creation, when we lived in Paradise without sin, who can prove that we sin in these pleasures so long as we do not pass the permitted limits?

Another objection is that sexual intercourse in marriage and the eating of delicious food are only allowed if they are done without pleasure. If this is so, they are allowed to be done in a way in which they never can be done. Such a concession is not reasonable. By what reasoning did the ancient law enforce marriage so that each should leave his seed to Israel? Or how did the apostle order wives to fulfil the mutual debt (1 Cor. 7, 3–5) if these acts could not be done without sinning? . . . I think it is clear that no natural physical delight can be accounted a sin, nor can man be guilty to delight in what, when it is done, must involve the feeling of pleasure.

Those called to office in the Church, from the bishop down to the simple clerk in minor orders, had appropriate rites and those above deacon were described as ordained. Like marriage, ordination was for life, and for most of the medieval period implied a consecration to celibacy.

D. Ayerst and A. Fisher, *Records of Christianity, vol. II: Christendom* (Oxford, 1977) p. 288

Ordination, by Walter Stapledon, Bishop of Exeter, 1315

September 20 – *Exeter*. Ordination held in Exeter Cathedral. Examiners for sub-deacons, deacons, and priests Masters R. de Coletone, then Official of the Lord Bishop; and N. de Hele; for the acolytes, J. de Lancestone; for those to receive the first tonsure, W. de Wolleghe.

Numbers ordained:

Boys given the first tonsure – 71

Acolytes 25 (including 1 with dispensation for his illegitimacy; 2 Dominican friars)
Coristes 6 (including 1 Franciscan, 1 Canon Regular)
Sub-deacons 28 (including 1 Dominican; 3 Canons Regular; 3 Rectors)
Deacons 31 (including 3 Canons Regular; 1 Rector)
Priests 44 (including 2 Monks of Ford; 3 Rectors; 1 Vicar)

At the moment of departure from this life the Church had an appropriate ceremony which prepared the dying for the next world which was seen as the fuller life.

Proficiscere

Go forth, Christian soul, out of this world. Go in the name of God the Father Almighty who created you. Go in the name of Jesus Christ, Son of the living God, who suffered for you. Go in the name of the Holy Spirit, who was given for you. Go in the name of Mary, Virgin Mother of God; in the name of blessed Joseph; in the name of the angels, archangels, thrones and dominations; in the name of the patriarchs and prophets; of the holy apostles and evangelists; of the holy martyrs, confessors, monks and hermits; of the holy virgins, and of all the Saints of God. May peace be yours this day, and may your home be in heaven . . .

Alongside the seven sacraments were many other signs and 'sacramentals' which were given by the Church, including various blessings and exorcisms.

F. E. Warren (trans.) *The Sarum Missal in English* (1913) part 1, pp. 13–15

Exorcism of water: blessing of salt and water

Blessing of salt and water. On all Sundays throughout the year, after prime and the chapter, the blessing of salt and water shall take place, at the step of the quire, by a priest, after the following manner.

I exorcize thee, O creature of salt by the living God, by the true God, by the holy God, by the God who commanded thee to be cast into the water by Elisha the prophet that the barrenness of the water might be healed, that thou mayest become salt [*Here shall the priest look at the salt*] exorcized for the salvation of them that believe, and that thou mayest be salvation of soul and body to all that take thee; and from that place where thou shalt have been sprinkled, let every delusion and wickedness, or craft of devilish cunning, when adjured, flee and depart. Through him who shall come to judge the quick and the dead and the world by fire. R. Amen.

The next collect follows without 'The Lord be with you,' *and only with* 'Let us pray.'

Collect

Almighty everlasting God, we humbly implore thy boundless loving-kindness [*Here the priest shall look at the salt*] that of thy goodness thou wouldest deign to bless and sanctify this creature of salt, which thou hast given for the use of mankind; that it may be unto all who partake of it health of mind and body; that whatsoever shall have been touched or sprinkled with it may be freed from all uncleanness, and from all assault of spiritual wickedness. Through our Lord Jesus Christ, thy Son, who liveth and reigneth with thee in the unity of the Holy Ghost, God, world without end. Amen.

Here follows the exorcism of the water.

I exorcize thee, O creature of water, in the name of God the Father almighty, and in the name of Jesus Christ his Son our Lord, and in the power of the Holy Ghost; that thou mayest become water exorcized for putting to flight all power of the enemy; that they mayest have power to root out and transplant the enemy himself with his apostate angels, by the power of the same Jesus Christ our Lord; who shall come to judge the quick and the dead and the world by fire.

R. Amen.

The next collect follows without 'The Lord be with you,' *but with* 'Let us pray.'

Collect

O God, who for the salvation of mankind has hidden [one of thy] greatest sacraments in the element of water graciously hearken unto our invocations, and pour upon this element [*Here shall the priest look upon the water*] prepared for divers purifications the power of thy blessing that this thy creature, serving in thy mysteries, may acquire the effectual power of divine grace for casting out devils, and for driving away diseases; and that on whatsoever in the houses or dwelling places of the faithful this water shall have been sprinkled, it may be freed from all uncleanness, and may be delivered from hurt. Let no pestilential spirit, no corrupting air, linger there. Let all the insidious attacks of the lurking enemy be dissipated; and if there be aught which threatens the safety or the peace of the inhabitants, let it be driven away by the sprinkling of this water, so that saved by the invocation of thy holy name they may be defended from all assaults. Through our Lord Jesus Christ thy Son, who liveth and reigneth with thee in the unity of the Holy Ghost, God, world without end.

Here shall the priest cast salt into the water in the form of a cross, saying thus, without inflection:

Let this mixture of salt and water alike be made in the name of the Father, and of the Son, and of the Holy Ghost. Amen.
V. The Lord be with you.
R. And with thy spirit. Let us pray.

Collect

O God, the author of unconquered might, and the king of unconquerable empire, who ever triumphest magnificently, who repressest the strength of adverse power, and overcomest the rage of the roaring adversary, and by thy might subduest the onslaughts of iniquity; with fear and humility we entreat and beseech thee, O Lord, that thou wouldest deign to accept [*Here shall he look upon the salt mixed with water*] this creature of salt and water; graciously illumine it, and by thy love and by thy pity sanctify it; that whenever it shall have been sprinkled, by the invocation of thy holy name, every attack of the unclean spirit may be parried, and dread of the venomous serpent may be driven far away; and may the presence of the Holy Ghost be vouchsafed to be with us, as we ask thy mercy in every place, through our Lord Jesus Christ thy Son.

While the water is being sprinkled the following Anthem shall be sung:

Thou shalt purge me, O Lord, with hyssop, and I shall be clean thou shalt wash me, and I shall be whiter than snow.

Ps. Have mercy upon me, O God, after thy great goodness.

Thou shalt purge me, etc. [Ps. li. 7, 1]

V. And according to the multitude of thy mercies, do away mine offences.

Thou shalt purge me, etc.

V. Glory be to the Father, etc. As it was, etc.

To be repeated. Thou shalt wash me, and I shall be whiter than snow.

Further Reading

C.W. Bynum, *Holy Feast and Holy Fast: the religious significance of food to medieval women* (Berkeley, 1986).

E. Duffy, *The Stripping of the Altars: traditional religion in England, 1400–1580* (London, 1992).

C. Harper-Bill, *The Pre-reformation Church in England, 1400–1530* (Harlow, 1989).

A. Jones, *A Thousand Years of the English Parish* (London, 2000).

R. Marks, *Image and Devotion in Late Medieval England* (Stroud, 2004).

G. R. Owst, *Preaching in Medieval England* (Cambridge, 1926).

M. Rubin, *Corpus Christi: the eucharist in late medieval culture* (Cambridge, 1991).

R. N. Swanson, *Catholic England: faith, religion and observance before the Reformation* (Manchester, 1993).

7 Theology

The intellectual life of the medieval world was rich in its diversity, and theology, the study of God, was seen as the high point of scholarship. The writing of theology was closely linked to its teaching and preaching, and great corpus of theological writing emerged. Medieval theology was deeply influenced by classical learning. The writings of the Patristic period, especially those of Augustine of Hippo (d. 430), remained standard texts throughout the period.

R. N. Bosley and M. M. Tweedale, *Basic Issues in Philosophy: selected readings presenting the interactive discourses among the major figures* (Ontario, 1999) pp. 512–514

St Augustine: from The Way of Life of the Catholic Church

What is the supreme good for human beings?

CHAPTER 3

(4) Let us inquire, then, how according to reason human beings ought to live. Certainly, we all wish to live happily. There is no human being who would not assent to this statement almost before it is uttered. However, in my opinion, neither one who lacks what he loves can be called happy, whatever it be, nor one who has what he loves if it be harmful, nor one who does not love what he has although it be the best. For he who desires what he cannot obtain is tormented, and he who has attained what he should not have desired is deceived, while he who does not desire what he should seek to attain is diseased. To souls such as these, there remains nothing but misery, and since misery and happiness are not accustomed to dwell in the same person simultaneously, none of these persons can be happy.

As I see it, however, a fourth alternative remains in which the happy life may be found – when that which is best for a human being is both loved and possessed. For what else is meant by enjoyment but the possession of what one loves? But no one is happy who does not enjoy what is supremely good for human beings, and whoever does enjoy it is not unhappy. We must possess our supreme good, therefore, if we intend to live happily.

(5) It follows that we must seek to discover what is the supreme good for human beings, and it cannot, of course, be anything inferior to humans themselves; for whoever strives after something inferior to themself becomes themself inferior. But all human beings are obliged to seek what is best. Therefore, the supreme good for human beings is not inferior to human beings.

Will it then perhaps be something similar to human beings themselves? It might well be so, provided there is nothing superior to human beings that they can enjoy. If, however, we find something that is both more perfect than human beings and which can be attained by the one loving it, who would doubt that they should, in order to be happy, strive to possess this thing, which is more excellent than they themselves who seek it? For if happiness is the possession of a good than which there is no greater, and this is what we call the supreme good, how can a person be said to be happy who has not yet attained their supreme good? Or how can it be called the supreme good if there is something better that they can attain? Such being the case, it follows that one cannot lose it against their will, for no one can be confident of a good they know can be snatched from them even though they wish to keep and cherish it. And if they lack this confidence in the good which they enjoy, how can they, in such fear of loss, be happy?

(6) Let us, then, attempt to discover what is better than human beings. And this will be very difficult unless we first discuss what human beings themselves are. But I do not think I should be expected to give a definition of human being here. Rather, it seems to me that since nearly everyone agrees (or at least, and it is sufficient, those with whom I am now dealing agree) that we are composed of body and soul, what should be determined at this point is what human beings themselves are. Of the two which I have mentioned, are they body alone or soul alone? For although these are two things, soul and body, and neither could be called a human being were the other not present (for the body would not be a human being if there were no soul, nor would the soul be a human being were there no body animated by it), it might happen, nevertheless, that one of these would be looked upon and be spoken of as a human being.

What do we call 'human being', then? Is the human a soul and body like a centaur or two horses harnessed together? Or shall we call him the body alone in the service of a governing soul, as is the case when we give the name lamp, not to the vessel and flame together, but to the vessel alone on account of the flame within it? Or shall we say that a human is nothing but the soul, inasmuch as it rules the body, just as we say that the horseman is not the horse and human together, but the human alone from the fact that he guides the horse? This is a difficult problem to solve, or, at any rate, even if its solution were simple, it would require a lengthy explanation involving an expense of time and labour which would not profit us here. For whether it be both body and soul or soul alone that goes by the name of 'human being,' that is not the supreme good for human beings which constitutes the supreme good of the body. But whatever is the highest good either of body and soul together or of the soul alone, that is the supreme good for human beings.

(7) If we ask what is the supreme good of the body, reason compels us to admit it is whatever causes the body to be at its best. But of all the things that give vigour to the body, none is better nor more important than the soul. Hence, the supreme good of the body is not sensual pleasure, nor absence of pain, nor strength, nor beauty, nor swiftness, nor whatever else is ordinarily numbered among the goods of the body, but the soul alone. For by its very presence, the soul provides the body with all the things we have enumerated and with that which excels them all besides, namely, life. Therefore, it does not seem to me that the soul is the supreme good for human beings, whether we call a human being soul and body together, or soul alone. For, as reason declares, the greatest good of the body is that which is better than the body and by which the body is given life and vigour, so, too, whether the body and soul together be the human being or the soul alone, we must still find out whether there is anything beyond the soul itself

which, when sought after, makes the soul more perfect in its own order. If we can discover some such thing, all of our doubts will be removed, for it will unquestionably merit the name of the supreme good for human beings.

(8) If the body be a human being, it cannot be denied that the supreme good for human beings is the soul. But, surely, when it is a question of morals – when we ask what kind of life we must lead in order to attain happiness – the commandments are not for the body, and we are not concerned with bodily discipline. In a word, good morals pertain to that part of us which inquires and learns, and these are acts of the soul. Therefore, when we are dealing with the attainment of virtue, the question is not one which concerns the body. But if it follows, as it does, that the body when ruled by a virtuous soul is ruled both better and more worthily and is at its best because of the perfection of the soul ruling it rightly, then that which perfects the soul will be the supreme good for human beings even though we call the body a human being. For if at my command the charioteer feeds and properly manages the horses in his care, and enjoys my generosity in proportion as he is obedient to me, who can deny that not only the charioteer but the horses, too, owe their well being to me? And so, whether body alone, or soul alone, or both together be the human being, the important thing, it seems to me, is to discover what makes the soul perfect, for when this is attained, a man cannot but be perfect, or at least much better than if it were lacking to him.

CHAPTER 6

(9) No one disputes the fact that virtue perfects the soul, but the question might well be asked as to whether virtue can exist by itself or only in the soul. This is another of those profound questions demanding lengthy discussion, but perhaps a summary will be adequate for our purpose. And I hope that God will grant His assistance, so that, to the extent our weakness of mind permits, we may treat this subject not only clearly but briefly as well.

Whichever it be – whether virtue can exist by itself without the soul, or whether it cannot exist except in the soul – doubtless, the soul seeks after something in order to attain virtue, and this must be either itself, or virtue, or some third thing. If the soul pursues itself in seeking virtue, it pursues something foolish, since the soul itself is foolish before it has acquired virtue. And since the supreme desire of all who seek is to attain what they are seeking, in this case either the soul must not wish to attain what it seeks, and there is nothing more absurd nor perverse than this, or, in pursuing its foolish self, it attains the very foolishness from which it flees. But if, in its desire to attain virtue, it seeks after it, how can it seek what does not exist? Or how can it desire to attain what it already has? Therefore, either virtue is outside the soul, or, if we must reserve the name of virtue only for that disposition or quality of the wise soul which cannot exist except in the soul, it remains that the soul must pursue something else in order that virtue may arise within itself. For neither by pursuing nothing nor by pursuing foolishness can the soul, in my opinion, reach wisdom.

(10) Consequently, this something else, through the seeking of which the soul becomes possessed of virtue and wisdom, is either a wise person or God. But as has been said above, it must be of such a nature that we cannot lose it against our will. Now who would hesitate to admit that a wise person, should we be satisfied to follow after him, can be taken from us, not only against our will, but even in spite of our resistance?

Only God remains, therefore. If we follow after Him, we live well; if we reach Him, we live not only well but happily. As for those who may deny that God exists, I cannot concern myself with arguments by which to persuade them, for I am not even sure that we ought to enter into discussion with them at all. To do so, in any event, would necessitate starting out all over again with a different approach, a different method, and different arguments from those we have taken up at present. I am now concerned only with those who do not deny God's existence and who, besides, acknowledge that He is not indifferent to human affairs. For I cannot believe there is anyone who considers himself religious who does not hold at least that Divine Providence looks after our souls.

The issues discussed by the Patristic writers were developed particularly in the eleventh and twelfth centuries by monastic theologians like St Anselm (d. 1109), who combined a deep reverence for the Scriptures with an acute logical mind.

Bosley and Tweedale, *Philosophy*, pp. 105–106

St Anselm: the being 'a greater than which cannot be thought': Proslogion, chs 1–4

Chapter 1

. . . O Lord, I acknowledge and give thanks that You created in me Your image so that I may remember, contemplate, and love You. But this image has been so effaced by the abrasion of transgressions, so hidden from sight by the dark billows of sin, that unless You renew and refashion it, it cannot do what it was created to do. Lord, I do not attempt to comprehend Your sublimity, because my intellect is not at all equal to such a task. But I yearn to understand some measure of Your truth, which my heart believes and loves. For I do not seek to understand in order to believe but I believe in order to understand. For I believe even this: that I shall not understand unless I believe.

Chapter 2

Therefore, Lord, Giver of understanding to faith, grant me to understand – to the degree You deem best – that You exist, as we believe, and that You are what we believe You to be. Indeed, we believe You to be something than which nothing greater can be thought. Is there, then, no such nature as You, for the Fool has said in his heart that God does not exist? But surely when this very Fool hears the words 'something than which nothing greater can be thought,' he understands what he hears. And what he understands is in his understanding, even if he does not understand [judge] it to exist. Indeed, for a thing to be in the understanding is different from understanding [judging] that this thing exists. For when an artist envisions what he is about to paint, he has it in his understanding, but he does not yet understand [judge] that there exists what he has not yet painted. But after he has painted it, he has it in his understanding and he understands [judges] that what he has painted exists. So even the Fool is convinced that something than which nothing greater can be thought exists at least in his understanding; for when he hears of this being, he understands [what he hears], and whatever is understood is in the understanding. But surely that than which a greater cannot be thought cannot be only in the understanding. For if it were only in the understanding, it could be thought to exist also in reality – which is greater [than existing only in the understanding]. Therefore, if that than which a greater cannot be thought existed only in the understanding, then that than which a greater cannot be thought would be that than which a greater can be thought! But surely this conclusion is impossible. Hence, without doubt, something than which a greater cannot be thought exists both in the understanding and in reality.

Chapter 3: God cannot be thought not to exist.

Assuredly, this being exists so truly that it cannot even be thought not to exist. For there can be thought to exist something whose non-existence is inconceivable; and this thing is greater than anything whose non-existence is conceivable. Therefore, if that than which a greater cannot be thought could be thought not to exist, then that than which a greater cannot be thought would not be that than which a greater cannot be thought – a contradiction. Hence, something than which a greater cannot be thought exists so truly that it cannot even be thought not to exist.

And You are this being, O Lord our God. Therefore, Lord my God, You exist so truly [really] that You cannot even be thought not to exist. And this is rightly the case. For if any mind could conceive of something better than You, the creature would rise above the Creator and would sit in judgment over the Creator – an utterly preposterous consequence. Indeed, except for You alone, whatever else exists can be conceived not to exist. Therefore, You alone exist most truly [really] of all and thus most greatly of all; for whatever else there is does not exist as truly [really] as You and thus does not exist as much as do You. Since, then, it is so readily clear to a rational mind that You exist most greatly of all, why did the Fool say in his heart that God does not exist? Why indeed except because he is foolish and simple!

Chapter 4: How the Fool said in his heart what cannot be thought.

Yet, since to say something in one's heart is to think it, how did the Fool say in his heart what he was not able to think, or how was he unable to think what he did say in his heart? Now, if he really – rather, since he really – both thought [what he did] because he said it in his heart and did not say it in his heart because he was unable to think it, then there is not merely one sense in which something is said in one's heart, or is thought. For in one sense an object is thought when the word signifying it is thought, and in another when what the object [i.e. its essence] is understood. Thus, in the first sense but not at all in the second, God can be thought not to exist. Indeed, no one who understands what God is can think that God does not exist, even though he says these words [viz. 'God does not exist'] in his heart either meaninglessly or else bizarrely. For God is that than which a greater cannot be thought. Anyone who comprehends (*bene intelligit*) this, surely understands (*intelligit*) that God so exists that He cannot even conceivably not exist. Therefore, anyone who understands that this is the manner in which God exists cannot think that He does not exist.

I thank You, good Lord, I thank You that what at first I believed through Your giving, now by Your enlightening I so understand that even if I did not want to believe that You exist, I could not fail to understand [that You exist].

Peter Abelard (d. c.1142) questioned the beliefs and arguments of his predecessors and was particularly concerned with the question of meaning within language. Like all medieval theologians, Abelard did not want to create a conflict between faith and reason but rather establish a lucid exploration of the intellectual basis of faith. Ultimately, like the monastic theologians who went before him, his life was a prolonged search for God.

A. O. Norton, *Readings in the History of Education* (Cambridge MA, 1909) pp. 19–20, 21

Peter Abelard (1079–1142): Sic et Non

In truth, constant or frequent questioning is the first key to wisdom; and it is, indeed, to the acquiring of this [habit of] questioning with absorbing eagerness that the famous philosopher, Aristotle, the most clear sighted of all, urges the studious when he says: 'It is perhaps difficult to speak confidently in matters of this sort unless they have often been investigated. Indeed, to doubt in special cases will not be without advantage.' For through doubting we come to inquiry and through inquiry we perceive the truth. As the Truth Himself says: 'Seek and ye shall find, knock and it shall be opened unto you.' And He also, instructing us by His own example, about the twelfth year of His life wished to be found sitting in the midst of the doctors, asking them questions, exhibiting to us by His asking of questions the appearance of a pupil, rather than, by preaching, that of a teacher, although there is in Him, nevertheless, the full and perfect wisdom of God.

Now when a number of quotations from [various] writings are introduced they spur on the reader and allure him into seeking the truth in proportion as the authority of the writing itself is commended. . . .

In accordance, then, with these forecasts it is our pleasure to collect different sayings of the holy Fathers as we planned, just as they have come to mind, suggesting (as they do) some questioning from their apparent disagreement, in order that they may stimulate tender readers to the utmost effort in seeking the truth and may make them keener as the result of their seeking. . . .

1 That faith is based upon reason, *et contra.*
6 That God is tripartite, *et contra.*
8 That in the Trinity it is not to be stated that there is more than one Eternal being, *et contra.*
14 That the Son is without beginning, *et contra.*
32 That to God all things are possible, *et non.*
56 That by sinning man lost free will, *et non.*
69 That the Son of God was predestinated, *et contra.*
79 That Christ was a deceiver, *et non.*
122 That everybody should be allowed to marry, *et contra.*

Scholasticism was a method which proceeded to its conclusions by a series of questions. Scholastics attempted to draw up lists of contradictory statements and through an understanding of the underlying arguments to reach an inner truth. Scholasticism flourished from the eleventh century to the Reformation. Its roots were in the Christian tradition and also in the rediscovery of the texts of Aristotle (d. 322 BC) especially through such writers as the Islamic Avicenna (d. 1037). The most important of the Scholastic theologians was the Dominican, Thomas Aquinas (d. 1274) whose life work was to identify the proper place of faith and reason in theological enquiry, an enquiry in which, as with all medieval theologians, the place of revelation was counted as paramount.

Bosley and Tweedale, *Philosophy*, pp. 114–117

St Thomas Aquinas, the five ways: Summa Theologiae

Does God exist?

In the third article we proceed as follows:

[1] It seems that God does not exist, because if one of two contraries were infinite it would totally destroy the other. But by the name 'God' we understand what is an infinite good. If, then, God existed, we would not find any evil existing. But we do find evil in the world. Therefore, God does not exist.

[2] Besides, what can be accounted for by a few principles is not to be accounted for by more. But it seems that all the things which we find in the world can be accounted for by other principles on the supposition that God does not exist. For natural things are traced back to the principle which is their nature, while things that result from purpose are traced back to the principle which is human reason or will. There is, then, no necessity for claiming that God exists.

But against the above: In Exodus we find God saying, 'I am who am.'

Reply: It should be said that it is possible to prove that God exists in five ways:

The first and more evident way is one which is based in motion. For it is obvious and apparent to the senses that some things in this world are in motion. But everything which is in motion is moved by something else. For something is in motion only in virtue of the fact that it has a potential for that toward which it is moving. But something moves something by being actual. Now, something can be taken from potency into act only by something actual. For example, something actually hot, like a fire, makes a piece of wood, which is potentially hot, be actually hot, and in so doing it moves and alters the stick. However, it is not possible that one and the same item is simultaneously actual and potential in respect of the same thing; rather this can only occur in respect of different things. For what is actually hot cannot at the same time be potentially hot; rather it is at that time potentially cold. Therefore, it is impossible that one and the same thing be both mover and moved in respect of the same motion, or that it put itself in motion. Thus it is necessary that everything which is in motion is moved by something else. Then, if that by which it is moved is itself in motion, it is necessary that it too be moved by something else. But there can be no infinite regress here, because, if there were, there would not be a first mover and consequently neither any other mover, since secondary movers only move things in virtue of the fact that they themselves are moved by the first mover. For example, a stick will not move anything unless because it is moved by a hand. Therefore, we have to arrive at some first mover which is not moved by anything, and this everybody thinks is God.

The second way derives from the notion of an efficient cause. For in the realm of things perceivable by the senses we discover that there is an ordering of efficient causes. Nevertheless, we do not find there, nor is it possible, that something is an efficient cause of itself, because if it were it would exist before itself, which is impossible. Moreover, there cannot be an infinite regress in efficient causes, for in every case of efficient causes in an ordered series the first is the cause of the intermediary and the intermediary is the cause of the last (allowing that the intermediary can be several causes or just one). Now if the cause is taken away, so is the effect. Therefore, if in these efficient causes there was no first, there would not be the last nor the intermediary. But if there is an infinite regress in efficient causes there will be no first efficient cause, and thus there will not be the final effect nor any intermediary efficient causes, which is obviously false. Therefore it is necessary to posit a first efficient cause, which everybody calls 'God.'

The third way is based in possibility and necessity and runs as follows: Among things we discover some for which both existing and not existing are possible, since some things are found to be generated and destroyed and as a result to exist and not to exist. But it is impossible that everything which exists is of this sort, because that for which not existing is possible, at some time does not exist. If then everything is such that not existing is possible for it, at some time there was nothing really existing. But if this were true, then right now there would be nothing, since what is not in existence begins to exist only in virtue of something which exists. If, then, there was nothing in existence, it was impossible for anything to begin to exist, and thus there would be nothing now, which is obviously false. Therefore, it is not the case that all beings are possible ones; rather, there must be something in reality that is necessary. Now every necessary thing either has its necessity caused by something else, or not. Nor is it possible to have an infinite regress in necessary things whose necessity has a cause, just as neither in efficient causes, as was shown. Therefore, we must posit something which is necessary through itself and does not have its necessity caused by something else, but which is a cause of necessity in other things. [And this everybody says is God.]

The fourth way is based in the degrees which we find in things. For in things we find that something is more or less good and true and noble, and so on for other cases of this sort. But different things are said to be more or less by the fact that they vary in their nearness to something which is a maximum. For example, that is more hot which comes closer to what is maximally hot. There is, then, something which is most true, most good, and most noble, and as a result is maximally a being; for, according to *Metaphysics II*, the things that are maximally true are maximally beings. Now, 'what is a maximum in some genus is the cause of everything in that genus,' for example, 'fire which is maximally hot is the cause of everything that is hot,' as he says in that same book. Therefore, there is something which is the cause of existence, and goodness, and every perfection in all things, and this we say is God.

The fifth way is based in the governance of things. For we see that some things which lack cognition, viz. natural bodies [i.e. the elemental bodies], function for an end. This is evident from the fact that they always or very frequently function in the same way and end up resulting in what is best. From this it is clear that it is not by chance but by purpose that they arrive at the end. But now those things which lack cognition do not tend towards an end unless they are directed by something with knowledge and intelligence, just as the arrow is directed by the archer. Therefore, there is some intelligent being who directs all natural things to an end, and this being we say is God.

To the first [1], then, we should say what Augustine says in Enchiridion: 'Since He is the highest good, God would never permit anything bad in his works if He were not omnipotent and good to the point of making even out of evil something good.' It belongs then to the infinite goodness of God that He allows evil to exist and from it brings forth good.

To the second [2], it should be said that, since a nature functions for a determinate end under the direction of some higher agent, it is necessary that the things which come to be by nature are also traced back to God as to a first cause. Likewise, also the things that come to be by purpose have to be traced back to some higher cause which is not human reason or will, for the latter are changeable and subject to failure, and everything subject to motion and capable of failure must be traced back to some first principle that is immobile and necessary through itself, as was shown.

A being which just is its own existence

Whatever does not belong to the thought of an essence or quiddity is something which comes from outside and makes a composition with the essence, because no essence can be thought of without the things which are parts of it. Now, every essence or quiddity can be thought of without anything being thought about its existence. For I can think of what a human being is, or what a phoenix is, and yet not know whether they have existence in the real world. It is clear, therefore, that existence is other than essence or quiddity.

There is perhaps an exception to this if there exists a thing whose quiddity is its existence. And there can be only one such thing, and it would be first, because it is impossible to plurify a something except either by the addition of some difference, as the nature of the genus is multiplied in its species, or by the reception of a form into diverse matters, as the nature of the species is multiplied in diverse individuals, or by this: that one is absolute and the other is received in something; for example, if there were a separated heat, it would by virtue of its very separation be other than heat which is not separated. Now, if we posit a thing which is just existence, such that the existence itself is subsistent, this existence would not receive the addition of a difference because it would no longer be just existence, but existence plus some form. And much less would it receive the addition of matter because it would no longer be a subsistent existence, but a material existence. Whence it remains that such a thing, which is its own existence, cannot be but one.

It follows that it is necessary that in any thing other than this one its existence is other than its quiddity, or its nature, or its form. Consequently, it is necessary that in the intelligence's existence is something besides the form, and this is why it was said that an intelligence is form and existence.

Now, whatever belongs to something is either caused by the principles of its nature, as the ability to laugh in human beings, or comes from some extrinsic principle, as light in the air from the influence of the sun. But it cannot be that the very existence of a thing is caused by the form or quiddity of that thing – by 'cause' here I mean an efficient cause – because then something would be its own cause, and would bring itself into existence, which is impossible. It is therefore necessary that every thing of the sort whose existence is other than its nature has its existence from something else. And because every thing which exists by virtue of something else is led back to that which exists by virtue of itself as to its first cause, it is necessary that there be some thing which is the cause of the existence of all things in virtue of the fact that it is just existence. Otherwise, there would be an infinite regress of causes, since every thing which is not just existence has a cause of its existence, as has been said. It is clear, therefore, that an intelligence is form and existence, and that it gets existence from the first being, which is just existence. And this is the first cause, which is God.

Bosley and Tweedale, *Philosophy*, pp. 401–403

Avicenna: the nature of universals, First Philosophy, V

I say, then, that 'universal' has three senses: (1) Something is called universal because it is actually predicated of many items, for example human being. (2) An intention is called universal when it is possible for it to be predicated of many, even if none of these items actually exist, for example, the intention of a seven-sided house. This is universal because its nature can be predicated of many; it is not necessary that those many items exist nor even some one of them. (3) An intention is called universal when nothing prevents its being thought to be predicated of many, because if something did prevent [its being predicated of many] it would prevent this by a cause by which this is proven. Sun and earth are examples, for so far as the idea of them is concerned the fact that sun and earth are thought does not prevent its being possible for their intention to be found in many. This is only prevented if we bring in an argument by which it may be known that this is impossible. And then this will be impossible because of an extrinsic cause, not because of the imagination of them.

All of these senses agree in this much: what is universal is something which in thought it is not impossible to predicate of many. The logical universal and whatever is similar to it must have this feature. Thus a universal, just from being a universal, is something, and from being something to which universality happens to belong it is something else. Thus one of the aforesaid terms is signified by 'universal' just because it has been made a universal, for, since it is human being or horse, the intention here, which is humanity or horseness will be something else outside the intention of universality.

For the definition of horseness is outside the definition of universality, and universality is not contained in the definition of horseness. Horseness has a definition which does not require universality; rather universality happens to belong to it. Consequently, horseness itself is just mere horseness. In itself it is neither many nor one, existent neither in sensibles nor in the soul, neither potential nor actual in such a way that this is contained within the essence of horseness; rather [it is what it is in itself] from the fact that it is mere horseness.

Animal can be considered on its own [*per se*] even though it exists with something other than itself, for its essence is with something other than itself. Therefore its essence belongs to it on its own. Its existing with something other than itself is something which happens to it or something which goes along with its nature, for example this animality and humanity. Therefore, this consideration precedes in being both the animal which is individual on account of its accidents, and the universal which is in these sensible items and is intelligible, just as the non-composite precedes the composite and as the part the whole. For from this being it is neither a genus nor a species nor an individual, nor one nor many; rather from this being it is merely animal and merely human being.

But doubtless being one or many goes along with this, since it is impossible for something to exist but not be one or the other of these, although they go along with it extrinsically.

Thus, just as animal in existing has many modes, so also in the intellect. In the intellect it is the abstracted form of animal in virtue of the abstraction we have talked of earlier, and in this mode it is said to be an intelligible form. And in the intellect the form of animal exists in such a way that in the intellect by one and the same definition it agrees with many particulars. On account of this, one form in the intellect will be related to a multiplicity, and in this respect it is universal. [It is a universal] because it is a single intention in the intellect whose comparison does not change no matter which animal you take, i.e. when you first represent the form of any of these in your imagination, if later the intellect strips away the accidents from its intention, you will acquire in the intellect this very form. Therefore, this form is what you acquire by stripping away from animality any individual imagination taken from its external existence, even though it does not have external existence, rather the imagination abstracts it. . . . Thus common things in a way have existence outside and in a way do not. But that a thing one and the same in number is predicated of many, i.e. predicated of this individual in such a way that this individual is it, and likewise this [other] individual, is obviously impossible.

The essences of things

The essences of things either are in the things themselves or are in the intellect. Thus they have three relationships: One relationship of an essence exists in as much as the essence is not related to some third existence nor to what follows on it in virtue of its being such. Another is in virtue of its existing in these singulars. And another is in virtue of its existing in the intellect. And then there follow on it accidents which are distinctive of this sort of existence. For example, supposition [i.e. standing for things], predication, universality and particularity in predicating, essentiality and accidentality in predicating, and others which you will get to know later. But in the items which are outside there is no essentiality or accidentality at all; neither is there some complex or non-complex item, neither proposition nor argument, nor anything else like these.

Let us take an example of a genus: animal is in itself something. And it is the same whether it is sensible or is apprehended in the soul by thought. But in itself it is neither universal nor singular. For if it were universal in itself in such a way that animality from the fact that it is animality is universal, no animal could possibly be singular; rather every animal would be universal. But if animal from the fact that it is animal were singular, it would be impossible for there to be more than one singular, viz. the very singular to which animality is bound, and it would be impossible for another singular to be an animal. . . .

Generality is called a logical genus, which means what is predicated of many items of different species in answer to the question 'What?'. It does not express or designate something because it is animal or something else. Just as a white item is in itself something thought of, but that it is a human being or a stone is outside its idea but follows on that, and is thought to be one, so also the logical genus. But the natural genus is animal according as it is animal, which is suited to having the comparison of generality added to its idea. For when the idea is in the soul it becomes suited to having generality understood of it. Neither the idea of Socrates nor the idea of human being has this aptitude. . . .

But if some one of the species is a genus, it has this not from its generality which is above it, but from those items which are under it. But the natural genus attributes to that which is under it its name and definition from its own naturalness, i.e. from the fact, for example, that animal is animal, and not from the fact that it is a natural genus, i.e. something which once it has been thought of tends to become a genus from the fact that it is the way it is. For it is impossible that the latter [i.e. the genus] not have what is beneath the former [i.e. the species].

And generally when it is said that the natural genus gives to that which is under it its name and definition, this is not really true except by accident. For it does not give this from the fact that it is a natural genus, just as also it did not give it its being a logical genus, since it gave it only a nature which is apt to be a natural genus. This nature by itself is not a natural genus just as it is not a logical genus.

But if a natural genus means only the primary nature on its own [*per se*] which is suited to generality, and natural genus is not understood as we understand it, then it is correct to say that a natural genus attributes its name and definition to that which is under it. And then animal is really a natural genus only because it is mere animal.

An individual does not become an individual until outside properties, either shared or unshared, are joined to the nature of the species and this or that particular matter is designated for it. However, it is impossible for properties apprehended by thought to be added to the species, no matter how many they are, because in the end they will not succeed in showing the individuating intention on account of which an individual is created in the intellect. For if you say that Plato is tall, a beautiful writer, and so on, no matter how many properties you add still they will not describe in the intellect the individuality of Plato. For it is possible that the intention which is composed from all of them is possessed by more than one item and shows you only that he exists, and is a pointing to the individual intention. For example, if we said that he is the son of this person and at a given time is a tall philosopher, [and] it happened at that time that no one else had those properties, and you happened to know this appearance, then you would know his individuality just as you would know that which is sensible if it were pointed out to you with a finger. For example, if Plato were pointed to at the third hour. For then his individuality would be determined for you, and this would be a case of pointing out his individuality to you. . . .

And the difference which there is between human being which is a species and individual human being, which latter is common not just in name but also by being predicated of many, is this: We say that the idea of human being, which is a species, is that it is rational animal. And what we say of individual human being is that that nature taken together with an accident which happens to belong to it is joined to some designated matter. It is just as though we said 'a certain human being,' i.e. 'some rational animal.' Thus rational animal is more common than that, for sometimes it is in the species, sometimes in the individual, i.e. in this one named item. For the species is rational animal just as the individual rational animal is rational animal.

Bosley and Tweedale, *Philosophy*, pp. 571–572

St Thomas Aquinas: from **Summa Theologiae**

Article 3: Can sexual lechery be a sin?

On the third question we proceed as follows:

[1] It seems that sexual lechery cannot be a sin, for by the sexual act semen is discharged and this is a surplus of nutriment, as The Philosopher makes clear. But no sin can be involved in the discharge of other surpluses; therefore, neither can there be any sin in sexual acts.

[2] Further, anyone can legitimately use as they see fit what is their own. But in the sexual act a person uses only what is their own, except probably in adultery or rape. Therefore, in sexual usings there can be no sin and so lechery of this sort is not a sin.

[3] Further, every sin has a vice that is its opposite. But no vice seems to be opposed to lechery. Therefore, lechery is not a sin.

But, in opposition to this, a cause is more powerful than its effect. But wine is prohibited on account of sexual lechery, according to The Apostle who says, 'Do not get drunk on wine because from that comes sexual lechery.' Therefore, sexual lechery is prohibited.

Further, in Galatians [5:19] over-indulgence in sex is listed among the works of the flesh.

Reply: We have to say that the more necessary something is the more the order of reason must be preserved with respect to it, and, consequently, the more vicious it is if the order set by reason is ignored. Now the use of sexual things, as we said [art.2], is very necessary to the common good of preserving the human race. Therefore, in this matter it is especially required to abide by the order set by reason, and consequently if in this matter something is done beyond what the order set by reason demands, it will be vicious. But it is part of the meaning of lechery that it exceeds in sexual matters the order and mode which reason sets, and thus doubtless sexual lechery is a sin.

To [1], then, we have to say, just as The Philosopher says in the same book: 'Semen is a surplus which is needed,' for it is a surplus left over from the activity of the nutritive faculty but is needed for the work of the generative faculty. The other surpluses from the human body are ones that are not needed and therefore it does not matter how they are discharged as long as social decencies are observed. The discharge of semen is not like this, since it ought to occur in a way that suits it to the end for which it is needed.

To [2], we have to follow The Apostle in saying against sexual lechery: 'You have been bought at a great price. Glorify and carry God in your body.' Therefore, by using their body in an inordinate way a person through over-indulgence in sex wrongs God, who is the original owner of our body. Thus Augustine too says [*Serm. ad popul.* IX, 10]: 'God, who governs his servants for their own benefit, not his, orders this, and commands it, so that his temple, which you have begun to be, is not defiled by wanton and illicit pleasures.'

To [3], we have to say that since humans are very prone to enjoying pleasures, the opposite of overindulgence is not often found. Nevertheless, the opposed vice falls under unfeelingness, and it occurs in a person who so dislikes using women that he does not even give his wife what is her due.

Aquinas was credited with the authorship of hymns for the liturgy which put his theology in accessible form.

J. R. Woodford (trans.) in P. Dearmer, R. V. Williams and M. Shaw, *Songs of Praise* (Oxford, 1925) no. 279

Thomas Aquinas: 'Adoro Te'

THEE we adore, O hidden Saviour, thee,
Who in thy Supper with us deign'st to be;
Both flesh and spirit in thy presence fail,
Yet here thy presence we devoutly hail.
O blest memorial of our dying Lord,
Who living bread to men doth here afford!
O may our souls for ever feed on thee,
And thou, O Christ, for ever precious be.
Fountain of goodness, Jesus, Lord and God,
Cleanse us, unclean, in thy most cleansing flood;
Increase our faith and love, that we may know
The hope and peace which from thy presence flow.
O Christ, whom now beneath a veil we see,
May what we thirst for soon our portion be,
To gaze on thee unveiled, and see thy face,
The vision of thy glory and thy grace.

Further Reading

H. Burns (ed.) *The Cambridge History of Medieval Political Thought* (Cambridge, 1988).

M. T. Clanchy, *Abelard: a medieval life* (Oxford, 1997).

P. Dronke, *Women Writers of the Middle Ages* (Cambridge, 1984).

J. R. Ginther and C. N. Still (eds) *Essays in Medieval Philosophy and Theology in Memory of Walter H. Principe: fortresses and launching pads* (Aldershot, 2005).

A. Murray, *Reason and Society in the Middle Ages* (Oxford, 1978).

S. Smalley, *The Study of the Bible in the Middle Ages* (Oxford, 1983).

R. W. Southern, *Scholastic Humanism and the Unification of Europe*, 2 vols (Oxford, 1995; 2001).

8   Mysticism

Prayer, according to St John Damascene (d. c.750), 'is the raising of one's mind and heart to God or the requesting of good things from God.' Prayer is conversation with God and, in the Christian tradition, Jesus Christ as the self-revelation of the Father, is the model of prayer. Christian prayer in the Middle Ages is based on Christ's own prayer. The Bible, in both the Old and New Testaments, is the word of God and the Psalter, the book of the Psalms in the Old Testament, is the place in which the word of God becomes the prayer of men and women. The Lord's Prayer in the New Testament is the perfection of verbal prayer and the inspiration for all meditative prayer in the Christian life.

J. E. Rotelle (ed.) *Augustine's Heritage: readings from the Augustinian tradition* (New York, 1973) vol. 1, p. 9

Prayers are the expression of our desires

He who knows how to give good gifts to his children urges us to ask and to seek and to knock.

Since he is well aware of what is needful for us before we ask him, our mind can be perturbed by his acting in this way, unless we realize that our Lord and God has no need to have our will made known to him since he cannot but know it. Rather he wishes our desires to be expressed in prayers so that we may be able to receive what he is ready to give. This is something very great, but we are too small and narrow to receive it.

Therefore, we are told: 'Open wide your hearts! Do not yoke yourselves in a mismatch with unbelievers.' Thus we shall receive that which is so great, which eye has not seen because it is not color, ear has not heard because it is not sound, nor has it entered the heart of man because the heart of man must enter into it. And we shall receive it in fuller measure in proportion as our hope is more well founded and our love more ardent.

Hence, words are necessary for us that we may be roused and be fully aware of what we are asking, but we are not to think that they are necessary for the Lord in order that he may be informed or be influenced. Thus, when we say 'Hallowed be thy name,' we inspire ourselves to desire that his name, which is always holy, should be held holy among men also, that is, that it should not be dishonored – something that benefits men not God.

Similarly, when we say 'Thy kingdom come,' it will come whether we wish it or not; however, we stir up our desire for that kingdom, that it may come in us and that we may deserve to reign in it.

When we say 'Give us this day our daily bread,' by the words 'this day' we mean 'at this time' when we either ask for that sufficiency, signifying the whole of our need by the name of bread which is the principal part of it, or for the sacrament of the faithful, which is necessary at this time for us to attain not so much this temporal happiness as our eternal one.

When we say 'Forgive us our trespasses as we forgive those who trespass against us,' we admonish ourselves as to what to ask and what to do in order that we may deserve to obtain mercy.

When we say 'Lead us not into temptation,' we admonish ourselves to ask not to be deprived of his help, not to give in to any temptation through deception, not to yield through affliction.

When we say 'Deliver us from evil,' we remind ourselves to reflect that we are not yet in that happy state where we shall suffer no evil.

With the heart, a person could pass into a loving relationship with God, a communion approached through humility and a prayerful study of texts, of which the Bible was the most important. Alcuin (d. 804) was confident that the human mind could seek after God and find him.

D. Dales, *A Mind Intent on God. The Prayers and Spiritual Writings of Alcuin: an anthology* (Norwich, 2004) pp. 36–37, 40–41, 43–46

The revelation of God

The entire authority of Holy Scripture enjoins us that in order to believe rightly in God we must love him wholeheartedly. But the vision of the human mind is incapable of beholding the surpassing light of the divine majesty, unless the righteousness of faith and love, given by divine grace, illuminates it with its splendour. Therefore this divine grace should be sought with all prayers so that the eye of the heart may be cleansed, to be able to see that the Trinity is properly the one and only true God, and also how the Father, the Son and the Holy Spirit are rightly to be described, believed and understood to be of one and the same substance and essence. No one can attain to the vision of this most holy blessedness except by the faith of a pure heart. For Truth himself has said: 'Blessed are the pure in heart, for they shall see God' (Matthew 5.8). Therefore this vision ought not to be reckoned as discernible by the eyes of the flesh, but by the intuition of a pure mind, even as the grace of the Holy Spirit deigns to illuminate the keenness of our minds.

For the scriptorium

Here sit those who copy the words of the holy law,
And also the sacred sayings of the holy fathers.
These guard lest they sow frivolity among their words,
Or commit folly because of the errors of their hands.

They seek out with the utmost care correct versions of books,
So that their pens may fly along the right paths.
They distinguish proper grammar and sense with colons,
Placing points each in their proper places:
Lest the reader in church reads falsely
Or suddenly falls silent before his devout brethren.
For it is a noble task to write out holy books,
Nor does the scribe wish for any reward himself.
It is better to copy out books than to till vines,
For one serves the stomach, but the other the mind.
The master can offer many volumes, old and new,
To a person who can read the holy sayings of the fathers.

How to use the Psalms

The prophetic Spirit was not at all times present to the minds of the prophets: aware that they did not always possess it, they acutely sensed it within themselves when they did have it. Thus it was that when the prophet Elijah wished to divine the future, and sensing the absence of the Spirit of prophecy from within him, it came upon him only as he sang praises with psalms and so filled his spirit with insight into the future (2 Kings 3–15). For the voice of psalmody, when aroused by the pure intention of the heart, becomes the means whereby the heart is again prepared by Almighty God, and filled with either an intent mind, or prophetic mysteries, or the grace of compunction. Thus it is written: 'Whoever offers the sacrifice of praise honours me, and prepares thereby a way that I may show him the salvation of God' (Psalm 50:23).

By this sacrifice of praise comes the revealing of the way to Jesus: for when through psalmody compunction is poured into the heart, the way is open within us by which we may come to him. For it is indeed fitting that as the mind grows strong in its awareness of all things, it should cleanse itself, and join itself to divine praises and spiritual realities, so that the things of heaven may be revealed to it. Nothing else in this mortal life can enable us to draw near to the presence of God than to abide in his praise. Nothing therefore, neither word nor intellect, can explain to us the power of the Psalms, except in so far as we avoid their superficial expression as we sing the praise of Almighty God with an intent mind.

In the Psalms may be found, if approached with an intent mind and a spiritual understanding, the incarnation of the Lord the Word, his passion, resurrection and ascension. With an intent mind you may also discover a secret prayer that you could in no way devise for yourself. In the Psalms you will find an intimate way of confessing your sins, and a sincere mode of prayer for the divine mercy of the Lord. You may also perceive through them the hidden work of divine grace in everything that happens to you. In the Psalms you may confess your weakness and wretchedness, and thereby draw to yourself the mercy of God: for you will find all manner of virtues in the Psalms, if you merit from God the revelation of their secrets.

If you wish to praise Almighty God and his majesty, and all his kindness towards the human race since the beginning of the world: consider his manifestation in the Old Testament towards the patriarchs and prophets, and in the New Testament in the incarnation of his eternal Son. For all of this we should be moved to give thanks; we should sing those Psalms that begin with the word 'Alleluia!' You will by so doing offer a sweet tribute of praise to Almighty God, sweeter than any honey or honeycomb, if you continually praise and magnify him with these Psalms.

If you wish to exercise your innermost heart in divine praises and precepts, the commandments of heaven, sing Psalm 119. You may contemplate and scrutinize the virtue of this Psalm until your dying day, but you will never, I think, be able perfectly to understand its meaning. Every verse in it speaks either concerning the way to God, or of his Law, with its divine commandments and precepts; or it speaks words of judgement, justification or admonition. All this is accomplished within you without you diffusing your soul through the reading of many books.

In the Psalms you have enough material until the end of your life for reading, reflection and teaching. In them you will find the spiritual meaning to some extent set forth and described of both the prophets, evangelists and apostles, and of all the divine books of Scripture. You may find within them prophecies concerning the first and second comings of the Lord. You may find also in the Psalms all the force of divine utterance concerning the incarnation and the passion, the resurrection and the ascension of the Lord himself. If you examine them carefully in your innermost mind, then by the grace of God you may arrive in your heart at an intimate understanding of them.

He who is the Truth has promised us, and in this he cannot deceive us: 'Knock and it will be opened to you' (Matthew 7.7). Let us therefore knock on the door of the Psalms: for he is both the door and the doorkeeper. Let us therefore pay careful heed to how we sing the Psalms, and we shall see how they can achieve more in prayer than human words can ever express. They contain the sweetest love of the divine law; they arm the soul with courage in spiritual warfare, and are also a formidable stronghold in times of tribulation. They expel the fear and sadness of this passing age, and gladden our minds with spiritual joy and happiness.

Mysticism was an integral part of Christian belief, not a marginal alternative. The aspiration to perfection was the goal of every Christian and the spiritual life a means of reaching that goal. Formal theology with clear concepts and arguments is complemented in the Christian tradition by a mystical theology which is not concerned with words but with symbols, rituals and silence. In the West, building on the deeply influential writings of Dionysius, the Pseudo-Areopagite (c.500), mystical writers saw the possibility of a loving union with God in which all intellectual operations are abandoned.

The methodology of reaching that loving union with God was commonly described in three related 'ways' – the purgative, the illuminative and the unitive. This meant that spiritual progress began with the eradication of bad habits and the following of the virtues, moved on to the illumination of the mind by meditation and contemplation and climaxed in unitive love.

Mystical theology was expressed both in traditional language and in poetic images.

B. Pennington (ed.) *The Works of Aelred of Rievaulx, vol. 1: treatises and the pastoral prayer* (Massachusetts, 1971) pp. 35–39

The commentary of the Venerable Aelred, Abbot of Rievaulx, on the passage from the Gospel: 'When Jesus was twelve years old . . . '

The moral sense

28. The first day, then, on which the soul that thirsts for God dwells in the delights of contemplation as if in Jerusalem, is the consideration of God's power. The second day is admiration of his wisdom. The third day is a sweet foretaste of his goodness and kindness. To the first belongs justice; to the second, knowledge; to the third, mercy. Justice terrifies, knowledge teaches, mercy cherishes. 'I will enter,' says the Prophet, 'into the mighty deeds of the Lord; Lord, I will remember your justice alone.' Behold justice. 'What is uncertain and hidden in your wisdom you have manifested to me.' Behold knowledge. 'For your mercy is better than life.' Behold mercy. And on the first day that fear which proceeds from the consideration of justice purifies the soul. When it has been purified wisdom enlightens it. When it has been enlightened goodness rewards it by communicating to it its sweetness. You see, if I am not mistaken, how necessary and how useful it is, amid the performance of good works, to spend these three days in the delights of Jerusalem. There fear provides you with the bread of sorrow, knowledge with the wine of exultation and goodness with the milk of consolation. I know you will not be surprised that sorrow is not absent from what I have called delights, since you have often experienced that the sorrow which proceeds from chaste fear is preferred by the contrite soul to all the delights of this world. Our slight experience in the matter enables us to say as much as this. But men of more outstanding merit, endowed with greater talents and with souls better purified make more sublime and more profound discoveries in these three things. In God's power they see the depths of his judgments; in his wisdom, his hidden purposes; in his goodness, the unutterable words of his mercy. So Paul, entering into the mighty deeds of the Lord and awestruck at the abyss of his judgments, says: O man, who are you to answer God? Does the clay say to him who fashions it: 'Why have you made me so?' In wonderment too at the treasures of his wisdom he cries out: 'O the depths of God's wisdom and knowledge.' Recalling also the wealth of his goodness, he says: 'Do you scorn the wealth of his goodness and forbearance?'

29. So 'at the end of three days they found him in the temple.' That is to say, Mary and Joseph, the one his mother, the other his foster-father. He who in spirit contemplates the things of the spirit is found not just anywhere in Jerusalem but in the temple. For Jerusalem has a courtyard, it has gates, it also has a temple. While the courtyard sometimes lies open even to enemies, the gates are opened only to friends and entrance into the temple is granted only to the perfect. The man who is able to see the eternal in the things of time, the heavenly in the earthly, the divine in the human, the Creator in the creature, may exult as if admitted to Jerusalem's courtyards. This far, into the courtyard, the philosophers, like enemies, were able to penetrate with their intellectual powers as the Apostle says: 'The knowledge of God is clear to their minds. For they have caught sight of his invisible nature as it is known through his creatures.' Whereas the man who, with veil removed and his face uncovered, can look upon God's glory in Sacred Scripture, may boast that he has entered Jerusalem's gates. But if upon the altar of your heart the flame of heavenly desire has set on fire the fatness

of interior love and the marrow of your affections so that fragrant smoke mounts up from your burning prayers and your mind's eye extends its gaze into heaven's secret places while the palate of your heart tastes the blessed savour of God's own sweetness, then you have been in Jerusalem's temple and offered there a most acceptable holocaust.

30. But while the holy soul lingers in these delights, its mother and foster-father grieve, complain and search; when at length they find it they upbraid it with gentle reproaches and take it back to Nazareth. This can be applied in particular to those spiritual men, who have been entrusted with preaching God's Word and caring for souls. Further our foster-father I would interpret most readily as the Holy Spirit and nothing is better fitted to serve as our mother than charity. These cherish us and make us advance, feed and nourish us, and refresh us with the milk of twofold affection: love, that is, for God and for neighbour. It is these that keep and uphold us in the pursuit of holiness, as if in Nazareth, it is these that comfort us in sorrow, advise us in doubt, strengthen us when we are weary, heal the contrite of heart and bind up their wounds. It is with their help that we pass on from Nazareth to Jerusalem, from toil to rest, from the fruit of good works to the secrets of contemplation. These by the eternal law command us not wholly to neglect the contemplation of God for the sake of our neighbour's welfare, nor again to neglect our neighbour's welfare for the delights of contemplation. Therefore it is not without good reason that, if we indulge in repose more than is fitting, fraternal charity as it were complains of us. It is dissatisfied with our stay in Jerusalem if it feels that our repose is fraught with harm for others who depend on our solicitude.

For often when we lay to one side all business to give ourselves to interior meditation or to private prayer, if we linger in such delights longer than is good for those under our care, the Spirit intervenes and charity prompts us. We suddenly remember the weak and take thought for this one in distress who is waiting for fatherly consolation, that one suffering temptation and wondering when his father will appear in public and bring him some comfort by his words. Another is provoked to anger and murmuring against his father because there is no one to whom he can make the confession that will heal him, ridding him of the poison he has imbibed. And there is yet another overcome by the spirit of spiritual weariness running hither and thither to find someone to talk to and to advise him. It is by means of such promptings originating in our brethren's hearts, that we hear mother charity upbraiding us as it were: 'Son, why have you behaved so towards us? I and your father have been looking for you in sorrow.' We do no wrong to the Holy Spirit or to charity when we say that they grieve or complain in holy men, even if still imperfect, since the Spirit himself intercedes for us with unutterable groanings, just as he is accustomed to speak and be sorrowful and behave in holy men.

31. But if the love of repose leads the soul's feelings to murmur against such necessities, as if to say: 'Ought I not to concern myself with my Father's business?' none the less the reasoning spirit considers that Christ died in order that he who lives may not live for himself. And he goes down with them in subjection to them. The man who goes down with such a foster-father and such a mother need have no fears. The man who is led by God's Spirit to put himself on the same level as his inferiors out of charity will be happy to go down. With these as my leaders I will gladly go down even to Egypt; only, if they lead me there, may they bring me back again, if they make me go down, may they make me come up again. Gladly will I submit myself to such masters, gladly

will I put my shoulder to any burden they may lay upon me, gladly will I welcome the yoke they may make me bear, well aware that their yoke is sweet and their burden light. But you also, my son, although Christ is still hiding you under his wings free from such cares, must be as careful to avoid scandalising your companions as superiors have to be not to endanger their subjects. They on occasion put the needs of those in their care before the delights of contemplation. You must show the same preference for the unity and peace of the community. Above all never rely on your own unaided judgment to discern the times of these spiritual alterations, that is to say, when you are to go down to Nazareth or go up to Jerusalem, but always ask the advice of your elders.

32. And so you have, dearest son, what you asked for. Though it is not worthy of your desire, your affection, your expectation, yet it is some token of my good will and an attempt of a sort to satisfy you. Realise that we have been concerned not so much to give an exegesis of the Gospel passage as to draw from it, as you asked, some seeds for meditation.

B. Pennington (ed.) *The Works of Aelred of Rievaulx, vol. 1: treatises and the pastoral prayer* (Massachusetts, 1971) pp. 112–113

Pastoral prayer 6

Special prayer for wisdom

> These things, my Hope,
> I need for my own sake.
> But there are others that I need
> not only for myself, but for the sake of those
> to whom you bid me be a power for good,
> rather than merely a superior.
> There was a wise king once, who asked
> that wisdom might be given him to rule your people
> His prayer found favour in your eyes,
> you did hearken thereto;
> and at that time you had not met the Cross,
> nor shown your people that amazing love.
> But now, sweet Lord, behold before your face
> your own peculiar people, whose eyes are ever on your
> Cross,
> and who themselves are signed with it.
> You have entrusted to your sinful servant
> the task of ruling them.
> My God, you know what a fool I am,
> my weakness is not hidden from your sight.
> Therefore, sweet Lord, I ask you not for gold,
> I ask you not for silver, nor for jewels,
> but only that you would give me wisdom,
> that I may know to rule your people well.
> O font of wisdom, send her from your throne of might,
> to be with me, to work with me,

to act in me, to speak in me,
to order all my thoughts and words and deeds and plans
according to your will,
and to the glory of your name,
to further their advance and my salvation.

F. M. Steele (trans.) *The Life and Visions of St. Hildegarde* (1914) pp. 130–137

Hildegarde of Bingen (d. 1179) Scivias, *the vision of the great mountain with many windows and the bright one above*

I saw as it were a great mountain, having the colour of iron, and above it a certain One sitting, of such exceeding great brightness that His brilliancy dimmed my sight. And out of both sides of Him stretched a soft shadow, like a wing of wonderful length and breadth. And before Him, at the foot of this same mountain, stood a certain image full of eyes round about it, and because of the multitude of the eyes, I was unable to discern any human form about it. And before this last image was another of a child clothed in a pale vestment, with white shoes, and upon his head descended so much brightness, from Him Who sat upon the top of the mountain, that I was not worthy to look upon His face, except through Him Who sat above. Many living sparks fell down which flew round these images with great gentleness.

In this same mountain many little windows were to be discerned, in which appeared as it were heads of men, some pale and some white. And behold, He Who sat above the mountain called out in a very strong and most penetrating voice, saying:

O man! fragile dust of the dust of the earth, and ashes of ashes, cry aloud and say concerning the entrance into incorruptible salvation: Forasmuch as those who are learned and see the inner meaning of the Scriptures, but wish neither to tell it nor to preach it because they are blind and tepid in preserving the righteousness of God, open to them the lock of these mysteries, which they timid ones conceal in a hidden field without fruit. Therefore write at large from a fountain of abundance, and so overflow in mystical erudition, that they may tremble at the profusion of your irriga-tion, who wished you to be considered contemptible on account of Eve's transgression.

But thou dost not get this profound knowledge from men, for thou receivest it from above, from the tremendous and heavenly judge, where in very clear light this serenity will shine strongly among the shining ones. Arise, therefore, cry aloud, and say: These things are manifested to thee by the strongest power of Divine help, because He Who governs every one of His creatures powerfully and benignly, pours forth Himself in the light of celestial illumination, upon those fearing Him and walking in His gentle love, in a spirit of humility, and leads those persevering in the way of righteousness, to the joys of the eternal vision.

From whence also, as thou seest, this great mountain having an iron colour means the strength and stability of the eternity of the kingdom of God, which by no means of change or decay is able to be exterminated. And He Who sitting above in such light that the brightness of the vision blinded thee, shows in the kingdom of blessedness, Him Who, governing all the world in the splendour of perfect serenity, is incomprehen-sible to the minds of men in His heavenly divinity.

But from each side of Him a soft shadow, like a wing of wonderful length and breadth, is extended: which is both in admonishing and chastising a sweet and gentle protection, showing justly and lovingly an ineffable justice in the perseverance of true equity.

And before Him at the foot of the mountain was standing a certain image, full of eyes every where: because the gazing into the kingdom of God in humility before Him, fortified by the fear of the Lord, and with the clearness of a good and just intention, trains in men earnest endeavour and divine stability: thus thou wast not able to discern any human form in it by reason of its eyes, because He mitigates, by the sharpest glance of His inspection, all that forgetfulness of the justice of God, which men in weariness of spirit often feel, for human inquiry in its weakness cannot shake off His vigilance.

And before this image was another of the age of a child, in a white tunic, and it appeared to be shod with white shoes, because those who are poor in spirit follow in the preceding fear of the Lord, in as much as the fear of the Lord, in humble devotion, holds fast firmly the blessedness of poverty of spirit, which does not desire vainglory nor elation of heart, but loves simplicity and sobriety of mind, not attributing its good works to itself but to God, as it were in the pallor of subjection, like the garment of a white tunic, but following faithfully the innocent footsteps of the Son of God.

So much brightness descended upon His head from Him Who sat above the mountain, that thou wast not able to see His face, because the serenity of His visitation, Who governs every creature laudably, infuses the power and strength of His beatitude, so much that thou with thy weak and mortal regard wast not able to grasp His riches, and he who has divine riches submits himself humbly to poverty.

But because many living sparks go out from Him, Who sits above the mountain, and fly round those images with great gentleness, this means that divers and very strong virtues shining in great brilliancy come from Almighty God, and embrace ardently and comfort those who fear God truly, and who love poverty of spirit faithfully, and are surrounded by His help and guardianship. Then in this same mountain as it were many little windows were seen at which appeared men's faces, some pale and some white, because in the highest height of the deepest and clearest knowledge of God, the endeavours of men are neither able to be hidden nor concealed when they very often show in themselves earnestness and beauty, for sometimes men fatigued in heart and action sleep in disgrace, and sometimes roused up they watch in honour, as Solomon testifies according to My will saying: 'The hand of the poor worketh extreme poverty, but the hand of the strong prepares riches' (Prov. x.).

For it is said that that man makes himself poor and weak, who is unwilling to do justice, or to blot out iniquity or to remit debt, when he remains careless in the wonderful things of the works of blessedness. But he who works the works of salvation running in the way of truth, he obtains a fountain of glory, in which he prepares for himself, both in heaven and on earth, the most precious riches.

And whosoever has the knowledge of the Holy Spirit and the wings of faith, he will not transgress my admonition, but will perceive it, embracing it in the joy of his soul.

Hugh of Saint-Victor: selected spiritual writings, translated by a religious of CSMV with an introduction by Aelred Squire (1962) pp. 52, 60–62, 62–63, 70, 79–80

Noah's ark (De Arca Noe Morali)

Book I

CHAPTER 7: THAT NOAH'S ARK IS THE FIGURE OF A SPIRITUAL BUILDING, THAT CORRESPONDS TO CHRIST'S WHOLE PERSON. FROM THE WORDS OF ISAIAH THE PROPHET

Now the figure of this spiritual building which I am going to present to you is Noah's ark. This your eye shall see outwardly, so that your soul may be fashioned to its likeness inwardly. You will see there certain colours, shapes, and figures which will be pleasant to behold. But you must understand that these are put there, that from them you may learn wisdom, instruction, and virtue, to adorn your soul. And because this ark denotes the Church, and the Church is the body of Christ, to make the illustration clearer for you I have depicted Christ's whole Person, the Head with the members, in a form that you can see; so that, when you have seen the whole, you will be able the more easily to understand what will be said hereafter with reference to the parts. And I want to represent this Person to you in such wise as Isaiah testifies that he beheld Him. So I shall quote Isaiah's words to you, and from them take the thing I want to show you; so that what the literal sense says, the prophecy may confirm.

Now what he says is this: 'I saw the Lord sitting upon a throne, high and lifted up.' It is high, because it is located in the height. It is lifted up, because from the depths it has been translated to the heights.

CHAPTER 12: THE VISIBLE SHAPE OF THE ARK ACCORDING TO THE LETTER, AND CERTAIN VIEWS RESPECTING ITS FIVE STOREYS

Those who want to make a closer study of the truth of what is told us about Noah's ark according to the letter have to search out two things in particular – namely, its shape and its size. Now Origen with reference to the shape says: 'I think myself that, from what is said about it, the ark must have rested on a quadrangular base, of which the corners, as they went up, were drawn together gradually, so that it narrowed at the top to the space of a single cubit.' Many things seem to refute this view; for one thing, this shape does not appear such as would keep afloat. For it is indisputable that so massive a structure, laden with so many and such large animals, and also with provisions, could not possibly keep afloat when the waters came, unless the greater portion of its bulk were at the bottom; this fact we can put to the proof today with ships that carry heavy loads. If, then, as is stated, the ark began to narrow from the bottom upwards, so that the sides sloping towards each other took the swelling billows and did not throw them back, and it was thus not so much the waters that carried the ark as the ark the waters, how was it that the whole thing did not forthwith sink to the bottom?

Another point. When it says, 'The door shalt thou set in the side below', it seems to mean the side *wall*, as distinct from the surface that formed the roof above, in which perhaps the window was located. And again it says that Noah 'opened the roof of the ark'; this makes it clear enough that the ark had walls below, over which the roof was placed, immediately above the top storey where the humans dwelt. For these and other reasons it seems to us that this ark must have had walls erected on four sides, over which was set the roof, narrowed at its ridge to the measure of a single cubit. Authority does not tell us what was the height of the walls themselves, but we infer that the walls reached to the base of the fourth storey. For the learned tell us that the door of the ark was between the second storey and the third, in such wise that its threshold was close to the base of the third, but its entrance was cut out above, in the side of the same storey; so that there were two floors below the door and three above it.

And they say that one was appointed to receive the animals' dung, the second for their food supplies, while in the third were the wild animals, in the fourth the tame ones, and in the fifth, which was at the top, the humans and the birds. And it is very likely that, when the ark was afloat, the two lower storeys were pressed down under water; whereas the third, in which were animals that needed fresh air to breathe, was the first to rise above the waters. Thus, for people approaching the ark from the water outside, the door was almost on the water-level.

That perhaps is what is meant when it is said, 'The door shalt thou set in the side below'. Or 'below' may mean that, in whichever storey it was located, the door had to be placed low down, so that the feet of those entering would be on the floor.

If, however, one asks whether or not the height of all the storeys was the same, we for our part cannot judge from authority what should be thought on this point. Nevertheless we ask to be allowed to put forward a suggestion which does not contradict it. For we divide things thus: we allow four cubits of height for the first storey, five for the second, six for the third, seven for the fourth, and eight for the fifth. Thus the height of the walls will be fifteen cubits, and the height of the roof also will be fifteen.

On the outer surface of the walls of this ark little nests or chambers were constructed, and these were fastened to the walls in such wise as to allow entrance to them from without, while on the inside the surface of the wall remained unbroken. And these nests are said to have been made for those animals that cannot live either always in the water or always in the dry, like the otter and the seal. So much for the shape of the ark.

CHAPTER 13: THE SIZE OF THIS SAME ARK RECKONED ACCORDING TO GEOMETRY, TOGETHER WITH CERTAIN VIEWS ABOUT THREE STOREYS

Of the size of the ark we are told as follows: 'The length shall be three hundred cubits, the breadth fifty cubits, the height thirty cubits.'

There are, however, some who say that these dimensions would not be sufficient to contain so many kinds of animals and foodstuffs to feed them for a whole year. The learned answer these objections on these lines: they say that Moses, who as Scripture testifies concerning him was 'learned in all the wisdom of the Egyptians', put the number of cubits in this place according to the laws of geometry, an art in which the Egyptians excel; and, according to that, one cubit is reckoned the equivalent of six. Certainly, if this method of reckoning be applied to the dimensions of the ark, it will afford length, breadth, and height fully sufficient to contain enough seed for the renewal of the entire world, and stock from which all living creatures could be bred anew.

It must be understood, moreover, that there was no need for the animals that are generated not by sexual union but from the moisture of the earth, or from dead bodies, or some other corrupting thing, or for those that are born of the union of two different kinds, such as the two sorts of mule, to be included in the ark at all. From these considerations the conclusion emerges that it would not have been impossible for a place of such capacity to contain sufficient stock to renew all living things.

There are some who say that there were only three storeys in the ark, and that of these one was a single chamber, the middle one was divided into two, and the topmost into three. And they say that Scripture calls these divisions in the storeys rooms, but the storeys themselves it calls floors. We have depicted this form in preference to the other, because we were unable to show the height of the walls in a flat drawing. For in this plan the ascending beams are gradually brought together until they meet in the measure of a single cubit.

These things have been spoken about Noah's ark according to the letter.

CHAPTER 16: OF THE MYSTICAL NUMBER OF CUBITS IN THE HEIGHT OF THE SEVERAL STOREYS

If, however, anybody wants to investigate the mysteries of the numbers which we have allotted to each storey, he will see the fitness of the number four for the first. For, because the human body is composed of the four elements, and joined together by the combination of the four humours, the life of carnal persons, who are slaves to the pleasures of the flesh, is rightly designated by the number four.

Next, because of the five senses, the number five aptly represents natural men who, though they are not shamefully dominated by carnal lusts, nevertheless pursue and love things that minister to the delight of their outward senses, since they do not know what spiritual delight means.

The number six suits spiritual persons, because of the perfection of their works. The number seven, signifying rest, is proper to the souls who rest in hope and in anticipation of the glory of the resurrection.

The number eight, which signifies beatitude, fits those who, having already received back their bodies, rejoice in blessed immortality.

Book II

CHAPTER 6: THE MEANING OF THE DOVE AND THE GREEN OLIVE BRANCH

The other three kinds of contemplation, however, are symbolized by the going forth of the dove who, when she was sent out and found no rest for her foot, returned at evening carrying in her mouth an olive branch in leaf. She went out empty, but she did not return so. For she found outside that which she did not have within, although the thing that she brought in she did not love outside.

The olive branch in leaf denotes a good state of soul. For it often happens that the more holy men gaze upon the works of their Creator, the more do they burgeon with an inward love for Him. For as a result of seeing the mutability of present things they lose their esteem for all that seems fair in this world and, as it were, return carrying the olive branch in their mouth; since they long to see the loveliness of their Creator all the more ardently for having found so little to their liking among things created. The soul is happy to find its food within, since no pleasure keeps it outside; and, having once been a shipwrecked mariner amid the billows of the world, now that it has been led back safely to the ark, its haven, it fairly jumps for joy.

Similarly, in the second kind of contemplation, as often as we learn to marvel at God's unseen power and wisdom in things visible, we bring back, as it were, olive branches from the waters to the ark; since in the changeable things exterior to ourselves we acknowledge Him whom we love unchangeably within ourselves.

Again, in the third kind of contemplation, when we pay attention to His judgements without, we are renewed inwardly by His fear and love.

C. Kirchberger (trans.) *Richard of Saint-Victor: selected writings on contemplation* (1962) pp. 131–146

Richard of St Victor (d.1173), **Of the Grace of Contemplation or Benjamin Major**

Book one

CHAPTER ONE: OF CONTEMPLATION AND ITS PRAISE

If we may have leave, by the gift of his inspiration who has the key of knowledge, we should like, by our small commentary, to unlock the mystical ark of Moses, at least to some extent. And if, in this treasury of divine secrets and storehouse of the sciences there is still anything which our poor efforts may disclose to the advantage of others, we shall not be slow to display it in public, and produce it for common use. Much has already been usefully said concerning this matter, but there yet remains much which may fruitfully be added. Before our time the doctors have already spoken of what this tabernacle signifies mystically, according to the allegorical sense, namely, in what way it signifies Christ, and minds more acute than mine have thoroughly investigated it. But let us not suppose that we shall be guilty of rashness if we write something on the moral sense of the text. Indeed, in order that the methodical study of this matter may be more attractive to us and that it may excite our desire more strongly to wonder, let us meditate on what that great man among the prophets felt about it who calls it an 'ark of sanctifications'. 'Arise, O Lord into thy rest: thou and the ark of thy sanctification.' [Psalm cxxxii, 8] Let us see whether this ark which is called sanctifying is named after the thing itself. We should note carefully and keep deep in our memory that this thing whatever it may be, is called the ark of your sanctification, for you whom our doctor taught, saying: 'Ye shall be holy for I am holy.' [Leviticus xi, 44] You therefore, who are sanctifying yourselves, today, tomorrow, and on the third day, [Exodus xix, so, ii] do not neglect to notice what is meant when it is called the ark of sanctification. If we rightly believe Moses, we know that whoever shall touch it shall be made holy. If this is indeed so, everybody will truly seek to touch it, if the power of holiness goes forth from it. O that one among you might be found like the man of Ramathaim, robed in glorious vestments as befits the high priest, might be worthy to enter the Holy of Holies so as not only to see, but also to touch that which is called the ark of sanctification and to be cleansed of all his uncleanness. But what should I say of him to whom, perchance, the key of knowledge may be given by 'Him who openeth no man shutteth', that he may see what there is within the ark of sanctification? For I think there is something precious enclosed in that ark. I would greatly like to know what this ark is which sanctifies those who come to it and so is truly called an ark of sanctification. I do not doubt but that it is that wisdom which overcomes evil. [Wisdom vii, 30] For I know surely that from the beginning, whoever is made whole is healed by wisdom. And this is certain that no man can please God unless wisdom be with him. Would any man doubt that sanctification includes the cleansing of a man from his uncleanness and the purgation of his mind from all malice and wickedness? For a man is defiled by these things. He is purified by wisdom [Wisdom ix, 19] when she overtakes malice with strength and triumphs over it until 'reaching from end to end mightily, she ordereth all things sweetly'. [Wisdom viii, i] And to be thus purged is, I think, to be sanctified. When the Lord was about to teach Moses how to construct the tabernacle, he first instructed him about building the ark so that he might understand thereby that all other things were to be constructed in relation to the ark. I am sure that no one would hesitate to say that the ark was the chief and principal shrine among all those objects which the tabernacle of the covenant contained. It will easily occur to anyone who asks, what grace can be signified by that shrine which excels all others, unless perchance he happens to doubt that Mary chose the best part. [S. Luke x, 42] Yet what is that best part that Mary chose but to wait and taste how sweet the Lord is? [Psalm xxxiv, 8] For while Martha, as the Scripture saith, was occupied in serving, Mary sat at the Lord's feet and heard his word. For thus the highest wisdom of God hidden in the flesh, which she could perceive by the eye of the flesh, she understood by hearing and saw by understanding, and in this way, sitting and listening, she was occupied in contemplation of the highest truths. This is that part which shall never be taken away from the elect and the perfect. This is the work which will never come to an end in time or eternity. For the contemplation of truth begins in this life but is carried on perpetually in the next. By the contemplation of truth man is instructed unto righteousness and prepared for glory. See therefore how true it is that the grace of contemplation is to be understood by that shrine, which for its dignity is distinguished amongst all others in God's tabernacle. O most special grace! most specially exalted, by which we are sanctified in this present world, and beautified in that which is to come! If then by the ark of sanctification the grace of contemplation is rightly to be understood that grace should indeed be sought, since he who receives it is not only cleansed but also sanctified. Truly nothing else so purifies the heart of all worldly affection, nothing inflames the soul more with heavenly love! It is this which purifies and this which sanctifies, so that a man may be made clean and hold the world in contempt by diligent contemplation of the truth and may be sanctified by the love of God.

CHAPTER TWO: HOW USEFUL IS THIS GRACE AND HOW FAVOURED ARE THOSE WHO MAKE PROGRESS THEREIN

This very thing which David calls the ark of sanctification is called by Moses, the ark of the covenant. But why an 'ark'? Why 'the ark of the covenant'? And not any man's ark but the Lord's? We know that precious things, gold, silver and precious stones are generally deposited in an ark. If we reflect upon the treasures of wisdom and knowledge we shall quickly discover what the container of this kind of treasure is. What is this ark fit for this purpose, but the intelligence of man? For this ark is fashioned and gilded by divine workmanship when the human intelligence is promoted to the grace of contemplation by divine inspiration and revelation. Yet when we attain to this grace in this life, what do we receive but the pledge of that future fulfilment where we may perpetually enjoy everlasting contemplation? We receive this grace as a token of the divine promise, as a pledge of divine love or as the bond of a covenant and memorial of mutual charity. Do you not see how rightly the ark of the covenant of the Lord is named, when in it and by it such grace is typified? How willingly should a man gird himself to any kind of labour if he desires, or thinks himself fit to receive, a token of such great love. I doubt not but that there are among you some who, like a Hebrew slave, would gladly serve six years for this grace, so that in the seventh year he might go forth a freeman, without price and henceforth be able to give himself freely to the contemplation of truth. Truly, if there be found among you one who is a Jacob, or who may be thought worthy of such a name, a strong man and powerful in battle, a mighty wrestler, an overthrower of vices so that he may overcome some by strength and supplant others by cunning, such a man will gladly serve seven years and seven more for such a grace, inasmuch as he will think the days to be few for the greatness of his love, so long as he may come to the embrace of Rachel, though late in time. He who would attain to that embrace must needs serve for Rachel seven years and seven more, that he may learn to be at rest, not only from evil works but also from idle thoughts. For many, even if they know how to be still bodily, are yet quite unable to be quiet in mind, not knowing how to make Sabbath on the Sabbath, and so they are not able to do what the Psalmist teaches: 'Be still and know that I am God.' [Psalm xlvi, 10] They are still in the body but their hearts wander about everywhere, nor shall they deserve to see how sweet the Lord is, how good is the God of Israel to those who are right in heart. [Psalm lxxiii, 1] And because of this 'their adversaries did mock at their sabbaths.' [Lamentations i, 7] But the true Jacob never ceases to labour till he comes to the goal of his desires, serving in the household of the true Laban, he who is truly shining white, because glorified, whom the Father glorified in himself with the glory which he had before the world was; [S. John xvii, 5] he whom it behoved to suffer and so to enter into his glory, that he might endue the form of a servant with the brilliance of glory and be truly shining, made whiter than snow, crowned with honour and glory and be made fair among the children of men, yea even in the sight of the angels and be such as the angels desire to look upon. Do you see how great is this grace for which he works with such long suffering and desire, which is acquired by so much travail and possessed with such great joy? In many places of his Scriptures, Moses treats of this same grace in symbolic terms, but here he discusses it more fully in a mystical description, dividing it into different species.

CHAPTER THREE: OF THE PROPERTIES OF CONTEMPLATION AND OF HOW IT DIFFERS FROM MEDITATION OR THINKING

In order that we may more easily understand and rightly judge those things which are to be said about contemplation, we ought first to seek to determine or to define what it is and how it differs from thinking or meditation. For we must realize that we may regard one and the same object in one way by thinking, examine it in another way by meditation, and wonder at it in yet another by contemplation. Although at times, these three may agree in studying the same object, they differ greatly in method. Thought and meditation may approach one and the same matter in different ways and contemplation in yet a third and widely divergent manner. Thinking, slow-footed, wanders hither and thither along bypaths, caring not where they will lead. Meditation with great mental industry, plods along the steep and laborious road keeping the end in view. Contemplation on a free wing, circles around with great nimbleness wherever the impulse takes it. Thinking crawls along, meditation marches and sometimes runs, contemplation flies around and when it wills, it hovers upon the height. Thinking is without labour and bears no fruit. Meditation labours and has its fruit. Contemplation abides untoiling and fruitful. Thinking roams about, meditation investigates, contemplation wonders. Thinking arises from the imagination, meditation from the reason, contemplation from the intelligence. Behold these three, imagination, reason, intelligence. Intelligence takes the highest place, imagination the lowest, reason lies between them. Everything which comes under the view of the lower sense, comes necessarily also under the view of the higher sense. Hence it follows that everything which is grasped by the imagination, is also, together with much that is above it, grasped by the reason. So also, all that the imagination and reason include, together with those things which they cannot include, fall under the view of the intelligence. Behold then how wide is the extent of the ray of contemplation, for it embraces all things. And it is right that one and the same thing may, by one man, be considered thoughtfully, by another meditatively, by another contemplatively, yet not by a different road but by a different movement. Thinking moves from one thing to another rambling aimlessly. Meditation is perseveringly intent on one thing only. Contemplation sheds the light of a single ray upon innumerable objects. The depth of the mind is given expanse and immensity by the intelligence and the point of the contemplating soul is sharpened that it may become capable of understanding many things, and acute to penetrate subtleties. Contemplation can never exist without some degree of liveliness in the intelligence. For as it is the work of the intelligence which fastens the eye of the mind upon material things, so by that same power, from that one intuition of material things the eye is dilated to comprehend innumerable objects. Therefore whenever the soul of the contemplative is enlarged to take in lower things, as often as it is raised to the heights and sharpened to penetrate inscrutable things, or with marvellous nimbleness carried away by innumerable interests, almost without respite, so often you may be quite sure that this is the work of the power of the intelligence. This is said on account of those who think that these lower powers are unworthy of the regard of the intelligence, or of being considered in any way to belong to contemplation. But in a special and strict sense, contemplation is so called when it treats of sublime things where the soul makes use of the pure intelligence. But nevertheless contemplation always deals with things, either manifested according to their nature or known intimately by study or made clear by revelation.

CHAPTER FOUR: DEFINITION OF CONTEMPLATION, MEDITATION AND THINKING, INDIVIDUALLY

It seems that they may be defined thus: Contemplation is a free and clear vision of the mind fixed upon the manifestation of wisdom in suspended wonder. Or indeed as it appeared to a distinguished theologian of our times who defined it thus: Contemplation is the clear and free glance of the soul bearing intently upon objects of perception, to its furthest limits. Meditation however, is an industrious attention of the mind concentrated diligently upon the investigation of some object. Or thus: meditation is the careful look of the soul zealously occupied in the search of truth. But thinking is the careless glance of the soul prone to restless wandering. It will thus be seen that all three have this in common and it is almost of their essence, that they are the sight of the soul. Where nothing is discerned by the mind they cannot be thus named or declared to exist. It is common to contemplation as to meditation that they are occupied with useful things, and engaged chiefly and intensively in the study of wisdom or knowledge. But in this they differ greatly from thinking, which is wont at all times to relax in vain and frivolous considerations, throwing off the bridle of discretion to interfere or rush headlong into everything. Contemplation and thinking have this in common that by free motion and according to spontaneous impulse they move hither and thither and are not hindered by any obstacle or difficulty from following their course. In this they differ greatly from meditation which always is intent, however laborious the effort and notwithstanding difficulties of the mind, to grasp hard things, to break through obstacles and penetrate hidden things. Yet it often happens that in the wanderings of our thinking, the soul meets with something which it passionately desires to know and presses on strongly towards it. But if the mind satisfying its desire applies itself with zeal to this kind of investigation it already exceeds the bounds of thinking by thinking, and thought passes over into meditation. The same thing happens in the case of meditation. For when a truth has been long sought, and is at last discovered, the mind usually receives it greedily, wonders at it with exultation and for a long time rests therein in wonder. And this already shows meditation exceeding its bounds and passing over into contemplation. For it is the property of contemplation to adhere with wonder to the object which brings it joy. And in this it differs both from meditation and thinking. For thought, as we have said, always moves about hither and thither with uncertain steps, but meditation always tends to its final object, proceeding deliberately.

CHAPTER FIVE: HOW THE MODE OF CONTEMPLATION OPERATES IN MANY WAYS

Although that clear ray of contemplation is always hovering over some object in the greatness of wonder, nevertheless it does not operate in one way or uniformly. For the liveliness of the intelligence in the soul of the contemplative sometimes comes and goes with wonderful quickness, sometimes it circles around, sometimes it draws itself into a point and remains motionless. If we consider the nature of this thing rightly, we can see examples of it daily in the birds of heaven. You see some now rising up on high, now sinking down to earth and often repeating these modes of ascent and descent. You see others moving off to the right and left, coming down on this side or the other and a little ahead or hardly moving at all, and often repeating the same movements of their flight with great perseverance. You see some pushing forward with great haste. But soon and equally rapidly they return to the rear and often repeat this performance and continue and prolong their advance and retreat frequently and at length. You may also watch others moving in a circle and see how often they do this or make like circles, some a little wider, some narrower, but always returning to the same point. You may see others who with beating and vibrating wings hold themselves suspended a long time in one and the same place, and though moving, maintain themselves motionless by their activity. And they do not depart at all from the place where they are resting but stay there a long time, as if by performing and persevering in this work they might seem to exclaim and say: 'It is good for us to be here.' [S. Luke ix, 33] According to this example of suggested similes, we may vary the flight of our contemplation in many ways, and it may take different forms according to the differences in men and their occupations. It may rise from lower to higher things or fall from higher to lower. It may move from the part to the whole, or from the whole to the part by the nimbleness of its reflections and derive its reasons on that which it seeks to know, from the major or the minor premises. It moves around, now in one direction, now in the opposite, and draws its knowledge of contrary things from the science of opposites, and is accustomed to vary the process of its reasonings according to the various kinds of opposites. Sometimes it runs forward and immediately returns back, when it apprehends the manner or essence of anything either by its effects or causes, together with the things which have gone before or follow. Sometimes our speculation leads us thus round and about when we consider what each thing has in common with others; or in defining any particular thing, the reason is drawn and applied now to similar things, now to things having likenesses with it or accidents in common. But the fixed attention of our thought remains almost motionless in one place when the gaze of the contemplative gladly attaches itself to one being of a thing, or to distinguishing or admiring its qualities. But lest our words may seem to savour of human philosophy or to depart from the even tenor of catholic doctrine let us say, perhaps more conveniently, that all these things, ascending and descending, going and coming, removing now hither now thither, or in a circle and yet cleaving to one thing, means nothing but that the soul by that nimbleness of mind may be satisfied in its appreciation of new things, by all these activities. . . . Behold truly, as we have said above, that the matter of our contemplation always depends upon and is developed by some one thing, while the soul of the contemplative gladly dwells on the beholding of his happiness, while he endeavours always to return to it or to hold himself motionless in it for a long time. Hearken to an example of that manner of contemplation which is wont to go back and forth: 'And the living creatures ran and returned as the appearance of a flash of lightning.' [Ezekiel i. 24] Take as an example of that kind in which the soul is caught up in separate things, running divers ways with great rapidity: 'The righteous shall shine and shall run to and fro like sparks among the reeds.' [Wisdom iii, 7] He who moves upwards and back again is signified in a few words in the psalms: 'They mount up to the heavens they go down again to the depths.' [Psalm cvii, 26] With regard to that way of contemplation which is led round about, the voice of the prophet admonishes thee: 'Lift up thine eyes round about and see.' [Isaiah lx, 4] So also the ray of contemplation that is fixed unmoving in one place as it were, which any Habakkuk may experience in himself: 'The sun and moon stood still in their habitation.' [Habakkuk iii, ii] This then is contemplation as we have taught it, limiting it and defining it. We must now divide it into its species, and therefore let us see what are the kinds of contemplation.

CHAPTER SIX: THE KINDS OF CONTEMPLATION AND THEIR CHARACTERISTICS

There are six kinds of contemplation divided from each other and subdivided. The first lies in the imagination and is according to the imagination only. The second is in the imagination but according to the reason. The third is in the reason according to the imagination. The fourth is in the reason and according to the reason. The fifth is above reason but not contrary to it. The sixth is both above reason and contrary to it. So two are concerned with the imagination, two with the reason, two with the intelligence.

Our contemplation certainly takes place in the imagination when the form of these visible things and their image is made an object of thought, so that our attention is held in amazement, and amazement arrests the attention. And these bodily things which we absorb by a bodily sense, are manifold: so great, so various, so fair and lovely. And in all things we reverence with wonder the power of that superessential creativity of God, his wisdom and bounty; we wonder and venerate. But our contemplation takes place in the imagination and is given shape by the imagination only, when we neither seek nor examine anything by reason, but the mind freely moves this way and that to whatever kind of observation our sense of wonder attracts it.

The second kind of contemplation is that which exists in the imagination but is given shape and proceeds by the power of reason. This takes place when we seek and find the reason for those things which arise in the imagination and which we have already said, belong to the first kind of contemplation; and when we have found these reasons and considered them we regard them with wonder. In the former case it is the things themselves, in the latter the reason for them, their order, disposition, the cause of any single thing, its manner and use; it is these which we explore, examine and wonder at. So that this kind of contemplation takes place in the imagination but according to the power of the reason, for it develops by reasoning upon that which is found in the imagination. And although this manner of contemplation seems to consist in some way in the reason inasmuch as it seeks the reason of visible things, yet it should rightly be attributed to the imagination, for whatever we seek or find in it by reasoning, we certainly relate it to what takes place in the imagination when we follow it up by reasoning about these things.

The third kind of contemplation, we said, is that which is formed in the reason but according to the imagination. We make use of this kind of contemplation when we are lifted up by the likeness of visible things to the consideration of invisible things. This speculation has its basis in the reason because it follows up only those things which go beyond the imagination by design or investigation; for it only aims at invisible things and especially those that are grasped by the reason. But it is said to be formed according to the imagination because in this speculation the image of visible things provides an illustration or similitude by which the mind is assisted in its enquiry into invisible things. And it is correctly asserted that this contemplation exists in the reason but according to the imagination for although it proceeds by reasoning, all its reasons and arguments are founded and based first in the imagination and it draws its reasons and assertions from the properties of things that can be imagined.

The fourth kind of contemplation is that which is formed in the reason and according to the reason. And this happens when having set aside all use of the imagination, the soul reaches out to those things only which the imagination does not know, but which the mind puts together by reasoning or understands through the reason. We follow this kind of speculation when we consider those invisible aspects of our ego which we know by our own experience and understand by our intelligence. And we rise from this consideration to the highest contemplation of celestial spirits and of the good things of the mind. This contemplation exists in the reason, for having put aside material things, it aims solely at the things of the mind. And this contemplation will appear to begin from and take as a basis, those invisible things of ours which the human soul knows by experience and understands by common intelligence. Yet nevertheless, this contemplation may be rightly ascribed to the reason, for these invisible things of our nature are grasped by the reason and therein do not exceed the category of reasoning. For this contemplation proceeds according to reason alone for it deduces by reasoning from invisible things, such facts as it cannot know by experience. In this contemplation the human soul first makes use of the pure intelligence and having cast away all use of the imagination, this intelligence of ours in this operation seems to understand itself by itself for the first time. For indeed it seems that in these earlier kinds of contemplation this intelligence was not absent but was present implicitly, in meditation by the reason or sometimes by the imagination. Here it is used almost as an instrument and functions like a mirror, for here it works by itself and the contemplation is direct. Here the intelligence stoops as far as it may, for by its nature it cannot be found in any lower category.

The fifth kind of contemplation we said was above reason but not contrary to it. We ascend this watch-tower of contemplation by lifting up the mind, when we know by divine revelation what we cannot fully understand by any human reason, and what we are not capable of investigating thoroughly by any human reasoning. For example, such things as we believe concerning the nature of the Godhead and the simple essence and which we prove by the authority of the Sacred Scriptures. Therefore our contemplation truly rises up above reason when the human soul discerns by an exaltation of the mind, that which transcends the limits of human capacity. Yet it is to be reckoned as being above reason but not contrary to it, when the human reason cannot contradict that which is discerned by the point of the intelligence but rather acquiesces readily in it and confirms it by its witness.

The sixth kind of contemplation concerns the things which exist above the reason and seem to be beyond it or even contrary to it. In this supreme speculation, most honourable of all contemplations, the soul truly rejoices and dances when it comes to know and consider by the radiation of divine light, those things against which all human reason protests. Such are almost all things concerning the Persons of the Trinity which we are commanded to believe. For when the human reason is referred to about these things, it can do nothing but contradict them.

CHAPTER SEVEN: WHAT THINGS ARE COMMON AND TO WHICH CATEGORY THEY BELONG

Of all these, two things exist in the imagination for they concern sensible things only. Two in the reason for they deal only with things intelligible. And two exist in the intelligence for they concern only the objects of the pure intelligence. I call 'sensible' those things which are visible and can be perceived by the bodily senses. I call 'Intelligible' those invisible things which can nevertheless, be grasped by the reason. I call in this place, 'intellectible', those invisible things which are incomprehensible to the human reason. Of these six kinds of contemplation the four lower kinds are concerned chiefly with created things and the two higher kinds with uncreated and divine things. . . .

The English mystics have attained popularity and celebrity through their rediscovery and use by modern poets and theologians, like T. S. Eliot (d. 1965), they were part of a continuing tradition and were part too of a deeply Christian spirituality which did not attempt to replace the Christian way but to encourage its deepening and understanding. In modern terms mysticism is often about cultic obscurity. In medieval terms it is about clarification and the removal of obscurity.

E. Underhill (ed.) *A Book of Contemplation the Which Is Called The Cloud of Unknowing, in the Which a Soul Is Oned with God* (1922) ch. 7

How a man shall have him in this work against all thoughts, and specially against all those that arise of his own curiosity, of cunning, and of natural wit.

AND if any thought rise and will press continually above thee betwixt thee and that darkness, and ask thee saying, 'What seekest thou, and what wouldest thou have?' say thou, that it is God that thou wouldest have. 'Him I covet, Him I seek, and nought but Him.'

And if he ask thee, 'What is that God?' say thou, that it is God that made thee and bought thee, and that graciously hath called thee to thy degree. 'And in Him,' say, 'thou hast no skill.' And therefore say, 'Go thou down again,' and tread him fast down with a stirring of love, although he seem to thee right holy, and seem to thee as he would help thee to seek Him. For peradventure he will bring to thy mind diverse full fair and wonderful points of His kindness, and say that He is full sweet, and full loving, full gracious, and full merciful. And if thou wilt hear him, he coveteth no better; for at the last he will thus jangle ever more and more till he bring thee lower, to the mind of His Passion.

And there will he let thee see the wonderful kindness of God, and if thou hear him, he careth for nought better. For soon after he will let thee see thine old wretched living, and peradventure in seeing and thinking thereof he will bring to thy mind some place that thou hast dwelt in before this time. So that at the last, or ever thou wit, thou shalt be scattered thou wottest not where. The cause of this scattering is, that thou heardest him first wilfully, then answeredest him, receivedest him, and lettest him alone.

And yet, nevertheless, the thing that he said was both good and holy. Yea, and so holy, that what man or woman that weeneth to come to contemplation without many such sweet meditations of their own wretchedness, the passion, the kindness, and the great goodness, and the worthiness of God coming before, surely he shall err and fail of his purpose. And yet, nevertheless, it behoveth a man or a woman that hath long time been used in these meditations, nevertheless to leave them, and put them and hold them far down under the cloud of forgetting, if ever he shall pierce the cloud of unknowing betwixt him and his God. Therefore what time that thou purposest thee to this work, and feelest by grace that thou art called of God, lift then up thine heart unto God with a meek stirring of love; and mean God that made thee, and bought thee, and that graciously hath called thee to thy degree, and receive none other thought of God. And yet not all these, but if thou list; for it sufficeth enough, a naked intent direct unto God without any other cause than Himself.

And if thee list have this intent lapped and folden in one word, for thou shouldest have better hold thereupon, take thee but a little word of one syllable: for so it is better than of two, for ever the shorter it is the better it accordeth with the work of the Spirit. And such a word is this word GOD or this word LOVE. Choose thee whether thou wilt, or another; as thee list, which that thee liketh best of one syllable. And fasten this word to thine heart, so that it never go thence for thing that befalleth.

This word shall be thy shield and thy spear, whether thou ridest on peace or on war. With this word, thou shalt beat on this cloud and this darkness above thee. With this word, thou shall smite down all manner of thought under the cloud of forgetting. Insomuch, that if any thought press upon thee to ask thee what thou wouldest have, answer them with no more words but with this one word. And if he proffer thee of his great clergy to expound thee that word and to tell thee the conditions of that word, say him: That thou wilt have it all whole, and not broken nor undone. And if thou wilt hold thee fast on this purpose, be thou sure, he will no while abide. And why? For that thou wilt not let him feed him on such sweet meditations of God touched before.

M. L. Del Mastro (trans.) *Revelations of Divine Love of Juliana of Norwich* (New York, 1977) pp. 179–180, 187–189, 191–192, 193

Julian of Norwich (d. c.1416): God our mother

It is a lofty understanding inwardly to see and to know that God, who is our maker, dwells in our soul, and it is a still loftier and greater understanding inwardly to see and to know that our soul, which is created, dwells in God's substance. From this substance we are what we are, by God.

I saw no difference between God and our substance, but saw it as if it were all God. And yet my understanding accepted the fact that our substance is in God; that is to say that God is God and our substance is a creature in God. For the Almighty Truth of the Trinity is our Father, for he made us and preserves us in himself; the deep wisdom of the Trinity is our mother, in whom we are enclosed; the lofty goodness of the Trinity is our Lord, and in him we are enclosed and he in us.

We are enclosed in the Father, we are enclosed in the Son, and we are enclosed in the Holy Spirit. The Father is enclosed in us – All-power, All-wisdom, and All-goodness: one God, one Lord.

God, the blessed Trinity, who is everlasting Being, just as he is endless from without beginning, so it was in his endless purpose to make man. This fair nature was first prepared for his own Son, the Second Person of the Trinity, and when he willed it with the full agreement of the whole Trinity, he made us all at once.

In our making he first knitted us and joined us to himself. By this joining we are kept as clean and as noble as we were created to be. By virtue of that same previous joining, we love our maker and become like him, praise him and thank him, and endlessly rejoice in him. And this is the work that is wrought continuously in every soul that shall be saved. This is the 'goodly will' I mentioned before.

And thus in our creation God Almighty is our natural father, and God all-wisdom is our natural mother, with the love and goodness of the Holy Spirit. These are all one God, one Lord. In the knitting and joining he is our real, true spouse and we are his loved wife and his fair maiden. . . .

In our Father Almighty we have our preservation and our bliss, as far as our natural substance, which we have from our creation without beginning, is concerned. In the Second Person we have our preservation, in wit and wisdom, as far as our sensuality, our restoring and our saving are concerned. For he is our mother, brother and saviour. And in our good Lord the Holy Spirit we have our rewarding and our harvest for our living and our bitter labour, endlessly surpassing all that we desire in his marvellous courtesy from his lofty, plenteous grace.

All our life is in three modes. In the first is our being. In the second we have our increasing. And in the third we have our fulfilling. The first is nature. The second is mercy. The third is grace.

... The Second, most precious, Person, who is our substantial mother has now become our sensual mother, for we are double by God's making, that is to say, substantial and sensual. Our substance is the higher part that we have in our father, God Almighty.

The Second Person of the Trinity is our mother in nature, in our substantial making. In him we are grounded and rooted, and he is our mother by mercy in our sensuality, by taking flesh.

Thus our mother, Christ, in whom our parts are kept unseparated, works in us in various ways. For in our mother, Christ, we profit and increase, and in mercy he reforms and restores us, and by virtue of his passion, death, and resurrection joins us to our substance. This is how our mother, Christ, works in mercy in all his beloved children who are submissive and obedient to him. . . .

Our substance is whole in each person of the Trinity, which is one God. Our sensuality is only in the Second Person, Christ Jesus, in whom are the Father and the Holy Spirit. In him and by him we are powerfully taken out of hell, and out of the wretchedness on earth, and are gloriously brought up into heaven and blissfully joined to our substance, increased in richness and nobility by all the virtue of Christ and by the grace and working of the Holy Spirit.

[Christ] Our natural mother, our gracious mother, because he willed to become our mother in everything, took the ground for his work most humbly and most mildly in the maiden's womb. . . . Our high God, the sovereign wisdom of all, arrayed himself in this low place and made himself entirely ready in our poor flesh in order to do the service and the office of motherhood himself in all things.

... A mother can give her child milk to suck, but our precious mother, Jesus, can feed us with himself. He does so most courteously and most tenderly, with the Blessed Sacrament, which is the precious food of true life. With all the sweet sacraments he sustains us most mercifully and graciously. That is what he meant in these blessed words, where he said, 'I am that which holy Church preaches and teaches you,' that is to say, 'All the health and life of the sacraments, all the virtue and grace of my word, all the goodness that is ordained for you in holy Church, that I am.'

To motherhood as properties belong natural love, wisdom and knowledge – and this is God. For though it is true that our bodily bringing forth is very little, low, and simple compared to our spiritual bringing forth, yet it is he who does the mothering in the creatures by whom it is done.

The natural loving mother, who recognises and knows the need of her child, takes care of it most tenderly, as the nature and condition of motherhood will do. And continually, as the child grows in age and size, she changes what she does, but not her love. When the child has grown older, she allows it to be punished, breaking down vices to enable the child to receive virtues and grace.

This work, with all that is fair and good, our Lord does in those by whom it is done. Thus he is our mother in nature, by the working of grace in the lower part of love for the higher. And he wills that we know it, for he wills to have all our love fastened to him.

In this I saw that all the debts we owe, by God's command, to fatherhood and motherhood by reason of God's fatherhood and motherhood, are repaid in the true loving of God. This blessed love Christ works in us. And this was showed in everything, especially in the noble, plenteous words, where he says, 'I am what you love.'

Further Reading

A. Bernau, R. Evans and S. Salih (eds) *Medieval Virginities* (Cardiff, 2003).

C. W. Bynum, *Docere verbo et exemplo: an aspect of twelfth-century spirituality* (London, 1978).

—— *Jesus as Mother: studies in the spirituality of the High Middle Ages* (London, 1992).

D. Davies, *God within: the mystical tradition of northern Europe* (London, 1988).

S. Flanagan, *Hildegard of Bingen, 1098–1179* (London, 1998).

M. Glasscoe, *English Medieval Mystics: games of faith* (London, 1993).

S. T. Katz (ed.) *Mysticism and Religious Traditions* (Oxford, 1983).

D. Knowles, *The English Mystical Tradition* (London, 1961).

J. Leclerq, *The Love of Learning and the Desire for God* (New York, 1961).

A. Louth, *The Origins of the Christian Mystical Tradition* (Oxford, 1981).

C. L. Sahlin, *Birgitta of Sweden and the Voice of Prophecy* (Woodbridge, 2001).

D. Watt (ed.) *Medieval Women in Their Communities* (Cardiff, 1997).

9   The Eastern Church

The Eastern Church, centred on the city of Constantinople or Byzantium, developed on separate parallel lines to that in the West. In its Greek language this was partly a question of cultural disparity. It became, too, a matter of contrasted theological emphases. The Council of Constantinople in 381 had declared that 'next to the Bishop of Rome, the Bishop of Constantinople shall have priority of rank because Constantinople is New Rome', but it was often the Eastern Emperor rather than the Bishop, or Patriarch as he became known, that provided the central leadership of the Church in what had been the eastern part of the Roman Empire. Constantinople itself in its great Church of Santa Sophia provided an eastern counterpart to the city of Rome. The liturgy of the Eastern Church was distinct from the Roman rite and was attributed to John Chrysostom (d. 407) although its language – Greek, Syriac, Coptic or Slavonic – was that of the local Church.

W. Lethaby and H. Swainson (trans.) *The Church of St. Sophia Constantinople* (New York, 1894) pp. 24–28, 42–52

Procopius describes the Hagia Sophia (dedicated by Justinian in 537)

The emperor, thinking not of cost of any kind, pressed on the work, and collected together workmen from every land. Anthemius of Tralles, the most skilled in the builder's art, not only of his own but of all former times, carried forward the king's zealous intentions, organized the labours of the workmen, and prepared models of the future construction. Associated with him was another architect [*mechanopoios*] named Isidorus, a Milesian by birth, a man of intelligence, and worthy to carry out the plans of the Emperor Justinian. It is indeed a proof of the esteem with which God regarded the emperor, that he furnished him with men who would be so useful in effecting his designs, and we are compelled to admire the wisdom of the emperor, in being able to choose the most suitable of mankind to execute the noblest of his works.

[St Sophia] is distinguished by indescribable beauty, excelling both in its size, and in the harmony of its measures, having no part excessive and none deficient; being more magnificent than ordinary buildings, and much more elegant than those which are not of so just a proportion. The church is singularly full of light and sunshine; you would declare that the place is not lighted by the sun from without, but that the rays are produced within itself, such an abundance of light is poured into this church. . . .

Now above the arches is raised a circular building of a curved form through which the light of day first shines; for the building, which I imagine overtops the whole country, has small openings left on purpose, so that the places where these intervals occur may serve for the light to come through. Thus far I imagine the building is not incapable of being described, even by a weak and feeble tongue. As the arches are arranged in a quadrangular figure, the stone-work between them takes the shape of a triangle, the lower angle of each triangle, being compressed where the arches unite, is slender, while the upper part becomes wider as it rises in the space between them, and ends against the circle which rests upon them, forming there its remaining angles. A spherical-shaped dome standing upon this circle makes it exceedingly beautiful; from the lightness of the building, it does not appear to rest upon a solid foundation, but to cover the place beneath as though it were suspended from heaven by the fabled golden chain. All these parts surprisingly joined to one another in the air, suspended one from another, and resting only on that which is next to them, form the work into one admirably harmonious whole, which spectators do not dwell upon for long in the mass, as each individual part attracts the eye to itself.

No one ever became weary of this spectacle, but those who are in the church delight in what they see, and, when they leave, magnify it in their talk. Moreover it is impossible accurately to describe the gold, and silver, and gems, presented by the Emperor Justinian, but by the description of one part, I leave the rest to be inferred. That part of the church which is especially sacred, and where the priests alone are allowed to enter, which is called the Sanctuary, contains forty thousand pounds' weight of silver.

Paul the Silentiary: the wonders of St Sophia

Above all rises into the immeasurable air the great helmet [of the dome], which, bending over, like the radiant heavens, embraces the church. And at the highest part, at the crown, was depicted the cross, the protector of the city. And wondrous it is to see how the dome gradually rises, wide below, and growing less as it reaches higher. It does not however spring upwards to a sharp point, but is like the firmament which rests on air, though the dome is fixed on the strong backs of the arches. . . . Everywhere the walls glitter with wondrous designs, the stone for which came from the quarries of seagirt Proconnesus. The marbles are cut and joined like painted patterns, and in stones formed into squares or eight-sided figures the veins meet to form devices; and the stones show also the forms of living creatures. . . .

A thousand others [lamps] within the temple show their gleaming light, hanging aloft by chains of many windings. Some are placed in the aisles, others in the centre or to east and west, or on the crowning walls, shedding the brightness of flame. Thus the night seems to flout the light of day, and be itself as rosy as the dawn. . . .

Thus through the spaces of the great church come rays of light, expelling clouds of care, and filling the mind with joy. The sacred light cheers all: even the sailor guiding his bark on the waves, leaving behind him the unfriendly billows of the raging Pontus, and winding a sinuous course amidst creeks and rocks, with heart fearful at the dangers of his nightly wanderings – perchance he has left the Aegean and guides his ship against adverse currents in the Hellespont, awaiting with taut forestay the onslaught of a storm from Africa – does not guide his laden vessel by the light of Cynosure, or the circling Bear, but by the divine light of the church itself. Yet not only does it guide the merchant at night, like the rays from the Pharos on the coast of Africa, but it also shows the way to the living God.

D. Geanakoplos (ed. and trans.) *Byzantium: church, society, and civilization seen through contemporary eyes* (Chicago, 1984) pp. 136–139

Preface to Justinian's Novella VI *(c.534)*

The greatest blessings of mankind are the gifts of God which have been granted us by the mercy on high: the priesthood and the imperial authority. The priesthood ministers to things divine; the imperial authority is set over, and shows diligence in, things human; but both proceed from one and the same source, and both adorn the life of man. Nothing, therefore, will be a greater matter of concern to the emperor than the dignity and honour of the clergy; the more as they offer prayers to God without ceasing on his behalf. For if the priesthood be in all respects without blame, and full of faith before God, and if the imperial authority rightly and duly adorn the commonwealth committed to its charge, there will ensue a happy concord which will bring forth all good things for mankind. We therefore have the greatest concern for true doctrines of the Godhead and the dignity and honour of the clergy; and we believe that if they maintain that dignity and honour we shall gain thereby the greatest of gifts, holding fast what we already have and laying hold of what is yet to come. 'All things,' it is said, 'are done well and truly if they start from a beginning that is worthy and pleasing in the sight of God.' We believe that this will come to pass if observance be paid to the holy rules which have been handed down by the Apostles – those righteous guardians and ministers of the Word of God, who are ever to be praised and adored – and have since been preserved and interpreted by the holy Fathers.

Photius Epanagoge: the powers of the patriarch (c.880)

The attributes of the patriarch are to be a teacher, to behave with equality and indifference toward all men, high as well as low; to be merciful in [administering] justice but reproving of the unbelievers, while speaking forcefully in behalf of truth and the vindication of [orthodox] doctrines before kings, and not to be ashamed.

The patriarch alone should interpret the canons adopted by those men of old and the decrees instituted by the holy synods.

The patriarch should take care of and decide whatever problems arise from what was done and arranged, in particular and in general, by the ancient Fathers in ecumenical synods and in provincial synods. . . .

Since the constitution, analogous to man, consists of parts and members, the highest and most necessary parts are the emperor and the patriarch. For this reason the peace and happiness of the subjects in soul and body lie in the agreement and harmony of kingship and priesthood in all respects.

The [episcopal] throne of Constantinople, honoured with dominion [over others], was declared by synodical votes to rank as the first [by the Second Ecumenical Council in 381]. Thus, those divine laws which followed decreed that matters brought before the other thrones should be referred to that [of Constantinople] for adjudication and decision.

Maximus the Confessor (d. 662): the limits of imperial power over the Church

None of the emperors was able, through compromising measures, to induce the Fathers, who were theologians, to conform to the heretical teachings of their time. But in strong and compelling voices appropriate to the dogma in question, they declared quite clearly that it is the function of the clergy to discuss and define the 'saving' dogmas of the universal church. And you said: 'What then? Is not every emperor a Christian and a priest?' To which I responded: 'He is not [a priest], for he does not participate in the sanctuary, nor, after the consecration of the bread, does he elevate it and say, "The holy things [belong] to the holy." He does not baptize nor perform the ceremony of chrismation; nor does he lay on hands and ordain bishops, priests, and deacons; nor does he consecrate churches; nor does he bear the symbols of the priest-hood, the *omoforion* [cloak] and the Gospel, as he does hear the symbols of his rule, the crown and the purple robe.'

Photius Epanagoge: to Caesar what is Caesar's; to God what is God's (c.880)

There are two kinds of courts. The one acts in accord with [civil] laws, the other with [church] canons. But there is also a third kind, which combines and administers what is taken from both [civil] laws and canons.

The tribunal of the *autokrator* and *basileus* is not subject to appeal, nor can its findings be reversed by another court, but it is constantly reviewed by itself. In the same way also Moses who saw God remitted to the law the authority to review judgments.

The tribunal of the patriarch is not subject to appeal nor can its decrees be reviewed by another court; it is in itself the basis and source of ecclesiastical courts. All the ecclesiastical tribunals derive from it, and they all return to and end in it. Yet it is not derived from any other, and it does not return to and end in any other. . . . It is reviewed only spiritually and that by itself.

. . . We do not allow anyone of the ranks of the clergy, either bishop, priest, deacon, or anyone registered among the clergy, to appear before a lay court, be it voluntarily or against his will. If anyone should do this [bring an ecclesiastic before a lay court against his will], he shall be reprimanded properly by Our Serenity. If an ecclesiastic should appear voluntarily before a lay court, or at his initiative prefer the judgment of that court to that of an ecclesiastical court, he is condemned by the holy canons, although he may believe he has received [fair] judgment from that court.

None of the officials has the authority to force the God-loving bishops to appear at court and give testimony. But let the judge send to the bishops some of those serving him, so that the bishops may testify what they know before God, as is proper.

The years 726 to 843 were dominated by the controversy over the sanctity of icons or holy images. During this period the eighth-century monk, John of Damascus, compiled what was later seen as a kind of semi-official statement of the teachings of the Orthodox Church, the *Fountain of Knowledge*.

M. H. Allies (trans.) *St. John Damascene on Holy Images* (1898) pp. 10–17

The veneration of icons

For the invisible things of God since the creation of the world are made visible through images. We see images in creation which remind us faintly of God, as when, for instance, we speak of the holy and adorable Trinity, imaged by the sun, or light, or burning rays, or by a running fountain, or a full river, or by the mind, speech, or the spirit within us, or by a rose tree, or a sprouting flower, or a sweet fragrance.

Again, an image is expressive of something in the future, mystically shadowing forth what is to happen. For instance, the ark represents the image of Our Lady, Mother of God; so does the staff and the earthen jar. The serpent brings before us Him who vanquished on the cross the bite of the original serpent; the sea, water, and the cloud the grace of baptism.

Again, things which have taken place are expressed by images for the remembrance either of a wonder, or an honour, or dishonour, or good or evil, to help those who look upon it in after times that we may avoid evils and imitate goodness. It is of two kinds, the written image in books, as when God had the law inscribed on tablets, and when He enjoined that the lives of holy men should be recorded and sensible memorials be preserved in remembrance; as, for instance, the earthen jar and the staff in the ark. So now we preserve in writing the images and the good deeds of the past. Either, therefore, take away images altogether and be out of harmony with God who made these regulations, or receive them with the language and in the manner which befits them. In speaking of the manner let us go into the question of worship.

Worship is the symbol of veneration and of honour. Let us understand that there are different degrees of worship. First of all the worship of *latreia*, which we show to God, who alone by nature is worthy of worship. Then, for the sake of God who is worshipful by nature, we honour His saints and servants, as Joshua and Daniel worshipped an angel, and David His holy places, when he says, 'Let us go to the place where His feet have stood.' Again, in His tabernacles, as when all the people of Israel adored in the tent, and standing round the temple in Jerusalem, fixing their gaze upon it from all sides, and worshipping from that day to this, or in the rulers established by Him, as Jacob rendered homage to Esau, his elder brother, and to Pharoah, the divinely established ruler. Joseph was worshipped by his brothers. I am aware that worship was based on honour, as in the case of Abraham and the sons of Emmor. Either, then, do away with worship, or receive it altogether according to its proper measure. . . .

Of old, God the incorporeal and uncircumscribed was never depicted. Now, however, when God is seen clothed in flesh, and conversing with men, I make an image of the God whom I see. I do not worship matter, I worship the God of matter, who became matter for my sake, and deigned to inhabit matter, who worked out my salvation through matter. I will not cease from honouring that matter which works my salvation. I venerate it, though not as God. How could God be born out of lifeless things. And if God's body is God by union, it is immutable. The nature of God remains the same as before, the flesh created in time is quickened by a logical and reasoning soul. I honour all matter besides, and venerate it. Through it, filled, as it were, with a divine power and grace, my salvation has come to me. Was not the thrice happy and thrice blessed wood of the Cross matter? Was not the sacred and holy mountain of Calvary matter? What of the life-giving rock, the Holy Sepulchre, the source of our resurrection: was it not matter? Is not the most holy book of the Gospels matter? Is not the blessed table matter which gives us the Bread of Life? Are not the gold and silver matter out of which crosses and altar-plate and chalices are made? And before all these things, is not the body and blood of our Lord matter? Either do away with the veneration and worship due to all these things, or submit to the tradition of the Church in the worship of images, honouring God and His friends, and following in this the grace of the Holy Spirit.

H. R. Percival (trans.) *The Seven Ecumenical Councils of the Undivided Church*, cited in P. Schaff and H. Wace (eds) *A Select Library of Nicene and Post-Nicene Fathers of the Christian Church* (Grand Rapids, 1955) 2nd series, vol. 14, pp. 543–544.

The Council of 754 condemns icons

Satan misguided men, so that they worshipped the creature instead of the Creator. The Mosaic law and the prophets cooperated to undo this ruin; but in order to save mankind thoroughly, God sent his own Son, who turned us away from error and the worshipping of idols, and taught us the worshipping of God in spirit and in truth. As messengers of his saving doctrine, he left us his Apostles and disciples, and these adorned the Church, his Bride, with his glorious doctrines. This ornament of the Church the holy Fathers and the six Ecumenical Councils have preserved inviolate. But the before-mentioned demiurgos of wickedness could not endure the sight of this adornment, and gradually brought back idolatry under the appearance of Christianity. As then Christ armed his Apostles against the ancient idolatry with the power of the Holy Spirit, and sent them out into all the world, so has he awakened against the new idolatry his servants our faithful Emperors, and endowed them with the same wisdom of the Holy Spirit. Impelled by the Holy Spirit they could no longer be witnesses of the Church being laid waste by the deception of demons, and summoned the sanctified assembly of the God-beloved bishops, that they might institute at a synod a scriptural examination into the deceitful colouring of the pictures which draws down the spirit of man from the lofty adoration [*latreia*] of God to the low and material adoration of the creature, and that they, under divine guidance, might express their view of the subject.

After we had carefully examined their decrees under the guidance of the Holy Spirit, we found that the unlawful art of painting living creatures blasphemed the fundamental doctrine of our salvation – namely, the Incarnation of Christ, and contradicted the six holy synods. These condemned Nestorius because he divided the one Son and Word of God into two sons, and on the other side, Arius, Dioscorus, Eutyches, and Severus [were also condemned by preceding ecumenical councils] because they maintained a mingling of the two natures of the one Christ.

Wherefore we thought it right, to show forth with all accuracy in our present definition the error of such as make and venerate these, for it is the unanimous doctrine of all the holy Fathers and of the six Ecumenical Synods, that no one may imagine any kind of separation or mingling in opposition to the unsearchable, unspeakable, and incomprehensible union of the two natures in the one hypostatis or person. What avails, then, the folly of the painter, who from sinful love of gain depicts that which should not be depicted – that is, with his polluted hands he tries to fashion that which should only be believed in the heart and confessed with the mouth? He makes an image and calls it Christ. The name Christ signifies God and Man. Consequently it is an image of God and man, and consequently he has in his foolish mind, in his representation of the created flesh, depicted the Godhead which cannot be represented, and thus mingled what should not be mingled. Thus he is guilty of a double blasphemy – the one in making an image of the Godhead, and the other by mingling the Godhead and manhood. Those fall into the same blasphemy who venerate the image, and the same woe rests upon both, because they err with Arius, Dioscorus, and Eutyches, and with the heresy of the Acephali. When, however, they are blamed for undertaking to depict the divine nature of Christ, which should not be depicted, they take refuge in the excuse: We represent only the flesh of Christ which we have seen and handled. But that is a Nestorian error. For it should be considered that the flesh was also the flesh of God the Word, without any separation, perfectly assumed by the divine nature and made wholly divine. How could it now be separated and represented apart?

. . . The only admissible figure of the humanity of Christ . . . is bread and wine in the holy Supper. This and no other form, this and no other type, has he chosen to represent his incarnation. Bread he ordered to be brought, but not a representation of the human form, so that idolatry might not arise. And as the body of Christ is made divine, so also this figure of the body of Christ, the bread, is made divine by the descent of the Holy Spirit; it becomes the divine body of Christ by the mediation of the priest who, separating the oblation from that which is common, sanctifies it.

The evil custom of assigning names to the images does not come down from Christ and the Apostles and the holy Fathers; nor have these left behind them any prayer by which an image should be hallowed or made anything else than ordinary matter.

If, however, some say, we might be right in regard to the images of Christ, on account of the mysterious union of the two natures, but it is not right for us to forbid also the images of the altogether spotless and everglorious Mother of God, of the prophets, apostles, and martyrs, who were men and did not consist of two natures; we may reply first of all: If those fall away, there is no longer need of these. But we will also consider what may be said against these in particular. Christianity has rejected the whole of heathenism, and so not merely heathen sacrifices, but also the heathen worship of images. The Saints live all eternally with God, although they have died. If anyone thinks to call them back again to life by a dead art, discovered by the heathen, he makes himself guilty of blasphemy. Who dares attempt with heathenish art to paint the Mother of God, who is exalted above all heavens and the Saints? It is not permitted to Christians, who have the hope of the resurrection, to imitate the customs of demon-worshippers, and to insult the Saints, who shine in so great glory, by common dead matter.

H. R. Percival (trans.) *The Seven Ecumenical Councils of the Undivided Church*, **cited in P. Schaff and H. Wace (eds)** *A Select Library of Nicene and Post-Nicene Fathers of the Christian Church* **(Grand Rapids, 1955) 2nd series, vol. 14, p. 550**

The Seventh Ecumenical Council condemns iconoclasm (787)

We, therefore, following the royal pathway and the divinely inspired authority of our Holy Fathers and the traditions of the Catholic Church (for, as we all know, the Holy Spirit indwells her), divine with all certitude and accuracy that just as the figure of the precious and life-giving Cross, so also the venerable and holy images, as well in painting and mosaic as of other fit materials, should be set forth in the holy churches of God, and on the sacred vessels and on the vestments and on hangings and in pictures both in houses and by the wayside, to wit, the figure of our Lord God and Saviour Jesus Christ, of our spotless Lady, the Mother of God, of the honourable Angels, of all Saints and of all pious people: For by so much more frequently as they are seen in artistic representation, by so much more readily are men lifted up to the memory of their prototypes, and to a longing after them; and to these should be given due salutation and honourable reverence [*proskynesis*], not indeed that true worship of faith (*latreia*) which pertains alone to the divine nature; but to these, as to the figure of the precious and life-giving Cross and to the Book of the Gospels and to other holy objects, incense and lights may be offered according to ancient pious custom. For the honour which is paid to the image passes on to that which the image represents, and he who reveres the image reveres in it the subject represented. . . .

   Those, therefore, who dare to think or teach otherwise, or as wicked heretics to spurn the traditions of the Church and to invent some novelty, or else to reject some of those things which the Church hath received, [the Gospels, the image of the cross, pictorial icons, or relics of martyrs], or evilly and sharply to devise anything subversive of the lawful traditions of the Catholic Church or to turn to common uses the sacred vessels or the venerable monasteries, if they be Bishops or Clerics, we command that they be deposed; if religious or laics, that they be cut off from communion.

D. Geanakoplos (ed. and trans.) *Byzantium: church, society, and civilization seen through contemporary eyes* **(Chicago, 1984) p. 157**

The iconoclast views of Emperor Leo V (815)

Why are the Christians suffering defeat at the hands of the pagans (*ethnoi*)? It seems to me it is because the icons are worshiped and nothing else. And (for this reason) I intend to destroy them. For you see that those emperors who accepted and worshiped them [the icons] died either as a result of exile or in battle. But those alone who have not worshiped them died each one in his own bed and after death were buried with honour in the imperial tombs at the Church of the Holy Apostles. Thus I too wish to imitate these latter emperors and destroy the icons in order that I and my son may live for a long time, and that our line may reign until the fourth and fifth generation.

In 843, at Hagia Sophia, the Empress Theodora, widow of the iconoclast Emperor Theophilus, called at an ecclesiastical council. At this council a permanent restoration of icons was effected.

D. Geanakoplos (ed. and trans.) *Byzantium: church, society, and civilization seen through contemporary eyes* (Chicago, 1984) p. 158

Acclamation of orthodoxy

> . . . As the Prophets prophesised, as the Apostles taught, as the Church has received, as the teachers have dogmatised, as the Universe has agreed, as Grace has shown forth, as truth has revealed, as error was repudiated, as wisdom has pronounced, as Christ awarded:
>
> Let us declare, let us assert, let us preach in like manner Christ our true God, and honour His Saints in words, in writing, in thoughts, in deeds, in Churches, in Holy Icons, worshipping Him as God and Lord and honouring them as His true servants.
>
> This is the faith of the Apostles, this is the faith of the Fathers, this is the faith of the Orthodox, this is the faith which sustains the Christian *Oikoumene*. . . .

The Seventh Ecumenical Council of 787, the Second Council of Nicaea, was the last of the Church councils to be regarded as ecumenical. In time the seven ecumenical councils were to be regarded as inviolable and the guarantee of Orthodox identity.

The monastic tradition, in its origins the same as that in the West, developed differently in the East. There was no proliferation of monastic orders, and the monastic way for men or women was seen in its perfection as the search for mystical union with God. The movement of Hesychasm (which can be translated as quietude), which flourished in the fourteenth century, considered itself the high point of a tradition which went back to the early Church.

D. Geanakoplos (ed. and trans.) *Byzantium: church, society, and civilization seen through contemporary eyes* (Chicago, 1984) pp. 183, 185–186

Barlaam attacks the Hesychasts (c.1340)

> I have been instructed by them [certain Athonite monks] in monstrosities and in ridiculous doctrines not even worthy of mention by one of sound mind or understanding – products of mistaken doctrines and reckless fantasy. Among such, they transmitted to me knowledge of certain wondrous disjunctions and reunions of the mind with the soul, the relations of demons with the soul, distinctions between red and white lights, and also intelligible entrances and exits which occur through the nostrils while breathing, vibrations present in the area of the navel [*omphalon*], and, lastly, the union of our Lord with the soul which occurs perceptibly within the navel and with full conviction of heart.

Symeon: methods of holy prayer and attention (eleventh century)

There are three ways of prayer and attention by which the soul raises itself or falls; it raises itself if these means are employed at the right time; it is cast down, if it undertakes them at the wrong time and in the wrong spirit. Sobriety [attention] and prayer are united like soul and body; one could not subsist without the other. The combination of the two is accomplished in two ways – first, sobriety opposes itself to sin like a cleanser and a guard that goes in front. As a result, prayer at once exterminates and reduces to nothing evil thoughts that one has tried to will away, since will power alone is not able to succeed. This then is the door of life and death – that is, attention and prayer. If we purify ourselves by sobriety, we improve ourselves. If, on the contrary, by letting ourselves go we neglect sobriety and soil it, we become evil.

Since we have indicated three kinds of attention and prayer, it is necessary to set forth all the features of each, so that he who wishes to acquire life and put it to work may do so without hesitation. Of these three states enumerated, choose the best and do not run the risk of accepting through ignorance the worst, that is, of being excluded from the best part.

The First Method of Prayer and Attention. The peculiarities of the first method are as follows: a man sets himself to pray and lifts his hands and eyes as well as spirit to heaven. The spirit, then forming one divine concept and imagining celestial beauties, hierarchies of the angels and dwellings of the mind, assembles briefly in his mind all that he has learned from the Holy Scriptures and excites his soul to divine love while gazing fixedly at the sky. It happens also that his eyes fill with tears, and his heart expands and he arises. He takes for divine consolation what he experiences and constantly wishes to devote himself to such an activity. There are signs of his errors, for the good exists only when he accomplishes it rightly. If then such a man devotes himself to utter silence, a solitary life without exterior relations, he can hardly escape from going out of his mind. But if, by chance, he does not fall into evil, it will at least be impossible for him to arrive at the possession of virtues and disinterest (apathy). It is this kind of attention that has strayed. Those are the sensitive ones who see light, perceive certain perfumes, hear voices, and [observe] many other similar phenomena. Some have been possessed entirely of a demon . . . and in their madness, wander from place to place; some others have been led astray, taking the devil for an angel of light, in which form he appeared to them without their recognizing him. . . . Some, instigated by the devil, have committed suicide . . . or hanged themselves. . . . From this, a man of sense can see what harm comes from this first method of attention and prayer – if it is considered as the final perfection in prayer. . . .

The Second Method of Prayer and Attention. The second method is this. When the spirit, retiring from external things and guarding against sensations from outside, and collecting all its thoughts, advances, forgetful of all vanities, the more it makes an examination of its thoughts, the more it applies its attention to the demands that the lips address to God, the more it attracts to itself captive thoughts, so that, overcome itself by passion, it uses violence to return to itself. To combat this, peace is impossible to arrive at and virtue too. . . . In his pride [the one who practices this] despises and criticizes others and praises himself, . . . and he is like a blind man who undertakes to lead the blind. Such is the second method. It does harm to the soul, and one should watch oneself carefully. Yet this method is better than the first, as moonlight is better than a dark night without a moon.

The Third Method of Prayer and Attention. Now we begin to speak of the third prayer. It is strange and hard to explain; for the ignorant . . . it is almost unbelievable. Few are those in whom one meets this. My view is that this great good has deserted us along with obedience. For obedience, disengaging its adherents from evil . . . frees them from cares and attachment to possessions, renders them constant and decisive in pursuit of their aim, if they find a sure guide at the same time. . . . The beginning of this third method is not gazing upward to heaven, raising the hands or keeping the mind on heavenly things. . . . Nor is it guarding the senses with the mind and directing all attention on this, not watching for the devil's onslaughts on the soul from within. This is the second method and those [who follow it] become enslaved by demons. . . .

The third method of attention and prayer is the following: the mind should be in the heart. . . . It should guard the heart while it prays, revolve, remaining always within, and from the depths of the heart, offer prayers to God. . . . In a word, he who does not have attention in himself and does not guard his mind, cannot become pure in heart and so cannot see God. . . . You should observe three things above all: Freedom from all cares, not only bad and vain but even about good things; in other words, you should become dead to everything; your conscience should be entirely clear, and denounce you in nothing. You should have complete absence of passionate attachment, so that your thought inclines to nothing worldly. Keep your attention within yourself (not in your head but heart). Wrestling thus the mind will find the place of the heart. This happens when grace produces sweetness and warmth in prayer. From that moment, whenever a thought appears, the mind at once dispels it, before it has time to enter and become a thought or image, destroying it by [repeating] Jesus' name [prayer], 'Lord Jesus Christ, have mercy upon me.'

Conflict between the Eastern and Western Churches was inherent in the development of papal authority, which was seen as antipathetic to the Eastern view that the five great sees were in an apostolic college. The sees of Rome, Constantinople, Alexandria, Antioch and Jerusalem formed the so-called pentarchy. In the eleventh century the Great Schism witnessed a permanent rift between Rome and the Eastern bishops.

D. Geanakoplos (ed. and trans.) *Byzantium: church, society, and civilization seen through contemporary eyes* (Chicago, 1984) pp. 208–212

Reciprocal excommunications (1054)

i   *Cardinal Humbert's anathema of the patriarch, Michael Cerularius*

Humbert, by the grace of God cardinal-bishop of the Holy Roman Church; Peter, archbishop of Amalfi; Frederick, deacon and chancellor, to all sons of the Catholic church:

The holy Roman, first, and Apostolic See, toward which, as toward the head, belongs the special solicitude of all churches, for the sake of the peace and benefit of the church, has deigned to appoint us *apocrisiarii* [legates] to this city, in order that, according to our instructions, we might come over and see whether in fact the clamour still continues which, without ceasing, comes to its [Rome's] ears or, if that is not so, in order that the Holy See might find out about it. Therefore, above all else, let the glorious emperors, the clergy, the Senate, and the people of this city of Constantinople, and the entire Catholic church, know that we have noted here a great good, on account of which we deeply rejoice in the Lord, but also we have perceived a very great evil because of which we are extremely saddened.

For, with respect to the pillars of the empire and its wise and honoured citizens, the City is most Christian and orthodox. However, with regard to Michael, falsely called patriarch, and his followers in folly, too many tares [*zizania*] of heresies are daily sown in its midst. For as the Simoniacs sell God's gift; as the Valesians castrate their guests and promote them not only to the priesthood but even to the episcopate; as the Arians rebaptise people already baptized (especially Latins) in the name of the Holy Trinity; as the Donatists affirm that, excepting for the Greek church, Christ's church and the true sacrifice [of the Mass] and baptism have perished from the whole world; as the Nicolaites permit and defend [carnal] marriage for ministers of the holy altar; as the Severians maintain that the law of Moses is accursed; as the Pneumatomachians [enemies of the Holy Spirit] or Theoumachians have deleted from the creed the procession of the Holy Spirit from the Son; as the Manichaeans declare, among other things, that anything fermented is alive; as the Nazarenes maintain the bodily cleanliness of the Jews to such a point that they deny baptism to infants who die before the eighth day after birth and [deny] communion to menstruating women or those about to give birth or if they [the women] were pagan they forbid them to be baptized; also, they [the Nazarenes], preserving their hair and beards, do not receive into communion those who, according to the custom of the Roman church, cut their hair and shave their beards. Although admonished by our Lord Pope Leo regarding these errors and many other of his deeds, Michael [Cerularius] himself has with contempt disregarded these warnings. Moreover, to us his [Leo's] ambassadors who are seeking faithfully to stamp out the cause of such great evils, he denied his presence and any oral communication, and he forbade [us the use of] churches to celebrate Mass in, just as earlier he had closed the Latin churches [in Constantinople], and, calling the Latins azymites [users of unleavened bread in communion], he hounded them everywhere in word and deed. Indeed, in the persons of its sons, he cursed the Apostolic See, in opposition to which he signed himself 'ecumenical patriarch.' Wherefore, not putting up with this unheard-of slander and insult to the first, holy Apostolic See, and seeing the Catholic faith assaulted in many ways, we, by the authority of the undivided and Holy Trinity and that of the Apostolic See, whose embassy we constitute, and by the authority of all the orthodox fathers of the seven [ecumenical] councils and that of the entire Catholic church, whatever our most reverend lord the pope has denounced in Michael and his followers, unless they repent, we declare to be anathematised:

'May Michael, false neophyte patriarch, who only out of human fear assumed the monastic habit, now known notoriously to many because of his extremely wicked crimes, and with him Leo the archdeacon called bishop of Ochrida, and his treasurer [*sacellarius*] Michael, and Constantine who with profane feet trampled upon the Latins' sacrifice [the Eucharist], and all their followers in the aforesaid errors and presumptions, be anathematised, Maranatha, with the Simoniacs, Valesians, Arians, Donatists, Nicolaites, Severians, Pneumatomachians, Manichaeans, and Nazarenes, and with all heretics, indeed with the devil and his angels, unless by some chance they repent. Amen. Amen. Amen.'

The patriarch, Michael Cerularius and the standing synod anathematize the papal legation

Decree in response to the bull of excommunication cast before the holy altar by the legates of Rome against the most Holy Patriarch Michael in the month of July of the 7th indiction [1054]:

When Michael, our most holy despot and ecumenical patriarch was presiding [over the Orthodox church] certain impious and disrespectful men (what else, in fact, could a pious man call them?) – men coming out of the darkness (they were begotten of the West) – came to this pious and God-protected city from which the springs of orthodoxy flow as if from on high, disseminating the teachings of piety to the ends of the ecumene. To this city [Constantinople] they came like a thunderbolt, or an earthquake, or a hailstorm, or to put it more directly, like wild wolves trying to defile the Orthodox belief by the difference of dogma. Setting aside the Scriptures, they deposited [an excommunication] on the holy altar according to which we, and especially the Orthodox church of God, and all those who are not in accord with their impiety (because we Orthodox want to preserve what is Orthodox and pious) are charged with, among other things, the fact that unlike them we do not accept the shaving of our beards. Nor did we want to transform what is natural for men into the unnatural [i.e., we favour marriage for the lower clergy, rather than celibacy]. In addition, we do not prohibit anyone from receiving communion from a married presbyter. In addition to all this, we do not wish to tamper with the sacred and holy creed, which holds its authority inviolate from synodal and ecumenical decrees, by the use of wrongful arguments and illegal reasoning and extreme boldness. And unlike them we do not wish to say that the Holy Spirit proceeds from the Father and the Son – O what artifice of the devil! – but rather we say that the Holy Spirit proceeds from the Father. But we declare that they do not follow the Scripture which says 'Do not shave your beards.' Nor do they want to fully understand that God the Creator in an appropriate way created woman, and he decreed that it was improper for men to be alone. But they dishonour the fourth [canon] of the Synod of Gangra, which says to those who despise marriage: 'If one would hesitate to receive communion from a married presbyter, let him be anathematised.' In addition, they respect and honour the sixth synod which says . . . that those who are about to become deacons or to be worthy of being ordained presbyters should not have relations with their wives. And we, who continue to observe inviolate the ancient canons of the apostolic perfection and order, wish to affirm that the marriage of ordained men [priests] should not be dissolved and they should not be deprived of having sexual relations with their wives which from time to time is appropriate. So if anyone is found to be worthy of the office of deacon or subdeacon, he should not be kept from this office and he should be restored to his lawful wife, in order that what God has himself ordained and blessed should not be dishonoured by us, especially since the Gospel declares 'Those whom God has joined together, let not man put asunder. . . .'

If someone then dares against the apostolic canons to remove anyone of the clergy, that is presbyter, deacon, or subdeacon, depriving him of his lawful bond with his wife, let him be excommunicated. And likewise if some presbyter or deacon wants to cast aside his wife on the pretext of piety, let him be excommunicated, and if he persists, let him be excommunicated.

Moreover, they [Latins] do not wish to comprehend, and insist that the Holy Spirit proceeds not only from the Father but also from the Son, although they have no evidence from the Evangelists [the Gospels] nor from the ecumenical councils for this blasphemy against the holy doctrine. For the Lord Our God speaks of 'the spirit of the Truth, [which] proceeds from the Father.' But the fathers of this new impiety speak of 'the Spirit which proceeds from the Father and the Son.' But if the Holy Spirit proceeds from the Father, then this property of his is affirmed. And if the Son is generated from the Father, then this property of the Son is likewise affirmed. But if, as they foolishly maintain, the Holy Spirit proceeds from the Son, then the Spirit which proceeds from the Father has more properties than even the Son. For the origin from the Father himself is common to both the Spirit and the Son. As to the procession of the Spirit from the Father, this is a property belonging alone to the Spirit, but the Holy Spirit does not also proceed from the Son. But if the Spirit has more properties than the Son, then the Son would be closer to the essence of the Father than the Spirit. And thus there would appear again on the scene the drama of the heresy of Macedonius against the Holy Spirit. And apart from what has been said, they do not wish at all to accept that what is not common to the omnipotent and consubstantial triad, belongs to only one of the three. But the procession of the Holy Spirit is not common to the three. Thus it is only the property of one of the three.

But they come against us and against the Orthodox church of God, not as from the elder Rome but as from some other place, arriving before the most pious emperor. But they intrigued against the faithful and even 'counterfeited' their arrival with the pretext that they came from Rome, and pretending that they were sent by the pope. But the truth is that they were sent by the fraudulent Argyrus [the Byzantine commander in Italy] and his numerous admonitions and counsels, and they arrived by their own accord and not at all as messengers of the pope. And they even produced fraudulent letters which allegedly had been given them by him. This fraud was detected, among other things, also from the seals which were clearly tampered with. This document written against us in Italian [Latin] letters was deposited by this impious man [Humbert?] in the presence of the subdeacons who were officiating in the second week on the holy altar of the Great Church of God. Later it was removed from the holy altar by the subdeacons, and the subdeacons suggested that it be taken back, but as the legates did not accept it, it was thrown on the ground and fell into many hands. And so that the blasphemies contained in it not be publicized, Our Mediocrity [Cerularius] took it. Then, after this, Our Mediocrity asked certain men, the protospatharios Kosmas, Romanus, Pyrrhus, and the monk John the Spaniard to translate it from Latin into Greek. After the document had been translated by them, the content of their words was as follows:

'Whoever contradicts the faith and the sacrifice of the Roman and Apostolic See, let him be anathema and not accepted as orthodox, but let him be called proazymite and the new Antichrist. Humbert, by the grace of God, bishop of the Holy Roman Church, Peter, archbishop of Amalfi, Frederick, deacon and chancellor of all the children of the Catholic church.'

. . . This was in essence the contents of the impious, distasteful document. Our Mediocrity, unable to tolerate such audacity and impudence against our piety by remaining silent or to permit it to remain unpunished, communicated this to our powerful and sacred emperor. And he, after it was reported to him (when the legates had been away from the city for only one day), sent messengers to bring them back to the great city, and they returned quickly. But they refused to come before Our Mediocrity or to face the holy and great synod and to give any answer about the impious acts they had committed. But besides delivering the document, they even insisted further that they had even more to say than what had been written [in the document] against our faith and would prefer to die rather than to come to face us and the synod. These things were reported to us and to the synod by the powerful and sacred emperor through the response of the noble magister, the master of petitions, and the chartophylax, the most beloved of God. When the legates did not want to appear before us and the synod, our powerful and sacred emperor would not allow them to be brought by force because they held the office of legates. But because it would be improper and completely unworthy for such impiety against our faith to go unpunished, the emperor found a perfect solution for the matter by sending an honourable and respectful letter to Our Mediocrity through Stephan, the most holy monk and *oikonomos* [steward] of the Great Church, John the magister and master of petitions, and Constans the vestiarius and consul of the philosophers (*Ilypatos ton philosophon*) I which read as follows:

'Most holy lord, Our Majesty, after examining what has happened, has found that the root of the evil was committed by the interpreters and by the party of Argyrus [the Latin commander of the Byzantine army in Italy, a political enemy of Cerularius]. And concerning those who are alien and foreign and have been influenced by others we can do nothing. But those responsible we have sent to Your Holiness in order that they might be instructed properly and through their example others may not do such foolishness. Let the document with the anathema be burned in the presence of all including those who have counselled, published, and written it, and even those who have some idea about it. For Our Imperial Majesty has commanded that the vestarches, the son-in-law of Argyrus, and the vestes his son, be incarcerated in prison, in order that they might be punished there, since they are responsible for the matter. In the month of July, the seventh indiction.'

So read the imperial and sacred decree. And in accordance with the foresight of our most pious emperor, that impious document and those who deposited it or gave an opinion on its composition were placed under anathema in the great secretum in the presence of the legates sent to the emperor. This was decreed on the fourth day, which is the first of the present week, on the twentieth of the present month of July, and the report of the fifth synod will be read, according to custom, before the people, and this impious document once more will be anathematised along with those who edited it, wrote it, or had something to do with it either in will or act. And the original of the impious document deposited by these irreligious and accursed men was not burned, but was placed in the depository of the chartophylax in order that it be to the perpetual dishonour of those who have committed such blasphemies against us and as permanent evidence of this condemnation. It should also be known that on the twentieth day of the present month, during which the blasphemies against the Orthodox faith were anathematised, there were also present those who convened today with us, the hierarchy and all the metropolitans of the standing synod and the archbishops, namely Archbishop Leo of Athens, the synkellos Michael Sylaios, the synkellos Nicholas Euchaneias, the synkellos Demetrius of Caria, and also Archbishop Paul of Lemnos, Leo Cotradia, and Antonius Ziccia.

The Crusades marked a low point in relations between East and West. The Fourth Crusade in 1204 led not only to the Sack of Constantinople but also to the establishment of a network of Latin states in Greece and the Aegean. A series of councils in the thirteenth and fourteenth centuries offered some hope of reconciliation. In 1453 Constantinople fell to the Turks and the Middle Ages ended with the Eastern Church in some disarray.

M. Philippides, *The Fall of the Byzantine Empire* (Amherst, 1980) pp. 128–130

Makaios Melisenos, The Chronicle of the Seige of Constantinople *(2 April–29 May 1453)*

By then, the whole host of the enemy were on our walls and our forces were put to flight. They abandoned the outer walls and were retreating to the inside ones through the gate, trampling over each other. As these events were unfolding, a shout was raised from the inside, the outside, and the areas of the harbour: 'The castle has fallen; Turkish standards and banners have been raised on the towers.' It turned our troops to flight and encouraged our adversaries, who, with their war cries, were fearlessly and eagerly climbing our fortifications.

When my unfortunate lord and emperor saw what was happening, he implored God, with tears in his eyes, and urged our soldiers to be brave. There was no hope of help and aid. He spurred on his horse and reached the spot where the Turks were coming in large numbers. He fought like Samson against the Philistines. In his first assault he pushed the impious from the walls. It was a strange and marvellous sight to the beholder: roaring like a lion and holding his drawn sword in his right hand, he killed many opponents, while blood was streaming from his legs and arms. Don Francisco from Toledo, whom I have already mentioned, surpassed Achilles; he happened to be by the right side of the emperor and, like an eagle with claws and beak, attacked and cut down the enemy. Similarly, when Theophilos Palaeologus perceived that the emperor was fighting and that the City was in danger, he shouted with loud voice and laments, 'Better to die,' and rushed into the middle with a war cry; all whom he met he put to flight, scattered, or killed. But John Dalmates, in the same spot, also fought, more bravely than any other in his efforts to check his adversaries. Whoever happened to be there could only admire the strength and bravery displayed by these excellent men. Twice, and even three times, were they attacked and a battle ensued; they put the impious to flight, killed a multitude, and even pushed others from the walls; in a hard struggle and contest did they perish but also inflicted heavy casualties on the enemy before they met their deaths. Other soldiers valiantly defending the same spot were also killed near the Gate of Saint Romanos, against which the Turks had positioned that great cannon. It was here that, after demolishing the City fortifications, they first entered it. I was not with my lord and emperor at that hour but had been inspecting another part of the City, according to his orders.

After the Turks had entered the walls, they scattered the Christians within the inner walls with missiles, bolts, arrows, and stones; they took control of the entire area, with the exception of the towers Basileios, Leon, and Alexios, which were manned by the Cretan sailors, who bravely continued the struggle into the sixth and seventh hour and killed many Turks. Although they saw their numbers and were aware that the whole

City was enslaved, they refused to be enslaved and maintained that death was preferable to life. When a Turk reported their bravery to the sultan, he ordered them to come down, under a truce; he declared that they, their ship, and all their equipment would remain free. Even so, the Turks had trouble persuading the Cretans to abandon the fight.

Along with many others, the two Italian brothers called Paolo and Troilo [Bocchiardi] also fought bravely in their assigned section, strongly repelled the enemy, and put up a noble fight. There was slaughter on both sides, opponents and defenders. Finally, Paolo looked back, saw that the enemy had already entered the City, and cried out to his brother: 'Shudder thou sun, groan thou earth: the City has fallen. The hour has passed for us to fight. Let us take thought for our own safety.'

Thus our enemy took possession of our City on Tuesday, May 29, about two and a half hours after dawn.

Book III, 10–12

As soon as the Turks were inside the City, they began to seize and enslave every person who came their way; all those who tried to offer resistance were put to the sword. In many places the ground could not be seen, as it was covered by heaps of corpses. There were unprecedented events: all sorts of lamentations, countless rows of slaves consisting of noble ladies, virgins, and nuns, who were being dragged by the Turks by their headgear, hair, and braids out of the shelter of churches, to the accompaniment of mourning. There was the crying of children, the looting of our sacred and holy buildings. What horror can such sounds cause! The Turks did not hesitate to trample over the blood and body of Christ poured all over the ground and were passing His precious vessels from hand to hand; some were broken to pieces while others, intact, were being snatched away. Our precious decorations were treated in a similar manner. Our holy icons, decorated with gold, silver, and precious stones were stripped, thrown to the ground, and then kicked. Our wooden decorations in the churches were pulled down and turned into couches and tables. The enemy's horses were clothed in priestly garments of silk embroidered with golden thread, which were also used as tablecloths. They stripped our saintly vessels of their precious pearls, they scattered and trampled over all sacred relics. Many other lamentable crimes of sacrilege were committed by these precursors of antiChrist.

Christ, our Lord, how inscrutable and incomprehensible your wise judgments! Our greatest and holiest Church of Saint Sophia, the earthly heaven, the throne of God's glory, the vehicle of the cherubim and second firmament, God's creation, such edifice and monument, the joy of all earth, the beautiful and more beautiful than the beautiful, became a place of feasting; its inner sanctum was turned into a dining room, its holy altars supported food and wine, and were also employed in the enactment of their perversions with our women, virgins, and children. Who could have been so insensitive as not to wail, Holy Church? Everywhere there was misfortune, everyone was touched by pain. There were lamentations and weeping in every house, screaming in the crossroads, and sorrow in all churches; the groaning of grown men and the shrieking of women accompanied looting, enslavement, separation, and rape. Venerable nobility commanded no respect, wealth afforded no protection. Misfortune manifested itself in squares and corners everywhere in the City. No place remained unsearched and

untouched. Christ, our Lord, protect all Christian cities and lands from similar affliction and sorrow! All gardens and houses within the walls were searched and dug to
yield possible hidden wealth; thus many old and recent treasures, as well as other
precious possessions, came to light and enriched our enemies.

When all resistance had ceased, the sultan entered our City. His immediate concern
was the fate of the emperor, as he was extremely anxious to discover whether he was
still alive. Some individuals came and declared that the emperor had escaped, some
that he had gone into hiding, and others that he had perished in the defence of the
City. An immediate search was ordered to locate the emperor's body among the heaps
of the slain. They washed the heads of many corpses, but the emperor could not be
identified. His body was finally spotted by means of the golden imperial eagles traditionally imprinted on the greaves and shoes of our emperors. The sultan rejoiced,
became cheerful, and directed some Christians to bury the emperor's body with imperial honours. Woe to me! Divine Providence should have decreed my death long before
this day.

My adored, most serene, and memorable emperor was forty-nine years, three
months, and twenty days old when he perished.

The sultan was elated with his great victory, became most vain, and demonstrated
his savage and merciless nature. Our grand duke Lord Loukas Notaras came to his
court, prostrated himself, and presented him with his huge treasure, which had been
concealed up to this day. It consisted of pearls, precious stones, and gems worthy of
royalty. The sultan and all his courtiers were amazed. Then Notaras spoke: 'I have
guarded this treasure for the beginning of your reign. Accept it, I beg you, as my
personal gift. I am now your liege man.' He had hopes that he and his household would
thus escape slavery.

The sultan responded: 'Inhuman halfbreed dog, skilled in flattery and deceit! You
possessed all this wealth and denied it to your lord the emperor and to the City, your
homeland? And now, with all your intrigues and immense treachery which you have
been weaving since youth, you are trying to deceive me and avoid the fate you deserve.
Tell me, impious man, who has granted possession of this City and of your treasure to
me?' Notaras answered that God was responsible. The sultan went on: 'Since God saw
fit to enslave you and all the others to me, what are you trying to accomplish here with
your chattering, criminal? Why did you not offer this treasure to me before this war
started or before my victory? You could have been my ally and I would have honoured
you in return. As things stand, God, not you, has granted me your treasure.'

Forthwith the sultan ordered his executioners to place Notaras under arrest and to
guard him closely. On the following day, Notaras was brought before the sultan's
throne. The sultan addressed him again: 'Why were you unwilling to assist the emperor
and your homeland with your immense wealth? Why did you not advise the emperor,
when I sent word to him, to surrender this City in peace? I would have transferred him
to another location in friendship and affection. Much blood and destruction would
have been prevented.' Notaras replied: 'I am not responsible for the emperor's actions.
The Venetians and the inhabitants of Galata [the Genoese] had convinced him that
their army and fleet were on the way to his aid.' The sultan spoke again: 'You are still
able to invent many lies, but they will be of no avail to you any longer.'

Then he ordered that on the following day, Notaras be taken to Xeros Hill and
witness the execution of his two sons, the ones who had aspired to the offices of grand

constable and grand chancellor, and then be put to death. So it happened, and Lord Loukas Notaras passed away in this manner.

The executions of many eminent noblemen followed, including the Venetian bailey and his son together with the Catalan consul and his two sons. Contarini and certain other nobles from Venice were able to escape their fate by bribing Zaganos Pasha, who then interceded on their behalf. The sultan then dispatched men to Galata, who arrested and executed many individuals. He showed no regard for his numerous pledges to the inhabitants of Galata but commanded them to be his tributaries.

Then he forced his attention to Halil Pasha, who was imprisoned in a tower and executed a few days later, because he had advocated peace with our City and had maintained that a Western expedition would come to our aid and force the Turks out of Europe, as I have already mentioned. Halil's death was lamented by many Turkish soldiers, as he was generally liked through the advice he had always offered to the sultan. . . .

D. C. Munro (trans.) *Translations and Reprints from the Original Sources of European History*, series 1, vol. 3:1 (rev. edn) (Philadelphia, 1912) pp. 15–16

Nicetas Choniates: the sack of Constantinople (1204)

. . . How shall I begin to tell of the deeds wrought by these nefarious men! Alas, the images, which ought to have been adored, were trodden under foot! Alas, the relics of the holy martyrs were thrown into unclean places! Then was seen what one shudders to hear, namely, the divine body and blood of Christ was spilled upon the ground or thrown about. They snatched the precious reliquaries, thrust into their bosoms the ornaments which these contained, and used the broken remnants for pans and drinking cups, – precursors of Anti-Christ, authors and heralds of his nefarious deeds which we momentarily expect. Manifestly, indeed, by that race then, just as formerly, Christ was robbed and insulted and His garments were divided by lot; only one thing was lacking, that His side, pierced by a spear, should pour rivers of divine blood on the ground.

Nor can the violation of the Great Church [the Hagia Sophia] be listened to with equanimity. For the sacred altar, formed of all kinds of precious materials and admired by the whole world, was broken into bits and distributed among the soldiers, as was all the other sacred wealth of so great and infinite splendour.

When the sacred vases and utensils of unsurpassable art and grace and rare material, and the fine silver, wrought with gold, which encircled the screen of the tribunal and the ambo, of admirable workmanship, and the door and many other ornaments, were to be borne away as booty, mules and saddled horses were led to the very sanctuary of the temple. Some of these which were unable to keep their footing on the splendid and slippery pavement, were stabbed when they fell, so that the sacred pavement was polluted with blood and filth.

Nay more, a certain harlot, a sharer in their guilt, a minister of the furies, a servant of the demons, a worker of incantations and poisonings, insulting Christ, sat in the patriarch's seat, singing an obscene song and dancing frequently. Nor, indeed, were these crimes committed and others left undone, on the ground that these were of lesser guilt, the others of greater. But with one consent all the most heinous sins and crimes were committed by all with equal zeal. Could those, who showed so great madness against God Himself, have spared the honourable matrons and maidens or the virgins consecrated to God?

Nothing was more difficult and laborious than to soften by prayers, to render benevolent, these wrathful barbarians, vomiting forth bile at every unpleasing word, so that nothing failed to inflame their fury. Whoever attempted it was derided as insane and a man of intemperate language. Often they drew their daggers against any one who opposed them at all or hindered their demands.

No one was without a share in the grief. In the alleys, in the streets, in the temples, complaints, weeping, lamentations, grief, the groaning of men, the shrieks of women, wounds, rape, captivity, the separation of those most closely united. Nobles wandered about ignominiously, those of venerable age in tears, the rich in poverty. Thus it was in the streets, on the corners, in the temple, in the dens, for no place remained unassailed or defended the suppliants. All places everywhere were filled full of all kinds of crime. Oh, immortal God, how great the afflictions of the men, how great the distress!

By the fourteenth century the power and influence of the Patriarch of Constantinople was outstripping the Emperor. The Patriarch had an authority which stretched far beyond the City State that the Empire had become. The Slavic world was a particular area of expansion. In Russia it was not Greek which became the dominant language but Slavonic. A Slavic alphabet was undertaken by Ss. Cyril (d. 869) and Methodius (d. 885), creating Church Slavonic. There is a rich literature of Slavonic as well as Greek writing which survives from medieval Russia, where Christianisation began in the late tenth century. As late as the closing years of the fourteenth century the Patriarch of Constantinople was still defending the hegemony of the Eastern Emperor against adverse remarks made by Vasily I, Grand Prince of Moscow.

S. A. Zenkovsky (ed. and trans.) *Medieval Russian Epics, Chronicles and Tales* (New York, 1974) pp. 101–105, 85–90

The martyrdom of Boris and Gleb (1015)

Sviatopolk [the elder brother of Boris and Gleb] settled in Kiev after his father's death, and after calling together all the inhabitants of Kiev, he began to distribute largess among them. They accepted it, but their hearts were not with him, because their brethren were with Boris. When Boris returned with the army, not having met the Pechenegs, he received the news that his father was dead. He mourned deeply for him, for he was beloved of his father before all the rest.

When he came to the Alta, he halted. His father's retainers then urged him to take his place in Kiev on his father's throne, since he had at his disposal the latter's retainers and troops. But Boris protested: 'Be it not for me to raise my hand against my elder brother. Now that my father has passed away, let him take the place of my father in my heart.' When the soldiery heard these words, they departed from him, and Boris remained with his servants.

But Sviatopolk was filled with lawlessness. Adopting the device of Cain, he sent messages to Boris that he desired to live at peace with him, and would increase the patrimony he had received from his father. But he plotted against him how he might kill him. So Sviatopolk came by night to Vyshegorod. After secretly summoning to his presence Putsha and the boyars of the town, he inquired of them whether they were wholeheartedly devoted to him. Putsha and the men of Vyshegorod replied: 'We are ready to lay down our lives for you.' He then commanded them to say nothing to any man, but to go and kill his brother Boris. They straightway promised to execute his order. Of such men Solomon has well said: 'They make haste to shed blood unjustly. For they promise blood, and gather evil. Their path runneth to evil, for they possess their souls in dishonour' (Proverbs, 1:16–19).

These emissaries came to the Alta, and when they approached, they heard the sainted Boris singing vespers. For it was already known to him that they intended to take his life. Then he arose and began to chant, saying: 'O Lord, how are they increased who come against me! Many are they that rise up against me' (Psalms, 3:1). And also: 'Thy arrows have pierced me, for I am ready for wounds and my pain is before me continually' (Psalms, 38:2, 17). And he also uttered this prayer: 'Lord, hear my prayer, and enter not into judgment with thy servant, for no living man shall be just before thee. For the enemy hath crushed my soul' (Psalms, 140:1–3). After ending the six psalms, when he saw how men were sent out to kill him, he began to chant the Psalter, saying: 'Strong bulls encompassed me, and the assemblage of the evil beset me. O Lord my God, I have hoped in thee; save me and deliver me from my pursuers' (Psalms, 22:12, 16; 7:1). Then he began to sing the canon. After finishing vespers, he prayed, gazing upon the icon, the image of the Lord, with these words: 'Lord Jesus Christ, who in this image hast appeared on earth for our salvation, and who, having voluntarily suffered thy hands to be nailed to the cross, didst endure thy passion for our sins, so help me now to endure my passion. For I accept it not from those who are my enemies, but from the hand of my own brother. Hold it not against him as a sin, O Lord!'

After offering this prayer, he lay down upon his couch. Then they fell upon him like wild beasts about the tent, and overcame him by piercing him with lances. They also overpowered his servant, who cast himself upon his body. For he was beloved of Boris. He was a servant of Hungarian race, George by name, to whom Boris was greatly attached. The prince had given him a large gold necklace which he wore while serving him. They also killed many other servants of Boris. But since they could not quickly take the necklace from George's neck, they cut off his head, and thus obtained it. For this reason his body was not recognized later among the corpses.

The murderers, after attacking Boris, wrapped him in a canvas, loaded him upon a wagon, and dragged him off, though he was still alive. When the impious Sviatopolk saw that he was still breathing, he sent two Varangians to finish him. When they came and saw that he was still alive, one of them drew his sword and plunged it into his heart. Thus died the blessed Boris, receiving from the hand of Christ our God the crown among the righteous. He shall be numbered with the prophets and the Apostles, as he joins with the choirs of martyrs, rests in the lap of Abraham, beholds joy ineffable, chants with the angels, and rejoices in company with the choirs of saints. After his body had been carried in secret to Vyshegorod, it was buried in the Church of St. Basil.

The impious Sviatopolk then reflected: 'Behold, I have killed Boris; now how can I kill Gleb?' Adopting once more Cain's device, he craftily sent messages to Gleb to the effect that he should come quickly, because his father was very ill and desired his presence. Gleb quickly mounted his horse, and set out with a small company, for he was obedient to his father. When he came to the Volga, his horse stumbled in a ditch on the plain, and broke his leg. He arrived at Smolensk, and setting out thence at dawn, he embarked in a boat on the Smiadyn. At this time, Yaroslav received from Predslava the tidings of their father's death, and he sent word to Gleb that he should not set out, because his father was dead and his brother had been murdered by Sviatopolk. Upon receiving these tidings, Gleb burst into tears, and mourned for his father, but still more deeply for his brother. He wept and prayed with the lament: 'Woe is me, O Lord! It were better for me to die with my brother than to live on in this world. O my brother, had I but seen thy angelic countenance, I should have died with thee. Why am I now left alone? Where are thy words that thou didst say to me, my brother? No longer do I hear thy sweet counsel. If thou hast received affliction from God, pray for me that I may endure the same passion. For it were better for me to dwell with thee than in this deceitful world.'

While he was thus praying amid his tears, there suddenly arrived those sent by Sviatopolk for Gleb's destruction. These emissaries seized Gleb's boat, and drew their weapons. The servants of Gleb were terrified, and the impious messenger, Goriaser, gave orders that they should slay Gleb with dispatch. Then Gleb's cook, Torchin by name, seized a knife, and stabbed Gleb. He was offered up as a sacrifice to God like an innocent lamb, a glorious offering amid the perfume of incense, and he received the crown of glory. Entering the heavenly mansions, he beheld his long-desired brother, and rejoiced with him in the joy ineffable which they had attained through their brotherly love.

'How good and fair it is for brethren to live together!' (Psalms, 133:1). But the impious ones returned again, even as David said, 'Let the sinners return to hell' (Psalms, 9:17). When they returned to Sviatopolk, they reported that his command had been executed. On hearing these tidings, he was puffed up with pride, since he knew not the words of David: 'Why art thou proud of thy evildoing, O mighty one? Thy tongue hath considered lawlessness all the day long' (Psalms, 52:1).

After Gleb had been slain, his body was thrown upon the shore between two tree trunks, but afterward they took him and carried him away, to bury him beside his brother Boris in the Church of St. Basil. United thus in body and still more in soul, ye dwell with the Lord and King of all, in eternal joy, ineffable light, bestowing salutary gifts upon the land of Russia. Ye give healing to other strangers who draw near with faith, making the lame to walk, giving sight to the blind, to the sick health, to captives freedom, to prisoners liberty, to the sorrowful consolation, and to the oppressed relief. Ye are the protectors of the land of Russia, shining forever like beacons and praying to the Lord in behalf of your countrymen. Therefore must we worthily magnify these martyrs in Christ, praying fervently to them and saying: 'Rejoice, martyrs in Christ from the land of Russia, who gave healing to them who draw near to you in faith and love. Rejoice, dwellers in heaven. In the body ye were angels, servants in the same thought, comrades in the same image, of one heart with the saints. To all that suffer ye give relief. Rejoice, Boris and Gleb, wise in God. Like streams ye spring from the founts of life-giving water which flow for the redemption of the righteous. Rejoice, ye who have trampled the serpent of evil beneath your feet. Ye have appeared amid bright rays, enlightening like beacons the whole land of Russia. Appearing in faith immutable, ye have ever driven away the darkness. Rejoice, ye who have won an unslumbering eye, ye blessed ones who have received in your hearts the zeal to fulfil God's only commandments. Rejoice, brethren united in the realms of golden light, in the heavenly abodes, in glory unfading, which ye through your merits have attained. Rejoice, ye who are brightly irradiate with the luminance of God, and travel throughout the world expelling devils and healing diseases. Like beacons supernal and zealous guardians, ye dwell with God, illumined forever with light divine, and in your courageous martyrdom ye enlighten the souls of the faithful. The light-bringing heavenly love has exalted you, wherefore ye have inherited all fair things in the heavenly life: glory, celestial sustenance, the light of wisdom, and beauteous joys. Rejoice, ye who refresh our hearts, driving out pain and sickness and curing evil passions. Ye glorious ones, with the sacred drops of your blood ye have dyed a robe of purple which ye wear in beauty, and reign forevermore with Christ, interceding with him for his new Christian nation and for your fellows, for our land is hallowed by your blood. By virtue of your relics deposited in the church, ye illumine it with the Holy Spirit, for there in heavenly bliss, as martyrs among the army of martyrs, ye intercede for our nation. Rejoice, bright daysprings, our Christ-loving martyrs and intercessors! Subject the pagans to our princes, beseeching our Lord God that they may live in concord and in health, freed from internecine war and the crafts of the devil. Help us therefore who sing and recite your sacred praise forever unto our life's end.'

Metropolitan Hilarion, 'The Sermon on the Law of Moses Given to Him by God, and on the Grace and Truth Brought to Earth by Jesus Christ' (written sometime between 1037 and 1050)

Blessed be the God of Israel, the God of Christianity who visited his people and brought them salvation. He did not disdain his creation, which was for ages possessed by pagan darkness and by worship of the devil, but he enlightened the Children of Abraham by giving them his Law tablets, and later he saved all nations, sending them his Son, his Gospel, and his Baptism, and by giving them resurrection to eternal life. . . .

Law was the precursor and the servant of Grace and Truth. Grace and Truth were the servants of the future life and immortal life. Law led its people of the Old Testament toward the blessing of Baptism, and Baptism led its sons to the life eternal.

Moses and the prophets announced the coming of Christ, but Christ and the Apostles announced resurrection and the future age. . . .

And what could the Law achieve? And what could Grace achieve? First was the Law and then Grace. Hagar and Sarah are the pictures of Law and Grace: Hagar was a handmaid and Sarah was free. First comes the handmaiden and then the free woman. And he who reads (the Bible) must understand this. Abraham, since his youth, had Sarah for his wife and she was free and not a slave, and so God decided before all ages to send his Son into the world that Grace might appear through him (but sent him to man only later). But Sarah was restrained from bearing children, since she was unfruitful. But she was not actually unfruitful, but was chosen by Divine Providence to bear in her old age. The wisdom of God was not revealed to anyone, but concealed from both angels and men. This wisdom was not shown, but was concealed to be revealed at the end of the age.

It was Sarah who said unto Abraham: 'Behold now, the Lord has prevented me from bearing children; go in to my maid; it may be that I shall obtain children by her.'

And so the Divine Grace (of the Son) announced to God, the Father: 'It is not yet my time for descending to the earth and to save the world. Descend to Mount Sinai and give them the Law.'

And, just as Abraham did as Sarah told him and went into Hagar, so God, the Father, did as he was told by the Divine Grace and descended to Mount Sinai.

And Hagar, the handmaid, bore from Abraham a servant (not a truly free man), and Abraham gave him the name Ishmael. And Moses brought from Mount Sinai the Law and not the Grace, the shade and not the Truth.

When Abraham and Sarah were old, God appeared to Abraham by the oaks of Mamre, as he sat at the door of his tent in the heat of the day. And he ran to meet him, and bowing lowly to the earth, he hastened into the tent (to Sarah). And so, when the end of the age was nearing, God appeared to the humankind, descended to the earth, and blessed the womb of the Virgin. And he was received by the Immaculate Virgin into the tent of the flesh. And the Virgin said to the angel: 'Behold I am the servant of the Lord; let it be to me according to your word.'

Once the Lord gave Sarah to bear a child, and she begat Isaac, the free son of a free mother. And, when once more our Lord visited the humankind, he appeared unknown and hidden from men and then was born Grace and Truth, but not the Law. And now it was the Son and not the servant.

And the child grew up and was weaned; and Abraham made a great feast on the day that Isaac was weaned. And when Christ was upon the earth Grace did not reveal itself and Christ was hiding himself until he was thirty. And when he had grown and was weaned, then there, in the river Jordan, Grace was revealed by a man. And Our Lord invited many and made a great feast and offered up the fatted calf of the age, His beloved Son, Jesus Christ, and God then called to this feast many of heaven and earth and they the angels and men into one (Church). . . .

This blessed faith spreads now over the entire earth, and finally it reached the Russian nation. And, whereas the lake of the Law dried up, the fount of the Gospel became rich in water and overflowed upon our land and reached us. And now, together with all Christians, we glorify the Holy Trinity, while Judea remains silent. . . .

The eulogy to our Kagan Vladimir

Rome, with voices panegyrical, praises Peter and Paul through whom they came to believe in Jesus Christ, the Son of God; Asia, Ephesus, and Patmus praise John the Theologian; India praises Thomas; Egypt, Mark. All lands, cities, and men honour and glorify their teacher who brought them the Orthodox Faith. Thus, let us, through our own strength, humbly praise our teacher and mentor, the great Kagan of our land Vladimir, the grandson of Igor of yore and son of glorious Sviatoslav, who ruled in their day with courage and valour, becoming famed in many lands for their victories and fortitude. And they did not reign in a poor and unknown land, but in Russia, which is known and celebrated by all to the ends of the earth. . . .

A good attestation of your devotion, blessed one, is the Holy Church of the Blessed Virgin, the Mother of God, which you build on the Orthodox foundation and where your valorous body now lays at rest and awaits the archangel's trumpet.

A good and certain attestation is your son, George [Yaroslav's Christian name], whom God has made the heir to your throne, who does not destroy your laws, but confirms them, who does not diminish works of piety, but extends them, who does not undo, but strengthens, who finishes that which you have left unfinished even as Solomon finished the works begun by David; who has built a great and holy temple to God's omniscience that it may hallow your city; who has embellished with all manner of things beautiful, with gold and silver and precious stones and with sacred vessels; so that the church is a wonder to all surrounding lands and so that the like cannot be found in all the northern land, nor in the east nor the west; who has given your famous city of Kiev the crown of glory, who has turned your city and its people to all-glorious Mother of God, who is always ready to succour Christians and for whom he has built a church with doors of gold in the name of the first Holy Day of the Lord of the Annunciation, that the veneration, which the archangel will offer to the Virgin, may also be upon this city.

To her he speaks, saying:

'Rejoice, Blessed One, the Lord is with you!'

And to the city he speaks, saying:

'Rejoice, faithful city, the Lord is with you!'

Arise from your grave, venerated prince, arise and shake off your sleep.
You are not dead, but only sleep until the day of resurrection of all.
Arise! You are not dead, for it is not right that you should die,
for you have believed in Christ, the Sustainer of the whole world.
Shake off your deep sleep and lift up your eyes that you might see what honour the
Lord has granted you, and you still live upon this earth, unforgotten through your sons.
Arise! behold your son George, your child, your beloved one! whom God has brought
forth from your loins.
Behold him embellishing the throne of your land.
Rejoice and be of good cheer!
Behold the pious wife of your son, Irina.
Behold your grandchildren and your great-grandchildren.
Behold how they live and how they are cared for by God.
Behold how they preserve devotion in your tradition, how they partake of the
Sacraments of the Holy Church, how they glorify Christ,
and how they venerate his Holy Name.
Behold your city radiant with majesty. Behold your blossoming churches, behold
Christianity flourishing.
Behold your city gleaming, adorned with holy icons and fragrant with thyme, praising
God and filling the air with sacred songs.
And beholding all this, rejoice and be of good cheer, and praise the Lord, the Creator
of all. . . .

D. Geanakoplos (ed. and trans.) *Byzantium: church, society, and civilization seen through contemporary eyes* (Chicago, 1984) pp. 143–144

Letter of Patriarch Anthony defending the emperor (1395)

The holy emperor has a great place in the church, for he is not like other rulers or governors of other regions. This is so because from the beginning the emperors established and confirmed the [true] faith in all the inhabited world. They convoked the ecumenical councils and confirmed and decreed the acceptance of the pronouncements of the divine and holy canons regarding the correct doctrines and the government of Christians. They struggled boldly against heresies, and imperial decrees together with councils established the metropolitan sees of the archpriests and the divisions of their provinces and the delineation of their districts. For this reason the emperors enjoy great honour and position in the Church, for even if, by God's permission, the nations [primarily the Ottoman Turks] have constricted the authority and domain of the emperor, still to this day the emperor possesses the same charge from the church and the same rank and the same prayers [from the church]. The *basileus* [note: the Greek term for emperor] is anointed with the great myrrh and is appointed basileus and autokrator of the Romans, and indeed of all Christians. Everywhere the name of the emperor is commemorated by all patriarchs and metropolitans and bishops wherever men are called Christians, [a thing] which no other ruler or governor ever received. Indeed he enjoys such great authority over all that even the Latins themselves, who are not in communion with our church, render him the same honour and submission which they did in the old days when they were united with us. So much more do Orthodox Christians owe such recognition to him.

Therefore, my son, you are wrong to affirm that we have the church without an Emperor for it is impossible for Christians to have a church and no empire. The *Basileia* [empire] and the church have a great unity and community – indeed they cannot be separated. Christians can repudiate only emperors who are heretics who attack the church, or who introduce doctrines irreconcilable with the teachings of the Apostles and the Fathers. But our very great and holy *autokrator*, by the grace of God, is most orthodox and faithful, a champion of the church, its defender and avenger, so that it is impossible for bishops not to mention his name in the liturgy. Of whom, then, do the Fathers, councils, and canons speak? Always and everywhere they speak loudly of the one rightful basileus, whose laws, decrees, and charters are in force throughout the world and who alone, only he, is mentioned in all places by Christians in the liturgy.

Further Reading

F. Dvornik, *Byzantine Missions amongst the Slavs: saints Constantine, Cyril and Methodius* (New Brunswick, 1970).
J. Gill, *Byzantium and the Papacy, 1198–1400* (New Brunswick, 1979).
J. Herrin, *Women in Purple: rules of Byzantium* (London, 2001).
C. Mayo (ed.) *The Oxford History of Byzantium* (Oxford, 2002).
D. Nicol, *Byzantium and Venice* (Cambridge, 1988).
D. Obolensky, *The Byzantine Commonwealth: eastern Europe, 500–1453* (London, 1971).
S. Runciman, *The Eastern Schism* (Oxford, 1955).
M. Whittow, *The Making of Orthodox Byzantium, 600–1025* (London, 1996).
N. G. Wilson, *Scholars of Byzantium*, 2nd edn (London, 1996).

10 Judaism and Islam

The place of minority religions in Christendom was problematic. The Catholic Church claimed a universal authority, and those outside the Church were almost by definition aliens. The Jews, with their separate traditions, were seen by the medieval Church as both critics of Christianity and as fellow believers in the one God. The history of the Jews in the Middle Ages is one of co-existence interrupted by active persecution. The conflict between Christians and Jews was fundamentally about the identity of Jesus, God incarnate in the Christian understanding, teacher of the Law in the Jewish one.

Islam was founded by Mohammed (d. 629) and its doctrine is laid down in the Qur'an and the Sunna, which contains the customs of the Prophet and his immediate successors. The central dogma of Islam is the absolute unity of God, and Jesus is not considered the only begotten Son of God, although he is a prophet. Its expansion in the Middle Ages and the crusading movement led to theological contacts with the Western Church, and there was some effort by the friars to convert Muslims to Christianity.

J. Parkes, *The Conflict of the Church and the Synagogue: a study in the origins of antisemitism* (New York, 1934) pp. 392–393

Justinian: Novella 146: On Jews

8.ii.553. Nov.146. Justinian to Areobindas, P.P.

> A Permission granted to the Hebrews to read the Sacred Scriptures according to Tradition, in Greek, Latin or any other Language, and an Order to expel from their community those who do not believe in the judgment, the Resurrection, and the Creation of Angels.

PREFACE

> Necessity dictates that when the Hebrews listen to their sacred texts they should not confine themselves to the meaning of the letter, but should also devote their attention to those sacred prophecies which are hidden from them, and which announce the mighty Lord and Saviour Jesus Christ. And though, by surrendering themselves to senseless interpretations, they still err from the true doctrine, yet, learning that they disagree among themselves, we have not permitted this disagreement to continue without a ruling on our part. From their own complaints which have been brought to us, we have understood that some only speak Hebrew, and wish to use it for the sacred

books, and others think that a Greek translation should be added, and that they have been disputing about this for a long time. Being apprised of the matter at issue, we give judgment in favour of those who wish to use Greek also for the reading of the sacred scriptures, or any other tongue which in any district allows the hearers better to understand the text.

CHAPTER I

We therefore sanction that, wherever there is a Hebrew congregation, those who wish it may, in their synagogues, read the sacred books to those who are present in Greek, or even Latin, or any other tongue. For the language changes in different places, and the reading changes with it, so that all present may understand, and live and act according to what they hear. Thus there shall be no opportunity for their interpreters, who make use only of the Hebrew, to corrupt it in any way they like, since the ignorance of the public conceals their depravity. We make this proviso that those who use Greek shall use the text of the seventy interpreters, which is the most accurate translation, and the one most highly approved, since it happened that the translators, divided into two groups, and working in different places, all produced exactly the same text.

i. Moreover who can fail to admire those men, who, writing long before the saving revelation of our mighty Lord and Saviour Jesus Christ, yet as though they saw its coming with their eyes completed the translation of the sacred books as if the prophetic grace was illuminating them. This therefore they shall primarily use, but that we may not seem to be forbidding all other texts we allow the use of that of Aquila, though he was not of their people, and his translation differs not slightly from that of the Septuagint.

ii. But the Mishnah, or as they call it the second tradition, we prohibit entirely. For it is not part of the sacred books, nor is it handed down by divine inspiration through the prophets, but the handiwork of man, speaking only of earthly things, and having nothing of the divine in it. But let them read the holy words themselves, rejecting the commentaries, and not concealing what is said in the sacred writings, and disregarding the vain writings which do not form a part of them, which have been devised by them themselves for the destruction of the simple. By these instructions we ensure that no one shall be penalised or prohibited who reads the Greek or any other language. And their elders, Archiphericitae and presbyters, and those called magistrates, shall not by any machinations or anathemas have power to refuse this right, unless by chance they wish to suffer corporal punishment and the confiscation of their goods, before they yield to our will and to the commands which are better and clearer to God which we enjoin.

CHAPTER II

If any among them seek to introduce impious vanities, denying the resurrection or the judgment, or the work of God, or that angels are part of creation, we require them everywhere to be expelled forthwith; that no backslider raise his impious voice to contradict the evident purpose of God. Those who utter such sentiments shall be put to death, and thereby the Jewish people shall be purged of the errors which they introduced.

CHAPTER III

We pray that when they hear the reading of the books in one or the other language, they may guard themselves against the depravity of the interpreters, and, not clinging to the literal words, come to the point of the matter, and perceive their diviner meaning, so that they may start afresh to learn the better way, and may cease to stray vainly, and to err in that which is most essential, we mean hope in God. For this reason we have opened the door for the reading of the scriptures in every language, that all may henceforth receive its teaching, and become fitter for learning better things. For it is acknowledged that he, who is nourished upon the sacred scriptures and has little need of direction, is much readier to discern the truth, and to choose the better path, than he who understands nothing of them, but clings to the name of his faith alone, and is held by it as by a sacred anchor, and believes that what can be called heresy in its purest form is divine teaching.

EPILOGUE

This is our sacred will and pleasure, and your Excellency and your present colleague and your staff shall see that it is carried out, and shall not allow the Hebrews to contravene it. Those who resist it or try to put any obstruction in its way, shall first suffer corporal punishment, and then be compelled to live in exile, forfeiting also their property, that they flaunt not their impudence against God and the empire. You shall also circulate our law to the provincial governors, that they learning its contents may enforce it in their several cities, knowing that it is to be strictly carried out under pain of our displeasure.

M. Goldstein, *Jesus in the Jewish Tradition* (New York, 1950) pp. 148–154

An anti-Christian view of Jesus

In the year 3671 in the days of King Jannaeus, a great misfortune befell Israel, when there arose a certain disreputable man of the tribe of Judah, whose name was Joseph Pandera. He lived at Bethlehem, in Judah.

Near his house dwelt a widow and her lovely and chaste daughter named Miriam. Miriam was betrothed to Yohanan, of the royal house of David, a man learned in the Torah and God-fearing.

At the close of a certain Sabbath, Joseph Pandera, attractive and like a warrior in appearance, having gazed lustfully upon Miriam, knocked upon the door of her room and betrayed her by pretending that he was her betrothed husband, Yohanan. Even so, she was amazed at this improper conduct and submitted only against her will.

Thereafter, when Yohanan came to her, Miriam expressed astonishment at behaviour so foreign to his character. It was thus that they both came to know the crime of Joseph Pandera and the terrible mistake on the part of Miriam. Whereupon Yohanan went to Rabban Shimeon ben Shetah and related to him the tragic seduction. Lacking witnesses required for the punishment of Joseph Pandera, and Miriam being with child, Yohanan left for Babylonia.

Miriam gave birth to a son and named him Yehoshua, after her brother. This name later deteriorated to Yeshu. On the eighth day he was circumcised. When he was old enough the lad was taken by Miriam to the house of study to be instructed in the Jewish tradition.

One day Yeshu walked in front of the Sages with his head uncovered, showing shameful disrespect. At this, the discussion arose as to whether this behaviour did not truly indicate that Yeshu was an illegitimate child and the son of a *niddah*. Moreover, the story tells that while the rabbis were discussing the Tractate *Nezikin*, he gave his own impudent interpretation of the law and in an ensuing debate he held that Moses could not be the greatest of the prophets if he had to receive counsel from Jethro. This led to further inquiry as to the antecedents of Yeshu, and it was discovered through Rabban Shimeon ben Shetah that he was the illegitimate son of Joseph Pandera. Miriam admitted it. After this became known, it was necessary for Yeshu to flee to Upper Galilee.

After King Jannaeus, his wife Helene ruled over all Israel. In the Temple was to be found the Foundation Stone on which were engraven the letters of God's Ineffable Name. Whoever learned the secret of the Name and its use would be able to do whatever he wished. Therefore, the Sages took measures so that no one should gain this knowledge. Lions of brass were bound to two iron pillars at the gate of the place of burnt offerings. Should anyone enter and learn the Name, when he left the lions would roar at him and immediately the valuable secret would be forgotten.

Yeshu came and learned the letters of the Name; he wrote them upon the parchment which he placed in an open cut on his thigh and then drew the flesh over the parchment. As he left, the lions roared and he forgot the secret. But when he came to his house he reopened the cut in his flesh with a knife and lifted out the writing. Then he remembered and obtained the use of the letters.

He gathered about himself three hundred and ten young men of Israel and accused those who spoke ill of his birth of being people who desired greatness and power for themselves. Yeshu proclaimed, 'I am the Messiah; and concerning me Isaiah prophesied and said, "Behold, a virgin shall conceive, and bear a son, and shall call his name Immanuel."' He quoted other messianic texts, insisting, 'David my ancestor prophesied concerning me: "The Lord said to me, thou art my son, this day have I begotten thee."'

The insurgents with him replied that if Yeshu was the Messiah he should give them a convincing sign. They therefore, brought to him a lame man, who had never walked. Yeshu spoke over the man the letters of the Ineffable Name, and the leper was healed. Thereupon, they worshipped him as the Messiah, Son of the Highest.

When word of these happenings came to Jerusalem, the Sanhedrin decided to bring about the capture of Yeshu. They sent messengers, Annanui and Ahaziah, who, pretending to be his disciples, said that they brought him an invitation from the leaders of Jerusalem to visit them. Yeshu consented on condition the members of the Sanhedrin receive him as a lord. He started out toward Jerusalem and, arriving at Knob, acquired an ass on which he rode into Jerusalem, as a fulfilment of the prophecy of Zechariah.

The Sages bound him and led him before Queen Helene, with the accusation: 'This man is a sorcerer and entices everyone.' Yeshu replied, 'The prophets long ago prophesied my coming: "And there shall come forth a rod out of the stem of Jesse," and I am he; but as for them, Scripture says "Blessed is the man that walketh not in the counsel of the ungodly."'

Queen Helene asked the Sages: 'What he says, is it in your Torah?' They replied: 'It is in our Torah, but it is not applicable to him, for it is in Scripture: "And that prophet which shall presume to speak a word in my name, which I have not commanded him to speak or that shall speak in the name of other gods, even that prophet shall die." He has not fulfilled the signs and conditions of the Messiah.'

Yeshu spoke up: 'Madam, I am the Messiah and I revive the dead.' A dead body was brought in; he pronounced the letters of the Ineffable Name and the corpse came to life. The Queen was greatly moved and said: 'This is a true sign.' She reprimanded the Sages and sent them humiliated from her presence. Yeshu's dissident followers increased and there was controversy in Israel.

Yeshu went to Upper Galilee, the Sages came before the Queen, complaining that Yeshu practiced sorcery and was leading everyone astray. Therefore she sent Annanui and Ahaziah to fetch him.

They found him in Upper Galilee, proclaiming himself the Son of God. When they tried to take him there was a struggle, but Yeshu said to the men of Upper Galilee: 'Wage no battle.' He would prove himself by the power which came to him from his Father in heaven. He spoke the Ineffable Name over the birds of clay and they flew into the air. He spoke the same letters over a millstone that had been placed upon the waters. He sat in it and it floated like a boat. When they saw this the people marvelled. At the behest of Yeshu, the emissaries departed and reported these wonders to the Queen. She trembled with astonishment.

Then the Sages selected a man named Judah Iskarioto and brought him to the Sanctuary where he learned the letters of the Ineffable Name as Yeshu had done.

When Yeshu was summoned before the queen, this time there were present also the Sages and Judah Iskarioto. Yeshu said: 'It is spoken of me, "I will ascend into heaven."' He lifted his arms like the wings of an eagle and he flew between heaven and earth, to the amazement of everyone.

The elders asked Iskarioto to do likewise. He did, and flew toward heaven. Iskarioto attempted to force Yeshu down to earth but neither one of the two could prevail against the other for both had the use of the Ineffable Name. However, Iskarioto defiled Yeshu, so that they both lost their power and fell down to the earth, and in their condition of defilement the letters of the Ineffable Name escaped from them. Because of this deed of Judah they weep on the eve of the birth of Yeshu.

Yeshu was seized. His head was covered with a garment and he was smitten with pomegranate staves; but he could do nothing, for he no longer had the Ineffable Name.

Yeshu was taken prisoner to the synagogue of Tiberias, and they bound him to a pillar. To allay his thirst they gave him vinegar to drink. On his head they set a crown of thorns. There was strife and wrangling between the elders and the unrestrained followers of Yeshu, as a result of which the followers escaped with Yeshu to the region of Antioch; there Yeshu remained until the eve of the Passover.

Yeshu then resolved to go the Temple to acquire again the secret of the Name. That year the Passover came on a Sabbath day. On the eve of the Passover, Yeshu, accompanied by his disciples, came to Jerusalem riding upon an ass. Many bowed down before him. He entered the Temple with his three hundred and ten followers. One of them, Judah Iskarioto apprised the Sages that Yeshu was to be found in the Temple, that the disciples had taken a vow by the Ten Commandments not to reveal his identity but that he would point him out by bowing to him. So it was done and

Yeshu was seized. Asked his name, he replied to the question by several times giving the names Mattai, Nakki, Buni, Netzer, each time with a verse quoted by him and a counter-verse by the Sages.

Yeshu was put to death on the sixth hour on the eve of the Passover and of the Sabbath. When they tried to hang him on a tree it broke, for when he had possessed the power he had pronounced by the Ineffable Name that no tree should hold him. He had failed to pronounce the prohibition over the carob-stalk, for it was a plant more than a tree, and on it he was hanged until the hour for afternoon prayer, for it is written in Scripture, 'His body shall not remain all night upon the tree.' They buried him outside the city.

On the first day of the week his bold followers came to Queen Helene with the report that he who was slain was truly the Messiah and that he was not in his grave; he had ascended to heaven as he prophesied. Diligent search was made and he was not found in the grave where he had been buried. A gardener had taken him from the grave and had brought him into his garden and buried him in the sand over which the waters flowed into the garden.

Queen Helene demanded, on threat of a severe penalty, that the body of Yeshu be shown to her within a period of three days. There was a great distress. When the keeper of the garden saw Rabbi Tanhuma walking in the field and lamenting over the ultimatum of the Queen, the gardener related what he had done, in order that Yeshu's followers should not steal the body and then claim that he had ascended into heaven. The Sages removed the body, tied it to the tail of a horse and transported it to the Queen, with the words, 'This is Yeshu who is said to have ascended to heaven.' Realizing that Yeshu was a false prophet who enticed the people and led them astray, she mocked the followers but praised the Sages.

The disciples went out among the nations – three went to the mountains of Ararat, three to Armenia, three to Rome and three to the kingdoms buy the sea, They deluded the people, but ultimately they were slain.

The erring followers amongst Israel said: 'You have slain the Messiah of the Lord.' The Israelites answered: 'You have believed in a false prophet.' There was endless strife and discord for thirty years.

The Sages desired to separate from Israel those who continued to claim Yeshu as the Messiah, and they called upon a greatly learned man, Simeon Kepha, for help. Simeon went to Antioch, main city of the Nazarenes and proclaimed to them: 'I am the disciple of Yeshu. He has sent me to show you the way. I will give you a sign as Yeshu has done.'

Simeon, having gained the secret of the Ineffable Name, healed a leper and a lame man by means of it and thus found acceptance as a true disciple. He told them that Yeshu was in heaven, at the right hand of his Father, in fulfilment of Psalm 110:1. He added that Yeshu desired that they separate themselves from the Jews and no longer follow their practices, as Isaiah had said, 'Your new moons and your feasts my soul abhorreth.' They were now to observe the first day of the week instead of the seventh, the Resurrection instead of the Passover, the Ascension into Heaven instead of the Feast of Weeks, the finding of the Cross instead of the New Year, the Feast of the Circumcision instead of the Day of Atonement, the New Year instead of Chanukah; they were to be indifferent with regard to circumcision and the dietary laws. Also they were to follow the teaching of turning the right if smitten on the left and the meek acceptance of suffering. All these new ordinances which Simeon Kepha (or Paul, as he was known to the Nazarenes) taught them were really meant to separate these Nazarenes from the people of Israel and to bring the internal strife to an end.

J. Jacobs (ed.) 'Gerald of Wales', in *The Jews of Angevin England: documents and records* (1893) pp. 283–285. Opera (rolls series) iv, 139

Gerald of Wales: two Cistercian monks turn Jews (before 1200)

A certain monk of the same order, or rather a certain demoniac in our own times, being as it were tired of the Catholic faith and worn out with the sweet and light burden of Christ's yoke, and scorning, at the instigation of the devil, any longer to walk in the way of salvation. . . . as if phrenetic and mad, and truly turned to insanity, fleeing to the synagogue of Satan. And to cut short the whole wretched story which we have dilated upon at great length to show our detestation, at last he caused himself to be circumcised with the Jewish rite, and as a most vile apostate joined himself, to his damnation to the enemies of the cross of Christ.

Also on the northern borders of England, in a house of the same order called Geroudon, a certain brother, likewise in our own days, by a similar error, or rather madness, presuming to set at naught the part of Christ and reconciling himself with Satan, opposing and exciting the mind to depravity by his depraved and pestiferous rites which he, the monk, had renounced with sacred laver and baptismal oath, and again put on his chains from which he had been freed, subjecting himself to eternal slavery as well as the punishment of hell. For he, too, fled with ruinous and ruin bearing ways to Judaism, the home of damnation and the asylum of this depraved reprobation.

But when that man, known for his distinguished fame and extent of writings, as well as gifted with wit, Walter Mapes, Archdeacon of Oxford, heard of these two having apostatised out of that order alone, wondering, he broke out in public into these words: 'It is remarkable,' said he, 'that those two wretches, since they wished to leave their former faith, as being so perverse and infested with so many poisonous vices, did not become Christians, adopting a safer and more salubrious plan,' as if he would say and hint, though indirectly and by sidelong words, that men of this order, on account of the stains of deliberate vice and cupidity, and their faults so manifest and so clearly unchristian, were not worthy to be called Christians.

But I myself am persuaded that those two wretches did not leave the truth and fly to a vain shadow with damnable exchange out of mere devotion or desire of increasing their religion. . . . but because they could no longer bear the harshness and rigour of that order, and instigated by the spirit of fornication they committed this crime.

J. C. Robertson, 'Materials for a History of Thomas Becket', iv., 151; in Joseph Jacobs (ed.) *The Jews of Angevin England: documents and records* (1893) p. 45

An Israelite bishop without guile (c.1168)

The easy terms on which English Jews and Christian mingled gave rise to this anecdote. Jacobs noted: 'Bishop' was the term applied in England to each of the three Dayanim or judges who constituted the Beth Din or ecclesiastical tribunal which decided cases between Jews.

> And so too that well known saying of Henry of London was heard by many. For there were one day in the Church of St. Paul at London many bishops and abbots taking cognisance of certain ecclesiastical cases by order of our lord the Pope, and with them a great multitude of clergy, citizens, soldiers, and others. There chanced to enter certain Jews of London, who mixed with these and others in seeking for their debtors if they might see them. And among them comes a certain Bishop of the Jews. And to him Henry said in joke: 'Welcome, Bishop of the Jews! Receive him among ye, for there is scarcely any of the Bishops of England that has not betrayed his lord the Archbishop of Canterbury, except this one. In this Israelite Bishop there is no guile.'

J. Marcus, *The Jew in the Medieval World: a sourcebook*, 315–1791 (New York, 1938) pp. 24–27

The expulsion of the Jews from France (1182)

[Philip Augustus had often heard] that the Jews who dwelt in Paris were wont every year on Easter day, or during the sacred week of our Lord's Passion, to go down secretly into underground vaults and kill a Christian as a sort of sacrifice in contempt of the Christian religion. For a long time they had persisted in this wickedness, inspired by the devil, and in Philip's father's time, many of them had been seized and burned with fire. St. Richard, whose body rests in the church of the Holy Innocents in the Fields in Paris, was thus put to death and crucified by the Jews, and through martyrdom went in blessedness to God. [Louis VII, then king, held the Jews guiltless in this death.] Wherefore many miracles have been wrought by the hand of God through the prayers and intercessions of St. Richard, to the glory of God, as we have heard.

And because the most Christian King Philip inquired diligently, and came to know full well these and many other iniquities of the Jews in his forefathers' days, therefore he burned with zeal, and in the same year in which he was invested at Rheims with the holy governance of the kingdom of the French, upon a Sabbath, the sixteenth of February [1180], by his command, the Jews throughout all France were seized in their synagogues and then bespoiled of their gold and silver and garments, as the Jews themselves had spoiled the Egyptians at their exodus from Egypt. This was a harbinger of their expulsion, which by God's will soon followed. . . .

At this time [1180–1181] a great multitude of Jews had been dwelling in France for a long time past, for they had flocked thither from divers parts of the world, because peace abode among the French, and liberality; for the Jews had heard how the kings of the French were prompt to act against their enemies, and were very merciful toward their subjects. And therefore their elders and men wise in the law of Moses, who were called by the Jews *didascali* [teachers], made resolve to come to Paris.

When they had made a long sojourn there, they grew so rich that they claimed as their own almost half of the whole city, and had Christians in their houses as menservants and maidservants, who were open backsliders from the faith of Jesus Christ, and *judaised* with the Jews. And this was contrary to the decree of God and the law of the Church. And whereas the Lord had said by the mouth of Moses in Deuteronomy

[23:20], 'Thou shalt not lend upon usury to thy brother,' but 'to a stranger,' the Jews in their wickedness understood by 'stranger' every Christian, and they took from the Christians their money at usury. And so heavily burdened in this wise were citizens and soldiers and peasants in the suburbs, and in the various towns and villages, that many of them were constrained to part with their possessions. Others were bound under oath in houses of the Jews in Paris, held as if captives in prison.

The most Christian King Philip heard of these things, and compassion was stirred within him. He took counsel with a certain hermit, Bernard by name, a holy and religious man, who at that time dwelt in the forest of Vincennes, and asked him what he should do. By his advice the King released all Christians of his kingdom from their debts to the Jews, and kept a fifth part of the whole amount for himself.

Finally came the culmination of their wickedness. Certain ecclesiastical vessels consecrated to God the chalices and crosses of gold and silver bearing the image of our Lord Jesus Christ crucified had been pledged to the Jews by way of security when the need of the churches was pressing. These they used so vilely, in their impiety and scorn of the Christian religion, that from the cups in which the body and blood of our Lord Jesus Christ was consecrated they gave their children cakes soaked in wine. . . .

In the year of our Lord's Incarnation 1182, in the month of April, which is called by the Jews Nisan, an edict went forth from the most serene king, Philip Augustus, that all the Jews of his kingdom should be prepared to go forth by the coming feast of St. John the Baptist [24th June]. And then the King gave them leave to sell each his movable goods before the time fixed, that is, the feast of St. John the Baptist. But their real estate, that is, houses, fields, vineyards, barns, winepresses, and such like, he reserved for himself and his successors, the kings of the French.

When the faithless Jews heard this edict some of them were born again of water and the Holy Spirit and converted to the Lord, remaining steadfast in the faith of our Lord Jesus Christ. To them the King, out of regard for the Christian religion, restored all their possessions in their entirety, and gave them perpetual liberty.

Others were blinded by their ancient error and persisted in their perfidy; and they sought to win with gifts and golden promises the great of the land counts, barons, archbishops, bishops that through their influence and advice, and through the promise of infinite wealth, they might turn the King's mind from his firm intention. [The lords appealed to were the political enemies of the king.] But the merciful and compassionate God, who does not forsake those who put their hope in Him and who doth humble those who glory in their strength so fortified the illustrious King that he could not be moved by prayers nor promises of temporal things. . . .

The infidel Jews, perceiving that the great of the land, through whom they had been accustomed easily to bend the King's predecessors to their will, had suffered repulse, and astonished and stupefied by the strength of mind of Philip the King and his constancy in the Lord, exclaimed with a certain admiration: 'Shema Israel!' ['Hear, O Israel'] and prepared to sell all their household goods. The time was now at hand when the King had ordered them to leave France altogether, and it could not be in any way prolonged. Then did the Jews sell all their movable possessions in great haste, while their landed property reverted to the crown. Thus the Jews, having sold their goods and taken the price for the expenses of their journey, departed with their wives and children and all their households in the aforesaid year of the Lord 1182.

N. P. Tanner (ed. and trans.) *Decrees of the Ecumenical Councils* **(Georgetown, 1990) vol. 1, pp. 263–267**

Decrees of the Fourth Lateran Council

68. That Jews should be distinguished from Christians in their dress

A difference of dress distinguishes Jews or Saracens from Christians in some provinces, but in others a certain confusion has developed so that they are indistinguishable. Whence it sometimes happens that by mistake Christians join with Jewish or Saracen women, and Jews or Saracens with Christian women. In order that the offence of such a damnable mixing may not spread further, under the excuse of a mistake of this kind, we decree that such persons of either sex, in every Christian province and at all times, are to be distinguished in public from other people by the character of their dress – seeing moreover that this was enjoined upon them by Moses himself, as we read. They shall not appear in public at all on the days of lamentation and on passion Sunday; because some of them on such days, as we have heard, do not blush to parade in very ornate dress and are not afraid to mock Christians who are presenting a memorial of the most sacred passion; and are displaying signs of grief. What we most strictly forbid, however, is that they dare in any way to break out in derision of the Redeemer. We order secular princes to restrain with condign punishment those who do so presume, lest they dare to blaspheme in any way Him who was crucified for us, since we ought not to ignore insults against Him who blotted out our wrongdoings.

69. That Jews are not to hold public offices

It would be too absurd for a blasphemer of Christ to exercise power over Christians. We therefore renew in this canon, on account of the boldness of the offenders, what the council of Toledo providently decreed in this matter: we forbid Jews to be appointed to public offices, since under cover of them they are very hostile to Christians. If, however, anyone does commit such an office to them let him, after an admonition, be curbed by the provincial council, which we order to be held annually, by means of an appropriate sanction. . . .

J. R. Marcus (trans.) *The Jew in the Medieval World: a source book, 315–1791* **(Cincinnati, 1938) pp. 45–46**

The Black Death and pogroms against the Jews (1349)

In the year 1349 there occurred the greatest epidemic that ever happened. Death went from one end of the earth to the other, on that side and this side of the sea, and it was greater among the Saracens than among the Christians. In some lands everyone died so that no one was left. Ships were also found on the sea laden with wares; the crew had all died and no one guided the ship. The Bishop of Marseilles and priests and monks and more than half of all the people there died with them. In other kingdoms and cities so many people perished that it would be horrible to describe. The pope at Avignon stopped all sessions of court, locked himself in a room, allowed no one to approach him and had a fire burning before him all the time. [This last was probably intended as some sort of disinfectant.] And from what this epidemic came, all wise teachers and physicians could only say that it was God's will. And as the plague was now here, so was it in other places, and lasted more than a whole year. This epidemic also came to Strasbourg in the summer of the above mentioned year, and it is estimated that about sixteen thousand people died.

In the matter of this plague the Jews throughout the world were reviled and accused in all lands of having caused it through the poison which they are said to have put into the water and the wells – that is what they were accused of – and for this reason the Jews were burnt all the way from the Mediterranean into Germany, but not in Avignon, for the pope protected them there.

R. B. Burke (trans.) *The Opus Majus of Roger Bacon* (Oxford, 1928) I, pp. 111–112.

Roger Bacon: the neglect of languages and of preaching to the infidel (1292–1294)

. . . For there is no doubt but that all nations of unbelievers beyond Germany would have been converted long since but for the violence of the Teutonic Knights, because the race of pagans was frequently ready to receive the faith in peace after preaching. But the Teutonic Knights are unwilling to keep peace, because they wish to subdue those peoples and reduce them to slavery, and with subtle arguments many years ago deceived the Roman Church. The former fact is known, otherwise I should not state the latter. Moreover, the faith did not enter into this world by force of arms but through the simplicity of preaching, as is clear. And we have frequently heard and we are certain that many, although they were imperfectly acquainted with languages and had weak interpreters, yet made great progress by preaching and converted countless numbers to the Christian faith. Oh, how we should consider this matter and fear lest God may hold the Latins responsible because they are neglecting the languages so that in this way they neglect the preaching of the faith. For Christians are few, and the whole broad world is occupied by unbelievers; and there is no one to show them the truth.

C. F. Horne (ed.) and E. H. Whinfield (trans.) *The Sacred Books and Early Literature of the East* (New York, 1917) vol. VIII: *Medieval Persia*, pp. 13–14

Omar Khayyam: profession of faith (c.1120)

Ye, who seek for pious fame,
And that light should gild your name,
Be this duty ne'er forgot
Love your neighbour harm him not.
To Thee, Great Spirit, I appeal,
Who can'st the gates of truth unseal;
I follow none, nor ask the way
Of men who go, like me, astray;
They perish, but Thou canst not die,

But liv'st to all eternity.
Such is vain man's uncertain state,
A little makes him base or great;
One hand shall hold the Koran's scroll,
The other raise the sparkling bowl
One saves, and one condemns the soul.
The temple I frequent is high,
A Turkish vaulted dome the sky,
That spans the world with majesty.
Not quite a Muslim is my creed,
Nor quite a Giaour; my faith indeed
May startle some who hear me say,
I'd give my pilgrim staff away,
And sell my turban, for an hour
Of music in a fair one's bower.
I'd sell the rosary for wine,
Though holy names around it twine.
And prayers the pious make so long
Are turned by me to joyous song;
Or, if a prayer I should repeat,
It is at my beloved's feet.
They blame me that my words are clear;
Because I am not what I appear;
Nor do my acts my words belie
At least, I shun hypocrisy.
It happened that but yesterday
I marked a potter beating clay.
The earth spoke out 'Why dost thou strike?
Both thou and I are born alike;
Though some may sink and some may soar,
We all are earth, and nothing more.'

E. A. Peers (trans.) *Blanquerna: a thirteenth century romance, translated from the Catalan of Ramon Lull* (1925) pp. 325–326, 330–331

Ramon Lull (d. 1315): plan for language teaching and the conversion of Saracens, Tartars, and Jews

3. After these words, the Pope and the Cardinals and the religious, to honour the glory of God, ordained that to all monks that had learning there should be assigned friars to teach divers languages, and that throughout the world there should be builded divers houses, which for their needs should be sufficiently provided and endowed, according to the manner of the monastery of Miramar, which is in the Island of Majorca. Right good seemed this ordinance to the Pope and to all the rest, and the Pope sent messengers through all the lands of the unbelievers to bring back certain of them to learn their language and that they at Rome might learn the tongues of these unbelievers, and that certain men should return with them to preach to the others in these lands, and that to those unbelievers that learned Latin, and gained a knowledge of the Holy

Catholic Faith, should be given money and garments and palfreys, that they might praise the Christians, who when they had returned to their own lands would continue to assist and maintain them.

4. Of the whole world the Pope made twelve parts, and appointed to represent him twelve men, who should go each one throughout his part and learn of its estate, to the end that the Pope might know the estate of the whole world. It came to pass that those who went to the unbelievers brought from Alexandria and from Georgia and from India and Greece Christians who were monks, that they might dwell among us, and that their will might be united with the will of our monks, and that during this union and relationship they might be instructed in divers manners concerning certain errors against the faith, and should then go and instruct those that were in their country. Wherefore the Pope sent also some of our monks to the monks aforesaid, and ordered that each year they should send to him a certain number of their friars, that they might dwell with us, and, while they dwelt among us, learn our language.

11. Throughout all the world went forth the fame of the holy life of the Pope and the great good which he did, and daily was valour increased and dishonour diminished. The good which came from the ordinance which the Pope had established illumined the whole world, and brought devotion to them that heard the ordinance recounted; and throughout all the world was sent in writing an account of the process of the making thereof. It chanced one day that the Pope had sent to a Saracen king a knight who was also a priest, and of the Order of Science and Chivalry. This knight by force of arms vanquished ten knights one after the other on different days, and after this he vanquished all the wise men of that land by his arguments, and proved to all that the Holy Catholic Faith was true. By messengers of such singular talent, and by many more, did the ordinance aforementioned, which was established by the Holy Apostolic Father, illumine the world.

13. In a certain land there were studying ten Jews and ten Saracens together with ten friars of religion; and when they had learned our holy law and our letters, the half of them were converted to our law, and they preached our law to other Jews, and to Saracens our holy Christian faith, in the presence of many that had not yet been converted, and thus did they daily and continually. And because the Papal Court did all that was in its power, and through the continuance of the disputation, and because truth has power over falsehood, God gave grace to all the Jews and Saracens of that country so that they were converted and baptized, and preached to others the Holy Faith. Wherefore the good and the honour which, through the Pope Blanquerna, was done to the Christian Faith, can in no wise be recounted.

H. Yule (trans.) *Cathay and the Way Thither* (1866) vol. 1, pp. 197–199

Missions to Cathay: John of Monte Corvino (1291–1305)

I, Friar John of Monte Corvino, of the order of Minor Friars, departed from Tauris, a city of the Persians, in the year of the Lord 1291, and proceeded to India. And I remained in the country of India, wherein stands the church of St. Thomas the Apostle, for thirteen months, and in that region baptised in different places about one hundred persons. The companion of my journey was Friar Nicholas of Pistoia, of the order of Preachers, who died there, and was buried in the church aforesaid.

I proceeded on my further journey and made my way to Cathay, the realm of the Emperor of the Tartars who is called the Grand Cham. To him I presented the letter of our lord the Pope, and invited him to adopt the Catholic Faith of our Lord Jesus Christ, but he had grown too old in idolatry. However he bestows many kindnesses upon the Christians, and these two years past I am abiding with him.

The Nestorians, a certain body who profess to bear the Christian name, but who deviate sadly from the Christian religion, have grown so powerful in those parts that they will not allow a Christian of another ritual to have ever so small a chapel, or to publish any doctrine different from their own.

To these regions there never came any one of the Apostles, nor yet of the Disciples. And so the Nestorians aforesaid, either directly or through others whom they bribed, have brought on me persecutions of the sharpest. For they got up stories that I was not sent by our lord the Pope, but was a great spy and impostor; and after a while they produced false witnesses who declared that there was indeed an envoy sent with presents of immense value for the emperor, but that I had murdered him in India, and stolen what he had in charge. And these intrigues and calumnies went on for some five years. And thus it came to pass that many a time I was dragged before the judgment seat with ignominy and threats of death. At last, by God's providence, the emperor, through the confessions of a certain individual, came to know my innocence and the malice of my adversaries; and he banished them with their wives and children.

In this mission I abode alone and without any associate for eleven years; but it is now going on for two years since I was joined by Friar Arnold, a German of the province of Cologne.

I have built a church in the city of Cambaliech, in which the king has his chief residence. This I completed six years ago; and I have built a bell-tower to it, and put three bells in it. I have baptised there, as well as I can estimate, up to this time some 6,000 persons; and if those charges against me of which I have spoken had not been made, I should have baptised more than 30,000. And I am often still engaged in baptising.

Also I have gradually bought one hundred and fifty boys, the children of pagan parents, and of ages varying from seven to eleven, who had never learned any religion. These boys I have baptised, and I have taught them Greek and Latin after our manner. Also I have written out Psalters for them, with thirty Hymnaries and two Breviaries. By help of these, eleven of the boys already know our service, and form a choir and take their weekly turn of duty as they do in convents, whether I am there or not. Many of the boys are also employed in writing out Psalters and other things suitable. His Majesty the Emperor moreover delights much to hear them chaunting. I have the bells rung at all the canonical hours, and with my congregation of babes and sucklings I perform divine service, and the chaunting we do by ear because I have no service book with the notes.

Further Reading

M. Cook, *Muhammad* (Oxford, 1983).

F. Heer, *God's First Love: Christians and Jews over two thousand years*, Eng. trans. (London, 1967).

B. Lewis, *The Arabs in History*, 6th edn (Oxford, 1993).

W. Montgomery Watt, *A Short History of Islam* (Oxford, 1996).

A. Rippin, *Muslims, their Religious Beliefs and Practices, in the Formative Period* (London, 1990).

C. Roth, *A History of the Jews in England*, 3rd edn (Oxford, 1964).

M. Ruthven, *Islam in the World*, 2nd edn (Cambridge, 2000).

K. R. Stow, *Alienated Minority: the Jews of medieval Latin Europe* (Cambridge MA, 1992).

Glossary

Abbess female head of a religious house

Abbey large religious house belonging either to one of the orders of the Benedictine family or to certain orders of the Canons Regular

Abbot the superior of a monastery (abbey) from the Latin *abbas* (father)

Absolution forgiveness of sins through the ministry of the Church or release from excommunication

Advowson right of appointing clerics to benefices

Agnus dei the depiction of a lamb as the symbol of Christ

Albigensians heretic sect of Cathars whose name derives from the Albi region of southern France

Anathema the solemnisation of excommunication

Annate a fee paid to the Pope for an ecclesiastical preferment, originally the whole of the first year's income from the office, thus the name from the Latin *annus*, year

Anti-pope rival factions in the Catholic Church from 1378 to 1417 led to the Great Schism or division of the Church. The unauthorised claimants to the papacy are designated Anti-popes

Apostles with the exception of St Paul, the apostles were Christ's closest friends and followers. Following his death and what Christians believe to be his resurrection and ascension into Heaven, the apostles served as the Church's first leaders and missionaries

Apostolic See the see, or diocese, of the apostle Peter, the person chosen by Jesus to lead the Church; hence, the bishopric of Rome, or the papacy (see also **Pope**)

Archbishop a bishop with authority over a group of territorially contiguous dioceses and their bishops; also known as a metropolitan

Archdeacon a cleric having a defined administrative authority delegated to him by the bishop in the whole or part of the diocese

Baptism the rite admitting an individual to the Church

Benedictine order of monks or nuns living according to the Rule of St Benedict

Benefice an ecclesiastical living or preferment which gave status and financial support to its holder

Bishop the principal priest of a diocese who exercised the apostolic authority in his area, ordaining priests and administering his see. The highest order of ministers in the Church. The word bishop is an Anglo-Saxon corruption of the Latin *episcopus*

Byzantine referring to the eastern Roman Empire, based in Constantinople, after the fall of Rome

Canon (1) a priest or cleric who is part of a corporation of clergy like a cathedral or a collegiate church, also applied to a member of a religious order living according to a rule (regular canons). Cathedral canons, not usually living a rule of life, are called secular canons. (2) an individual item of legislation

Canonisation the process of making saints in the Catholic Church in which men and women are enrolled in the *canon* or list of saints

Canon law the law of the Church, imposed by authority in matters of faith, morals and discipline

Cardinal from the Latin *cardo* (a hinge), a member of what amounted to the senate of the Roman Church who, during the course of the Middle Ages, emerged as the electors of the Pope. The College of Cardinals consisted of cardinal bishops, priests and deacons

Carthusian a monastic order, dedicated to solitary contemplation, founded at Chartreuse, in France, in the eleventh century

Cathar a heretical movement found in Germany, Italy and France in the eleventh to thirteenth centuries, based on a dualist belief in two gods, one of good and one of evil; also known as Albigensians

Cenobite from Greek for 'living in community': a religious in vows living in a community as contrasted to a hermit, living alone

Chantry an endowed chapel for the celebration of masses for the dead

Chartophylax an ecclesiastical official in the Byzantine Church

Cistercian monastic order derived from the Benedictine, reformed order from the French monastery of Citeaux in the twelfth century

Cluniac reform movement, in the Benedictine tradition beginning in Burgundy in the tenth century

Collegiate church a church served by a body of canons or prebendaries; not housing the throne of a bishop and therefore not a cathedral; served by secular canons rather than monks

Commutation (Latin *arreum*) substitute either in payment or in kind for a penance which the penitent could not enact. From commutation comes the idea of indulgences, the remission by the Church of the temporal penalty due to forgiven sin

Confession the rite of confession of sins to a priest in order to obtain absolution

Confirmation the sacrament of anointing which follows baptism, requiring the recipient to affirm their faith in the presence of a bishop

Conversi a name used for lay brothers in monasteries, presumably alluding to their 'conversion' in maturity

Corpus Christi literally, *Christ's body*, a feast instituted in 1264 to celebrate the real presence of Christ in the Eucharist

Council a meeting of ecclesiastics, also known as a synod, which dealt with Church disputes and resulted in legislation in the form of canons

Curia the court or place where the sovereign resided with his chief officials and household. Term frequently applied to the papal court

Deacon the rank in the ministry below the priest, with a major role in the collection and distribution of alms

Decretal papal letter written in response to a question, and having the authority of law

Diocese territory ruled by a bishop; also known as a **see**

Dominican order of mendicant friars founded in the early thirteenth century by the Spanish St Dominic; also known as the Friars Preacher or the Black Friars

Dorter the communal sleeping area of a monastery; also known as the dormitory

Ecumenical from the Greek for 'the whole inhabited world', is often attached to the Ecumenical Councils, assemblies of bishops and others representing the whole Christian world

Episcopal in relation to the authority of a bishop

Eremetical relating to the life of a hermit

Eucharist one of the seven sacraments and the principal ritual of the Church, in which bread and wine becomes the body and blood of Christ; the ritual must be administered by a priest

Excommunication the ritual exclusion of a person or church by the appropriate authority

Feretory a shrine in which a saints' relics are venerated

Feria in ecclesiastical language a *feria*, despite its literal meaning as a feast, is applied to a day on which no feast falls

Franciscan order of friars founded by St Francis of Assisi in the early thirteenth century in Italy; also known as the Friars Minor or the Grey Friars

Frater the communal refectory of a monastic establishment

Friars religious brotherhood more centralised than the monastic orders and dedicated to poverty and preaching

Gospel the books of the New Testament of the Bible detailing the life of Christ and the immediate aftermath of his death and resurrection; comprises the books of Matthew, Mark, Luke and John

Heresy a mistaken belief about the central teachings of the Christian faith

Heretic person who has expressed formal denial or doubt of any defined doctrine of the Church

Hesychasm in the Eastern Church, the tradition of mystical prayer, associated especially with the monks of Mount Athos. The word comes from the Greek for 'quietness'.

Holy communion the sacrament of the Eucharist

Holy orders the higher grades of the Christian ministry; those of bishop, priest and deacon

Holy See the diocese of the Bishop of Rome; commonly used to denote the authority and jurisdiction of the papacy

Hussites followers of Jan Hus (d. 1415), the Bohemian reformer, condemned for heresy by the Council of Constance in 1414

Indulgence see **commutation**

Interdict Church prohibition of ecclesiastical functions imposed on persons or places

Investiture public transfer of property or rights marked by a public ceremony and often involving symbols of office

Jubilee year in which a special 'indulgence' is given, sometimes called a 'holy year'. The first was in 1300

Laity persons who are not members of the clergy

Lay brother member of a religious order who is not bound to the recitation of the divine office and is occupied in manual work, generally adult converts to the monastic life; also known as *conversi*

Lay sister female member of a religious order who is not bound to the recitation of the divine office and is occupied in manual work, generally adult converts to the monastic life

Lectio literally, reading, from the Latin. Applied to slow meditative reading for monks

Legate an ecclesiastic of high rank, usually a cardinal, representing the Pope on a mission

Liturgy prescribed order of a church service

Lollards followers of John Wycliffe (d. 1384), condemned as heretics

Marriage the ceremony of union of man and wife was a sacrament of the Church

Martyr member of the Church who suffered death for their faith and ranking before all other saints

Mass the principal ritual of the Church, the service at which the sacrament of the Eucharist, or Holy Communion, is performed

Mendicant a beggar in a literal sense, often applied as a title to friars who, in theory, owned nothing and depended on charity

Metropolitan a bishop with authority over a group of territorially contiguous dioceses and their bishops; also known as an archbishop

Minor orders the lower ranks of the Christian ministry

Monk a religious who lives under a rule of life in the enclosure of a monastery and takes vows of obedience, renunciation and stability

Mystery plays religious dramas performed at major festivals, commonly performed out of doors

Obedientaries officials of monasteries

Office of the dead service for the benefit of the souls of the dead

Opus Dei Latin for 'work of God'. Applied to monastic work of liturgy and the canonical hours

Orders the status of clerk or holy orders was divided into the major orders of bishops, priests and deacons (who had sacramental authority) and minor orders which gave status but not authority. Entry to the clerical state was controlled by the bishops and shown by a tonsure or clerical haircut

Ordination the rite of admission into the ministry of the Church; only admission to the major orders of the ministry was considered to be a sacrament

Orthodox name given to the Eastern Church, especially after the split or schism of Rome and Byzantium in 1054

Pallium circular band of white woollen material with two hanging straps and marked with black crosses worn by the Pope and given to archbishops to show metropolitan status

Papacy see **Pope**

Papal relating to the office of the Pope

Papal bull legal document issued under the authority of the Pope

Papal curia the central government of the Western Church (Latin *curia*, meaning court)

Parish an area under the pastoral care of a priest, himself under the jurisdiction of a bishop; the parish church was the centre of worship for the parish

Patriarch a title, current since the sixth century, for the bishops of the Pentarchy. They ordained their dependant bishops or metropolitans. The title was extended later to the heads of some 'autocephalous' (or independent) churches like those in Russia and Bulgaria

Patristic with reference to the early fathers of the Church

Penance a form of punishment whereby one who has confessed his sins to a priest can obtain absolution. Penance means *poena* or punishment

Penitentials books for confessors which include lists of sins and the appropriate penance for each offence.

Pentarchy the five chief bishoprics or patriarchies of Christendom: Rome, Alexandria, Antioch, Constantinople and Jerusalem

Pilgrimage a journey to a holy place from motives of devotion, to obtain spiritual help, or as a form of penance

Pope the bishop of Rome, known as *papa* (father) of the Western Church. Also known as *Pontifex Maximus*, thus pontiff or pontifical

Prelate a holder of high office in the Church, from the Latin *prelatus*, meaning 'set over' others

Primate the chief bishop of a single state or people

Province a group of dioceses under the jurisdiction of an archbishop

Sacrament Defined by St Augustine (d. 430) as 'the visible form of invisible grace' and applied widely in the Middle Ages to sacred actions. Gradually, in the West, restricted to seven: baptism, confirmation, Eucharist, penance, anointing of the sick, holy orders and matrimony

Schism formal separation from the unity of the Church based not on doctrine (as with heresy) but rather on misunderstanding

Scholasticism method used by medieval thinkers founded on logic and intended to assist in the exposition and reconciliation of the Bible, the writings of the Church Fathers and classical philosophical texts, especially Aristotle, to create a unified system

Secular (1) in relation to clergy, priests living in the world, not under a rule, who may possess property, working under the authority of a bishop; (2) more generally, refers to people who are not clergy, the laity

See properly, the official 'seat' of a bishop. Commonly used for the territorial unit of administration in the Church, governed by a bishop; also known as a **diocese**

Simony the attempt to purchase spiritual gifts with money, taken from Simon Magus in the *Acts of the Apostles*. It became particularly associated with the buying and selling of church offices

Synkellos a liaison official between emperor and patriarch in the Byzantine Church

Synod see **council**

Transubstantiation the doctrine that the bread and wine of the Eucharist is changed into the real presence of the body and blood of Christ through the action of the priest

Unction anointing with consecrated oil as part of a ceremony of consecration

Waldensians sect organised in the twelfth century in Lyons; the founder became a mendicant preacher and expounded against the worldliness of the established Church; the sect survives today

Bibliography

A Descrition or Briefe Declaration of all the Ancient Monuments, Rites, and Customes Belonging or Beinge within the Monastical Church of Durham before the Suppression. Written in 1593 (Felinfach, 1998).

A Word in Season: monastic lectionary for the divine office (Pennsylvania, 1991).

M. N. Adler, *The Itinerary of Benjamin of Tuledo: critical text, translation and commentary* (New York, 1907).

M. H. Allies (trans.) *St. John Damascene on Holy Images* (London, 1898).

R. J. Armstrong, J. A. Wayne Hellmann and W. J. Short (eds) *Francis of Assisi: early documents, vol. 1: The Saint* (New York, 1999).

Augustine of Hippo, *The Monastic Rules*, with a commentary by G. Bonner (New York, 2004).

D. Ayerst and A. Fisher, *Records of Christianity, vol. I: in the Roman Empire* (Oxford, 1971).

—— *Records of Christianity, vol. II: Christendom* (Oxford, 1977).

J. Barmby, *The Book of Pastoral Rule and Selected Epistles of Gregory the Great*, Nicene and Post-Nicene Fathers, vol. XII (New York, 1895).

D. A. Bellenger, *The Carthusians of Somerset* (Bath, 2003).

J. F. Benton (ed.) and C. C. Swinton Bland (trans.) *Self and Society in Medieval France: the memoirs of Abbot Guibert of Nogent* (New York, 1970).

J. Bertram (trans.) St Aelred of Rievaulx, *Life of St. Edward the Confessor* (London, 1997).

Richard N. Bosley and Martin M. Tweedale, *Basic Issues in Philosophy: selected readings presenting the interactive discourses among the major figures* (Ontario, 1999).

E. Brehaut (trans.) Gregory of Tours, *History of the Franks*, Records of Civilization 2 (New York, 1916).

R. B. Burke (trans.) *The Opus Majus of Roger Bacon* (Oxford, 1928).

W. Butler-Bowdon (ed.), *The Book of Margery Kempe, 1436* (London, 1936).

H. J. Coleridge (ed.) *The Dialogues of St. Gregory the Great* (London, 1874).

C. G. Coulton (ed.) *Life in the Middle Ages*, vol. 1 (New York, 1910).

D. Dales, *A Mind Intent on God. The Prayers and Spiritual Writings of Alcuin: an anthology* (Norwich, 2004).

Elizabeth A. S. Dawes (trans.) *The Alexiad of the Princess Anna Comnena* (London, 1918).

P. Dearmer, R. V. Williams and M. Shaw, *Songs of Praise* (Oxford, 1925).

M. L. Del Mastro (trans.) *Revelations of Divine Love of Juliana of Norwich* (New York, 1977).

S. J. Eales (trans.) and J. Mabillon (ed.) *The Life and Works of St. Bernard of Clairvaux* vol. III (London, 1896).

J. France (ed.) and Radulf Glaber, *The Five Books of the Histories* (Oxford, 1989).

C. Garton (trans.) *The Metrical Life of St Hugh* (Lincoln, 1986).

D. Geanakoplos (ed. and trans.) *Byzantium: church, society, and civilization seen through contemporary eyes*, (Chicago, 1984).

M. Goldstein, *Jesus in the Jewish Tradition* (New York, 1950).

E. F. Henderson (trans.) *Select Historical Documents of the Middle Ages* (London, 1910).

P. Henderson (ed.) *A Pilgrim Anthology* (London, 1994).

James Hogarth (trans.) *The Pilgrim's Guide: a 12th century guide for the pilgrim to St James of Compostella* (London, 1992).

C. F. Horne (ed.) and E. H. Whinfield (trans.) *The Sacred Books and Early Literature of the East, vol. VIII: medieval Persia* (New York, 1917).

R. Hudleston (ed.) Sir Tobie Matthew, *The Confessions of Saint Augustine* (London, 1927).

Hugh of Saint-Victor: selected spiritual writings, translated by a religious of CSMV with an introduction by Aelred Squire, OP (London, 1962).

Idung of Prüfening, *Cistercians and Cluniacs, the Case for Citeaux. A dialogue between two monks, an argument on four questions* (Kalamazoo, 1977).

J. Jacobs (ed.) Gerald of Wales, *The Jews of Angevin England: documents and records* (London, 1893).

Jacobus de Voragine, *The Golden Legend, Book III* (London, 1900).

J. Johnson, *A Collection of the Laws and Canons of the Church of England*, vol. I (Oxford, 1850).

K. L. Jolly, *Popular Religion in Late Saxon England: elf charms in context* (Chapel Hill NC, 1996).

A. Kemp-Welch (trans., intro. and notes) *Of the Tumbler of Our Lady and other Miracles, now Translated from the French* (London, 1909).

M. H. King (trans.) *The Life of Christina of St-Trond by Thomas of Cantimpre* (Saskatoon, 1986).

C. Kirchberger (ed. and trans.) *Richard of Saint-Victor: selected writings on contemplation* (New York, 1962).

H. Lawrence (trans.) *Documentary Sources for the Canonisation Process for Edmund of Abingdon, Archbishop of Canterbury, 1234* (London, 1990).

H. C. Lea, *A History of the Inquisition of the Middle Ages*, vol. 1 (New York, 1887).

T. Mackintosh-Smith, *The Travels of Ibn Battutah* (London, 2003).

S. R. Maitland (trans.) *History of the Albigenses and Waldenses* (London, 1832).

Essulouk li Mariset il Muluk Makrisi, 'The Road to Knowledge of the Return of King', in Henry G. Bohn (ed.) *Chronicles of the Crusades* (London, 1848).

J. R. Marcus (trans.) *The Jew in the Medieval World: a source book, 315–1791* (Cincinnati, 1938).

J. McCann (ed. and trans.) *The Rule of St Benedict* (Aldershot, 1952).

M. L. McClure and C. L. Feltoe (eds and trans.) *The Pilgrimage of Etheria* (London, 1919).

C. E. McCracken (ed.) and A. Cabaniss (ed. and trans.) *Early Medieval Theology* (Philadelphia, 1957).

J. B. McLaughlin (trans.) *St. Antony the Hermit, by St. Athanasius* (London, 1924).

A. O. Norton, *Readings in the History of Education* (Cambridge MA, 1909).

D. N. Orlandi and H. J. Robinson (eds and trans.) *Sermons* (Siena, 1920).

E. C. E. Owen (trans.) *Some Authentic Acts of the Early Martyrs* (Oxford, 1927).

J. Parkes, *The Conflict of the Church and the Synagogue: a study in the origins of antisemitism* (New York, 1934).

E. A. Peers (trans.) *Blanquerna: a thirteenth century romance, translated from the Catalan of Ramon Lull* (London, 1925).

B. Pennington (ed.) *The Works of Aelred of Rievaulx, vol. 1: treatises and the pastoral prayer* (Massachusetts, 1971).

E. Peters (ed. and trans.) *Heresy and Authority in Medieval Europe: documents in translation* (London, 1980).

M. Philippides, *The Fall of the Byzantine Empire* (Amherst, 1980).

B. Pullan, *Sources for the History of Medieval Europe from the Mid-eighth to the Mid-thirteenth Century* (Oxford, 1971).

J. C. Robertson, 'Materials for History of Thomas Becket', iv, 151; in Joseph Jacobs (ed.) *The Jews of Angevin England: documents and records* (London, 1893).

P. Robinson (trans.) *The Writings of Saint Francis of Assisi* (Philadelphia, 1905; 1906).

E. F. Rogers, *Peter Lombard and the Sacramental System* (New York, 1917).

J. E. Rotelle (ed.) *Augustine's Heritage: readings from the Augustinian tradition*, vol. 1 (New York, 1973).

A. Saunders, J. Hillier, A. Halliwell and C. Rudge, *The Chichester Reliefs*, Otter Memorial Paper, no. 5 (Chichester, 1989).

P. Schaff and H. Wace (eds) *A Select Library of Nicene and Post-Nicene Fathers of the Christian Church* (Grand Rapids, 1955).

H. J. Schroder (trans.) *Disciplinary Decrees of the Ecumenical Councils* (St Louis MO, 1937).

D. Scott, *An Anglo-Saxon Passion* (London, 1999).

J. Scott (trans.) William of Malmesbury, *De Antiquitate Glastonie Ecclesie* (Woodbridge, 1981).

A. M. Sellar (trans.) *Bede's Ecclesiastical History of England* (London, 1907).

D. Sherlock, *Signs for Silence: the sign language of the monks of Ely in the Middle Ages* (Ely, ND).

F. M. Steele (trans.) *The Life and Visions of St Hildegarde* (London, 1914).

R. Steele and A. Moring (eds) *Kings' Letters: from the days of Alfred to the coming of the Tudors*, vol. I (London, 1900).

C. Stephenson and F. G. Marcham (eds and trans.) *Sources of English Constitutional History: a selection of documents from AD 600 to the present*, vol. VI (New York, 1937).

C. H. Talbot (ed. and trans.) *The Life of Christina of Markyate: a twelfth century recluse* (Oxford, 1959).

N. Tanner, *Heresy Trials in the Diocese of Norwich, 1428–31*, Camden Fourth Series, vol. 20 (London, 1977).

N. P. Tanner (ed. and trans.) *Decrees of the Ecumenical Councils*, vol. 1 (Georgetown, 1990).

Oliver J. Thatcher (ed.) *The Library of Original Sources, vol. v: the early medieval world* (Milwaukee, 1907).

The Bible, New Revised Standard Version (London, 1993).

Translations and Reprints from the Original Sources of European history, vol. II, no. 4 (Pennsylvania, 1897?–1907?).

Translation by a priest of Mount St Melleray, *St. Bernard's Treatise on Consideration* (Dublin, 1921).

E. Underhill (ed.) *A Book of Contemplation the Which Is Called The Cloud of Unknowing, In the Which a Soul Is Oned With God* (London, 1922).

R. Vaughan (ed.) *Tracts and Treatises of John de Wycliff* (London, 1845).

C. Waddell, *Cistercian Lay Brothers: twelfth-century usages with related texts* (Citeaux, 2000).

F. E. Warren (trans.) *The Sarum Missal in English*, parts 1 and 2 (London, 1913).

C. Wordsworth and D. MacLeane (eds) *Statutes and Customs of the Cathedral Church of the Blessed Virgin Mary of Salisbury* (London, 1915).

H. B. Workman and R. M. Pope (eds) *The Letters of John Hus* (London, 1904).

D. Wright (trans.) Geoffrey Chaucer, *The Canterbury Tales* (Oxford, 1986).

H. Yule (trans.) *Cathay and the Way Thither*, vol. 1 (London, 1866).

S. A. Zenkovsky (ed. and trans.) *Medieval Russian Epics, Chronicles and Tales* (New York, 1974).

Index

Related titles from Routledge

Christianity and Sexuality in the Early Modern World
Merry E. Wiesner-Hanks

In this lively and compelling study, Professor Wiesner-Hanks examines the ways in which Christian ideas and institutions shaped sexual norms and conduct from the time of Luther and Columbus to that of Thomas Jefferson. Providing a global overview, and including chapters on Protestant, Catholic and Orthodox Europe, Latin America, Africa, Asia and North America, this volume examines marriage, divorce, fornication, illegitimacy, clerical sexuality, witchcraft and love magic, homosexuality and moral crimes.

ISBN10: 0-415-14433-7 (hb)
ISBN10: 0-415-14434-5 (pb)

ISBN13: 978-0-415-14433-9 (hb)
ISBN13: 978-0-415-14434-6 (pb)

Available at all good bookshops
For ordering and further information please visit:
www.routledge.com

Related titles from Routledge

Women and Religion in Early America, 1600–1850
Marilyn J Westerkamp

Women in Early American Religion, 1600–1850 explores the first two centuries of America's religious history, examining the relationship between the socio-political environment, gender, politics and religion. Drawing its background from women's religious roles and experiences in England during the Reformation, the book follows them through colonial settlement, the rise of evangelicalism, the American Revolution, and the second flowering of popular religion in the nineteenth century. Tracing the female spiritual tradition through the Puritans, Baptists and Shakers, Marilyn Westerkamp argues that religious beliefs and structures were actually a strong empowering force for women.

ISBN10: 0-415-09814-9 (hb)
ISBN10: 0-415-19448-2 (pb)

ISBN13: 978-0-415-09814-4 (hb)
ISBN13: 978-0-415-19448-8 (pb)

Available at all good bookshops
For ordering and further information please visit:
www.routledge.com

Related titles from Routledge

Religion in World History
John C. Super and Briane K. Turley

Individuals and groups have long found identity and meaning through religion and its collective expression. In Religion and World History, John C. Super and Briane K. Turley examine the value of religion for interpreting the human experience in the past and present. This study explores those elements of religion that best connect it with cultural and political dynamics that have influenced history.

Working within this general framework, Super and Turley bring out three unifying themes:

- the relationship between formal and informal religious beliefs, how these change through time, and how they are reflected in different cultures
- the relationship between church and state, from theocracies to the repression of religion
- the ongoing search for spiritual certainty, and the consequent splintering of core religious beliefs and the development of new ones.

The book's unique approach helps the reader grasp the many and complex ways that religion acts upon and reacts to broader global processes.

ISBN10: 0-415-31457-7 (hb)
ISBN10: 0-415-31458-5 (pb)

ISBN13: 978-0-415-31457-2 (hb)
ISBN13: 978-0-415-31458-9 (pb)

Available at all good bookshops
For ordering and further information please visit:
www.routledge.com

Related titles from Routledge

The Reformation of Ritual: An Interpretation of Early Modern Germany

Susan Karant-Nunn

In The Reformation of Ritual Susan Karant-Nunn explores the function of ritual in early modern German society, and the extent to which it was modified by the Reformation. Employing anthropological insights, and drawing on extensive archival research, Susan Karant-Nunn outlines the significance of the ceremonial changes. This comprehensive study includes an examination of all major rites of passage: birth, baptism, confirmation, engagement, marriage, the churching of women after childbirth, penance, the Eucharist, and dying. The author argues that the changes in ritual made over the course of the century reflect more than theological shifts; ritual was a means of imposing discipline and of making the divine more or less accessible. Church and state cooperated in using ritual as one means of gaining control of the populace.

ISBN10: 0-415-11337-7 (hb)
ISBN13: 978-0-415-11337-3 (hb)

Available at all good bookshops
For ordering and further information please visit:

www.routledge.com